10/02

Scorned Literature

Recent Titles in
Contributions to the Study of Popular Culture

Scorned Literature

Essays on the History and Criticism of Popular Mass-Produced Fiction in America

Edited by Lydia Cushman Schurman
and Deidre Johnson

Foreword by Madeleine B. Stern

Contributions to the Study of Popular Culture, Number 75

Greenwood Press
Westport, Connecticut • London

Library of Congress Cataloging-in-Publication Data

Scorned literature : essays on the history and criticism of popular mass-produced fiction
in America / edited by Lydia Cushman Schurman and Deidre Johnson ; foreword by Madeleine
B. Stern.
    p. cm.—(Contributions to the study of popular culture, ISSN 0198–9871 ; no. 75)
    Includes bibliographical references and index.
    ISBN 0–313–32033–0 (alk. paper)
      1. American fiction—History and criticism—Theory, etc. 2. Popular literature—United
States—History and criticism—Theory, etc. 3. Criticism—United States—History—20th
century. I. Schurman, Lydia Cushman. II. Johnson, Deidre. III. Series.
    PS374.P63S36 2002
    813.009—dc21   2001042801

British Library Cataloguing in Publication Data is available.

Library of Congress Catalog Card Number: 2001042801
ISBN: 0–313–32033–0
ISSN: 0198–9871

First published in 2002

Greenwood Press, 88 Post Road West, Westport, CT 06881
An imprint of Greenwood Publishing Group, Inc.
www.greenwood.com

Printed in the United States of America

The paper used in this book complies with the
Permanent Paper Standard issued by the National
Information Standards Organization (Z39.48–1984).

10 9 8 7 6 5 4 3 2 1

Contents

Foreword

This provocative and seminal book on scorned literature immediately recalled to me the day that, at age thirteen, I confronted my Sunday School librarian and asked if I might borrow a book by Horatio Alger. The horror with which she regarded me entitles her to inclusion among the scorners of what has been denigrated as subliterature. Yet today, Horatio Alger is a subject of scholarly appraisal in Ralph Gardner's *Horatio Alger, or The American Hero Era*. Gardner's title is a telling one. Alger's scorned stories, rejected from my Sunday School library, do indeed reflect the idea and era of the American hero.

Unlike Horatio Alger, however, few authors of cheap literature for the masses have been restored to the library, to academe, to the canon. This innovative study, edited by Lydia Cushman Schurman and Deidre Johnson, will do much to open the gates of scholarship to them.

Comprehensive in scope, the volume covers the colorful varieties of so-called subliterature over almost two centuries: the dime novels and series books, the story papers and juvenile fiction, the Westerns and boys' series, the pulps and the comic books. Popular literature in general and individual works in particular are subjected to the scrutiny of contributors who ingeniously address the reasons for denigration of those genres by elitist critics. The results of such denigration are clearly presented: the lack of academic study accorded such writings, the inadequate scholarship assigned them, their absence not just from Sunday School libraries but from most libraries.

Yet it must be acknowledged that this enormous body of cheap literature was produced for the masses of American readers, distributed to the masses, and vividly consumed by the masses. Must it not also be acknowledged that such "subliterature"—page-turners for the millions—must reflect the climate of their times, the mores and the morality, as well as the nature of popular taste more accurately than more rarefied literary productions.

As this volume on scorned literature indicates, the books selected for analysis do indeed disclose concepts of society and gender that were in the air between about 1830 and the post-1950s. They reveal—if only between their lines—the antifeminism and the profeminism of the time, the conventions of the day, notions of the heroic and the antiheroic, of violence and racism. This is indeed what the editors call "the rich potential of such fare," the "value" of these "undervalued genres." From this collection of thoughtful essays the reader can contemplate writings that once earned their authors a penny a word but now yield historical and cultural riches to us.

The huge gap in American scholarship that has resulted from the exclusionary attitude of elitist critics must be filled. We need to be reminded of the lasting value of the ephemeral, the importance of retrieving the throwaway, of studying the ill-considered. *Scorned Literature*, addressing those problems and helping to fill that gap, takes a long and fascinating step in that direction.

Madeleine B. Stern

Introduction

Indeed, being out of the canon *signifies* being out of social prestige and power.
—Catharine R. Stimpson
"Reading for Love: Canons, Paracanons, and Whistling Jo March"

"A book on scorned literature? What would it include?" colleagues asked when first learning of this project. Then, as they thought more about it, they set about answering their own questions, offering examples and suggestions from their reading experiences. Almost everyone, it would seem, encounters—and even savors—some "subliterary fiction"; in recent years a growing number of scholars have discovered the rich potential of such fare. We believe the essays here provide illuminating insights into the scope of inexpensive, mass-produced, popular literature scorned in the United States over the last two centuries—from the story papers, dime novels, "libraries," and seminal series of the nineteenth century, through the pulp magazines, comics, juvenile series, paperback mysteries, and romance novels of the twentieth. The essays in this collection touch on almost every literary subgenre—detective fiction, Westerns, horror stories, romances, war adventures—and recognize scorned literature's appeal to a variety of audiences, its ability to reach readers from diverse age groups, social classes, and educational backgrounds. Scorn, like beauty, is apparently in the eye of the beholder, and, as we discovered when suggestions and submissions began to arrive, encompasses vast and fluid boundaries.

The essays in the book all share certain characteristics: They analyze popular literature scorned by librarians and other custodians of high culture in the United States from the 1830s to the present. We define literature loosely, as print-based, mass-produced, fictionalized narrative. This definition allows the inclusion of a visually oriented genre, comic books (a traditional target for criticism), but excludes nonfiction and amateur publications, such as the rapidly growing body of Internet-based fiction. Taken together, the essays in this collection provide an illuminating look at the scope of material scorned, at specific devalued authors or works, at critics and their reasons for denigrating certain publications, and at the effects of such reactions.

The book is unique in its focus on a broad spectrum of scorned literature in America and in its analysis of this material through scholarly lenses. The essays adopt a variety of approaches: some consider reasons for scorn; others reclaim previously scorned texts by examining them from a fresh perspective; still others work to develop a history of a scorned genre or subject and its impact on the culture. A few even suggest that some of the criticism was justified. Woven into these discussions are myriad reasons for scorn as well as frequently recurring motifs. Across the span of two centuries, the genres analyzed in this study have been categorized as unworthy, the same reasons cyclically repeated: sensational and formulaic plots, cheap and crude formats, commodified and mass-produced fiction. Critics have expressed fears about their impact on children, taste, publishing trends, culture, and even the country's future.

MASS PRODUCTION AND SCORN

One element common to the materials discussed in the essays is that all are mass-produced, and this sense of mass production, mechanized production, is a crucial concept. The mid-nineteenth century and subsequent years witnessed an array of "technological transformations" that ushered in a new era of cheap fiction. Wood pulp paper, the rotary press, stereotyped and electrotyped plates, and more extensive railway systems all made it possible to produce and distribute publications more rapidly and economically than ever before.[1] This emphasis on speed and efficient production, however, was not limited to the physical aspects of bookmaking but soon extended into the writing, with a perhaps predictable outcome: hastily written manuscripts (combined with the resultant literary sloppiness) and a mechanical approach to the process, both of which provided fuel for critics' scorn. On the simplest level, the rapid writing accounts for narrative flaws mentioned in criticisms of the various genres—poor grammar, narrative slippages, underdeveloped characters, and formulaic plots. Of greater concern, the very nature of most mass-produced fiction—a new publication each week, month, or year depending on the stated schedule—argues against a work of art produced by inspiration and honed by careful crafting, stressing instead the regularity of appearance and the necessity of grinding out a manuscript by a deadline regardless of its readiness to see print. Indeed, the idea of production rather than creation became so ingrained that "production metaphors" regularly appear in discussions of progenitors of such fare.[2] The term "fiction factory" has been applied to writers like Erle Stanley Gardner, producers such as the Stratemeyer Literary Syndicate, and publishers like Street and Smith.[3] The drive for greater speed and mechanized production is also evident in another oft-criticized element of such fiction, the use of prefabricated outlines or detailed plot formulas as a means of ensuring more standardized stories.[4]   Such standardization, in turn, promotes speed of consumption, another integral element in the mass production equation. As one critic remarked, appealing to a mass market involves "[streamlining] the aesthetic vehicle of . . . ideas to make it a common carrier so that the average man could ride along without effort."[5] Charging that such streamlining takes the form of more simplistic writing with heavy reliance on dialogue, short sentences and paragraphs for fast reading, a predilection for formula to produce "more of the same,"[6] or an emphasis on sensation or sentiment for easy emotional thrills, critics aver that reading such fiction requires little skill or intellectual effort. As one sniffed, "Kitsch pretends to demand nothing of its customers except their money—not even their time."[7]

Mass-produced is also often equated with commodification, of the process of viewing "books as economic commodities rather than as intellectual or aesthetic artifacts,"[8] and thus of "convincing [the public] to consume that commodity repetitively."[9] Commodification extends into all areas of production: from hack writing, which encourages quicker reading and thus hastens the need for another literary "fix," to faster production methods, which make the product available more quickly, to radical changes in distribution practices and in format, which promote more frequent and rapid purchases. This new approach to distribution involved establishing ubiquitous merchandising outlets; scorned publications were viewed as products and sold at newsstands, drug and department stores, and even in barrooms and backrooms. The rage for cost-effective and readily recognizable products also affected format: a standardized size and design, coupled with the use of cheap material and binding, made mass-produced publications into inexpensive, ephemeral entities—easy to buy, easy to discard. The once aesthetic, carefully crafted book became a commonplace item, sold alongside scented soap, patent medicines, and chewing tobacco. In essence, this new business philosophy advocated bookselling as "analogous to the trade in hams and sugar,"[10] transforming the book into "the quietest of merchandise."[11] Through such a devaluation of the book, "[t]he act of reading becomes . . . an act of genuine consumption (not of rereading and preservation) in which the product is digestible, disposable, and replaceable."[12]

Since mass production also requires mass consumption, an awareness of audience invariably becomes part of the scorners' rhetoric. The extensiveness of audience—that is, a work's popularity—is a magnet for scorn and, whether it be dime novels, series books, or Spillane's bloodbaths, high sales trigger a disproportionate amount of attention. Critics of mass-produced fiction question the intended audience's experience, mental capacity, and taste. Perhaps one of the most hotly contested areas of fiction is that aimed at children, where critics fear for everything from the mental health of young readers to their physical well-being. Genres that attract both adult and child readers—for example, dime novels, story papers, and comic books—draw the heaviest criticism in relation to their perceived effects on the young. Even genres with fewer juvenile readers are sometimes seen as appealing to "metaphorical children" or immature readers.[13] This audience includes the marginalized and disempowered: the working-class readers who devoured inexpensive fare and were castigated for their taste; the women who savored Harlequin romances and were accused of tacitly supporting patriarchal values.[14]   Even when critics do not explicitly invoke mention of readers' childlike intelligence or limitations, they often conjure up the idea of protecting youth by claiming that the growth or popularity of a particular type of publication promotes attitudes that will taint the future of the next generation—our "*children's* world."[15]

Finally, critics warned that mass production might promulgate a mass culture with all the social and philosophical consequences: as an early critic put it, "At its worst, mass culture threatens not merely to cretinize our taste, but to brutalize our senses while paving the way to totalitarianism."[16]   Or, as a current cultural scholar, Janice Radway, more gently stated, "mass culture critics can show how the consciousness created by popular literature reconciles readers to a social order dominated by others."[17]   All of these criticisms suggest that popular literature has been scorned for numerous reasons—but, as Alison Scott argues in an essay in this volume—these are "reasons that have little to do with their potential to reward serious inquiry."[18]   Indeed, the rise of cultural studies has encouraged a new consideration of such material. Scholars have "argued that while 'elite' literature might be taken as evidence for the beliefs of a particular section of the American population, assertions based upon it could not easily be extrapolated to wholly different classes or ethnic groups. . . . if accurate statements were to be made about more 'ordinary' Americans, the popular literature produced for and consumed by large numbers ought to become the primary focus of culturally oriented scholarship."[19]   Similarly, interdisciplinary fields such as American Studies and Women's Studies have begun explorations into the intersections among history, the literary canon, and popular literature—another indication that the tenor of the times is changing. As the essays in this volume demonstrate, scorned literature yields a rich harvest worthy of scholarly attention.

CONTENTS

The first five essays in this book are all specific studies of one element within a scorned genre—an author, an idea, a text, a series, or a character. The initial essay, Jesse Berrett's "Gresham's Law of Culture: The Case of Mickey Spillane and Postwar America," is ideal for beginning the collection, for it not only examines responses to Spillane and his fiction but also introduces many of the reasons for scorn highlighted throughout this book. Berrett's title encapsulates the core fear of scorners, that the object of scorn will drive out culture and by extension negate cultural authority.   Berrett singles out a specific object of scorn, as do the next four contributors, but Frantz, Dean, Palumbo, and Holsinger adopt a different approach, providing close readings of one or more scorned texts. Sarah Frantz's "'Expressing' Herself: The Romance Novel and the Feminine Will to Power" returns to another concept introduced in Berrett—that even within a traditionally scorned genre, certain authors or works receive more criticism than others. Like Frantz, Janet Dean, in "Calamities of

Convention in a Dime Novel Western," argues that a rereading of such works through a feminist lens may provide an interpretation that elevates or reclaims a particular type of story. Within this context, both Frantz and Dean allude to the threat scorned texts make to established societal or cultural values with respect to gender roles. In analyzing the modern romance, Frantz finds a blurring of gender roles that empowers women and challenges sources of men's authority. Similarly, Dean, in her discussion of a dime novel Western, observes that elements frequently considered narrative flaws instead actually help to create a "flexible identity" and thus a "challenge to the traditional concept of gender."

In "Marvel's *Tomb of Dracula*: Case Study in a Scorned Medium," Donald Palumbo also uses critical theory to reclaim texts in an undervalued genre, arguing that "comic books can and often do have significant literary merit . . . and thus can be profitably analyzed through the same methodologies applied to elite literature." Although he draws on New Criticism rather than feminist criticism and focuses primarily on character study, Palumbo also mentions a blurring of roles, this time of hero, antihero, and villain. Examining the construct of Dracula in several comic book series, Palumbo postulates that comic book authors use the same types of traits associated with heroic characters but link them with the villain. Like Palumbo's essay, M. Paul Holsinger's "'Blood in the Sky': The World War II-Era Boys Series of R. Sidney Bowen" examines a series of narratives with recurring characters and one in a genre frequently criticized for its violence and gore. Drawing on his experience as a young reader and simultaneously examining the books within an historical context, Holsinger finds that war adventure series, amid exciting narratives and patriotic prose, also promoted unrealistic expectations and may even have encouraged a costly and perhaps unnecessary participation in subsequent conflicts. In an unusual twist in this collection, Holsinger suggests that critics' concerns were justified when leveled at war series for children, that "daily doses of death, bloodshed, and constant gore coupled with unremitting racism and bigotry were the wrong prescriptions for the future."

If the first five essays could be said to take a microscope approach, providing an in-depth analysis of a specific element within a scorned genre, the next five may thus be viewed as taking a telescopic approach—in broader terms delineating the history of the genre and reactions to it. The authors focus on the genre itself or the history of scorn when directed at that genre. Taken in sequence, the essays provide a panoramic view of the progression of scorn and also a reminder that, whatever the period, many of the same ideas resonate in the comments of critics. Dawn Fisk Thomsen's "'It is a pity it is no better': The Story Paper and Its Critics in Nineteenth-Century America" surveys the development and reception of one of the earliest forms of mass-produced literature in the United States and examines publishers' strategies to combat scorn. Several of the major story paper publishers mentioned in Thomsen's essay also issued paperbound libraries during the last three decades of the nineteenth century; these libraries form the focus of Lydia Cushman Schurman's "The Effect of Nineteenth-Century 'Libraries' on the American Book Trade." Schurman's essay traces the powerful impact of cheap reprint editions of pirated European classics on standard American publishers and analyzes their complex responses, which involved competitive marketing strategies, public denunciations of rivals, and calls for postal reform and copyright legislation. The rivalry between publishers of mainstream and cheap literature also informs Erin A. Smith's "'The ragtag and bobtail of the fiction parade': Pulp Magazines and the Literary Marketplace." Indeed, some of the same publishers closely associated with story papers, dime novels, and paperbound libraries issued pulp magazines, too. In addition to giving an illuminating overview of the evolution of the pulps, Smith also details the intricate relationship among pulp writers, editors, and readers.

Although "From Abbott to Animorphs, from Godly Books to Goosebumps: The Nineteenth-Century Origins of Modern Series" by Deidre Johnson also examines the development of a scorned genre, her essay places less emphasis on publishers' strategies and responses to critics than the preceding three essays. Instead, Johnson shows how the design and marketing of modern-day series are founded on successful strategies invented by authors of the past century and scrutinizes the gradual emergence and cyclical nature of scorn directed at juvenile series. Amy Kiste Nyberg's "Poisoning Children's Culture: Comics and Their Critics" also examines a genre predominantly consumed by juvenile readers. She provides an overview of criticisms leveled at comic books, concerns about their effect on children, and studies in the field by academics.

The final two essays consider the institutional aspect of scorn. In "'Wise Censorship': Cultural Authority and the Scorning of Juvenile Series Books, 1890–1940," Kathleen Chamberlain studies the discourse of cultural authorities involved in censuring juvenile fiction. Explicating the history of these controversies, Chamberlain examines "the lengthy cultural process" by which the focus changed from "what do children read?" to "what *should* children read?" asserting that the debates disclose the processes involved in "the establishment of intellectual authority, the politics of canon formation, [and] the professionalization of librarianship and teaching." She further contends that examining this dialogue reveals "a great deal about the construction of American cultural identity during the Progressive Era." Concluding the collection, Alison M. Scott's "Romance in the Stacks; or, Popular Romance Fiction Imperiled" demonstrates all too persuasively the effects of such scorn—the absence of particular types of popular fiction from academic and research libraries and the resulting restrictions in terms of scholarship. Although Scott's argument foregrounds gender preferences in terms of selection—that is, women's fiction is less valued than that read by men and thus less frequently catalogued or preserved—her basic argument about librarians' failure to appreciate and thus to collect and maintain various categories of popular fiction can be extended to all the genres of scorned literature discussed in this collection. As the essays in this book indicate, readers have loved and been moved by these scorned materials, just as scholars have been intrigued by them. It is our hope that this volume will encourage further exploration and preservation of these genres and spur scholarly research in areas of popular literature yet unexamined.

Deidre Johnson
Lydia Cushman Schurman

NOTES

1. Bill Brown, ed., *Reading the West: An Anthology of Dime Westerns* (Boston: Bedford Books; 1997), 20.

2. Erin A. Smith, "'The ragtag and bobtail of the fiction parade': Pulp Magazines and the Literary Marketplace," chapter 8 in this volume.

3. In her biography of Erle Stanley Gardner, *Erle Stanley Gardner: The Case of the Real Perry Mason,* Dorothy B. Hughes notes that Gardner "referred to himself as a 'Fiction Factory'" (New York: William Morrow & Company, 1978), 16. Various sources have referred to Stratemeyer and his Literary Syndicate as a "Fiction Factory"; the allusion even occurs in the subtitle of Carol Billman's book *The Secret of the Stratemeyer Syndicate: Nancy Drew, the Hardy Boys, and the Million Dollar Fiction Factory* (New York: Unger, 1986). Similarly, Quentin Reynolds's history of Street and Smith was titled *The Fiction Factory; or, From Pulp Row to Quality Street* (New York: Random House, 1955).

4. The Stratemeyer Syndicate's use of prefabricated outlines and plot formulas—and the criticism related to same—is discussed briefly in Deidre Johnson's "From Abbott to Animorphs," chapter 9 in this volume. Somewhat similar charges have occasionally been leveled at romance publishers as can be seen in Alison Scott's "Romance in the Stacks; or, Popular Romance Fiction Imperiled," chapter 12 in this volume.

5. Ernest Van Den Haag, "Of Happiness and Despair We Have No Measure," in *Mass Culture: The Popular Arts in America,* eds. Bernard Rosenberg and David Manning White (New York: The Free Press, 1957), 521.

6. Margaret Mackey, "Filling the Gaps: The *Baby-Sitters Club,* the Series Book, and the Learning Reader," *Language Arts* 67 (September 1990): 487.

7. Clement Greenberg, "Avant-Garde and Kitsch," in *Mass Culture: The Popular Arts in America,* eds. Bernard Rosenberg and David Manning White (New York: The Free Press, 1957), 102.

8. Kathleen Chamberlain, e-mail to Lydia Cushman Schurman, 25 January 2000.

9. Janice A. Radway, *Reading the Romance: Women, Patriarchy, and Popular Literature* (Chapel Hill: University of North Carolina Press, 1984), 23.

10. "International Copyright," *American Bookseller* 23 (2 January 1888); quoted in Lydia Cushman Schurman, "The Effect of Nineteenth-Century 'Libraries' on the American Book Trade," chapter 7 in this volume.

11. "Mr. Wanamaker's Book Business," *Publishers' Weekly* 27 (3 January 1885): 8; quoted in Schurman.

12. Brown, 20.

13. Smith, chapter 8 in this volume.

14. Sarah Frantz's "'Expressing' Herself: The Romance Novel and Feminine Will to Power," chapter 2 in this volume, discusses attitudes toward romance readers.

15. Philip Wylie, "The Crime of Mickey Spillane," *Good Housekeeping* 140 (February 1955): 54; quoted in Jesse Berrett, "Gresham's Law of Culture: The Case of Mickey Spillane and Postwar America," chapter 1 in this volume.

16. Bernard Rosenberg, "Mass Culture in America," in *Mass Culture: The Popular Arts in America*, eds. Bernard Rosenberg and David Manning White (New York: The Free Press, 1957), 9.

17. Radway (1984), 6.

18. Scott, chapter 12 in this volume.

19. Introduction, Janice A. Radway, *Reading the Romance: Women, Patriarchy, and Popular Literature* (1984; reprint, with a new introduction, Chapel Hill: University of North Carolina Press, 1991), 3. Similarly, a recent column by critic Alison Lurie, discussing the phenomenal popularity of K.A. Applegate's Animorphs and similar juvenile series, concludes, "The real fears and fantasies of children appear in the books they like best, just as ours do in the ones we read," again privileging the popular over the canonical. "Reading at Escape Velocity," *New York Times Book Review*, 17 May 1998: 51.

Chapter 1

Gresham's Law of Culture: The Case of Mickey Spillane and Postwar America

Jesse Berrett

"The taste of the public is as mysterious as the taste of critics," Raymond Chandler complained to his publicist in 1952. "Look at the success a fellow called Mickey Spillane is having. . . . Pulp writing at its worst was never as bad as this stuff. It isn't so very long since no decent publisher would have touched it." Six years later, still fuming over his rival's unaccountable popularity, Chandler wrote one critic that "Spillane is perhaps an extreme example of the sadistic writer, but I may be wrong. I can't read him." Neither could Chandler's hero, Philip Marlowe. In *Playback*, the author's last novel (also published in 1958), the detective essays his own brand of literary criticism. Marlowe "picked a paperback off the table and made a pretense of reading it. It was about some private eye whose idea of a hot time was a dead naked woman hanging from a shower rail. . . . I threw the paperback into the wastebasket, not having a garbage can handy at the moment."[1]

Chandler was hardly alone among detective novelists in his distaste for Spillane. Early in a career that rejected the hard-boiled tradition for psychoanalytically informed rummages through troubled family histories, the young Ross Macdonald protested his publisher's demand that his new novel provide more action: "between Spillane and Charybdis is where I am." Spillane, he told his friend Hugh Kenner, had "pulled the plug" on the tradition in which he had chosen to write.[2]

Many outside the genre shared Chandler's and Macdonald's pessimism; for them Spillane loomed over the landscape, driving out everything worthwhile throughout American letters and American culture. The iconoclastic critic Philip Wylie, who had introduced "Momism" to the language in his controversial *Generation of Vipers*, worried in the staid pages of *Good Housekeeping* that Spillane menaced the future itself: "He has a wife and children, yet this is the vulgar, gruesome tripe he spews on the public. What a great, wonderful contribution he is making to the world—his *children's* world!" Surveying the book trade in the mid-1950s, the eminent literary critic Malcolm Cowley made slightly less grandiose claims but still considered Spillane worthy of serious scrutiny. His best-selling fiction, Cowley felt, "illustrates the worst side of the paperbacks as a cultural phenomenon." Even the State Department joined in. When it removed "politically suspect" writers like Lillian Hellman and Henry Wallace from the shelves of its overseas libraries in the spring of 1953, along with them went Spillane, politically unobjectionable but artistically suspect. Fellow mystery writers, book critics and intellectuals, government officials—even, we shall see, screenwriters and actors—agreed: Mickey Spillane was positively dangerous.[3]

Hovering uncertainly on the margins between "serious" literature and pulp, mystery fiction has always enjoyed a precarious critical reputation. Whereas writers as disparate as Dashiell Hammett, Dorothy Sayers, and Ruth Rendell have occasionally been permitted to escape the confines of genre for various canons, Mickey Spillane remains unquestionably the most critically savaged writer in the history of the form. Histories of the genre treat him as at best a straggler in its upward march to quality, at worst an utter debasement of everything detective fiction should represent. In his encyclopedic survey of the popular arts in America, for instance, pioneering cultural historian Russel Nye protested the monstrous success of Spillane's "inept, vulgar, savage" novels, "the ultimate degradation" of the hard-boiled detective tradition.[4] But why should one particular novelist, even one with Spillane's popularity, attract such universal opprobrium? And why then? Given that his production remained vigorous into the 1970s (with sporadic resumptions since), why was it Spillane's initial early-1950s burst of popularity that so agitated so many?

In part, these reactions were entirely appropriate to both the magnitude of Spillane's success and the publicity campaigns that helped create that success. Between 1950 and 1954 he was more or less inescapable to anyone who beheld the literary scene: promoted aggressively, his novels sold by the bushel and made him a popular celebrity—the very model, it seemed, of the modern writer. (Attempting to get his friend Neal Cassady a book deal in the mid-1950s, Jack Kerouac was astounded to discover that an editor at Gold Medal Books had counseled Cassady to read Spillane's novels, which would open for him the secrets of reaching heretofore inaccessible audiences.[5])

In truth, the highly visible changes then taking place in the publishing industry would have made *any* best-selling paperback author a target of criticism. Yet the fact remains that Spillane attracted far more than his share of such antipathy. More important than his role as vanguard of the paperback world, then, was Spillane's capacity to condense a wide variety of seemingly unrelated questions: the rise of mass culture, a defining issue for 1950s intellectuals; the onrush of paperback publishing and mass advertising, a longtime question for the book industry and its observers; and the creation of new kinds and sources of authority in Cold War culture, a matter of great concern throughout postwar American life. That collection of disparate issues suggests that Spillane became the core of what sociologist Stanley Cohen calls a "moral panic": "a condition, episode, person or groups of persons emerges to become defined as a threat to societal values and interests; . . . the moral barricades are manned."[6] An examination of that moral panic, centered around Spillane and his work, reveals how thoroughly and effectively such scorned literature can define and articulate—even generate—the central concerns of a culture. By inflating Spillane into a social menace and then attacking that menace, his opponents made all the more plain their own interpretations of and fears about the directions American culture was taking.

Born in Brooklyn in 1918 to working-class parents, Frank Morrison Spillane earned a reputation as a storyteller while still a child; in high school he sold several pieces to pulp magazines. After a brief stint at a teachers' college in Kansas that encouraged his distaste for the academy—an antipathy that later skirmishes with the intelligentsia would only reinforce—he returned to the East Coast and found work churning out plots for comic strips. (He was well suited to the task and is reputed to have produced in a single day as much copy as any three average writers.) In World War II he enlisted and trained Air Force pilots in Mississippi; at its end, he married the first of his four wives, returned to New York, and began to write. In only nineteen days he turned out his first Mike Hammer novel, *I, the Jury*. As even this brief period may have seemed too "literary," in later accounts, the author revised the figure downward to nine days. Though many in the firm were markedly unenthusiastic ("it isn't in the best of taste, but it will sell," one editor said resignedly) E.P. Dutton published it in hardcover in 1947.[7]

Most critics received the novel with equal distaste. The *Saturday Review of Literature* characterized it as "lurid," while the *Chicago Sun*'s James Sandoe blasted it as "a shabby and rather nasty little venture." The reviewer for the *New York Times* found the book a bit extreme, perhaps, but certainly not outlandish: "the story will measure up to the expectation of those mystery fans who must have the impact 'right between the eyes.'" In the *San Francisco Chronicle*, Anthony Boucher, America's preeminent mystery critic, struck a politicocultural note that anticipated later jeremiads. He was outraged that the book had even been published, because *I, the Jury* was "so vicious a glorification of force, cruelty and extra-legal methods that the novel might be made required reading in a Gestapo training school."[8]

These condemnations had no apparent effect on readers, at least on those who purchased the paperback edition that appeared the next year. Issued by New American Library (NAL) in December 1948, the twenty-five-cent reprint of *I, the Jury* enjoyed strong sales at once. By March 1949, 525,000 copies were already in print, and demand remained consistent for the rest of the year. Three years later, 2,250,000 copies had been sold; with its fiftieth printing in early 1960, the more than 5,000,000 copies sold made it Spillane's most popular novel.[9]

Though issued with little expectation that it would become a bestseller, *I, the Jury*'s instant success made Spillane's paperback publishers eager for more. (Pushing their authors to write as much as possible, and recruiting hordes of new and untried novelists from the ranks of pulp fictioneers, upstart publishing houses of the 1950s like NAL aggressively outpromoted their older, more staid hardcover siblings.[10]) The short novel that Spillane penned in 1948, *Whom the Gods Would Destroy*, was withheld until 1966 because the publisher feared it was too implausible for mass appeal, but Spillane hit his stride in 1950 and 1951, churning out five novels—*My Gun Is Quick, Vengeance Is Mine, One Lonely Night, The Big Kill*, and *The Long Wait*. Their sales made Spillane simultaneously America's most popular writer and a lightning rod for criticism. By December 1951, the newspaper columnist Max Lerner was describing a desperate flight from city to city, pursued by "mounds of . . . Mickey Spillane quarter mysteries spilling violence and sadism from every drugstore rack." Lerner's vision, horrific though it was, accurately reflected the magnitude of what both joyful publishers and enraged critics termed "the Spillane phenomenon." In the previous five months alone, 6,300,000 copies of Spillane's novels had been sold in America. *One Lonely Night* sold an astounding 1,500,000 copies within a month of its release in August 1951, an achievement dwarfed in December by *The Big Kill*, whose record-setting first printing of 2,500,000 copies sold out in just three weeks.[11]

Such sales figures remain impressive today, but at the time they were unprecedented, almost beyond belief. Spillane was clearly the best-selling author of 1951, Joseph Henry Jackson recognized in *Publishers' Weekly* in early 1952, but "since no one has yet plumbed the depth of the two-bit reprint market there is no way to be sure of how good this is." (Nor did the publishing industry see fit to take such questions seriously enough to provide answers until 1955, when *Publishers' Weekly* compiled its first list of paperback bestsellers and *Paperbound Books in Print* was published.) Spillane had sold "Thirteen Million Books of Sex and Slaughter," according to the cover of *Life*, by the summer of 1952; in that year alone, sales of his novels amounted to a full one-quarter of all paperback nonfiction. Checking the bookstands around Stamford, Connecticut, in early 1953, NAL editor in chief Victor Weybright complained that he had to visit seven or eight in order to find all of Spillane's titles. By year's end sales had reached nearly 24,000,000. Nor could the citadels of respectable literature resist him: Spillane's 1952 novel *Kiss Me, Deadly* made both the *New York Times* and *New York Herald Tribune* hardcover bestseller lists, the first time that a mystery had been so listed. Even in 1960, despite the fact that Spillane had not written a new novel in eight years, sales of his works exceeded 250,000 in a six-month period. By 1963 his novels had sold almost 75,000,000 copies across the globe. To a critic who despaired that he had written seven of the top ten bestsellers of all time, Spillane snarled, "Shut up; you're lucky I didn't write three more." As late as 1989 a solid core of popularity remained, and worldwide sales totaled an estimated 180,000,000; the most popular novelist of the paperback era, Spillane trailed only Dr. Spock in total books sold.[12]

As his editor at New American Library, Marc Jaffe, commented, Spillane did much to create the public image that sold his books: "Mickey was active, and he loved to promote, and so he was out and around quite a bit." He threw himself into the star-making machinery with a zest that suggested it was an affair of the heart, pioneering the coast-to-coast book tour, delighting in visits to book-sellers' conventions to press the flesh, and autographing stacks of his novels. Cultivating (and enjoying) what one scholar terms a "literary antireputation," Spillane infuriated critics with deliberately outrageous pronouncements. By his own admission "just a comic-book writer," he was usually photographed glower-ing in his trademark slouch hat in what his editor termed a "beer and firearms atmosphere." Crew-cut and hard-drinking, Spillane emphasized that he simply satisfied public demand: "the public is the only critic. And the only *literature* is what the public reads." Had his readers desired Thomas Wolfe, Spillane claimed, he'd have written in that style, "only ten times better." He compared his novels to jokes geared entirely toward the "punch line," the outrageous final scene, typing them single-spaced in less than two weeks because "that way there's no room for corrections . . . the first one will always be the best." Cou-pled with this disdain for conventional notions of artistic inspiration and produc-tion was his oft-repeated avarice. "Creative urge, hell," he once proclaimed. "I get a money urge." To aspiring writers he offered three words of advice: "write for MONEY!"[13]

But the selling of Mickey Spillane was only possible in a changed literary marketplace. After a century and a half of wide gaps between "serious" and "popular" markets, the postwar paperback "revolution" (the third such in Ameri-can history) drew the two inexorably together and permanently altered the con-tours of the nation's social and cultural landscapes.[14] In 1953 an estimated 300,000,000 paperbacks were printed; more than a third of the entire book mar-ket was paperbound. Providing "good reading for the masses," as New Ameri-can Library's slogan put it, paperbacks promised to efface much of the cultural hierarchy upon which intellectuals had come to rely; whereas clear qualitative distinctions had, in their view, previously demarcated literature from pulp, re-fined from mass taste, paperbacks now blurred them, making a much wider array of material available to many more readers. (As one retailer sneered, paperbacks welcomed "new customers who rarely buy regular books" into the world of reading.) But most observers echoed Frank Schick, who in 1958 surveyed the paperback market and rejoiced that "never before in the history of the printed book have so many readers simultaneously been offered such a variety of books at such a low price." For although many paperbacks merely eased the acquisi-tion of the sort of low-grade junk previously relegated to pulp magazines, inex-pensive university press books and quality softcover lines such as NAL's Mentor and Doubleday's Anchor made high culture accessible to millions.[15]

Paperbacks posed spatial as well as social dangers. They could be sold not just in urban bookstores but in "five-and-dimes, drug stores, supermarkets, roadside rests, newsstands, and even an occasional bookie joint and undertaking parlor." Their forerunners had typically flourished in locations outside the intel-lectual ambit—train stations and department stores, for example—but these new sites, "the greatest buying terrain of them all," according to one excited retailer, were alike in their unabashed commerciality. Thus it became clear to many critics that paperbacks were fostering an unwonted spirit of hucksterism and promotion. "There is at bottom little difference today," observed Basil Woon in his 1952 survey of the publishing industry, "between selling books and selling beef." If to Woon paperback publishers were butchers, to Schick they resembled the fast-food chains that were beginning to dot the nation's highways: "light fiction, Western stories, light romances, mysteries, detective stories and science fiction are written to be hastily and superficially indulged in and seldom to be remembered or reread."[16]

Constantly reminded by such remarks that Spillane's fiction was simultaneously lucrative and dangerous—his novels were banned in India, South Africa, West Germany, Australia, Denver, Milwaukee, and Boston, among other locations—NAL adopted a strategy that paid close attention to the bottom line while nodding in the direction of art. This strategy required that Spillane be nudged toward greater explicitness yet restrained from outright obscenity—a balance between sobriety and titillation that was especially important because NAL had originally split from Penguin Books, its British parent, in part over the latter's reluctance to promote its products with sufficient vigor. (In turn, Penguin's Allen Lane had been so distressed by Weybright's initial selections, including James T. Farrell and James M. Cain, that he sneered that the fledgling publishing house should dub itself Porno Books.) As its slogan indicated, NAL strove to walk the tightrope between commerce and culture; authors like Spillane—and, to a lesser extent, Erskine Caldwell, whose lurid prose was deemed part of his authentic regional vision—constantly threatened to overbalance its reprintings of Faulkner and Gide and its prestigious Mentor line of nonfiction, pitching it headlong into the chasm of mediocrity.[17]

Still, any—indeed every—paperback author might seem able to do Spillane's job. For if paperbacks threatened (or seemed to) old ways of doing literary and intellectual business, if they promised to sweep under the accustomed structures of the intellectual world, then surely any of the era's big sellers—Grace Metalious, say (1956's *Peyton Place*), or Kathleen Winsor (1945's *Forever Amber*, issued in paperback in 1950)—might have served just as well as a critical foil. (Or, a decade or so later, Jacqueline Susann.) Yet although both authors were briefly taken to task for their alleged hastening of the decline of national culture, neither attracted anything like the pervasive attention devoted to Spillane. Why, then, did the author who created "the gum-chewer's gumshoe," as *Newsweek* termed him, fulfill this function so often?[18]

The answer lies in the sheer variety of buttons he pushed and the tenacity with which he pushed them. Metalious and Winsor wrote only one bestseller each; Spillane wrote seven, six of them in a mere three years. But quantity was manifestly not the only concern, for Erle Stanley Gardner published at least two Perry Mason novels every year between 1933 and 1965 without managing to attract anything near the same level of criticism. Quality (or the lack thereof), that is, counted just as much. Gardner's inoffensive assembly-line prose and seamless, repetitive plotting positively discouraged critical attention and barred readers from investing themselves emotionally in the text. Spillane, on the other hand, courted (and won) strong reactions by stuffing his novels with raging, often self-contradictory polemics—for, variously, vigilantism and law and order; sexual license and sexual restraint—thereby offering every part of the spectrum something to aim at or invest in. As the cultural-studies scholar John Fiske observes, by their very nature certain mass-produced formulaic narratives encourage such interpretive latitude: "many industrially-produced texts have producerly characteristics that stimulate popular productivity in a way that official art-works cannot. . . . [S]uch popular productivity works better on industrial texts with their contradictions, inadequacies and superficialities, because it is these very qualities that make the text open and provocative rather than completed and satisfying."[19] Fiske's argument is part of a larger claim about audience creativity, but his analysis of mass media's producerly qualities can profitably be applied to critics as well: the sheer messiness and intellectual incoherence of Spillane's work—unlike Gardner's, which staked no larger claims and asked for no readerly response—yielded ample opportunity for enterprising critics intent on scoring points on any pressing issue, intellectual, political, or cultural. The very same quick, emotional composition that made Spillane such an appealingly unliterary figure to his readers also made him useful to gatekeepers in a wide range of fields. A brief survey of their reactions makes clear the unique importance they attributed to Spillane.

A few critics acceded to the publisher's careful balance of titillation and restraint by placing Spillane in the same chest of forbidden pleasures in which Victorians had stowed sensation literature and its more prurient cousin, pornography. (Indeed, their rhetoric echoes that of nineteenth-century moralists warning of the dangers of unrestrained consumption of murder stories and Wilkie Collins novels.) "Here's a bedtime story to be placed on the shelf alongside the earlier Spillane opus, *I, the Jury*," wrote the *San Francisco Chronicle*'s Edward Dermot Doyle. "We're talking about the shelf with the padlock on it so that neither the children nor granny will have the daylights shocked out of them . . . [but] you'll read on for sensation's sweet sake." "I can't recommend this because I am a serious literary critic and a moral leader of the community," the *Houston Post*'s Carl Little confessed. "But, confidentially, I had a hell of a swell time."[20]

To the majority of literary and cultural observers, however, Spillane's success represented the onslaught of an aggressive, smotheringly populist, lowbrow mass culture of suffocating idiocy. Though they did begin with such standard literary-critical considerations as plotting and prose style, their critiques did not merely read the aesthetic as political. Instead, they quickly decided that the truest understanding of the Spillane phenomenon required the social sciences. Applying sociological and psychological analysis to Spillane's titanic sales, his critics reached a consensus: not only did this author's popularity further prove Mencken's aphorism that no one would ever go broke underestimating the intelligence of the American public, but it also foretold the doom of American intellectual life.

Yet paradoxically enough, these critics' reactions to Spillane endowed him with a sociopolitical status he had not courted. Spillane himself always claimed to be little more than a mercenary. "I have no fans," he informed one reporter.

"You know what I got? Customers."[21] As in any moral panic, that is, the great-est claims for Spillane as a force of history came from his enemies, those quar-ters more threatened by what *they* took him to mean than by what he took *himself* to mean. That fundamental disparity suggests that he was less actual threat than useful rallying cry, a convenient and effective means of mustering critical and intellectual energies in defense of a position under siege.

There were solid reasons for such intellectual aggression. Galvanized by their declining hegemony, postwar American intellectuals made a stand on the unstable terrain of mass culture. For as television aerials sprouted on rooftops and paperbacks flooded drugstores, newsstands, and, increasingly, bookstores, the intellectuals began to fear expulsion from their cherished positions as cultural gatekeepers. Their ability to quarantine bad art from the mass of Americans, they hoped, would restore the political and cultural authority they felt slipping from their grasp. In this "struggle against kitsch and Khrushchev," as Bernard Rosenberg termed it, Spillane posed exactly the kind of problem that demanded immediate resolution. "This brew of sadism, eroticism and the glorification of 'the thrill of running something down and pumping a slug into it,'" Anthony Boucher complained of *My Gun Is Quick,* "is enough to make even the staunch-est member of the American Civil Liberties Union waver for just a second." Similarly, the critic James Sandoe deemed *The Long Wait* "so gross that the author might be testing the elasticity of the obscenity laws." As these not-quite demands for censorship demonstrate, these critics saw him as a perfect opportu-nity to man civilization's castle walls: they knew what was acceptable, what was not, and were not afraid to say so.[22]

Those who took a longer view seized upon Spillane as a symbol of cultural and political changes that seemed to portend the demise of American intellect. Such warnings issued regularly from the pages of *Partisan Review* in this pe-riod—"by the mid-1950s," according to Maurice Isserman, "the debate on mass culture had become the opiate of formerly radical intellectuals"—and Spillane proved an especially apposite figure. In a reversal of Matthew Arnold's famous dictum, he came to furnish critical shorthand for the worst that had been thought and said in America. To Dwight Macdonald he embodied "Gresham's Law of Culture," bad art's remorseless push to drive out the good. For David Dempsey the "horrendous Spillane" was the burden of progress, "the price we must pay in a democratic culture, for being able to buy *A Passage to India* for 25 cents." Or as Bernard Rosenberg put the case, "what makes mass culture so tantalizing is the implication of effortlessness. Shakespeare is dumped on the market along with Mickey Spillane." Spillane became an object of "sociological piety," a conveniently packaged means of quick analysis—both exemplar of and metaphor for the new mass culture that so exercised 1950s social critics.[23]

Spillane's novels also filled more politically minded critics' lenses. They typified the kind of cultural product that those American intellectuals influenced by the pessimism of Frankfurt school emigrés like Max Horkheimer and Theodor Adorno feared and resented. Material of this low quality, they held, would inevi-tably breed a uniform, lowbrow taste and thereby produce a monotonous, hideously standardized populace. (Openly extolling a man with a gun as the most effective solution to social problems, Spillane's work is a perfect instance of the fascistic potential of mass art.) Accordingly, there was open talk of a "Spillane menace": he was a "vicious and dangerous commodity," one reader worried; "the prototype of an American storm trooper," according to another. In an especially notorious attack, Christopher La Farge blasted Spillane in 1954 as "the logical conclusion, almost a sort of brutal apotheosis, of McCarthyism." Writing in *Commonweal* in 1949, Norbert Muhlen anxiously contrasted the "older, democratic hero" of Sir Arthur Conan Doyle or Dorothy Sayers with the "pre-totalitarian" detective of today. The Gestapo or the KKK, Muhlen worried, had "precisely the same status. . . . [The contemporary detective] is paid by his client and permitted by society to break the laws." Such heroes, he worried, "warn us of tremors beneath the surface of the society."[24]

So concentrated was this enmity that "Spillane" became a ready-made insult that cropped up in entirely unexpected contexts. When denigrating the prose style of Winston Churchill, the critic and Beat scholar Lawrence Lipton could think of nothing worse than to compare it to Spillane's outpourings. Writing in defense of the quality programming to be found on television, *Los Angeles Mirror* columnist Hal Humphrey pronounced himself "sorry for that little band of TV snobs who claim they can find nothing on the medium to merit their time. This is like saying you never read books because you can't stand Mickey Spillane." Six years later, during a turn-of-the-decade symposium on the nation's future, an English professor took issue with the underlying principles of what we would today call cultural relativism (phrased here as "one man's opinion is as good as another's") because it opened the door to aesthetic doom: it "indicates a resentment of any standards of excellence—'You like Shakespeare, I like Mickey Spillane. Who are you to say that your tastes are better than mine?' That comes down to cultural anarchy, or barbarism." By 1960, the intellectual consensus was clear: whenever one heard talk of the decline of Western civilization, one reached for Spillane.[25]

Even within the precincts of mass culture, Spillane's presence was so powerful—as inescapable for his popular-cultural contemporaries as for Harold Rosenberg—that parodies of and allusions to his work abounded. (Walt Kelly's *Pogo* gleefully presented the gory adventures of "Meat Hamburg, Private Eye, Ear, Nose, Throat, and Leg Man," in *The Bloody Drip* by "Mucky Spleen." The humorist Jean Kerr also parodied him in one of her columns.) The responses of fellow popular artists like Paddy Chayefsky and Vincente Minnelli drew finer distinctions: they took Spillane seriously and strove to create a popular art that responded to his. If tastemakers feared him as the leading edge of an army of trash, these artists saw Spillane threatening to replace *their* mass art—intelligent, refined, thoughtful—with *his*—degraded, crude, thoughtless. In several ways their perspective was actually more accurate than that of the credentialed intellectuals, for while Spillane by no means brought the critical world to its knees, his brand of mass art did help to squeeze out theirs. He was not solely, or even primarily, responsible, of course, but his work augured the future; theirs fell by the wayside.

The pervasiveness of Spillane's cultural presence becomes especially clear in *Marty* and *The Band Wagon*. Late in Paddy Chayefsky's *Marty*, the hero faces a momentous choice. Thirty-four-year-old Marty's only pleasure is cruising for girls with his best friend, Angie. One night at the Stardust Ballroom, he meets Clara, a schoolteacher, and, for the first time, words begin to spill from Marty's mouth: he tells Clara of his frustrations, his dreams, his fears. But when the pair meet Angie, he charges that Marty has deserted him, then storms off.[26] The next day Angie poses Marty's options more starkly. As Marty, Angie, and their friend Ralph lounge around Marty's apartment, Ralph describes the conclusion of *I, the Jury* with great relish. "What I like about Mickey Spillane," Ralph explains, "is he knows how to handle women." "Boy, that Mickey Spillane . . . he sure could write," Angie replies. After the men pass around a girlie magazine, Angie forces Marty to choose: "Listen, you wanna come with me tonight [to pick up girls] or you wanna go with that dog?"[27]

Climaxing a scene punctuated by repetitive invocations of Mickey Spillane, Angie's demand clearly articulates the alternatives: either Marty will remain trapped within his traditional world of ethnic blue-collar masculinity, where male social interchange takes place through talk *about* women; or he will escape that suffocating morass for upwardly mobile suburban maturity where men talk *to* women and learn to express themselves. Spillane serves here not just as a totem for the undershirted denizens of bars and bowling alleys, but as a central authority in their lives. Ralph, for instance, had previously put Spillane's knack for "handling" women to good use by offering Marty a "sure thing" with a lusty nurse if he would only dump Clara.

An element of rivalry certainly animated Chayefsky's attack: he saw Spillane as distracting an audience better served by the realistic, socially aware television dramas with which he was making his name. Yet for him, Spillane was in the end an essentially adolescent pleasure, a state through which one marched along the road to full adulthood. While Clara's choice of leisure activity is never specifically contrasted to Angie's, her profession of schoolteacher clearly signals that her pleasures are of a more mature, literate order than his, which are shown to stunt his intellectual and emotional development. The play ends on a note of hope: like Marty, Chayefsky hopes, American men will put away childish things and emerge from their pool halls and bowling alleys, blinking in the light of adult behavior, adult relationships, and adult mass culture—and the first step is to stop reading Mickey Spillane.

Where *Marty* proposes its own artistic virtues as a better alternative for the enormous audience Spillane is damaging, Vincente Minnelli's *Band Wagon* asks what "popular entertainment" should be in the light of Spillane's success.[28] Its answer is equal parts mockery and envy, for Spillane embodies a vulgar, exuberant, lowest-common-denominator popular art whose heroic posturing is as risible as its appeal is irresistible. In the film, Tony Hunter (Fred Astaire), an old song-and-dance star, tries to make a comeback on Broadway, but his first attempt is hijacked by an artsy director whose musical version of *Faust* is so inaccessible that it closes on opening night. Clearly, pretense does not make for good mass art, so Astaire and friends remake the show to feature "laughs and entertainment." On opening night in New York, the show runs through an array of crowd-pleasing numbers before concluding with a rambunctious tribute/parody/homage to Spillane called "Girl Hunt: A Murder Mystery in Jazz," in which Astaire plays a hard-boiled but balletic detective named Rod Riley. Lurid paperback covers for the novels of "Mickey Starr," which include *Dames Kill Me* and *Stab Me, Sugar*, litter the backdrop. Emulating the opening of *Kiss Me, Deadly*, published the year before, "Girl Hunt" begins with a blonde in a raincoat being menaced by hoodlums in trenchcoats; when Riley comes to her rescue the hoods beat him up. The next few minutes provide a quick précis of Spillane's novels, including a number of fights and a tantalizing dark-haired woman described in authentic Spillane similes: "She came at me in sections, [with] more curves than a scenic railway. She was bad. She was dangerous. I wouldn't trust her any further than I could throw her. She was selling hard, but I wasn't buying." After a somewhat incoherent series of episodes, Riley shoots the blond woman, snarling (in an obvious echo of *I, the Jury*), "Now I knew who the killer was, but it didn't matter. Killers have to die!" The blond woman crumples to the floor, though not before giving Riley one last kiss; he then embraces the dark one, at which point the audience at the play explodes in a standing ovation. It has been a spectacular finale, one that will surely ensure the show's future prospects. Tony and his cohorts, tutored by Mickey Spillane, have rediscovered real entertainment.

On the one hand, "Girl Hunt" overtly parodies Spillane's plotting and language in the same way that *Pogo* ridiculed "Meat Hamburg." The routine assumes that the audience will recognize the Spillane allusions and laugh at the willowy Astaire's tough-guy pretensions. Yet in a more fundamental sense, the scene also respects the magnitude of Spillane's cultural presence: the ballet does, after all, bring the house down; it offers the audience (for both the film itself and that for the show within the film) the accessible, exciting narrative it quite obviously demands, rather than the highbrow aridity the film has already mocked. As Astaire and Charisse sing in the closing number, which reprises the movie's theme song, "the art that appeals to the heart/that's entertainment." So although *Band Wagon* renders Spillane risible, a clownish celebrity (or "Starr") who jolts his readers with the blasts of simpleminded, ritualized violence his titles announce, it also pays him his due, for it demands precisely the kind of climax in which he specialized. Even while the film laughs at his pretensions to masculine authority, in short, it craves (and borrows) his surefire mass appeal. The song makes the admission the film can never quite bring itself to make: *that* is entertainment.

Were Dwight and Ross Macdonald, Bernard and Harold Rosenberg right? In retrospect, it is abundantly clear that Spillane did not single-handedly bring the end of intellectual life to pass, nor did he bleed dry the market for literary fiction. He has since become, if anything, something of a curio, a relic from a lost cultural and intellectual world. "The red-blooded Mike Hammer, after all," the critic James Wolcott argued in 1983, "belongs as indubitably to the boxy, bulky fifties as Sherlock Holmes does to the gaslight and wet cobblestones of the turn of the century." On the other hand, the movie musical and the "quality" television program did more or less die out, although in each case industry imperatives had far more to do with the form's demise; Spillane (and paperbacks more generally) played marginal roles at best. More prescient were those observers who worried that Spillane would sensationalize the publishing profession; Chandler's rather unsalacious *Playback* itself bears the imprint of Spillane's popularity, the excerpt placed inside the front cover featuring a woman ripping her own shirt off. Indeed, "Spillane's work," argue the compilers of a recent anthology of hard-boiled fiction, "far more than that of any other writer, dictated which sort of crime fiction was to be published as paperback originals over the next twenty years. . . . [His influence] cannot be ignored or underestimated." And it is certainly true that over the past forty years the publishing industry has grown more and more obsessed by what one analyst has termed "the blockbuster complex": huge print runs, enormous bonuses for ghostwritten celebrity "autobiographies" and self-help tomes, massive waves of promotion that sell authors rather than books.[29]

Yet even so, while Spillane certainly rode the waves of change in publishing to the best of his ability, he did not set them off. What the moral/cultural/literary/political panic over his work seems most of all to reflect is the extraordinarily febrile *mentalité* of the early Cold War, one in which apocalypses of many sorts seemed constantly to impend, and a good many transient issues assumed the character of major national crises: not a mountain out of a molehill, certainly, but rather a case of critics lashing out at shadows, desperate to find something tangible, to capture and solidify the changing contours of their world. They were certainly not completely wrong to latch onto Spillane, but neither were they entirely right. He was at most a symbol of change, a standard-bearer rather than a leader—and certainly no simple solution to the question of what had caused such enormous cultural shifts.

NOTES

1. *Selected Letters of Raymond Chandler*, ed. Frank McShane (New York: Dell Publishing, 1987), 310–11, 476; Geoffrey O'Brien, *Hardboiled America: Lurid Paperbacks and the Masters of Noir*, expanded ed. (New York: Da Capo Press, 1997), 105.

2. Ross Macdonald, "Farewell, Chandler," *Ross Macdonald: Inward Journey*, ed. Ralph B. Sipper (Santa Barbara, CA: Cordelia Editions, 1984), 37–42; Matthew J. Bruccoli, *Ross Macdonald* (San Diego: Harcourt Brace Jovanovich, 1984), 49, 51.

3. Philip Wylie, "The Crime of Mickey Spillane," *Good Housekeeping* 140 (February 1955): 54; Malcolm Cowley, *The Literary Situation* (New York: Viking, 1954), 107; Richard Pells, *Not Like Us: How Europeans Have Loved, Hated, and Transformed American Culture since World War II* (New York: Basic Books, 1997), 82.

4. Russel B. Nye, *The Unembarrassed Muse: The Popular Arts in America* (New York: Dial Press, 1970), 263.

5. Ann Charters, *Kerouac* (New York: Warner Paperback Library, 1974), 146.

6. Stanley Cohen, *Folk Devils and Moral Panics: The Creation of the Mods and the Rockers* (New York: St. Martin's Press, 1980), as quoted in Simon Watney, *Policing Desire: Pornography, AIDS and the Media*, 2d ed. (Minneapolis: University of Minnesota Press, 1989), 39.

7. Max Allan Collins and James Traylor, *One Lonely Knight: Mickey Spillane's Mike Hammer* (Bowling Green: Popular Press, 1984), 5–6; Richard Johnston, "Death's Fair-Haired Boy," *Life* 32 (23 June 1952): 89; Art Harris, "Mickey Spillane, Still Hammering," *Washington Post*, 24 October 1984, D1, D9.

8. "The Criminal Record," *Saturday Review of Literature* 30 (3 August 1947): 31; *Book Review Digest* (1947): 846; Jack Glick, "Criminals at Large," *New York Times Book Review*, 3 August 1947, 15; *San Francisco Chronicle This World*, 3 August 1947, 19.

9. Victor Weybright to John Macrae, 17 February 1949, *I, the Jury* Folder, Box 68, Folder 1706 [hereafter ITJ], New American Library Files, Fales Library, NYU; Weybright to John Edmondson, 16 October 1951, General Correspondence Folder 1700 [hereafter GC1], New American Library Files, Fales Library, NYU; "Mickey Spillane Printing History as of 12/12/51," GC1; memo from HG, 24 September 1959, ITJ.

10. The best treatment of the paperback world of the 1950s remains Kenneth Davis, *Two-Bit Culture: The Paperbacking of America* (Boston: Little, Brown, 1984).

11. Max Lerner, "Sex and Death," *New York Post*, 13 December 1951, 42; Schedule of Payments to Farrar, Straus on Spillane Accounts, 3 October 1951, GC1; publicity release by Al Dreyfus, 24 October 1951, GC1; Johnston, "Death's Fair-Haired Boy," 80; "After Hours," *Harper's* 204 (May 1952): 99. For the sake of comparison, a survey of the book trade published in 1949 described a "huge printing" as 150,000 copies. (William Miller, *The Book Trade* [New York: Columbia University Press, 1949], 336.)

12. Joseph Henry Jackson, "Fiction Is Neither What It Was nor What It Might Be," *Publishers' Weekly* 161 (19 January 1952): 198; Frank L. Schick, *The Paperbound Book in America* (New York: R.R. Bowker, 1958), 90–91, 95; "Thirteen Million . . . " is on the cover of *Life*, 23 June 1952; memo from Weybright, 3 February 1953, General Correspondence Folder 1702 [hereafter GC3], New American Library Files, Fales Library, NYU; Theodore Walker to Arthur Baker, 12 May 1954, GC3; bestseller list in *Publishers' Weekly* 162 (22 November 1952): 2111; Weybright to Allan Adams, 15 December 1952, GC3; "The Boom in Paper-Bound Books," *Fortune* 48 (September 1953): 150; memo from PG on Spillane reprints, 4 November 1953, GC3; Terry Southern, "An Investigation of the Mid-Century Literary Phenomenon in Which Mr. Spillane, a Popular Novelist of the Day, Chooses to Assay the Role of His Hero, Mike Hammer, in a Motion Picture Interpretation of a Book, Thereby Inciting Curious Speculation," *Esquire* 60 (July 1963): 74; Gay Talese, "It's a New Killer for Mike Hammer," *New York Times*, 19 June 1962, 29; "Dutton Hopes to Make a Killing with Spillane's Latest Mike Hammer," *Publishers' Weekly* 236 (6 October 1989): 59; "So Big," *Publishers' Weekly* 235 (26 May 1989): 531.

13. Marc Jaffe, interview with author, Mount Kisco, New York, 6 January 1992; the phrase "literary antireputation" is from John Raeburn, *Fame Became of Him: Hemingway as Public Writer* (Bloomington: Indiana University Press, 1984), 7; Southern, "An Investigation," 76; J. Kenneth van Dover, *Murder in the Millions* (New York: Ungar, 1984), 99; Mickey Spillane, "Life Is a Thriller," *Ulisse 2000* 75 (June 1990): 196, 200; Collins and Traylor, *One Lonely Knight*, 20; William Ruehlmann, *Saint with a Gun: The Unlawful American Private Eye* (New York: New York University Press, 1984), 98;

Fanny Butcher, "'I Write for the Money That's in It!' Spillane Says He Gives the Public What It Wants," *Chicago Sunday Tribune Magazine of Books*, 19 July 1953, 9.

14. On previous "paperback revolutions," see Schick, *Paperbound Book in America*, 3–19, 22–66; Lewis Coser, Charles Kadushin, and Walter Powell, *Books: The Culture and Commerce of Publishing* (New York: Basic Books, 1982), 20–23; Thomas Bonn, *Undercover: An Illustrated History of American Mass-Market Paperbacks* (New York: Penguin, 1982).

15. "Boom in Paper-Bound Books," 123; Carl Kaestle, "Literacy and Diversity: Themes from a Social History of the American Reading Public," *History of Education Quarterly* 28 (1988): 523–49; for a dissent see David D. Hall, "Readers and Reading in America: Historical and Critical Perspectives," *Proceedings of the American Antiquarian Society* 103 (1993): 337–57; *How to Run a Paperback Bookshop* ed. Sidney Gross and Phyllis B. Steckler (New York: R.R. Bowker, 1963), 58; Schick, *Paperbound Book in America*.

16. Wallis Howe, "Breaking into New Markets," *Publishers' Weekly* 148 (27 January 1945): 428–31; Basil Woon, *The Current Publishing Scene* (New York: Exposition Press, 1952), 13; Schick, *Paperbound Book in America*, 119.

17. On the history of NAL, see especially Thomas Bonn, *Heavy Traffic and High Culture: New American Library as Literary Gatekeeper in the Paperback Revolution* (New York: New American Library, 1980). See also Davis, *Two-Bit Culture*, 115, 177–80, on the "Great Contradiction" throughout the industry between the (usually unprofitable) serious nonfiction and the mass-marketed category fiction whose profits paid for it.

18. "Just Like the Slobs," *Newsweek* 57 (19 June 1961): 104.

19. John Fiske, "The Cultural Economy of Fandom," *The Adoring Audience: Fan Culture and Popular Media*, ed. Lisa A. Lewis (London and New York: Routledge, 1992), 47.

20. Edward Dermot Doyle, review of *My Gun Is Quick*, *San Francisco Chronicle*, 12 February 1950, 16; Jaffe, editorial dopesheet for *Kiss Me, Deadly*, 23 January 1953, *Kiss Me, Deadly* Folder, Box 68, Folder 1711 [hereafter KMD], New American Library Files, Fales Library, NYU.

21. Harris, "Mickey Spillane, Still Hammering," D9.

22. This understanding of American intellectuals' mission as cultural inspectors is derived from Andrew Ross, *No Respect: Intellectuals and Popular Culture* (New York: Routledge, 1989), 42–64; see also Neil Jumonville, *Critical Crossings: The New York Intellectuals in Postwar America* (Berkeley: University of California Press, 1991), 151–85; Anthony Boucher, "Trigger-Happy," *New York Times Book Review*, 12 February 1950, 14; James Sandoe, review of *The Long Wait*, *New York Herald Tribune Book Review*, 18 November 1951, 24.

23. Maurice Isserman, *If I Had a Hammer . . . : The Death of the Old Left and the Birth of the New* (New York: Basic Books, 1987), 101; Dwight Macdonald, "A Theory of Mass Culture," *Mass Culture: The Popular Arts in America*, ed. Bernard Rosenberg and David Manning White (Glencoe, IL: The Free Press, 1957), 61; Davis, *Two-Bit Culture*, 187; Bernard Rosenberg, "Mass Culture in America," *Mass Culture*, ed. Rosenberg and White, 5; "After Hours," 100.

24. An influential Frankfurt School critique is Max Horkheimer and Theodor Adorno, *Dialectic of Enlightenment*, trans. John Cumming (New York: Continuum, 1972); Christopher LaFarge, "Mickey Spillane and His Bloody Hammer," *Mass Culture*, ed. Rosenberg and White, 176–85; for the "Spillane menace," see letters to *Saturday Review of Literature* in response to LaFarge's article, 4 December 1954, 25 and 27 Novem-

ber 1954, 25; letter to NAL, 18 August 1951, GC1; letter to NAL, 19 December 1948, GC1; Norbert Muhlen, "The Thinker and the Tough Guy," *Commonweal* 51 (25 November 1949): 216–17.

25. Lawrence Lipton, letter to *The Nation* 182 (30 June 1956): 540; Hal Humphrey, "Boots and Bravos," *Los Angeles Mirror*, 16 February 1954, II, 7; "What's Wrong—What's Right with Today's America," *US News and World Report* 48 (22 February 1960): 70.

26. For a similar description of Spillane fans, see H.H.T., "Spillane's 'The Long Wait' at Criterion," *New York Times*, 3 July 1954, 9; see also John Steinbeck's description of male bonding cemented by drinking and "paperback thrillers . . . loaded with sex and sadism." (*Travels with Charley: In Search of America* [New York: Bantam, 1962], 111.)

27. Dialogue taken from *Marty*, directed by Delbert Mann (United Artists, 1955), 91 min., videocassette; Chayefsky's original television play had posed Marty's dilemma less elegantly: Ralph's lines in the film are delivered in the play by a character sneeringly described as "Critic," characterized only as a "thirty-two-year-old man"—as if the combination of his age and appreciation of Mickey Spillane mark him as a terminal adolescent. (Paddy Chayefsky, *Television Plays* [New York: Simon & Schuster, 1955], 169–70, 174–75, 176.)

28. *The Band Wagon*, directed by Vincente Minnelli (MGM, 1953), 111 min, videocassette.

29. James Wolcott, "A Shot in the Dark," *New York* 16 (2 May 1983): 77–78; *Hard-Boiled: An Anthology of American Crime Fiction* ed. Bill Pronzini and Jack Adrian (New York: Oxford University Press, 1995), 13; Thomas Whiteside, *The Blockbuster Complex: Conglomerates, Show Business, and Book Publishing* (Middletown: Wesleyan University Press, 1981); Michael Korda, "Wasn't She Great?" *The New Yorker* 71 (14 August 1995): 66–72; more recently, see Robin Pogrebin, "The Naked Literary Come-On," *New York Times Book Review*, 17 August 1997, 31.

Chapter 2

"Expressing" Herself: The Romance Novel and the Feminine Will to Power

Sarah S.G. Frantz

A week after our child was born,
you cornered me in the spare room
and we sank down on the bed.
You kissed me and kissed me, my milk undid its
burning slip-knot through my nipples,
soaking my shirt.

—Sharon Olds, "New Mother"

It has been "a truth universally acknowledged" that modern romance novels are unacceptable reading material for the liberated woman of the twentieth century—and yet they continue to thrive, both paperback and hardback romances infiltrating even the *New York Times* bestseller lists.[1] The romance novel has suffered under the criticism of both the literary world and the feminist establishment. Disgusted critics have created the image of the bored housewife reading her "soft-porn" instead of doing housework or taking care of her children, while disgusted feminists have created the image of the repressed housewife reading her "soft-porn" instead of fighting the injustices of patriarchy.[2] Kay Mussell recalls that romance critics "shared the political perspective of feminism that romances were patriarchal structures that encouraged women to become reconciled to their social conditions."[3] While admitting that "romance reading originates in very real dissatisfaction and embodies a valid, if limited, protest," Janice Radway claims in her important examination of the romance and its readers, *Reading the Romance*, "when viewed from the vantage point of a feminism that would like to see the women's oppositional impulse lead to real social change, romance reading can also be seen as an activity that could potentially disarm that impulse."[4] However, both the readers and authors of the romance oppose these images and all that they imply, as Radway herself admits: "many of the writers and readers of romances interpret these stories as chronicles of female triumph."[5] Best-selling romance author Susan Elizabeth Phillips elaborates:

> Gradually I began to realize that the romance novel was providing me with a fantasy of which I was very much in need. But it wasn't the fantasy that I had always assumed romance writers were offering their readers—that of a wonderful man or a glamorous, fulfilling career. *I already had those things.* Instead, the fantasy these novels offered me was one of command and control over the harum scarum events of my life—a fantasy of female empowerment.
>
> For me, there was nothing more satisfying than the illusion that I was in command of all the external forces that so frequently frazzled and threatened me in real life, and as I talked to other women, both writers and readers, it became evident that I wasn't the only one experiencing this feeling.[6]

Furthermore, romance readers and authors claim, increasingly and almost without exception, that there is "no conflict between our feminist views and the content of the books we were reading," or in Lynn Coddington's words: "I write romance novels myself. I also consider myself a feminist."[7]

Although the romance novel is written for an almost exclusively female audience by writers who are also almost exclusively female and claim to be feminists, most non-romance-reading feminist critics continue to view the romance novel as deservedly entrenched in the category of scorned literature because they assume that the female empowerment readers claim is a form of false consciousness, a conservative social force. The seemingly contradictory convictions revealed in this debate can be reconciled by examining the elements in the romance by which the readers feel they are being empowered and by which feminist critics think the readers are being subjugated. The element that overwhelms the romance's landscape—the delight of its readers and the despair of its critics—is the hero, that "[d]angerously handsome, dangerously powerful, dangerously sleek, dangerously . . . *dangerous*" man.[8] The hero represents patriarchal power in all its glory by being the richest, or the strongest, or the most beautiful, or the most masculine, or the most emotionally distant man that the heroine has ever known, and it is this embodiment of patriarchy that, in author Penelope Williamson's words, "for all his fierceness, is quite literally brought to his knees to propose marriage and declare his undying love. The savage beast is tamed by love: such is the allure of the fantasy."[9] Author Jayne Ann Krentz describes the critical dilemma the hero presents: "These males are the tough, hard-edged, tormented heroes that are at the heart of the vast majority of best-selling romance novels. These are the heroes who carry off the heroines in historical romances. These are the heroes feminist critics despise."[10]

The inclusion of the hero's perspective in the narrative is the biggest change that the romance has undergone in the last fifteen years.[11] In *The Romance Revolution*, Carol Thurston surveyed romance readers and found that in 1982, readers "expressed a desire to see 'a well-developed hero point of view,' and by 1985 'mixed heroine-hero point of view' was at the top of the list of the five most-wanted story attributes. Readers are no longer satisfied with seeing only how the

New Hero responds, they now want to look inside his head to discover what and how he thinks, why he responds as he does, what his motivations and problems are, and what he is feeling."[12]   Unfortunately, and symptomatic of feminist criticism of romance, Thurston does not analyze this phenomenon further, but author Laura Kinsale adds to the discussion of this change with her claim that *"the man carries the book,"* because "readers are actually asking for emotional identification with the hero, not simply his viewpoint," which signals, in her opinion, "a plain rejection of heroine-identification in favor of hero-identification."[13]   Susan Elizabeth Phillips concurs: "The key to whether or not a romance novel gives me that satisfying sense of having some control over my life lies not so much with the personality of the heroine as with the type of hero the book depicts." With readers clamoring for the hero's perspective and romances complying with their requests, critics can no longer automatically assume that readers identify solely with the heroine.[14]

Consequently, Janice Radway's groundbreaking and admittedly insightful theories of the romance are not adequate for an evaluation of the increase in the hero's point of view, because they are too heavily predicated on the reader's heroine-identification and make few allowances for the increase in the hero's perspective that has transformed the romance since Radway finished her project. Using Nancy Chodorow's psychoanalytic theories from *The Reproduction of Mothering*, Radway hypothesizes that romance readers suffer from a "lack of institutionalized emotional support" in their roles as mothers and wives. The "lack of emotional nurturance combined with the high costs of lavishing constant attention on others is the primary motivation behind the desire to lose the self in a book." Because the heroines that "they most appreciated were virtually always provided with the kind of attention and care the Smithton women claimed to desire and further that the hero's ministrations were nearly always linked metaphorically with maternal concern and nurturance," the reader, "as a result of her identification with the heroine, feels herself the *object* of someone else's attention and solicitude. Ultimately, the romance permits its reader the experience of feeling cared for and the sense of having been reconstituted affectively, even if both are lived only vicariously."[15]   This theory, however, is now outdated, because the reader's need to crawl inside the hero's head cannot fully be explained by a need to feel nurtured through identification with the heroine. In fact, by showing the hero's thoughts as he falls in love, the romance provides its readers with something that Radway thought was missing from the romances she evaluated: the ability "to explain convincingly exactly why and how each individual heroine is able to translate male reticence and cruelty into tenderness and devotion."[16]

The heroine's musings in Mary Balogh's Regency romance *The Incurable Matchmaker* highlight the inadequacies of Radway's theories for evaluating the modern romance:

And though she could feel his body with every part of her own and had one arm about his broad shoulders and one hand twined in his thick dark hair, and though her own mouth had come open to his, she felt no uncontrollable physical passion.

Only something far, far worse. Only a deep feeling of affection. Only a craving to get behind his mask—because he assuredly did wear one, however much he denied doing so. Only a longing to know the man as he was and to find that after all he was likable and lovable. Only a need to deny reality and find her fantasy lover again.[17]

The heroine wants to get behind her hero's mask in order to understand "the man as he is," to feel that he, and therefore patriarchy, is lovable and controllable, because understandable. She wants knowledge of her hero's heart and head, not nurturance from him. This is the knowledge that is granted to the reader through the hero's perspective in the romance. The emotional climax of Susan Elizabeth Phillips' *Kiss an Angel* is when the hero looks into his heart and acknowledges, "*Love*. That's what this feeling was he hadn't understood, the feeling that had begun with a melting inside him. He'd been learning how to love. Daisy had seen it. She'd known what was happening to him, but he had denied it."[18] Being able to witness the hero's thought processes as he realizes he's in love with the heroine allows the reader to recognize that the hero does indeed love the heroine as she—heroine and reader—loves him, and to rejoice in the hero's confirmation of feminine knowledge and power. Conversely, when reading the *heroine's* thoughts, the reader is merely able to identify with what she, the reader, already knows, because she knows what it feels like to be a woman falling in love with an enigmatic man who embodies the power of a patriarchal society, a society in which women have little power. It is not a privilege for the reader, nor does it serve any purpose, to be able to examine the heroine's thoughts. The reader believes that if only she could see what the hero is thinking as he falls in love with the heroine; and once the hero's thoughts are revealed, if only she could recognize them as similar to her own thoughts when she falls in love; and once the similarity is noticed, if only the hero could come to recognize that her way of thinking is the better way—then, for the reader, the hero and the patriarchal power that he represents can be knowable, understandable—controllable.

In order to attempt to understand the romance reader's desperate and increasing need for the hero's viewpoint, it is necessary to advance beyond Radway's heroine-centered theories of nurturance to Michel Foucault's analysis of power gained through confession defined in the first volume of *The History of Sexuality*. Foucault's discussion of the "widening of [the] domain" of the confession that results from the addictive "perpetual spirals of power and pleasure" that the confession produces in both the person confessing and the listener is very easily adapted to an analysis of the romance's increasing preoccupation with the hero's thoughts as he falls in love with the heroine.[19] Knowledge of a subject creates power over that subject, and, in a Foucauldian reversal, power creates knowledge, and it is the confession, Foucault claims, that "became one of the West's most highly valued techniques for producing truth," which, in turn, produces power and knowledge.[20] Foucault describes the confession as:

a ritual that unfolds within a power relationship, for one does not confess without the presence (or virtual presence) of a partner who is not simply the interlocutor but the authority who requires the confession, prescribes and appreciates it, and intervenes in order to judge, punish, forgive, console and reconcile; a ritual in which the truth is corroborated by the obstacles and resistances it has had to surmount in order to be formulated; and finally, a ritual in which the expression alone, independently of its external consequences, produces intrinsic modifications in the person who articulated it: it exonerates, redeems, and purifies him; it unburdens him of his wrongs, liberates him, and promises him salvation.[21]

The female reader interprets the hypermasculine, "alpha male" hero's confessions as a symbol of his "purification," colonizing the patriarchal economy of use and transforming it into the "salvation" of a matriarchal power based on a female economy of exchange.[22] To produce more knowledge and therefore more power through the hero's confessions, it "is no longer a question of simply saying what was done . . . and how it was done; but of reconstructing, in and around the act, the thoughts that recapitulated it, the obsessions that accompanied it, the images, desires, modulations, and quality of the pleasure that animated it," because the "intensity of the confession renewed the questioner's curiosity; the pleasure discovered fed back to the power that encircled it."[23] By having ever-increasing access to the inner confessions of the hero's mind, the reader can trust in his romantic transformation as he abandons his belief in a masculine economy of use (hence all the rakes and libertines among romance heroes), and recognizes the superiority of and adopts a feminine economy of exchange (hence the requisite exchange of vows at the end of the romance). By having ever-increasing access to the hero's mind, the reader can recognize—and revel in the triumph of—her own thoughts in a patriarch's head. Rather than responding to patriarchy's failure with a "promise" of the restitution of masculine emotional nurturance that only further entrenches patriarchal control, as Radway claimed, the modern ideal romance provides the reader with the addictive promise of power *over* patriarchy, by supposedly granting her knowledge about it, through access to the hero's thoughts.[24]

In Jayne Ann Krentz's *Grand Passion*, the heroine has written and published a novel, *The Mirror*, that signifies all romance novels. This novel within a novel provides a fascinating, Foucauldian conjunction between *The Mirror* and Cleo's own romance with her hero. We are told: "The critics had, generally speaking, responded very favorably to *The Mirror*. Only Cleo knew that none of them had really understood it. They had thought the book was a work of autoeroticism; that the female narrator was locked in a fantasy of startling intimacy with the masculine elements of her own nature. They did not comprehend the significance of the man in the mirror."[25] Although the critics were wrong about the meaning of *The Mirror*, even those who were sympathetic to it, the hero, of course, understands it, and recognizes that even though "the sensual fantasies in the book were so vibrantly female in nature that they felt alien" when he read them, they still "compelled him, seduced him, captivated him."[26] When he has finished reading *The Mirror*, he tells the heroine and the reader what he sees in her fantasies:

"The portrayal of a female view of sexuality in *The Mirror* was nothing short of riveting," Max offered as he poured more tea into Cleo's cup. "The reader has the sense that the narrator is both the seducer and the one who is seduced. It brings up several interesting questions about the matter of reader identification, as far as I am concerned. . . .

"The reader must ask himself, for example," Max said in measured, pedantic tones, "just who is the seducer in *The Mirror*? Is it a work of autoeroticism? Is the narrator actually seducing herself when she looks into the mirror?"

That was certainly what the reviewers had believed, Cleo thought. She waited with a sense of impending fate to hear what Max had to say about it. . . .

. . . "Personally, I think something far more complex is going on. Women writers, after all, are interested in relationships. I believe that the figure in the mirror is the *other*, and that, initially, at least, he is actually the seducer. But there's another problem in the book. I think the man in the mirror is just as trapped in his own world as the narrator is in hers."

Cleo froze. None of the reviews that had appeared on *The Mirror* had understood that fundamental fact. Her eyes met Max's, and she nearly fell off the bar stool when she saw the deep, sensual understanding in his gaze.[27]

Max, like the perfect romance hero he is, recognizes the beauty, value, and rightness of the feminine economy of emotional exchange represented by *The Mirror* and, in an interesting twist, uses his insights to seduce the heroine. He, quite rightly, questions reader identification in romances, and understands, as no one else in *Grand Passion* has or can, that the attraction of romances is its promise to the reader of the liberatory power of freeing the patriarch from his own cage of patriarchy into the emancipation of feminine exchange. The romance fantasy is written by women, for women, in order that they may recognize themselves in patriarchy—in this case, because patriarchy recognizes itself in the female fantasy—and thereby appropriate its power.

As Tania Modleski hints, romances seem to be "violat[ing] the cardinal rule of patriarchy, famously articulated by Jacques Lacan: the Phallus must remain veiled."[28] In lifting the veil from the hero's thoughts, romances are pretending to readers that all the secrets of patriarchy are revealed as secrets they already know and control. However, the romance hero's confessions are of course *not* representations of what a "real" man thinks—the narrator *is* seducing herself when she looks into the mirror of the romance novel. The reader believes that she is lifting patriarchy's veil to find, as Modleski describes, "mortal men standing behind it, somewhat sheepish, perhaps, at having been exposed, but maybe a little relieved as well."[29] However, female authors and readers are actually lifting the veil to reveal a nonthreatening phallus that they themselves have created, one that bears little relation to the reality of patriarchal power structures besides their own fantasies about it, as the heroine in *Grand Passion* knows: "But she had created the mirror, she reminded herself. The only things she saw in the glass were the things she, herself, projected into it."[30] In *The Heroine's Text*, Nancy K. Miller discusses what she calls posed, feminocentric novels of the eighteenth century—novels written by men that pretend to explore the "female experience," but are actually "masculine representation[s] of female desire produced ultimately for an audience not of women readers, but of men." As both producers and consumers of the novels, men generated a "fictionalization of what is taken to be the feminine at a specific cultural moment," that is actually "auto-referential: a self-congratulatory and self-addressed performance destined to be celebrated by other men; an anxious simulation of alterity that would rewrite otherness as sameness."[31] By reversing the genders of Miller's analysis and applying it to the act of romance reading, it is possible to theorize that the modern romance's intense focus on the hero's perspective is a feminine representation of masculine desire produced by and for women, an attempt by women to rewrite masculine otherness as feminine sameness, through the medium of the utterly masculine hero's confessions, in order to appropriate patriarchal power for themselves.

Herein lies the key to the dilemma of the contradictory views of the romance, on which hinges both the romance's attraction for its readers and its downfall in the eyes of nonreader feminist critics. Following the trajectory Foucault predicted, romance authors and readers claim that the power the hero's confessions grant them is real precisely because they demand it and are then needed to interpret its importance, because it destroys all the obstacles of the hero's alpha-male masculinity in order to be spoken, and because the confession promises the hero the liberation of a feminine exchange economy that validates the readers' own involvement in that economy. Feminist criticism, however, questions the value of the liberatory power that the hero's confessions provide to the female romance reader, just as Radway questioned the value of male nurturance provided by the earlier romances, because the power that the reader claims is still contingent on the existence of the power of patriarchy and because the power is merely a temporary fantasy without basis in reality. However, any attempt to resolve the contradiction between these opinions by evaluating the nature of the romance's power through readings of actual romances is difficult because the proliferation of romance subgenres complicates the ability to generalize a theory for all romance novels. Sandra Booth argues "that the increasing fragmentation in the genre is a result not only of readers seeking novelty but of searching for different romance fantasies," making it increasingly unfeasible, as Mussell points out, "to imagine [the subgenres] sharing an audience at all."[32] One way to generalize among the subgenres in order to examine the power of the romance is to return to a constant, ineradicable presence in the romance—the body.[33]

The scenes I will be examining span the whole genre as little else in the romance does because they are an integral part of the individual romance's sex scenes. These particular scenes are, however, themselves sometimes scorned by both critics and readers, making them doubly interesting. Occasionally when the heroine has just given birth, the hero breast-feeds from her in scenes to which readers' reactions are, according to one reader, "extreme—no in-between. Loved it or hated it. Erotic or silly."[34] The scenes range in length from a brief interruption of the narrative to lengthy spectacles from and around which the novel's themes are constructed. In a brief scene in Mary Balogh's short story "The Anniversary," the hero tastes his wife's milk on his son's mouth when he kisses him, and reflects: "It was sweet-tasting, he thought irrelevantly as he walked downstairs to the dining room, wondering what awaited him there. He had not expected a mother's milk to taste sweet. He wanted to taste it again. He felt an unwelcome stabbing of physical desire."[35] This is the sole reference to the heroine's milk in Balogh's story, whereas the relationship between the hero and the heroine in Sandra Brown's *Sunset Embrace* is entirely predicated on her ability to wet-nurse his son, and his desire for her is established and "expressed"—pun intended—through breast-feeding scenes. By examining the interactions between the hero's and the heroine's perspectives of the power relations in the breast-feeding hero scenes, it is possible to evaluate the romance's worth to or subjection of its readers.

The sweeping changes that the romance has undergone in language and character perspective are noticeable in the following two brief scenes. In Bertrice Small's *Skye O'Malley*, published in 1980, Skye and Niall make love after their final reconciliation:

His hands reached up to play with the perfect round fruits of her breasts, and he lifted his head to nurse on a dark nipple, eyes widening in surprise at the milk that suddenly filled his mouth. Fascinated, he continued suckling, and more excited than she had ever been, Skye found her hips moving in the age-old rhythm of pleasure. She was shocked by herself, and by him, for neither of them could stop. Unable to control herself any longer, Skye pulled away from him and, arching her body, threw back her head, and took her release. Her pleasure increased when she felt him taking his as well.[36]

In the style of old romances, the language in this excerpt—"perfect round fruits of her breasts"—is obviously the "purple prose" derided by critics of the romance, and although the hero's point of view is included, the reader is returned relentlessly to Skye's perspective, symbolized by the fact that the book's title is the heroine's name, rather than a reference to the hero as is increasingly the case today. The suckling here merely provides a "shocking" addition to the sex scene.

A similar scene in Sandra Brown's *Hawk O'Toole's Hostage*, originally published in 1988, uses more realistic prose and indicates the more equal distribution of point of view in the modern romance, again symbolized by the title which refers to both the hero, Hawk O'Toole, and the heroine, his hostage.[37] In the novel's Epilogue, after their first son is born, Hawk vocalizes his love for his heroine for the first time:

"Have I mentioned how much I miss you, how empty my bed is without you, how much I love you?"
"Not today."
He kissed her again, keeping it innocent, until her tongue came in search of his. With a moan of longing, his mouth sank down upon hers. His hand moved to her gown and opened it. He covered her breast fondly and possessively. When he felt the sticky moisture, he raised his head and gazed down at her. "I love to watch my son nurse."
"I know. I love watching you watch him."

Hawk lightly stroked her dusky nipple and a bead of milk formed on the pad of his thumb. "He didn't drink it all. You've still got milk left."

"Plenty," she replied huskily.

His inquiring eyes flew up to hers. They held for several misty seconds. Then Randy lovingly curved her hand around the back of his head and drew it down.[38]

This ending leaves the reader with the image of Hawk's suckling as the culmination of a psychological characterization that is in direct opposition to Radway's theory of male nurturance of the heroine/reader. Hawk is of Indian heritage, born on a reservation. His mother died in another childbirth and his father died in a state institution for alcoholics. "He still mourns his mother and the brother who died at birth. He misses his grandfather," the heroine is told, but "Hawk didn't shed a single tear" when his father died.[39] Although a successful engineer, he feels tied to the reservation because his father betrayed it—the sins of the father are visited on the son by the son, and "he was shackled to it by guilt." At the novel's climax, Randy confronts Hawk with his need for her: "I know you desire me. I suspect you even love me, though you don't want to admit it. More than anything, you *need* me, Hawk O'Toole. You need me to hold you in the night when you're alone. You need my reinforcement when you're in doubt. You need my love. And I need yours."[40] Being loved by Hawk is not as important to Randy's involvement in their relationship as being needed by Hawk to love him in a very maternal manner: she wants him to need her to hold him at night when he is lonely and to need her to reinforce his opinions. In the final scene, Hawk wordlessly asks for permission to suckle, expressing his own desire silently and passively, and Randy controls the action, fulfilling their joint desire by drawing Hawk's head down, presumably to her breast, her "lovingly" curved hand neither sexual nor maternal, and yet both. Hawk's desire to suckle (to be suckled) at his wife's breast, when read against his whole character, can be read as the desire to return to the mother's nourishment that he never received as a child, as his need for his lover to embody his mother and his mother to be his lover. Randy's motivation to suckle (to be suckled by) her husband is more problematic. Previously in the epilogue, immediately after Randy "brushe[s] a strand of hair off his forehead," she reflects, "For a while after they were married, she had been hesitant to openly express her affection for him except when they were in bed. Soon, however, she had discovered that Hawk enjoyed her spontaneous caresses, probably because he'd experienced so little affection in his lifetime."[41] Randy's musings label her maternally coded action of brushing Hawk's hair off his forehead as a sexual "spontaneous caress" that would normally happen in bed. Therefore, Randy's active participation in, indeed her instigation of, the suckling scene can be read either as an extension of her self-described maternal role in their sexual relationship or as her sexual desire manifesting itself in a maternal moment. Either way, Radway's theory of male nurturance of the heroine is applicable to this scene only if the reader identifies with Hawk as the recipient of emotional nurturance, rather than with Randy. This need to switch reader-identification to accommodate Radway's theory itself questions the theory, but without a distinct character's perspective in the scene, it is difficult to analyze the reader's access to power.

Such an analysis can be done, however, by comparing two scenes that raise similar issues from different perspectives in relation to the breast-feeding—one told from the heroine's point of view, one from the hero's. Diana Gabaldon's epic tetralogy-and-counting time-travel novels have been the focus of much critical attention from the romance industry. The heroine Claire, a married woman from the 1940s, is thrown back in time to the 1740s in Scotland and falls in love with a Highlander, Jamie. He marries her but sends her, pregnant, "back to the future" to save her from English retribution against the 1745 Scottish Uprising. The breast-feeding scene in the third book, *Voyager*, initiates Claire's acceptance of a return to marital relations with her modern husband, even though the child for whom she has milk is Jamie's:

> Instead of leaving or answering, he took the pump from my hand and laid it down on the table. As though it moved of its own will, without direction from him, his hand rose slowly through the warm, dark air of the nursery and cupped itself gently around the swollen curve of my breast.
>
> His head bowed and his lips fastened softly on my nipple. I groaned, feeling the half-painful prickle of the milk rushing through the tiny ducts. I put a hand behind his head, and pressed him slightly closer.
>
> "Harder," I whispered. His mouth was soft, gentle in its pressure, nothing like the relentless grasp of a baby's hard toothless gums, that fasten on like grim death, demanding and draining, releasing the bounteous fountain at once in response to their greed.
>
> Frank knelt before me, his mouth a supplicant. Was this how God felt, I wondered, seeing the adorers before Him—was He, too, filled with tenderness and pity?[42]

Claire's musings attempt to appropriate for herself and the reader the position of the most potent patriarch, God—an empowering undertaking. However, in order to believe in Claire's ability to assume the position of arch-patriarch by feeling God's "tenderness and pity" toward the supplicant male, the reader needs to recognize in the supplicant hero emotions and thoughts similar to hers when she is the supplicant. If the hero's supplicating thoughts can be recognized, God's ultimate patriarchal power can be seized. Male confession in this excerpt is unfortunately unavailable, but is also inappropriate because the man is not the hero, not the ultimate representation of the patriarchy the reader is attempting to control. Nevertheless, it is still clear that Claire's husband has been initiated into a feminine exchange economy because, in exchange for resuming sexual relations that Claire does not particularly welcome, he provides her with relief. He does not just take her body. Because Frank is not Claire's "true love," the romance's normal sexual relief through orgasm is inappropriate, so Frank exchanges sex with relief from the maternal pain of a full breast. His continued acceptance of the superiority of feminine exchange economy in their marriage after this episode is demonstrated because he supports Claire's decision to become a doctor by assuming child-care duties—a difficult decision considering that the child is not his and that this section of the novel is set in the 1950s.

The reader can enter the mind of the supplicant man by reading the hero's reaction immediately after he breast-feeds from the heroine in Susan Johnson's *Silver Flame*:

> Like a small, flaunting goddess of fertility, [Trey] thought, Empress lured and beckoned. *Touch me and I'll give you pleasure*, she enticed, *suckle me and I'll give you sustenance*. His warm palms drifted over the flamboyant curve of her breasts, trailed down her ribs and narrow waist, traced the smooth roundness of her hips, gliding slowly to the splendid juncture of her thighs. Stroking the smooth, heated flesh and her pale silky hair, he felt her rise into the pressure of his hand, and his calm assessment abruptly ceased, his own intemperate passion flaring in response. The goddess offered more than pleasure and sustenance; she offered glory in the heated, sweet center of her body, a glory he wanted so badly, he could feel a pulsing ache creep up his spine.[43]

Trey himself grants to Empress the role of God(dess), and believes that she offers him pleasure, sustenance, and uncontrollable glory. The sustenance she extends is maternally coded—after all, he has just suckled her dry of her milk. The pleasure she grants is mutual sexual pleasure—all their encounters are represented as intensely mutually satisfactory. The glory she offers is the glory of receiving a God's love—the glorious promise of power bequeathed by a deity to her supplicant through her love. The reader sees through Trey's eyes a blurring of sexual roles that all result in power for her: the woman has become the patriarchal God, the man is her worshiper. This confusion of sexual roles is represented physically by Empress's "erection"—Trey feels "her rise into the pressure of his hand." Not only does Empress represent the Judeo-Christian God imparting the glory of her love, but she also owns the phallus, causing her hero to lose control of himself. The glory of God's love therefore becomes the glory that a woman's love can provide to the hero who realizes that he desperately needs her and her love. Not only is the heroine appropriating patriarchal power for herself, but she is also then generous enough to return some to the hero, who continues to embody patriarchal power, thereby validating feminine exchange economy from a position of power.

In a similar blurring of sexual roles through physical responses in *Silver Flame*, Empress's milk itself is a symbol of her own investment in the value of exchange by uncontrollably betraying her unwanted sexual arousal:

> "But I see," he went on in the same insolent tone, "you're becoming interested. Cooperative at last—"
> "I *am not*," she repudiated hotly, his derisive murmur impelling her heated rebuff.
> "Then what's that?" He raised a slender bronzed hand and languidly gestured.
> Shamed, Empress felt milk oozing from her breasts, dripping on the rumpled clothes at her feet, her senses immune to her hot-tempered offense at Trey's barbaric conduct.[44]

Her sexual arousal is incontrovertibly embodied in the uncontrollable semen-like flow from her protruding sexual organs, her breasts, as the romance hero's uncontrollable desire for the heroine is betrayed by his erection and eventual ejaculation. By leaking milk and then allowing Trey to suckle her, Empress becomes male in a very female way by not being able to control or hide her own initial and continued arousal, contributing to a blurring of gender roles that is increased and validated when the reader views Empress, through Trey's eyes, as a God(dess), imparting glory. Because the patriarchal expulsion of Trey's semen has a parallel in Empress's milk, both become a symbol for the characters' feminine exchange of love for each other in a scene that is fraught with contested power dynamics.

Breast-milk in Alexis Harrington's *Harper's Bride* serves a similar function of symbolizing exchange between the characters, creating an intimate confusion of character perspective:

> She threaded her hands in his hair to guide him toward her breast. His lips followed the path his fingertips had taken until he encountered her tight nipple. He closed his mouth over it and tugged, then was startled by a stream of warm milk that flowed into his mouth. Instantly, Dylan's raw need burned higher and hotter, and he rocked his hips against her thigh.
>
> Melissa caught her breath and squirmed under the unexpected pleasure of Dylan's hot, moist mouth at her breast. Every nerve on her skin seemed alive and sensitive to the lightest touch. With each light pull of her nipple, she felt spears of fire shoot through her belly to the place that even now prepared the way for their joining.

Two pages later, the scene is duplicated:

> Running his hands up her ribs, he skimmed the side of her breast with his palm. His kisses made a leisurely path down her throat, and his hair brushed lightly over her skin, sending tantalizing shivers through her. Then he dipped to suckle her again and groaned as he took her milk greedily from each breast. His erection, heavy and full, pulsated against her thigh.
>
> An insistent throbbing began between her legs, one that she had never known before. With it grew a demanding desire to have Dylan inside her, because she knew that only he could ease the ache.[45]

The scenes are almost identical to each other and that very parallel highlights the importance of the differences between them. In the first scene, Melissa guides Dylan to her breast, offering him her milk even though he does not expect it. The milk heightens Dylan's arousal, while his suckling, not the milk itself, heightens Melissa's arousal. The paragraphs are precisely separated into one depicting Dylan's point of view and then one depicting Melissa's. During the second scene, Dylan knows what to expect when he suckles Melissa. Although the second paragraph depicts Melissa's point of view, the first paragraph is more nebulous. It starts in Dylan's perspective, running his hands up Melissa's ribs, switches to Melissa's tantalizing shivering, transfers back to Dylan groaning as he receives the milk, and then joins the two characters in the feeling of his erection—the phallus—pulsing against her thigh. During the first scene, the milk is unexpected, and although the gift of it is arousing to both, the hero and the heroine are still separate personalities. In the second scene, Dylan's expectation of the milk fuses him and Melissa into one character perspective: only Dylan can know that his erection is full, but only Melissa can know that it is heavy, and both feel it pulsate against her thigh. Suckling the heroine's milk has completed the exchange between and uniting of the characters, symbolized by coownership of the phallus.

The importance of the heroine's milk as a symbol for feminine exchange economy is demonstrated by performing another comparative evaluation of two breast-feeding scenes that are both represented from the hero's perspective. Both of these books involve the heroine wet-nursing the hero's son after the hero's much-loved wife dies in childbirth. In Candice Proctor's *Night in Eden*, the heroine, Bryony, refuses to wet-nurse. She tells the hero, Hayden, "I'm not going to feed that baby with my milk. I'm not a—a cow," because she feels "for some reason, the thought of having this man use her body to suckle his son seemed only marginally better than having him use her body to slacken his lust. . . . Her entire being rose in revolt. Her milk was *Phillip's*, not his!"[46] Bryony does not own her own milk—it is her dead son's milk, and because she disclaims ownership, it cannot be used as a symbol of the hero's acceptance of the superiority of a feminine exchange economy, and instead, becomes a symbol for masculine use economy. Consequently, the hero, Hayden, lacks interest in her milk except as it pertains to his son. Observing Bryony's breast while she feeds his son, "Hayden stood there for a long time, watching his son guzzle greedily at the rich flow of life-giving milk. The skin of her breasts was fine, he noticed, almost translucent; he could clearly see the blue tracery of the veins that ran beneath where one of Simon's tiny hands rested against the pearly fullness beside his cheek."[47] Hayden appraises Bryony's aristocratically coded blue-veined breast, but the business of love, represented by sex, does not cross with the business of continuing the patrilineal heritage. Milk is used, not exchanged. Bryony's milk is represented neither as the object of Hayden's desire, nor as inciting him to sexual desire, and when he finally possesses her breasts, her milk is never mentioned. Hayden admits to Bryony after they become lovers, "I've even found myself envying Simon for his ready access to what I've wanted so badly."[48] However, Hayden's desire for access is the "typical" masculine desire for female breasts as secondary sexual characteristic, not Hawk O'Toole's desire for the maternally sexual/sexually maternal female, nor Trey's desire for the glory of the God(dess)'s love. The child, Simon, is portrayed as having usurped the hero's patriarchal prerogative as possessor and exploiter of the heroine's breasts, and when he is finished nursing, the hero takes over. To Hayden, breasts represent only sex and milk is merely a life-giving liquid for his son's use.

In contrast to Hayden's reaction, Ross of Sandra Brown's *Sunset Embrace* is almost instantly attracted to the heroine, Lydia—much to his own disgust and frustration and despite the fact that his wife died twenty-four hours before their first meeting—precisely because of Lydia's milk: "Most disgraceful of all was the stab of envy he felt toward Lee. His son knew what she tasted like."[49] Ross wants to "taste" his heroine's milk, rather than merely desiring "ready access" to her breasts as Hayden does. In fact, Ross finds the act of nursing itself to be inherently arousing precisely because of Lydia's milk: "The baby was sucking gustily at her generous breast. Milky bubbles foamed on his eager mouth and around the dusky areola."[50] The eroticism of Lydia's "generous breast" and "dusky areola" and the physical presence of her milk bubbling up from the baby's gusty sucks contrasts with the sterile manner in which Hayden observes Bryony's breast while she feeds Simon. In *Sunset Embrace*, it is the very tangibility of the transfer of milk that is the emblem of the hero's attraction to the heroine and, therefore, to feminine exchange. Ross watches the process of feeding and fixates on the medium of the exchange. He feels another stirring of attraction for the heroine when he contemplates Lydia's breast for the second time: "The only thing marring its creamy perfection was the faint blue veins rivering toward the dark nipple like lines on a map. Ross was fascinated by it and had to force his eyes upward to the girl's face."[51] Although contemplating Lydia's breast, not her milk, Ross follows the path of the rivers of milk flowing toward her nipple, unlike Hayden who merely regards the surface of Bryony's breast. Watching his son feed is arousing for Ross, but the milk itself, the symbol of exchange, is the reason for his arousal. At the end of the book, he recalls the scenes quoted above: "'That first night you were brought to me, I remember seeing this'—his finger outlined the areola—'pearly with your milk. I wanted you even then. God forgive me, but I did.'"[52] The milk is used as the symbol of Ross's immediate recognition of Lydia's importance to him, which indicates to the reader his rapid but unconscious acceptance of the feminine economy of exchange.

This symbol can be examined further when Ross finally tastes Lydia's milk as Lee is nursing:

> Ross didn't plan it, would have been horrified by the mere thought of doing it. But it was done before he realized he had even moved. He reached across Lydia, lifted the droplet of milk from her breast with his finger, and then brought it to his own mouth and licked it free with his tongue.
>
> Realizing too late what he had done, he lay perfectly still, paralyzed by his own reflexive action.[53]

Lydia falls asleep without commenting on Ross's action, but Ross himself is unable to "get over what he had done. And still he couldn't move away. And still he could taste it."[54] He finally falls asleep, "[w]ith the essence of her lingering on his tongue," and "[u]nconsciously," "[u]nknowingly," "instinctively," curls around Lydia: "To his subconscious mind, it felt right."[55]

In this scene, Lydia's milk is her "essence," belonging to her, not to the child between them, and when Ross tastes it, they both view the milk as stolen from her—he is a "guilty culprit caught in a crime."[56] Ross might take Lydia's milk without permission, as Hayden did Bryony's milk, but because Lydia, unlike Bryony, owns her own milk, the milk is a symbol of feminine exchange economy that leads to love, rather than masculine use economy that leads merely to sex. Indeed, so powerful is this symbol that Ross's theft, far from enabling him to act on the overwhelming attraction he feels for Lydia, paralyzes him, leaving him, in effect, impotent, because he still does not consciously recognize the importance of the exchange of love. Powerless, immobilized, and confused, Ross "couldn't get over what he had done," finding it "earthshattering" when the symbol of exchange is stolen.[57] The reader, recognizing herself in Ross's confusion, knows that Ross is yearning for love, but only his subconscious mind knows how to make everything "right" by sharing warmth during sleep.

Ross's preoccupation with Lydia's milk, further signified by his belief that she "still taste[s] milky"[58] months after her milk has stopped, is a powerful enough emblem of Ross's ultimate recoverability into exchange value that it plays an important role of redemption when he rapes Lydia in a jealous, drunken rage: "He didn't let himself touch her breasts. A remnant of sanity in his alcohol-ridden mind warned him that if he caressed her, he might begin to feel tenderness for her. That mustn't happen."[59] Ross's latent tenderness when considering Lydia's breasts, the origin of the milk that fascinates him so, signifies to the reader that he is not on the same level with Lydia's previous abuser, her stepbrother Clancy, who was incapable of tenderness. It is here that feminist critics would say that the romance is failing its readers. Rape is patriarchy's ultimate expression of the use and subjugation of women's bodies and nothing should pardon it—not the powerful symbolism of exchange represented by Lydia's milk that is established before the rape, and certainly not the fact that after he penetrates her, Ross gentles his possession of her and Lydia begins to enjoy the encounter. The reader, however, is reassured about the hero's motivations concerning the rape by being able to read Ross's mind, to hear his confessions of tenderness and need, both before and after he penetrates Lydia. Not only is he left with regret as soon as he enters her, but pleasure "saturated him" even though "he didn't want to feel" it.[60] In the code of the romance novel, that regret is his first emotion exonerates him, and the intense pleasure he feels—"the highest physical gratification he had ever known"[61]—indicates that he recognizes the heroine's power over him, and therefore recognizes the superiority of exchange over use, symbolized by his attempt to arouse her after he consummates the rape. If Sandra Brown had not included Ross's point of view of the rape, it would feel too much like a real rape to the reader—an unmotivated, malignant, random exercise of patriarchal power. Indeed, Brown follows Ross's rape of Lydia with Clancy's brutal beating, rape, and murder of a prostitute, told entirely from the woman's perspective, indicating to the reader the difference between Clancy's incomprehensible exercise of patriarchal power and Ross's jealous act of desperation. Being able to see inside Ross's head grants the reader power over the perpetrator of a rape by allowing her to see him at his most helpless against the power of the heroine, even as she is at her most helpless. This reciprocal helplessness is foreshadowed in Ross's helplessness when he tastes Lydia's milk and is reinforced in a scene after the rape that refers to Lydia's milk. Ross begins by kissing Lydia "rapaciously," but gentles to "nibbles" and "lovebites." Lydia asks him if he remembers the taste of her milk and wishes for its return, because "I would gladly feed you."[62] The use of "rapacious" recalls Ross's rape of Lydia, but her willingness to share her milk with him changes the recollection of the rape to emphasize the exchange rather than the use it represents. Male confession and the symbolism of breast-milk exchange work in conjunction to allow the romance reader power over one of the more terrifying dangers of patriarchy.

The merged character perspective found in *Harper's Bride*, and the parallel, gender-blurring perspectives found in *Silver Flame, Sunset Embrace*, and *Hawk O'Toole's Hostage*, are reminiscent of Hélène Cixous's definition of the effects of *écriture feminine* in "The Laugh of the Medusa": "Bisexuality: that is, each one's location in self of the presence—variously manifest and insistent according to each person, male or female—of both sexes, nonexclusion either of the difference or of one sex, and, from this 'self-permission,' multiplication of the effects of the inscription of desire, over all parts of my body, and the other body."[63] The hero and the heroine in the romance become one perspective in the breast-feeding scenes, giving and taking—exchanging—together. The reader, whether identifying with one or the other, has the possibility of identifying with both, of feeling the power of both because she has knowledge of both. "She gives," Cixous writes, "that there may be life, thought, transformation. This is an economy that can no longer be put in economic terms."[64] The economy of patriarchal use is overturned in the romance novel by the reader's intimate knowledge of both the subordinate and superior power positions.

No matter how powerful this transformation is, however, it is still internal to the romance, with little or no bearing on real patriarchal structures of society, which is precisely what galls feminist critics about the romance. To recall Radway's words: "when viewed from the vantage point of a feminism that would like to see the women's oppositional impulse lead to real social change, romance reading can also be seen as an activity that could potentially disarm that impulse."[65] In Radway's view, the romance does not establish a nonpatriarchal reality, merely a romantic fantasy to which its readers must return time and again in order to renew it, making real social change more difficult to accomplish. In response, author Laura Kinsale argues that the romance hero and all the power that he grants the reader "may be fictitious with regard to genuine males (and only the most oblivious of women wouldn't know it), but he exists nevertheless."[66] Quoting authors Ann Maxwell and Jayne Ann Krentz, Kinsale explains that "we do not read . . . for a reality check":

Not an external reality check, at any rate, but perhaps an internal one. I suspect that for a woman a romance may be a working-through of her own interior conflicts and passions, her own "maleness" if you will, that resists and resists giving in to what is desired above all, and yet feared above all [love], and then, after the decisive climax, arrives at a resolution, a choice that carries with it the relief and pleasure of internal harmony.

The oft-derided happy ending is no infantile regressive daydream; it is a dramatization of the integration of the inner self, an integration that goes on day by day, moment by moment, in the lives of women and men all over the world, because—yes—civilization and family and growing up require of all of us, male *and* female, a certain turning away from adventure, from autonomy, from what-might-have-been, and we mourn the loss and must deal with it.[67]

Here, Kinsale is actually agreeing with the feminist arguments about the romance—readers are indeed abandoning the ability to go out and conquer the real world when they read their romances. If women can find triumph in a fantasy world, they turn away from the "what-might-have-beens" of a changed society and accept what the real patriarchal world allots to them, good or bad. However, Kinsale continues, "Romance novels aren't the only manifestation of this fact. Pro football, male buddy movies, and men's genre fiction exist for a reason."[68] Obviously, however, male fantasies are much more popularly accepted than the scorned romance. If the world—feminists included—could come to accept and valorize the romance as it does male fantasies, might not that celebration of female power change the world as much as if romance readers forced themselves to abandon their fantasies of power and attempted to change the world without being renewed by the power they gain from believing they can recognize themselves behind patriarchy's mask? The romance hero's acceptance of the superiority of the feminine economy of exchange might be transferable to the real world of patriarchal use if the romance were not quite so scorned. Scorn, ridicule, derision, after all, keep the scorned object in its place, thereby implying that the object has some ability to threaten the power structure that scorns it.

NOTES

1. Because of the romance's status as scorned literature, most feminist critics of the romance find it difficult to confess that they are themselves avid readers of the novels—in fact, from reading scholarly analyses of the romance, it is much easier to recognize who is not a reader (Janice Radway) than trying to guess who is (Kay Mussell and Tania Modleski—see their articles in *Para-Doxa*). I wish to confess to this part of my reading history immediately: since my preteens I have avidly read romance novels of all varieties. It was in analyzing my own reading habits that I became interested in the subjects of this paper. Although I do not claim a universal understanding of all romance readers and their reactions to their own favorite romances, I have talked with enough readers who seem to read their romances in similar ways and for similar reasons as I do that I believe I am speaking for more than myself in my evaluation of readers' attraction to romance.

2. Ann Douglas's important early article on the romance was entitled "Soft-Porn Culture," *New Republic* (30 August 1980), a label that proromance critics have labored to overcome.

3. Kay Mussell, "Where's Love Gone? Transformations in Romance Fiction and Scholarship," *Where's Love Gone?: Transformations in the Romance Genre*, special issue of *Para-Doxa* 3, nos. 1–2 (1997): 9.

4. Janice Radway, *Reading the Romance: Women, Patriarchy, and Popular Literature*, (1984; 2d ed., with a new introduction by the author, Chapel Hill: University of North Carolina Press, 1991), 220, 213. Perpetuating the stereotypical view of the romance reader, the cover of the second edition of Radway's book pictures a woman sitting on a couch, engrossed in a romance, with a child's toy lying neglected behind her, implying that the woman is neither fighting patriarchy, nor putting her house in order, but is wasting her time reading a romance ironically entitled *Glory Days*.

5. Radway, 54.

6. Susan Elizabeth Phillips, "The Romance and the Empowerment of Women," in *Dangerous Men and Adventurous Women: Romance Writers on the Appeal of the Romance*, ed. Jayne Ann Krentz (1992; New York: HarperPaperbacks, 1996), 69–70. Emphasis in the original.

7. Phillips, 66. Lynn Coddington, "Wavering between Worlds: Feminist Influences in the Romance Genre," *Where's Love Gone?: Transformations in the Romance Genre*, special issue of *Para-Doxa* 3, nos. 1–2 (1997): 58.

8. Elizabeth Lowell, *Dark Fire* (New York: Silhouette Books, 1988), 17. Emphasis and ellipse in the original.

9. Penelope Williamson, "By Honor Bound: The Heroine as Hero," in *Dangerous Men and Adventurous Women: Romance Writers on the Appeal of the Romance*, ed. Jayne Ann Krentz (1992; New York: HarperPaperbacks, 1996), 156.

10. Jayne Ann Krentz, "Trying to Tame the Romance: Critics and Conventions," in *Dangerous Men and Adventurous Women: Romance Writers on the Appeal of the Romance*, ed. Jayne Ann Krentz (1992; New York: HarperPaperbacks, 1996), 132.

11. In "Where's Love Gone?" Kay Mussell defines the major changes in romances as increasing "portrayals of female sexuality, increasing emphasis on careers and equality, more male point of view," a proliferation of subgenres, characters who "look more like America" (the hero no longer has to be the richest man in the world) and who "live in an expanded social world" with extended families and more sympathetic friends (fewer isolated heroines), wider subject matter with plots with "more psychological depth," all of which contribute to an overall quality that is "generally higher" than earlier romances. Mussell finishes her list by admitting, "I have stopped using the term 'formula' to describe romances" because the word "is simply too loaded and pejorative to describe romances now," 3–6.

12. Carol Thurston, *The Romance Revolution: Erotic Novels for Women and the Quest for a New Sexual Identity* (Urbana: University of Illinois Press, 1987), 99.

13. Laura Kinsale, "The Androgynous Reader: Point of View in the Romance," in *Dangerous Men and Adventurous Women*, 44, 41, 41. Emphasis in the original. Kinsale continues, providing an example: "Significantly, now that the trend has swung firmly toward a substantial dose of masculine viewpoint, we hear no more cries at all for 'more of the heroine's point of view.' In my own historical romance, *The Prince of Midnight*, the heroine's character is virtually inaccessible for almost half the book, with little of her viewpoint and less explanation of it. The only comments I received from readers on the topic were complaints that they were frustrated *on behalf of the hero* because the heroine treated him so coolly. Because this same frustration was one of the hero's dominant emotions in the course of the book, I am led to the conclusion that these readers were comfortable identifying with him, not her" (42–43). Having read this book, I agree with Kinsale. In fact, she is my favorite romance author precisely because of her concentration on her heroes.

14. Phillips, 69. Even the romance industry made the mistake of believing firmly in heroine-identification. Kinsale recalls: "Indeed, until the 1980s, writers of Harlequin romances had to struggle to maintain clear and vivid 'internalizable' heroes without entering the male point of view. At that time, authors were actually prevented from using the male viewpoint by their publishers, who clearly operated solidly within the idea that the reader always identifies with the heroine" (42).

15. Radway, 96, 94, 13, 97. Emphasis in the original. Smithton is the pseudonym for the town in which Radway performed her research. In her new Introduction, Radway herself admits that "the book's argument is a product of a very particular historical moment" (1).

16. Radway, 128.

17. Mary Balogh, *The Incurable Matchmaker* (New York: Signet Regency Romance, 1990), 149.

18. Susan Elizabeth Phillips, *Kiss an Angel* (New York: Avon Books, 1996), 328.

19. Michel Foucault, *The History of Sexuality. Volume I: An Introduction*, trans. Robert Hurley (New York: Vintage Books, 1990), 63, 45.

20. Foucault, 59.

21. Foucault, 61–62.

22. The title "alpha male" is usually attributed to Jayne Ann Krentz, "The Alpha Male," *Romance Writers Report* 10, 1: 26–28. Author Kathleen Gilles Seidel reflects, "[S]o far as I know, this is the only piece of jargon that has originated from the authors themselves, even though we are a close-knit community with astonishing lines of communication. . . . The term 'alpha male' came into use, I believe, because some authors were engaged in a struggle with editors about a certain type of hero and needed a vocabulary for the discussion" ("Judge Me by the Joy I Bring," in *Dangerous Men and Adventurous Women*, 223–224).

23. Foucault, 63, 44–45.

24. Radway claims that the "Ideal Romance" grants the readers "The Promise of Patriarchy" that they are denied in their everyday lives—emotional nurturance (Title to Chapter Four), 119.

25. Jayne Ann Krentz, *Grand Passion* (New York: Pocket Star Books, 1994), 52.

26. Krentz, *Grand Passion*, 76.

27. Krentz, *Grand Passion*, 135–136.

28. Tania Modleski, "My Life as a Romance Reader," *Where's Love Gone?: Transformations in the Romance Genre*, special issue of *Para-Doxa* 3, nos. 1–2 (1997): 17.

29. Modleski, 26.

30. Krentz, *Grand Passion*, 129.

31. Nancy K. Miller, *The Heroine's Text: Readings in the French and English Novel, 1722–1782* (New York: Columbia University Press, 1980), x, 150.

32. Sandra Booth, "Paradox in Popular Romances of the 1990s: The Paranormal Versus Feminist Humor," *Where's Love Gone?: Transformations in the Romance Genre*, special issue of *Para-Doxa* 3, nos. 1–2 (1997): 94. Although I agree with this part of the argument, Booth falls into the trap of expecting heroine-identification when she continues, "Put simply, different readers seek validation of the heroine (and indirectly their own gender) by different methods," 94. Mussell claims that "subgenres have proliferated, enough so that the generic term 'romance' seems even less adequate than before to describe the variety available to readers," 3.

33. Besides the ubiquitous sex scenes, another way to analyze the romance's power is to examine the changes to and meanings of the endings. The increasing focus on the hero's realization that he loves the heroine, rather than on the heroine's realization that her hero loves her, as it used to be, reveals the transformation of the reader's motivation in reading the romance, from a need for nurturance, as Radway claims, to a need for power through knowledge over the hero's mind.

34. The reader I quote (with permission) is a participant of the Prodigy Romance listserv. My evaluation assumes the reader reacts to the scenes as erotic, a reaction partly validated by the Prodigy reader's observation: "I did notice there was quite a flurry of buying 'breast milk books,' so it evidently wasn't too offensive." Personal message, 25 November 1997.

35. Mary Balogh, "The Anniversary," in *From the Heart: Five Regency Love Stories* (New York: Signet Books, 1994), 53.

36. Bertrice Small, *Skye O'Malley* (New York: Ballantine Books, 1980), 458.

37. For an interesting discussion of the "coded" language of the romance, see "Beneath the Surface: The Hidden Codes of Romance," by Linda Barlow and Jayne Ann Krentz, in *Dangerous Men and Adventurous Women*, 17–36. Language, however, can be "coded" for the romance without having to be quite as laughable as is the prose in the passage from *Skye O'Malley*.

38. Sandra Brown, *Hawk O'Toole's Hostage* (1988; New York: Bantam, 1997), 198.

39. Brown, *Hawk O'Toole's Hostage*, 137.

40. Brown, *Hawk O'Toole's Hostage*, 138, 192. Emphasis in the original.

41. Brown, *Hawk O'Toole's Hostage*, 197.

42. Diana Gabaldon, *Voyager* (New York: Dell, 1994), 41–42.

43. Susan Johnson, *Silver Flame* (1988; New York: Bantam Books, 1993), 360. Emphasis in the original.

44. Johnson, 358.

45. Alexis Harrington, *Harper's Bride* (New York: Topaz, 1997), 267, 269.

46. Candice Proctor, *Night in Eden* (New York: Ivy Books, 1997), 16, 15–16.

47. Proctor, 21.

48. Proctor, 242.

49. Sandra Brown, *Sunset Embrace* (1985; New York: Warner Books, 1992), 59.

50. Brown, *Sunset Embrace*, 23.

51. Brown, *Sunset Embrace*, 25.

52. Brown, *Sunset Embrace*, 358.

53. Brown, *Sunset Embrace*, 90. Copyright permissions do not permit the extensive excerpting of the novel that I would like. Please see the appropriate pages in *Sunset Embrace* for the longer passages. The beauty of this scene especially is its very length and importance to the themes of *Sunset Embrace*.

54. Brown, *Sunset Embrace*, 91.

55. Brown, *Sunset Embrace*, 91.

56. Brown, *Sunset Embrace*, 90.

57. Brown, *Sunset Embrace*, 90.

58. Brown, *Sunset Embrace*, 358.

59. Brown, *Sunset Embrace*, 195.

60. Brown, *Sunset Embrace*, 195.

61. Brown, *Sunset Embrace*, 196.

62. Brown, *Sunset Embrace*, 279.

63. Hélène Cixous, "The Laugh of the Medusa," *Signs: Journal of Women in Culture and Society* 1, no. 4 (1976): 884.

64. Cixous, 893.

65. Radway, 213.

66. Kinsale, 45.

67. Kinsale, 48.

68. Kinsale, 48.

Chapter 3

Calamities of Convention in a Dime Novel Western

Janet Dean

In the opening scene of Edward Wheeler's 1878 dime novel Western *Deadwood Dick on Deck; or, Calamity Jane, the Heroine of Whoop-Up*, the grizzled miner Colonel Joe contemplates the peculiarities of gender construction in the Wild West. While "ther female sex ginerally war begarbed in petticoats, an left ther male representatives ter wear ther breeches" in Joe's home state east of the Mississippi, the conditions of the West require women to dress and act more like men. "I reckon ye kno' how it is out hayr in ther Hills," he tells his partner, "ef a female ken't stand up an' fight fer her rights, et's durned lettle aid she'll git."[1] Colonel Joe's comments are in qualified defense of the novel's heroine, Calamity Jane, a woman who both wears "breeches" and stands up for her rights, and they profoundly complicate assumptions that make the late-nineteenth-century West the last best place of reliable gender distinctions in the popular imagination. In the dominant understanding, the space Theodore Roosevelt termed the "masculine West" offered an ideal environment for the restoration and nourishment of American masculinity in the face of increasing challenges to traditional gender norms. The West was the place where men could be—and must be—men. Yet if the West masculinizes, Colonel Joe suggests, it does so indiscriminately, making "men" of women, as well. In opposition to Roosevelt's conception, which figures masculinity as a natural condition that the West could revive to its full potential in (white) American men, the example of Calamity Jane calls attention to the ways gender is *constructed* by the social environment "out hayr in ther Hills." Gender depiction in this seemingly conventional novel goes startlingly against convention: because masculinity is available to anyone in the West of *Deadwood Dick on Deck*, it quickly loses its cultural privilege.

As Calamity Jane's dress in "breeches" extends and thereby challenges the concept of Western masculinization, it also gives the lie to critical assumptions of our own age that the popular West inscribes conventional gender roles.

Among scholars of gender the dime novel Western has long been scorned literature because of its presumed conventionality. Critics presume that caricatured
exemplars of strong and valiant Western manhood, frail and fainting Eastern
womanhood populate dime novel Westerns, reinscribing the sexist social norms
of the nineteenth century. But such assumptions ignore evidence of the complexities of gender in the production and consumption of these texts, which fueled American fantasies about the West from roughly 1860 to 1900. The introduction to a recently published anthology of dime novel Westerns, for instance,
describes the pulp Western tradition as "an enterprise of men writing for men
about men," even as it recognizes that the first dime novel Western was written
by a woman and about a woman (Ann S. Stephens's *Malaeska, the Indian Wife
of the White Hunter*, 1860).[2] Recent research has shown that women authored
dime novel Westerns in substantial numbers, and while it is difficult to determine
with certainty who read these books, the inclusion of so many women characters
may reflect publishers' appeals to female readers.[3] Moreover, dime novel Westerns of the last half of the nineteenth century nurtured examples of a diversity of
gender types, including the feminized "cowboy dandy" and the masculinized,
gun-slinging frontierswoman.[4] The latter was especially pervasive, and a survey
of pulp Western titles reveals an intriguing handful: "Queen Helen, the Amazon
of the Overland"; "Wild Edna, the Girl Brigand"; "Rowdy Kate from Right-
bower"; "Backwoods Belle"; "Mustang Madge, Daughter of the Regiment";
"Hurricane Nell"; "The Tigress of Texas." As their names suggest, these heroines make a calamity of late-Victorian-era gender definitions of "womanliness"
by acting like Western men: not only do many wear "breeches," but they also
wield revolvers and lariats, shoot and play cards, own profitable businesses and
ride fast horses, fight, steal, cheat, and smoke cigars.

Such characters reflect an imagined space (the West) and a genre (the dime
novel) in which identity in general can be surprisingly unstable. The masculinized frontierswoman poses a challenge to conventional gender norms not unlike
that posed by the urban "New Woman." Where gender identity becomes relatively fluid—where women can be masculine—what keeps men from becoming
feminine? Further, where gender identity, that most elemental of cultural markers, is made flexible or put into question, how can other types of identity categories remain stable? And what are the implications of flexible identity categories
to pervasive critical assumptions about the construction of gender in the popular
imagination? *Deadwood Dick on Deck* and dime novel Westerns in general serve
as important, if improbable, sites for the investigation of such questions.

THE SCORNED DIME NOVEL WESTERN

Given the readily apparent complexities of gender identity in dime novel
Westerns and their influence on generations of American readers, why have
scholars of literature and gender scorned the genre? Perhaps the most obvious
reason for the neglect is the critical assumption that dime novel Westerns are
subliterary cultural products, in Henry Nash Smith's view evidence of the

"progressive deterioration in the Western story as a genre."[5] Produced in vast numbers for quick sale, dime novel Westerns are replete with narrative slips, lapses in logic, convoluted plots, and hasty and artificial conclusions. But to dismiss the genre altogether based on such criteria leaves a critical gap in our understanding of the imagined West; as Bill Brown argues, "[T]hough we can write a coherent history of the Western by jumping quickly from Cooper's *The Pioneers* to Wister's *The Virginian*, it is by reading the mass market fiction between those novels that we begin to see how fragile that coherence was."[6] Moreover, as this essay will demonstrate, by paying close attention to the narrative "flaws" of dime novel Westerns we can better understand the ideological contests in play in the popular consciousness.

Scorn for dime novel Westerns also stems from the theory that products of mass culture reinforce standardized social structures (such as patriarchy) and are geared toward the demands of hegemony, a view that begins with Theodor Adorno and Max Horkheimer's seminal reading of popular culture as "mass deception."[7] This view has been called into question in terms of mass-produced fiction by such critics as Michael Denning, who reads in the dime novel efforts to counter the encroachment of late-nineteenth-century capitalism.[8] While Denning's focus on the relationship between class and culture has garnered attention, it has not led others to investigate the similar relationship between gender and culture in the genre. Yet his identification of the dime novel as "a contested terrain, a field of cultural conflict where signs with wide appeal and resonance take on contradictory disguises and are spoken in contrary accents" invites closer consideration of the ways gender is negotiated on that terrain.[9]

A third, and less scrutinized, assumption behind the critical scorn for dime novel Westerns involves gender identity but in an overriding theory that fails to accommodate figures like Calamity Jane. This is the entrenched critical consensus that follows Roosevelt in seeing the West of popular imagination as a space with strictly enforced, strictly conventional gender roles—a view recently reiterated in Jane Tompkins's study of twentieth-century Westerns, *West of Everything*. This theory relies on a concept of the West as a place of simple and inviolable "classical oppositions": good and bad, nature and culture, words and things, illusion and truth, and encompassing all of these oppositions, man and woman.[10] Popular Westerns, according to this theory, are guided by a fixed, even sacred, gender binarity, a system in which women function only to demonstrate, by contrast, the masculinity of Western men. While such readings are useful in their critiques of Western masculinity, they overlook fictional figures whose behavior and appearance evade strict gender categorization. The prevalence of women characters and the evidence of women writers suggest that the dime novel Western was more gender inclusive than its offspring, the modern Western and the Western film. Moreover, the prevalence of women characters who act and dress like men in dime novel Westerns points to a fluidity of social categories and identities unrealized in other popular Western forms.

Deadwood Dick on Deck offers a fascinating example of the ways gender identity—and, by extension, other categories of social identity, as well—can be made fluid in the pages of the dime novel Western. Close examination of the cross-gender performances by Calamity Jane and other women in *Deadwood Dick on Deck* reveals how they effect a transformation of Western masculinity, as well as Eastern femininity, in the imagined West. Other identity categories, in turn, come into question. Indeed, the genre itself encourages a fluidity of identity, since the condition and character of mass-produced fiction leaves narrative and rhetorical "flaws" that reveal the pressures of and underlying resistance to conventional identity categories. Rereading gender and other identity categories in a dime novel Western, this essay calls for a revision of the critical consensus that mythologizes the popular West as a place of fixed, conventional identities and simultaneously dismisses the dime novel Western as overly conventional. The essay's title plays on Calamity Jane's name and suggests how the text itself threatens a calamity, "a great misfortune or disaster,"[11] of conventional social and cultural forms. A new understanding of the fluidity of identity in *Deadwood Dick on Deck* reveals the ways dime fiction contests with dominant ideologies and the ways the imagined West provides an ideal arena for that contest.

GENDER CALAMITIES

Published in 1878, *Deadwood Dick on Deck* presents a particularly rich context for exploring the fluidity of gender identity in the dime novel Western because it includes more than one example of cross-gender performance. The title is misleading: Calamity Jane and a mysterious young miner named Sandy are the protagonists of the novel, and Deadwood Dick makes only rare, if climactic, appearances. But two other female characters play crucial roles in the novel, and, like Calamity Jane, their behavior or appearance confuses gender distinctions. "Dusty Dick" is a young woman masquerading as a man in order to escape a husband, the Honourable [*sic*] Cecil Grosvenor, who wants to murder her to gain her inheritance. Sandy sees through Dusty Dick's disguise, but, honoring her wishes to keep her identity secret, takes her on as a mining partner and cabin-mate. Madame Minnie Majilton is also a central figure. Majilton, Grosvenor's first wife, has moved to Deadwood to become the successful owner of a gambling hall; she has earned a reputation for her feminine beauty as well as her propensity for drinking whiskey, smoking cigars, and earning money like a man. She, too, has been abused by Grosvenor, and, disguised as Mad Marie, "a woman shootist," she enacts revenge by robbing her husband when he appears in Deadwood and later murdering him.[12] Unlike Calamity Jane and Dusty Dick, Minnie Majilton does not wear "breeches," but her economic independence and her performance as a violent road agent make her as significant a challenge to traditional gender codes as the cross-dressing heroines.

Alongside the heroines in masculine attire, the novel includes a male character marked by his distinctly unmanly clothes, at least in terms of the conventions of Western culture. In a text in which descriptions of clothing are given considerable space, Grosvenor's attire is described in notable detail: he appears in "an elegant suit of broadcloth, silk hat, patent-leather boots, gloved hands, [with a] gold-headed cane, along with a cluster diamond pin on his immaculate shirt front."[13] While Grosvenor's costume marks him as unlike the miners and cowboys of Deadwood, an Eastern "dandy," it also suggests something about the range of gender identities in the West: just as not all women in the West wear petticoats, not all men wear the standard "breeches."

In fact, the prevalence of cross-gender dress and performance in *Deadwood Dick on Deck* reflects a preoccupation with questions of male and female identity that is evident from the novel's opening pages. High in the Black Hills, Colonel Joe and his mining partner listen to an unseen singer with a voice "clear and strong, with power and sustenation [*sic*], and capable of instant modulation to the softest, sweetest degree." The variations of power and softness in the voice leave the gender of its owner uncertain. "A woman, wa'n't it?" asks Sandy. Joe cautiously affirms that the mysterious singer, Calamity Jane, *is* a woman, but his response reflects a lingering uncertainty: "Yas, a woman . . . At least they say she's o' the feminine sex, fer which I can't sw'ar, purtic'lar . . . I ken't say as I really doubt et, fer I s'pect et's a solid fac' thet she ar' one o' ther lineal descendants o' thet leetle fruitful scrape in a certain garden, yeers ago."[14] The contradictory terms Joe uses (he cannot swear to yet does not doubt Calamity Jane's womanhood) and his vacillation between Calamity's masculine attributes and the presumption of her womanhood ("She's a woman," though she can "drink whisky, shute, play keerds or sw'ar"; "She's a woman . . . tho' thar's many who lay claim ter that name who ar below par") reveal the problem posed by her presence, which calls into question the very criteria that determine conventional gender categories.[15] Calamity Jane exhibits none of the conventional gender markers—dress, behavior, choice of social activities—that would register her womanhood, and even her voice cannot be called feminine. Indeed, Colonel Joe cannot say what makes Calamity Jane a woman; he can only point to her distinctly *un*womanly characteristics while anxiously reiterating her position in the category "woman."

As Calamity Jane's soft and strong voice echoes in the Black Hills, the questions about gender her presence raises seem to linger as well. The text describes Sandy in terms that at once challenge and attempt to reaffirm conventional gender identity. Colonel Joe, who knows little about his partner, associates Sandy with women, first by commenting on his resemblance to Joe's own "little golden-haired daughter," and then by worrying privately about supporting both his estranged wife and the partner with whom he is currently "consolidated," Sandy.[16] Having called into question Sandy's masculinity, however, the text works to reaffirm it, with a description that seems bent on answering the questions posed by the young man's long blonde hair and gender-neutral name: "Twenty-four or five years of life which had passed over his head had left a man in every sense of the word—a man in physical and mental development—a man in will and great force of character—a man so quiet and retired as to seem almost a recluse; yet when gazing scrutinizingly at him, you could but be impressed with the peculiar force of the expression—'still waters run deep'."[17] The repetition that Sandy is "a man" echoes Colonel Joe's tautological reassurance that Calamity Jane is indeed "a woman . . . o' the feminine sex" and points to the gender anxiety produced by her presence. Following so quickly after the association of Sandy with a daughter and a wife, the passage betrays a need to reassert conventional gender identity: if Calamity Jane's gender is uncertain, the text insists, Sandy's most certainly is not. The gesture is only partially successful, for while the passage insists on the existence of the category "man" in its repetition of the word, it fails to offer more than the most general criteria for that designation. Sandy is a man merely "in every sense of the word"; manhood itself is as mysterious and unfathomable as the proverbial still waters. Even as they seem to work toward definitive gender identification of the two main characters, these introductory passages have the effect of shaking confidence in the adequacy of the social categories "man" and "woman."

The opening descriptions of Calamity Jane and Sandy set the stage for multiple challenges to conventions of gender identity inscribed by both nineteenth-century middle-class culture and twentieth-century literary criticism of the imagined West. To begin with, the novel inverts the conventional plot of nineteenth-century frontier fiction, described by Leslie Fiedler and others, in which men move West in a flight from suffocating domestic space controlled by women.[18] As Nicole Tonkovich has pointed out, *Deadwood Dick on Deck* depicts *women* in flight from a *masculine*-controlled home front: all three women have come to the Dakota territories fleeing harmful domestic arrangements.[19] Both Minnie Majilton and Dusty Dick are escaping an abusive husband. Calamity Jane's history is less clear, but it is rumored she had been either deserted at the altar or married to a "Nevada brute," from whom she fled West. In any case, she swears to kill the man who "robbed Jane Forrest of her maiden name, but never of her honor."[20] Even where the novel partially reconstructs the traditional domestic scene, in Dusty Dick's role as Sandy's cook and "pard," it does much to reverse convention. Describing to a fellow miner how he and Dusty Dick became associates, Sandy explains he "took a notion to [Dusty Dick] and domesticated him."[21] Dusty Dick, in turn, resists the bonds of domesticity and feminine passivity. When rumors spread that she is a woman and Sandy's honor is questioned, she leaves the shanty for the hills. In leaving the shanty she asserts her independence from the restrictive domestic space and shows *her* need to protect *him*.

Dusty Dick's resistance and Calamity Jane's promise of revenge reflect the ways women in this novel take control over male-female relationships in distinctly unfeminine ways, and, as Sandy's need to "domesticate" Dusty Dick hints, that control poses a challenge to masculine, as well as feminine, norms. The challenge to Sandy's masculinity posed by the three independent, masculinized women becomes increasingly evident as the novel unfolds. Calamity Jane and Minnie Majilton both fall in love with Sandy, and both assert themselves in ways that mimic masculine convention. Predictably, each role-reversing encounter leaves Sandy defending his own masculinity. When Minnie Majilton proposes marriage to him, Sandy angrily rejects her and reasserts his masculine authority, declaring, "When I want a wife I shall do the picking and proposing myself."[22] Calamity Jane's habit of coming to Sandy's rescue—guiding him off a precarious mountain ledge, warning him of an impending mine explosion, or defending him against a group of angry fellow miners—presents an even greater threat to Sandy's masculinity. He is grateful for her protection but also uncomfortable with it: "I reckon I can look out for myself, ma'am," he tells her.[23] Still, Sandy must contend with the heroine's continual efforts to protect and aid him: she offers to "keep an eye out"[24] for his enemies and to "lick the cuss" who speaks against him.[25] Indeed, Calamity Jane is far more likely to come to Sandy's rescue than is Deadwood Dick.

When Calamity Jane flies to Sandy's aid against a gang of suspicious miners, she makes an explicit comparison between *her* power and *his* that thoroughly confounds any lingering sense of the reliability of gender categories. "You did handsome," she tells him, "but you should have shot a couple of the cusses to show them ye warn't afraid. That's the only way to git along out hayr. See what a change my comin' made? They know I'm business clean through."[26] Calamity Jane gives Sandy lessons on how to be a Western man, and thereby proves herself more a man than he. Not surprisingly, in the next scene she takes over his manly role altogether. Informed of Dusty Dick's disappearance, she volunteers to find and return her, as she knows the hills better than Sandy. Appropriating Sandy's role as defender of his female love interest, Calamity Jane undercuts his identity as a male; he can only retreat to the domesticated space of his shanty.

As Calamity Jane indicates in advising Sandy that a Western man should shoot more and talk less, firepower is the most legitimate source of authority in the West. It is a power all three women skillfully wield: Dusty Dick "always wore a single revolver at the waist" and could use it handily;[27] Calamity Jane is renowned for her skills with a gun; and Minnie Majilton proves herself as a most successful "woman shootist."[28] The phallic implications of the female gunslinging are clear: in the West of fact and fiction, a gun-toting woman would be threatening, in Ona Russell's words, "not only because she was physically dangerous, but because she was emasculating, because in taking up arms, she took control of the very object that made a man a 'man'."[29] Minnie Majillton understands and articulates her emasculating power when she robs Grosvenor at gunpoint. "Go, now, and if any one tells you you've lost your pin and purse, tell them Deadwood Dick's men robbed you. Don't for the world let any one know that a weak woman played road-agent to you."[30] The comment attacks Grosvenor's masculinity on two levels, since it at once denigrates him for falling victim to a "weak woman" and marks his possessions as already feminine, as the reference to "pin and purse" recalls the earlier description of the Eastern dandy's clothing.[31]

CATEGORICAL CALAMITIES

Masculinity in women, then, seems to bring to the surface femininity in men in this novel, exposing Sandy's domesticity and ineffectuality and Grosvenor's effeteness and weakness. By this reading, *Deadwood Dick on Deck* appears to uphold a strict gender binarity in the popular Western. Even if it reverses convention, the text still seems to require an antithetical relation between masculine and feminine behavior; though men and women switch roles in the novels, the roles themselves, at first reading, remain relatively stable. But the emphasis on clothing and its relation to identity throughout the novel moves beyond gender binarity to express, instead, the artificiality and performativity of gender in general.

The emphasis on Grosvenor's attire points up by contrast the most visible challenges to conventional gender categories, the cross-dressing habits of Calamity Jane and Dusty Dick. As many critics have noted, cross-dressing and cross-gender performances highlight the artificiality of gender construction, which depends so much on exterior markers, and suggest an unexpected fluidity of gender options. Writing on sexual disguise in modern film, Annette Kuhn has argued that "[b]y calling attention to the artifice of gender identity . . . [c]ross-dressing . . . may denaturalize that phenomenon held in our culture to be most evidently and pre-eminently natural: sexual difference."[32] Calamity Jane herself comments on the artificiality of gender construction when she encounters her former sweetheart, Charley Davis, just arriving in the Black Hills. Asked why she dresses as a man "when the attire of your own sex is more becoming," Calamity answers with haughty assurance. "I don't allow ye ken beat men's togs much fer handy locomotion an' so forth, an' then, ye see, I'm as big a gun among the men as any of 'em."[33] The description of easy locomotion in men's clothing is particularly apt, for in addition to practical reasons for dressing as a man, Calamity Jane indicates that her clothes allow her to move freely across the bounds of traditional gender options. Her status is not contained within convention. Calamity Jane identifies herself not as one of the men, but as a "big gun" on the frontier, and she chooses to dress the part. Identity in these terms has not so much to do with biology *or* with details of costume as it does with authority: authority to defend oneself and others in the lawless frontier and authority to *define* oneself independently of social convention.

Conventional identity categories lose meaning in the text. If Calamity Jane's cross-dressing allows her to define her own identity as a "big gun," it puts Charley's identity into crisis. The moment produces what Marjorie Garber calls a "category crisis," or "a failure of definitional distinction, a borderline that becomes permeable, that permits of border crossings from one (apparently) distinct category to another."[34] While acts of transvestism most obviously challenge the border between genders, Garber insists they produce "not just a category crisis of male and female, but the crisis of category itself";[35] they "[put] in question identities previously conceived as stable, unchallengeable, grounded, and 'known.'"[36] Directly after justifying her own clothing, Calamity Jane comments on Charley's in terms that suggest just such a "crisis of category." "[I]f ye're goin' to Whoop-Up, let me advise ye in one respect: snatch off thet b'iled shirt, an put on a flannel or caliker. Reckon they'd set you up as a swell ef ye war ter go in thet way."[37] Like Sandy and Grosvenor, Charley becomes less of a Western man as he is confronted with a masculinized woman. But the encounter between Calamity Jane and Charley reveals the crisis of other categories. With its dual connotations of effeteness and fashionableness, "swell" suggests that not just gender identity is at risk but also class identity. In Whoop-Up, Charley's clothes place him in gender and class categories entirely other than those he occupies as an Eastern police detective.

Calamity Jane goes on to reiterate the idea that usually reliable categories are now obsolete when Charley criticizes her clothes as "unmaidenly": "'Maidenly—unmaidenly!' Calamity muttered, staring hard at him. 'Charley Davis, when you left me, with a betrothal kiss clinging to my lips, I was a maiden, and as modest as they make 'em. But terrible changes have come since then. I am now a world's dare-devil, people say.'"[38] As Calamity Jane indicates, the blurring of boundaries produced by her and Charley's dress is not just between man and woman, but between virgin and whore, working-stiff and middle-class professional, cowboy and dandy, Easterner and Westerner. Or, rather, in the context of the Wild West, the clothes Calamity Jane and Charley wear make all kinds of conventional identity categories meaningless.

Clothes, then, indicate nothing if not the flexibility of identity in the dime novel Western. Calamity Jane's clothes reflect her rejection of arbitrary categorical boundaries. Her encounter with Charley is in keeping with a novel in which, as in most dime novels, costumes and disguise play a primary part in the unfolding drama: Minnie Majilton disguises herself as Mad Marie; Deadwood Dick masquerades as a Regulator; and at one point Calamity Jane disguises herself as Deadwood Dick disguised as an old man. Writing on the prevalence of disguise in nineteenth-century cheap fiction, Michael Denning has argued that it marks a break from the conventions of the bourgeois novel. Traditionally, highbrow narratives of disguise "[work] on a law of self-identity": a character's disguise is only a detour on the road to possessive individualism, revealed in a conclusion in which the "truth" of identity is disclosed or in which, in the novel of development, a character evolves through experience with disguise into his or her "true" self. In dime fiction, to the contrary, disguise is "the narrative equivalent of metaphor, working synchronically rather than diachronically, vertically rather than horizontally." A character may be a nobleman who works as a miner, Denning says, but neither identity negates the other; the miner "*is*, the is of metaphor, a noble."[39] In other words, where disguise in highbrow novels confirms the stability of identity, disguise in mass-produced novels reflects its instability.

Through disguise, dime fiction characters do not just mask a "true" identity; rather, they challenge the "either-or" presumptions of conventional identity categories. Accordingly, Dusty Dick maintains her disguise and her masculine performance both outside the shanty and within, and the narrative refers to her as "Dusty Dick" even after it has been revealed that she is the heiress Edna Sutton. Still more surprisingly, she remains "universally known" as Dusty Dick even after her marriage to Sandy, who also retains his alias.[40] Her masculine clothing does not simply mask her feminine identity; instead, it reflects the ways she embodies both identities, the ways she *is*, "the is of metaphor," Dusty Dick. Similarly, Calamity Jane's clothes are not so much disguise as uniform, and, as she indicates, they have the same effect of challenging "either-or" presumptions such as those made by Colonel Joe and Sandy in the opening scene of the novel. Calamity Jane's "breeches" represent her liberation from gender categories altogether.

NARRATIVE CALAMITIES

The challenge to the stability of social categories is reproduced in, and sustained by, the narrative character of the dime novel Western. As the opening passages of *Deadwood Dick on Deck* demonstrate, uncertainty and anxious reiteration strike a dominant note in the narrative. Such rhetorical faltering reflects the calamity produced by challenges to conventional gender codes; the text itself reproduces the effects of cross-gender dress and behavior. Elsewhere in the text awkward grammatical phrasing, narrative slippage, and an open-ended conclusion can reveal the ways the text embodies the contest with dominant ideology. While it would be a mistake to conclude that Edward Wheeler, about whom little is known, intended his dime novel Western to be a radical challenge to prevailing Victorian gender codes, the evidence of the text suggests that the very condition and character of the dime novel—its hasty production, its reliance on literary formula and cliché, its adherence to the requirements of seriality—bears the imprint of an unconscious struggle against restrictive identity categories in ways that other cultural forms may not. The text itself becomes inflected by the challenge to gender binarity raised by its plot.

Attention to textual "flaws" can make clear the ways the rhetoric and narrativity test conventional gender bounds, if, perhaps, inadvertently. A striking example comes in a description of Dusty Dick's skill with a gun, a narrative moment that indicates both the flexibility of gender identity and the category crisis it creates. Dusty Dick quickly learns to shoot, the narrator reports, and "despite the general *feminine* terror of fire-arms, *he* was no novice at a shot."[41] The awkward disjunction of adjective and pronoun in this sentence is symptomatic of a plot that continually undermines the reliability of gender identity, one in which conventional terms are increasingly inadequate. "No longer female even among her own sex," Dusty Dick is also not quite male, as references to her gentleness and soft hands suggest.[42] Rather, she is a "feminine . . . he" in the terms of the narrative, which fails fully to restore a "correct" gender identity even in its revelatory conclusion: the reader cannot assume Dusty Dick wore a dress to her own wedding, since the narrative makes no comment on her appearance.

A second narrative "flaw" appears at the conclusion of the novel and revisits the question of Sandy's gender identity. Sandy is revealed to be Earl Beverly, a man accused of forgery and suspected of murder who fled West to escape prosecution. When Charley Davis presents evidence that clears the hero of guilt, Sandy is so deeply relieved that he "staggers and falls in a swoon, strong, self-controlled man that he was."[43] The clash of novelistic clichés here, the traditionally feminine swoon and the traditionally masculine assertion of self-control, suggests that neither convention is quite adequate for the new kinds of gender identity the text has brought forth. Like the awkward "feminine . . . he" and the failure to return Dusty Dick to conventional female attire and thus "stabilize" her female identity in the conclusion, the jarring appearance of a masculine "swoon" might be attributed to hurried, inattentive writing and editing. What is important here, however, is not the aesthetic incoherence of the text, but the way its production inevitably exposes fissures in the conventional conception of gender identity as natural or "true."

Indeed, the novel's hasty conclusion leaves multiple identities unfixed. One might argue that there is something liberating in the typical dime novel conclusion, a revelatory scene that only *seems* to restore stable identity in the way high culture novels do, but in its abruptness often muddies the line between perceptions of "true" and "false" identities. Hence, Dusty Dick is revealed to be a woman but retains her masculine posture and name; Sandy preserves his "honor, as a man" by marrying Dusty Dick, but his conventional swoon is that of a woman. Minnie Majilton's "true" and "false" identities also merge: when she enacts revenge by murdering her husband, she *becomes* what she was disguised as, a "woman shootist." As is typical of dime novels, the conclusion ostensibly reveals the secrets of identity, but it simultaneously insists that all the identities in the novel are valid and "true."

Moreover, the seriality of dime novel Westerns allows for an open-endedness that well serves the underlying fluidity of identity. The commercial demands governing the form require that recognizable central figures remain unchanged enough to function in similar ways in sequels. Serial dime novels are often characterized by a distinct lack of the kind of narrative closure common in higher literary forms, in which the central character changes fundamentally by the closing scenes. For heroines of highbrow novels of the nineteenth century and earlier, that closure typically meant marriage.[44] Interestingly, the final page of *Deadwood Dick on Deck* nods to highbrow convention when it raises the rumor that Calamity Jane and Charley Davis married. But, true to the open-endedness of serial fiction, the novel quickly rejects this possibility. "As to the truth of this, I cannot say," the narrator reports; "I doubt much if Calamity Jane will ever marry."[45] In this gesture, *Deadwood Dick on Deck* preserves Calamity Jane's unconventionality to the very end, when she rides into the proverbial sunset.

Unlike the narrator, twentieth-century critics have been hard pressed to imagine possibilities for Calamity Jane outside of conventional gender categories. Smith, for example, sees Calamity Jane's failure to marry as evidence that she has been ruined by her unladylike dress and behavior: in his words, her "prospects . . . have suffered sadly from her neglect of appearances."[46] Unwilling or unable to see beyond the categories of "maidenly" or "unmaidenly" that Calamity Jane herself rejects, Smith misreads the open-ended conclusion as tragic and final, the conventional end of a conventional woman whose only possibilities for social roles are attractive lady or whore. Tonkovich, a more recent critic, is more appreciative of the novel's radicalism, but she nonetheless repeats Smith's gesture of imposing conventional gender categories on the novel. Focusing on the theme of marital wrongs, Tonkovich concludes that "domestic issues dominate" the text, making it more like a domestic novel than a Western.[47] Surprisingly, Tonkovich supports her reading by pointing to instances of female revenge in the novel, actions altogether antithetical to domestic ideology. Reading domestic issues into the Western, she reiterates the conventional assumptions she sets out to challenge: where there are women, her argument suggests, there must be that convention of womanhood, domesticity. *Deadwood Dick on Deck*, to the contrary, refuses the easy association of women and even the alternative domestic arrangements Tonkovich foregrounds, especially in its ending, which eschews the closure of marriage for two of the three women characters.

Such readings as Smith's and Tonkovich's resemble Colonel Joe's attempts to pin down Calamity Jane's gender in the opening scene of the novel. Like Colonel Joe, both critics insist "she's a woman" in the most conventional sense of the term despite all evidence to the contrary. In reality, Calamity Jane remains unfettered by gender categories. She is free of the confines of both the literary convention that requires a heroine to marry at the end of a traditional novel and the conventions of womanly behavior that require her to be either fallen or saved; she is free, that is, of conventions of both genre and gender. Even the terms of the concluding comment on her marital status, the assertion of rumor and the narrator's doubt, suggest flexibility. Here, characters are not required to inhabit the presumably universal conventions of identity.

Closer inspection of the narrative "flaws" in *Deadwood Dick on Deck* goes far to explain the text's status as scorned literature, for the rhetorical slippages and narrative fissures call attention to the novel's refusal to adhere to the dichotomies on which the myth of the "masculine West" depends. Theories of simple and inviolable "classical oppositions" fail to stand up against the example of Calamity Jane and others like her who repeatedly challenge the boundaries between genders. The breaking of these boundaries, moreover, should alert us to the challenges posed by the novel, and the form, to other binary codes. Such dime novel Western "hero outlaws" as Deadwood Dick, Michael Denning has shown, defy the divisive moral codes of good and evil.[48] The idea that Deadwood Dick is likely based on a decidedly unconventional real-life Westerner, the African-American cowboy Nat Love, hints at the ways popular fiction might test the conceptual boundaries between black and white even as it rewrites history in service of dominant racial ideologies.[49]   Far from an arena of sacred dichotomies, the West of dime novel Westerns is a frontier in the truest sense: a space of undetermined, shifting boundaries, a space where conventional identity categories are tested and contested. Accordingly, *Deadwood Dick on Deck* is a strikingly representative frontier text. It is a text that should help us to rethink, in fundamental ways, how the popularized West reconstructs identity and enacts difference.

NOTES

1. Edward Wheeler, *Deadwood Dick on Deck; or, Calamity Jane, the Heroine of Whoop-Up*, Beadle's Half-Dime Library #73 (1878), 1.

2. Bill Brown, "Reading the West: Cultural and Historical Background," in *Reading the West: An Anthology of Dime Westerns* (Boston: Bedford Books, 1997), 32. Countering the critical consensus and acknowledging the legacy of Stephens, June Johnson Bube has recently drawn attention to the many examples of dime novel Westerns written by women and featuring central women characters. See "From Sensational Dime Novel to Feminist Western: Adapting Genre, Transforming Gender," in *Change in the American West: Exploring the Human Dimension*, ed. Stephen Tchudi (Reno: University of Nevada Press, 1996), 64–70.

3. On women authors of dime novel Westerns, see Bube, 68. For a discussion of dime novel readership in America, see Michael Denning, Chapter Three, "'The Unknown Public': Dime Novels and Working Class Readers," in *Mechanic Accents: Dime Novels and Working Class Culture in America* (New York: Verso, 1987), 27–46; and Daryl Jones, *The Dime Novel Western* (Bowling Green: The Popular Press, 1978), 14–15. Bill Brown also acknowledges that women characters in dime novel Westerns may have been calculated to attract women readers; see Brown, 37.

4. Christine Bold, *Selling the Wild West: Popular Western Fiction, 1860–1960* (Bloomington: Indiana University Press, 1987), 13.

5. Henry Nash Smith, *Virgin Land: The American West as Symbol and Myth* (New York: Vintage Books, 1950), 134.

6. Brown, 14.

7. Theodor Adorno and Max Horkheimer, "The Culture Industry: Enlightenment as Mass Deception," in *The Cultural Studies Reader*, ed. Simon During (New York: Routledge, 1993), 29–43.

8. Denning, 157–166. Class issues are certainly alive in *Deadwood Dick on Deck*; as Denning notes, Sandy is "an enthusiast on the labor question," and his resistance to Eastern capitalists who want to take over his mine is an underlying theme (Wheeler, 5).

9. Denning, 3.

10. Jane Tompkins, *West of Everything: The Inner Life of Westerns* (New York: Oxford University Press, 1992), 48.

11. *The Random House Dictionary of the English Language.* 2d ed.

12. Wheeler, 5.

13. Wheeler, 3.

14. Wheeler, 1.

15. Wheeler, 1.

16. Wheeler, 2.

17. Wheeler, 2.

18. Leslie Fiedler, *Love and Death in the American Novel* (1966; New York: Anchor, 1992).

19. Nicole Tonkovich, "Guardian Angels and Missing Mothers: Race and Domesticity in *Winona* and *Deadwood Dick on Deck*," *Western American Literature* 32:3 (Fall 1997): 245.

20. Wheeler, 13.

21. Wheeler, 4.

22. Wheeler, 10.

23. Wheeler, 6.

24. Wheeler, 6.

25. Wheeler, 12.

26. Wheeler, 10.

27. Wheeler, 6.

28. Wheeler, 5.

29. Ona Russell, "What's in a Name Anyway?: The Calamity of Calamity Jane," *American Studies* 35 (Fall 1994), 28.

30. Wheeler, 5.

31. Wheeler, 3.

32. Annette Kuhn, "Sexual Disguise and Cinema," in *Popular Fiction: Technology, Ideology, Production, Reading*, ed. Tony Bennett (New York: Routledge, 1990), 173.

33. Wheeler, 11.

34. Marjorie Garber, *Vested Interests: Cross-Dressing and Cultural Anxiety* (1992; New York: Routledge, 1997), 16.

35. Garber, 17.

36. Garber, 13.

37. Wheeler, 11.

38. Wheeler, 11.

39. Denning, 146-47.

40. Wheeler, 15.

41. Wheeler, 6, emphasis added.

42. Wheeler, 7, 8.

43. Wheeler, 14.

44. On this convention and twentieth-century subversions, see Rachel Blau Du-Plessis, *Writing beyond the Ending: Narrative Strategies of Twentieth-Century Women* (Bloomington: Indiana University Press, 1985). In a subsequent Wheeler dime novel Western, Calamity Jane and Deadwood Dick marry, but their joint status as outlaws means that even the marriage is unconventional; see Edward L. Wheeler, *Deadwood Dick of Deadwood: or, The Picked Party*, Beadle's Half-Dime Library #156 (1880).

45. Wheeler, 15.

46. Smith, 134.

47. Tonkovich, 244.

48. Denning, 157–60.

49. Tonkovich, 243; see also Blake Allmendinger, Chapter One, "The White Open Spaces," *Ten Most Wanted: The New Western Literature* (New York: Routledge, 1998), 17–32.

Chapter 4

Marvel's *Tomb of Dracula*: Case Study in a Scorned Medium

Donald Palumbo

Comic books are to this day a "scorned" literary medium—at the very least, a narrative vehicle that is still almost completely ignored (and certainly underappreciated) by critics, just as it continues to be misunderstood by the general public. This scorn is fostered in large part by several widespread and tenacious misconceptions supported by a few fifties-era sociological studies, such as Fredric Wertham's particularly influential *Seduction of the Innocent*,[1] that "compete in their merciless castigation of the comics, heaping blazing coals upon them for their excesses of violence and gore, their often unwholesome treatment of sex, and their frequently low level of writing and drawing."[2] These midcentury studies perceive comic books not only as a medium marketed essentially to a vulnerable and undiscriminating audience of children, but also as the vehicle for badly illustrated cartoon versions of such lowbrow literary genres as detective, Western, horror, fantastic, and science fiction—pulp-narrative forms that were nearly as likely as the comics to elicit scorn in the fifties, even when their narratives were not presented via a medium that many infer is subliterate only because it communicates primarily through pictures. But, while these various genres of popular literature themselves have enjoyed a distinct critical rehabilitation in the past several decades—and even though certain atypical comic books created explicitly for an adult audience, such as Art Spiegelman's *Maus*, seemed to suggest "the emergence of comic books as a respectable literary form in the 1980s" and did prompt an increase in the positive critical attention afforded comic books[3]—the mass perception of the comic-book medium itself has not greatly changed. Despite their midcentury "castigation" and "the long decades of cultural scorn"[4] that followed, however, a close and unbiased look at typical mass-market comic books published since the fifties clearly reveals that comic books can and often do have significant literary merit in the traditional sense, and for this reason can be profitably analyzed through the same methodologies applied to elite literature.

Jean-Paul Gabilliet performs just such an analysis in his study of Marvel Comics' Silver Surfer, focusing archetypal and cultural criticism on the eighteen-issue run of *Silver Surfer*, volume 1 (1968–1970), to demonstrate that "it was possible for the comic book medium to achieve a shift from stereotypes to narrative myth by means of an exploration of a genre's ideological margins."[5] Positing that "superhero comic books . . . generally contain strongly stereotyped plots" that present good and evil in terms of "the preservation of 'legitimate' property links between persons and goods," and thus reinforce "Manicheanism and Capitalism . . . the two sides of . . . the ideology propagated by American popular culture," Gabilliet examines the literary and visual "devices used to . . . shift from stereotyped forms to a mythical structure" in *Silver Surfer*, which employs "a narrative structure analogous to that found in literary myths" that allows it "to initiate a reflection on personal morality in the contemporary world" as well.[6] He finds that "the Silver Surfer is at the center of a mythical structure which . . . acknowledges the existence of a transcendental morality" and presumes "the fundamental superiority of intrinsic morality over any political contract" in proposing a "hierarchization of ethical values" in which "personal desire is subordinate to submission to political power, which in turn is always superseded by morality."[7] And in doing so he validates this mythical structure's integrity while explicating *Silver Surfer*'s use of "psychoanalytical" and "archetypal" symbolism, "Christian imagery," and "the character's obvious analogies with Jesus Christ" to reveal "the Surfer's ambiguous position as a fallen angel" who confronts "ethical choices and is made to question the necessity of being good" while embodying "the existential contradiction experienced by one caught between unqualified selflessness and the impossibility to live up to it."[8]

Many of my own published articles over the past twenty years have used close textual analysis, that old "new criticism" methodology developed expressly to examine the aesthetics of elite literature, to investigate additional publications of the Marvel Comics Group, which (with Detective Comics) has dominated the comic-book industry over the past four decades. These studies too reveal that such mass-market comic books, as narrative vehicles, employ the same aesthetics as elite literature quite effectively, that "the publications of the Marvel Comics Group warrant serious consideration as a legitimate narrative enterprise that is frequently both literate and technically and philosophically sophisticated."[9] Plot analysis of a ten-issue *Avengers* story-line from 1978 discovers that

[w]ithin the confines of the story's beautifully orchestrated, skillfully balanced plot structure, one brief but dynamic scene in the second episode foreshadows both the two classic plot twists in the ninth and tenth episode climaxes and all three elements of the tenth episode resolution. Moreover, the story also contains numerous crucial ironies as well as resonant subplots, impressively articulated character development, and an intriguing use of metaphor, allusion, and graphic symbolism. . . . This simplified analysis shows that comics can be used to demonstrate the concepts of plot structure, climax, and

resolution, and the distinction between plot and story, as well as . . . foreshadowing. These issues . . . also use subplots to echo and foreshadow elements of the main plot . . . and . . . contain much comic relief that depends on ironic juxtaposition for its effect.[10]

A far more extensive study of the hundreds of comic books in which Marvel's most popular character, Spider-Man, had appeared throughout the sixties and seventies reveals that

Spider-Man exhibits within the confines of his comic-book universe nearly all the . . . characteristics of the existentialist hero. Both the constant and the ephemeral situations in which he finds himself are hopelessly absurd as well as improbably and hyperbolically ironic. . . . His most prominent trait is a crushing, encyclopedic alienation: he is not only an orphan, but he also feels responsible for the death of his foster father . . . and is surrounded by a host of hostile father-figures; his alienation-from-self is evident in his dual, diametrically dissimilar identities . . . and he is a social outcast and loner in both of them; his spider-powers clearly set him apart from normal humanity; and his career as a super-hero also sabotages his sex life, his already-precarious friendships, and his school work. He is sometimes the victim of hallucinations and frequently feels that his split life-style is driving him insane. His primary motivation for maintaining his Spider-Man identity . . . is a deep-seated feeling of guilt . . . and any failure or mistake on his part brings this . . . guilt crashing down upon him. His spider-powers are a type of freedom, and he sees them as an unasked for and an unwanted burden. However, . . . in the best existentialist hero tradition, he concludes that the absurdity he encounters in his world must be both accepted and combatted, that meaning is to be found only through struggle and that defeat lies only in capitulation.[11]

Indeed, these comics explicitly compare Spider-Man (whose favorite authors are Sartre, Camus, and Jung) to Franz Kafka's existential protagonist Gregor Samsa and, implicitly, not only to other Kafka protagonists but also to such existential icons as Sartre's Roquentin, Camus' Dr. Rieux and Orestes, and such "other unlikely existential Christ-figures" as Dostoyevsky's Raskolnikov, Faulkner's Joe Christmas and Benjy Compson, Joyce's Leopold Bloom, and Kesey's R.P. McMurphy.[12]

A study of one of Marvel's most interesting minor characters during this same time period reveals that Adam Warlock "is a carefully delineated cosmic Christ figure" who turns up in the comic-book equivalent of two "unusually philosophical and relentlessly allegorical science fiction novels."[13] By 1980 Warlock had appeared in "only two plots; each of these concludes with Warlock's death, resurrection, and ascension. The first contains numerous and obvious early prefigurations of his deaths and rebirths, while the second . . . contains shadowings of this same archetypal fantasy theme coupled with an ingenious, multilayered doppleganger motif' set in an intricate time-travel plot.[14] In pursuing their extraordinarily sophisticated reinterpretations of Christ, these two plots contain allusions and parallels to Wells' *Island of Dr. Moreau*, Dostoyevsky's "Dream of a Ridiculous Man" and the "Grand Inquisitor" chapter from *The Brothers Karamasov*, and Milton's *Paradise Lost* and *Paradise Regained*, as well as to "Genesis" and *The New Testament*.

Thus, it is not at all surprising that a much broader, subsequent study reveals that

Marvel Comics . . . liberally seed their stories with allusions to the Bible; to historical and contemporary figures and events; to Gothic and fantasy literature; to mainstream literary classics, particularly Shakespeare's plays; to Greek, Roman, Egyptian, and Norse mythology, non-western mythologies, and Arthurian and other folk legends; and to popular culture itself——especially science fiction, film, television, popular music, advertising, and, of course, the comics. . . . Marvel Comics are as much a mirror of western culture, substituting contemporary American references for those of turn-of-the-century Dublin, as is James Joyce's *Ulysses*, and the references in both occur in roughly the same ratio of historical to Judeo-Christian to mythological to Shakespearian to fantastic to popular. . . . Marvel Comics has, in this respect, accomplished through inevitable circumstance what Joyce had attempted by design: to hold a mirror to Western culture. As these comics are the labor of hundreds of people working continuously over a period of several decades, they are almost through statistical necessity . . . a faithful, measured reflection of the culture in which their many contributors are steeped.[15]

And in the early nineties these comics also experimented extensively with metafiction in *The Sensational She-Hulk*, a title that reinvents as a "postmodern" heroine the less-successful, initial version of a character first introduced a decade earlier. This title too is highly allusive as one facet of its being "relentlessly inventive in exploiting the revamped She-Hulk's awareness that she is a comic-book character."[16] While habitually indulging in a continuous stream of hip references to popular culture in general and contemporary comic books in particular, the revised She-Hulk "reads and shamelessly plugs her own books, chronicles her life in terms of issue numbers, refers jeeringly to her editor, invokes the comics code . . . notes how many pages of the story are left, and talks directly to her audience."[17] A comic-book superheroine for the nineties, the new She-Hulk "is the opposite of her initial, failed persona—the afflicted hero": Marvel has

recast her as a comic sex-goddess who loves her super-heroine identity, uses it to her advantage, and has taken control of her own life. . . . Not only is she woman-as-victor, and not (as she was portrayed originally) woman-as-victim, but she also possesses an almost unique insight into the nature of her existence—a special, ontological superiority. While it provides seemingly endless opportunities for absurdist metafictional comedy, the innate one-upmanship of this existential awareness combines with the revamped She-Hulk's self-confident, in-control, woman-as-victor persona to make her appealing as a strong female character to a contemporary audience.[18]

The following examination of Marvel's reinterpretations of Dracula demonstrates yet again that the typical, mass-market comic book of the late twentieth century is often, and very likely characteristically, the vehicle for complex narratives and characterizations that appeal to a sophisticated literary sensibility—even though, as in this instance, it may simultaneously recapitulate the content of yet another "scorned" genre, horror fiction. Actual comic-book consumers constitute a far more demanding and aesthetically mature audience than Wertham and his ilk had assumed existed, and Marvel comics respond to this market reality. Just as the more complex, highly innovative version of the She-Hulk succeeded with this audience while the earlier, more formulaic version had failed, so too did Marvel's more sophisticated, nuanced characterization of Dracula in the seventies succeed in finding and holding an audience while a simplistic, one-dimensional characterization of Dracula abortively attempted in the nineties did not. Just as Marvel Comics in general are highly allusive, so too does the Wolfman/Colan treatment of Dracula in the seventies allude extensively, not only to Bram Stoker's novel (as one might expect), but also to the historical figure on whom the Dracula legend may be based, Vlad Tepes. And just as such characters as Warlock, to a lesser extent the Silver Surfer, and even Spider-Man are developed as comic-book Christ-figures, so too can Marvel's seventies treatment of Dracula be seen as a species of conversion narrative in which the Lord of the Undead slowly comes to embrace explicitly Christian values.

From 1971, with his resurrection in *Tomb of Dracula* #1, to 1983, with the extinction of all vampires in *Doctor Strange* #62 (until they returned again in 1994's *Blade: the Vampire Hunter* #1), Count Dracula regularly stalked the pages of Marvel Comics. In seventy issues of *Tomb of Dracula* (1971–79), thirteen issues of the black-and-white, magazine-format *Dracula Lives* (1973–75), and scattered appearances in other Marvel titles, Dracula's character and mythos were manipulated—primarily by writer/editor Marv Wolfman and artist Gene Colan—to conform to the requirements of the hero-centered comic-book medium. Initially depicted as an inhuman fiend in the same unsympathetic vein first fanged by Bram Stoker's titular antagonist, Marvel's Dracula gradually developed into a tragic antihero, a tormented underdog of heroic stature who was often more sinned against than sinning, often more a savior than a devil, and who—while still a thing of evil—came to possess a sympathetic human dimension.

In the first ten issues of *Tomb of Dracula*, however, the Count almost always played the villain; these stories focus on the heroism of a small band of vampire hunters who hound him. While Frank Drake—an American and Dracula's last male descendant—explores the Transylvanian castle he has recently inherited, Clifton Graves, a duplicitous friend, discovers Dracula's crypt and revives the vampire by removing the stake lodged in his ribs. Dracula almost immediately transforms Frank's fiancée, Jean, into a vampire and Clifton into his mindless human slave. He subsequently reveals an ignoble nature in saving himself by thrusting another vampire, one of his former lovers, into the path of a crossbow shaft meant for him; in using a group of children and then a pack of decaying corpses as his pawns; and in coldly abandoning Clifton to a gruesome death once he has outlived his usefulness.[19]

These issues depict Dracula as a thing of "ancient evil"[20]—bloodthirsty, unfeeling, and treacherous. He has long since lost any reverence or concern for human life and regards his thousands of past victims, such as Lucy Westenra, as "mere sustenance."[21] Yet even here, in two of these first ten issues, Dracula is treated more sympathetically and all the techniques of his subsequent rehabilitation are sounded. In issue #4 he is presented as both a sympathetic underdog and a foil to the foolish. Outnumbered by relentless enemies and at a disadvantage when pitted against contemporary technology, he survives through cunning and courage. In the process he outwits and dispenses poetic justice to a vain old woman who tries to use him to regain her youthful beauty by becoming a vampire. In issue #9, while again the underdog, he displays positive human emotions and is a savior as well as a despoiler. Out of gratitude, he advises a youth who had aided him, pledges his "protection and friendship,"[22] and saves the youth from being victimized by two other vampires.

In issue #11 Dracula usurps the vampire hunters as the comic book's center of interest, in effect becoming the hero. Subsequently, he is presented as a survivor, as a man doomed to suffer a hideous fate who surmounts overwhelming odds through his possession of such admirable qualities as willpower, courage, strength, intelligence, and endurance. He foils those who deserve to be thwarted—not only the foolish but also corrupt, vicious men and supernatural horrors as evil as he is, or worse—and saves sympathetic characters from such unredeemed villains. He exhibits the ability to love as well as the will to persevere, and through demonstrating such positive emotions is gradually humanized. This process of humanization is reinforced both by stories that recount his human origins and by those that portray events from his perspective by assigning him the role of first-person narrator.

But the series' first heroes are the vampire hunters, and they must surrender some of their initial heroic stature if Dracula is to acquire it. In addition to Frank Drake, the vampire hunters include Rachel Van Helsing, great granddaughter of Bram Stoker's Dr. Van Helsing; Taj, Rachel's mute East Indian manservant; Quincy Harker, their wheelchair-bound leader and the son of Stoker's Jonathan and Mina; Blade, a black vigilante whose mother was slain by a vampire at the moment of his birth; Hannibal King, a vampire-detective who eschews the taste of human blood; and Harold Harold, the group's comic relief, a struggling hack writer for *True Vampire Stories*.[23] The moral distinction between the hunters and the hunted soon blurs, however. Except for King and Harold, the vampire hunters become as obsessive and ruthless in their pursuit of Dracula, himself a hunter, as Dracula is in his lust for blood. And Dracula hunts to survive, after all, while the vampire hunters are motivated primarily by a lust for vengeance—and come to recognize that their pursuit of Dracula is the only thing that gives their lives meaning.

Rachel's consuming hatred, which renders her incapable of love, stems from Dracula's murder of her parents when she was a child, just as Frank's vendetta stems from Dracula's murder of his fiancée. Taj had lost his vocal cords in a struggle with Dracula in which his wife had been crippled and his son, whom he eventually slays, transformed into a vampire. Similarly, decades earlier Dracula had crippled Quincy and driven his young wife to suicide—and more recently had transformed Quincy's grown daughter, Edith, into a vampire, forcing Quincy to slay her. And Blade seeks Deacon Frost, the vampire who had killed his mother and had also infected Hannibal King.[24]

As Dracula grows in compassion and love, the vampire hunters become ever more steeped in hatred. Moreover, they have chosen the role of de-stroyer—while Dracula, who never chose to be a vampire, is cast as their harried victim. Domini, the Madonna-like beauty who becomes Dracula's beloved human wife, accuses the vampire hunters, and specifically Rachel, of seeing "things only in terms of black and white [. . .] your eyes are so hard and cold . . . and your heart is so empty! [. . .] When was the last time you felt anything but hatred? When was the last time bitterness did not paint your every judgment? [. . .] When was the last time you felt love?"[25] And the vampire hunters are sometimes more ignoble than their prey: After they once temporarily join forces with Dracula to defeat an even more dangerous mutual foe, the disembodied brain of Dr. Sun, it is they who first seize the opportunity to break the truce and treacherously turn on the vampire, not vice versa, as soon as the mutual danger is past.[26]

Unlike Dracula, who remains basically evil (having fully accepted his vampiric nature) while exhibiting heroic qualities, Hannibal King is a true vampire hero—and thus is a foil to both Dracula and the vampire hunters. In his years as a vampire he never kills for blood; he even refuses to metamorphose into a mist or bat, except under the most dire exigency, because he so loathes his condition. Also, while he sometimes crosses paths with Dracula and the vampire hunters in investigating a case as a private detective, he does not seek vengeance for its own sake on Deacon Frost or Dracula. As King has never killed as a vampire, Marvel's Sorcerer Supreme Dr. Strange is ultimately able to restore his humanity. Rachel, on the other hand, is finally bitten by Dracula, becomes a vampire, and is slain at her own request. Quincy blows himself up in an almost-successful last attempt to slay Dracula. Taj returns to his wife in India. Harold Harold, after participating in numerous comic adventures while seeking copy for *True Vampire Stories*, finally becomes a vampire himself—and then a successful television sit-com writer—before he is exterminated with nearly all the other vampires. And Blade slackens his pace after he and King slay Deacon Frost; eventually, with Frank Drake, he retires from vampire hunting. It is only the most obsessed of the vampire hunters, Quincy and Rachel, who are destroyed by their obsession.[27]

While he continues to victimize the innocent, Dracula becomes a more sympathetic character—and often at least acts the part of a hero—in also terrorizing the guilty and demonic. As in *Tomb of Dracula* #4, he sometimes merely metes out poetic justice to the foolish: for example, when he turns on and kills the fanatical leader of a revivalist movement who publicly resurrects him—after the vampire hunters once succeed in hammering a stake through his heart—in a bid to attract followers to his congregation, or when he co-opts a devil-worshiping cult that mistakes him for Satan.[28] In such instances he is both a vehicle of justice and admirably superior, like Ben Jonson's Volpone, to the pitifully self-deceived and venal fools he thwarts. More often, however, he is the vehicle of well-deserved retribution to more truly evil men. But he most often combats, and saves humanity from, other supernatural villains who are at least as foul and threatening as he is—but are less tragically portrayed.

In *Tomb of Dracula* #11 the Lord of Vampires not only saves Quincy Harker's life—albeit unintentionally, by causing the death of a hired killer who threatens it—but also chooses as his prey a mugger rather than the young woman who would otherwise have been the mugger's victim. While Dracula often saves women from molestation, he sometimes does so only then to molest them himself. However, with no ulterior motive, he does once save a drug-addicted prostitute from being murdered by mobsters—and is labeled a "shy hero" by the police.[29]

It is in *Dracula Lives*, in which he is portrayed more consistently as an admirable character than in *Tomb of Dracula*, that Dracula is presented most often as the persistent foil of evil, as a bloodthirsty vigilante, almost as a superhero. In one episode he murders two drug addicts and a cynical imposter (a parody of L. Ron Hubbard). In another he plagues some cruel Nazis who occupy Castle Dracula during World War II and amuse themselves by torturing, raping, and massacring gypsies. In the seventeenth century he engineers the downfall of a sadistic countess who bathes in the blood of her murdered maidservants to preserve her youth. And, back in the twentieth century, he confronts and horribly executes a bomb-wielding terrorist hijacker (although most of the jet's passengers die as a result), a crazed mass murderess, and a mafia don.[30]

In preferring to slay scum, criminals, and maniacs, Dracula is much like his daughter, Lilith, even though father and daughter hate one another. In a tale in which she emasculates an uncouth bully, decimates a dockload of murderous stevedores, and upsets the operation of some drug pushers to save an innocent man from a frameup, we are told that the "cruel . . . brutal . . . merciless . . . unforgiving" Lilith "has learned that such excesses are far more gratifying . . . when the target of the wrath is deserving."[31] And in a story in which she kills both a psychopathic murderer and a knife-wielding rapist (whom she invites, as she methodically breaks his arm, to "relax . . . and enjoy it"), we learn that Lilith prefers to inhabit New York City because she "finds no joy in sucking the blood of innocents."[32]

It is in confronting supernatural evils like himself, often other vampires, that Dracula is most clearly heroic. Soon after he is captured by the Turks and transformed into a vampire by a vengeful gypsy, Dracula is attacked by other vampires and forced to fight a duel with their vampire lord for supremacy among the undead. That same year, 1459, he engages in a supernatural conflict with Father Bordia, a false priest and vampire who has pledged his soul to Satan. In contemporary times, Dracula defeats a super-vampire created and controlled by Dr. Sun, saves a young widow and her family from her brutish and possessively jealous vampire husband, and battles an army of vampires who had betrayed their allegiance to him to follow demons. Toward the end of his career—after his vampire hordes have all abandoned him because he has left Transylvania, married a human, forsaken Satan, and even wielded a crucifix to protect a group of children from their vampiric assault—he is persecuted by his own daughter, twice more attacked by legions of vampires, and forced to fight their new lord, Torgo, who plans to enslave humanity and breed men like cattle as food for the undead.[33]

Dracula's arch-nemesis is the diabolical Dr. Sun, the disembodied brain of an evil Red Chinese scientist who plots to steal Dracula's vampiric powers and transfer them to a loyal minion "who will rule all the undead . . . in the name of Doctor Sun. . . . He will supply me not only with the blood I need to survive—but with an invincible army with which to eventually rule the world itself."[34]   Quincy sees the choice the vampire hunters must make between Dracula and Sun as "the ever-so-sweet paradox of the devil you know versus the devil you don't,"[35] and eventually decides that Dracula is the lesser evil. Even Rachel roots for Dracula in the battle in which he is defeated by Sun's zombie-like henchman, Juno. Thus, when Dracula is destroyed, the vampire slayers resurrect him themselves—knowing that, in wreaking his vengeance on Sun, Dracula will eradicate an even more dangerous menace to mankind than himself. Of course, Dracula does defeat Sun in their next encounter, only then to be betrayed by his temporary allies.[36]

Another of Dracula's sinister enemies is Anton Lupeski, the leader of the devil-cult that mistakes Dracula for Satan. Himself undeceived, Lupeski hopes to use Dracula to consolidate his power over the cult and then to destroy him. Toward this treacherous end Lupeski enlists the aid of the vampire hunters—who this time choose the more diabolical, more ignoble antagonist because their hatred of Dracula warps their judgment. After Dracula's and Domini's infant son is accidentally killed in the final confrontation with Lupeski, Dracula crushes Lupeski's skull in his grief and rage but, at Domini's request, spares the remorse-stricken vampire hunters.[37]

The vampire hunters reciprocate this and several similar instances of Dracula's compassion toward them only once, immediately after Dracula is humbled in his sole encounter with Satan. On the two other occasions when the vampire hunters spare Dracula, they do so only under extreme duress: once because he is their sole hope of defeating Dr. Sun, and once because his vampire legions hold Rachel hostage and threaten to kill her if their master is harmed. Dracula likewise twice saves his enemies for a base motive: He once protects Taj when both are trapped in a hostile other dimension, and once saves Rachel when both are lost in a blizzard in the Transylvanian Alps, because in each case his foe is his last sure source of human blood, to be preserved against possible future need. Dracula also saves Rachel from Sun's supervampire because he covets the eventual satisfaction of draining her blood himself. However, Dracula later saves Harold from Sun's weaponry—immediately after Sun has been destroyed—purely to honor the alliance the vampire hunters will betray a moment later. Foreshadowing his clemency following his son's death, and likewise at Domini's request, he also releases rather than slays all of the vampire hunters on the night of his son's birth—an event the vampire hunters had defiled by mounting an attack against Dracula that ends in their capture.[38]

In his climactic confrontation with Satan, Dracula is victimized by this archetypal embodiment of evil, thwarts his will, and ultimately renounces him. Satan claims that in having married a human, Domini, and sired a son, Janus, who is reincarnated after his death as an angel of light, Dracula has upset the cosmic balance of good and evil in favor of good—and must be destroyed. Yet Dracula allies himself with the reborn Janus against Satan, and not only saves himself, but also saves another whom Satan has marked for death, Topaz, a woman whom Satan claims has the potential to undermine his evil hold over humanity. In retribution Satan strips Dracula of his vampiric traits and abilities, thus making him human again, and humbles him further by turning his former subjects, the vampires, against him—thus confronting Dracula with his innate mortality and prompting him for the first time in 500 years to fear death. Having thus broken Dracula, Satan makes him a vampire once more. Yet Dracula has by now cursed and renounced Satan, by whom he had previously sworn, and swears instead by the God whose icon, the crucifix, still causes him anguish.[39]

Dracula's encounter with Satan not only casts him in the role of hero confronting primal evil but also develops most fully two other techniques employed to transform him from a fiend into a sympathetic character: his portrayal as an underdog who survives through courage, cunning, and force of will, and as a once-human victim who still retains some positive, redeeming human emotions. Particularly vulnerable after he is stripped of his powers by Satan, Dracula is now not only at the mercy of human mobs and other vampires, including his daughter, but is also stalked by a ruthless professional killer hired by a mobster to avenge the death of one of the innumerable women Dracula has slain. Even without his vampiric powers, however, Dracula eludes his human and vampiric enemies and overcomes the cool, heavily armed mercenary through exercising his courage and indomitable will.[40]

Even Harker acknowledges that "there is more to Dracula than meets the eye . . . When he lived—five hundred years ago—viciousness was a necessary trait to prevent the enemy from invading your country. To his people, Dracula was not only a tyrant, but a hero. These days, Dracula does nothing without reason. He kills to survive."[41] And Dracula's brief reversion to humanity through the power of Satan is an objective correlative of the humanity within him that five centuries as a vampire has not yet completely extinguished. The final issue of *Tomb of Dracula* concludes with the words "Dracula was a Man . . . and never should that be forgotten."[42] *Dracula Lives* emphasizes Vlad Dracula's humanity by recounting his origins as a dashing, fearless Transylvanian warlord finally defeated in battle and captured by the Turks: Taken to a gypsy camp to be cured of his wounds, he is instead infected by a gypsy vampire, Lianda, who thus avenges on him the harm his policies have done her people; the Turks then rape and murder his beloved wife, Maria, before his eyes, and it is in his grief over Maria's death and his own lost humanity that he swears to wreak eternal vengeance on mankind as a vampire.[43]

Dracula never chose to be a vampire, sometimes curses his undead existence and the fate that made him what he is, and over the centuries has sought a cure for vampirism; when he is once compelled by sorcery to relive his greatest fear, he recalls being bitten by Lianda. He tries in vain to prevent Domini from resurrecting Janus because he does not want his own fate to befall his child, whom he fears will lose all innocence if reborn. And when another vampire once beseeches him to plunge a stake through her heart, he understands her desire for eternal rest and complies.[44]

In revealing such emotions as compassion, gratitude, understanding, grief, pity, and even fear of death, Dracula is humanized. He also sometimes exhibits a human sense of justice, although with a perverse twist, as when he turns an already dying woman into a vampire so that she can wreak vengeance on her murderer; kills a father for abusing his child; or conspires with a vengeful woman to slay four men who have betrayed her, then transforms them into vampires and looses them on the woman to extract their revenge in turn. He is even capable of feeling guilt and remorse.[45]

However, the emotion that most eloquently testifies to Dracula's remaining humanity is his capacity to love. Dracula habitually spares women who remind him of his beloved Maria, his first wife, and has had more than one brief love affair.[46] When one of the women he saves from a supernatural horror, Shiela Whitter, falls in love with him only later to commit suicide, he feels remorse and mourns at her grave.[47] Dracula's greatest love as a vampire, however, is Domini, who bears his child. His love for her amazes him, as he had thought he had lost the ability to love, and he is further surprised to find himself looking forward to fatherhood.[48] During this interval he spares a woman only because she has her child with her,[49] relocates a battle in progress out of concern that Domini might be injured,[50] and even comes to hope that "for perhaps the first time in five long centuries—perhaps I have found that ever-elusive thing men call peace."[51] Janus' death shatters that illusion of peace, but the unbridled grief with which Dracula mourns his lost son signifies the depth of his love.[52]

To have him sometimes tell his story himself is a final narrative strategy employed to make Dracula a more sympathetic character. On occasion the tale is presented as an entry in Dracula's diary (which is stolen and eventually falls into the hands of hack writer Bram Stoker), and at other times Dracula expresses his point of view in lengthy soliloquies. In both his diary and his monologues Dracula frequently alludes to his mortal past, laments his lost humanity, engages in philosophical speculation, and reveals a mawkish Victorian sentimentality. One diary entry begins:

"Once I was called Vlad, and I was the proud ruler of a people who embraced life with unfettered joy, and hailed me as the saint who preserved their joy.
"But no more.

"Once I was a freedom fighter, a man who exulted in the act of leading his army against those who would prey on the innocent. And once I was the head of more than a kingdom—I was the head of a family.

"But no more. No more am I *any* of these things. Now I am only Dracula."[53]

Regardless of its content, a first-person narrative intrinsically prompts some degree of identification with the narrator, inviting the reader to share his point of view and to be something of an accomplice in it.[54]

Yet Marvel's Dracula, while sympathetically portrayed, remains a comic-book villain. He too seeks world domination, although at a leisurely pace, and is not satisfied to be Lord of the Undead only. He once acquires an Atlantean idol that grants its possessor great power over material reality, but it is destroyed by Shiela Whitter. On another occasion he attempts to control Britain's Parliament by murdering, terrorizing, blackmailing, and mesmerizing its ministers, but is thwarted by the vampire hunters. And he allows himself to become involved with Anton Lupeski's devil worshipers because he hopes to achieve world domination by attracting the powerful to the cult with his charisma and then usurping Lupeski.[55]

Dracula's last, most ambitious bid for absolute power results in the "permanent" extinction of all vampires. (Although "permanent" in this case means a hiatus of eleven years in which no classic vampires appeared in Marvel Comics, this is still an extraordinarily long interval for a major Marvel character—much less an entire class of prominent supernatural beings—to remain "dead.") After the debacle involving Lupeski's devil worshipers and his humiliating encounter with Satan, Dracula gains control over the Darkholders, a cult dating back to precataclysmic Atlantis that worships the Elder God Chthon and seeks to recover and master the spells in The Darkholder "Book of Sins," parchments transcribed by Chthon that contain the arcane knowledge of the Elder Gods, knowledge rooted in such evil that employing it corrupts the soul. The first Darkholders, a small circle of Atlantean mystics, had used the "Book of Sins" to create the first vampires, fallen enemies whom they had planned to resurrect as soldier-slaves, but the vampires slew their creators and fled Atlantis. The Darkhold was lost in the island continent's subsequent destruction, but has resurfaced over the course of millennia in the possession of various scholars, priests, and sorcerers, most of whom were corrupted by it.[56]

Through his association with the Darkholders, Dracula attains a new plateau of power and gains immunity from all the substances that weaken vampires: crosses, silver, wood, garlic, and sunlight. However, his more human, sympathetic traits are eclipsed by his now obsessive lust for power, and toward the conclusion of this plot—and coincident with his being no longer the central character in his own book—he reverts to the pure, inhuman villainy that had characterized his presentation in the first ten issues of *Tomb of Dracula* and preys on such mainstream Marvel superheroes as the Asgardian Goddess Sif, the X-Men, and the Avengers.

Possession of the Darkhold itself would endow Dracula with invincibility, great mystic power, and true immortality, but the tome also contains the counterspell to that incantation used to create vampires that could purge the Earth of vampirism—the Montesi Formula, named for the medieval monk, long since slain by Dracula, who had discovered and first tried to use it. Thus, Dracula and the remaining vampire hunters, aided by Dr. Strange, vie to be the first to recover and use the Darkhold. Finally, Dracula locates the "Book of Sins" and overcomes the vampire hunters, only to be defeated on a mystic plane by Dr. Strange, who then recites the Montesi Formula and cleanses the Earth of all vampires save Hannibal King, the true vampire-hero, whose humanity Strange restores through his sorcery.[57]

In having recently been resurrected again, and this time (apparently) as an unmitigated villain once more, Dracula has come full circle in his career as Marvel Comic's lord of vampires. Blade discovers that the Montesi Formula has finally "collapsed"[58] and that Dracula, with other vampires, has returned "to prey on the living and rule the dead."[59] Laughing at the idea that Blade hopes "to struggle once more against overwhelming odds to save mankind" from him, this more traditional, thoroughly villainous Dracula gloats that "they don't want saving! They relish the dark, sensual perversity of what I offer them."[60] Moreover, Blade's ally Bible John has "been shown the affliction to come . . . a New York yet to be . . . The sky blazed and the streets echoed with the agonized cries of tortured souls. Cresting the city like a black sunrise was Count Dracula . . . reveling in the carnage, glutted on gore."[61]

This is a step backward from the complexity of the humanized Dracula who was presented as a protagonist for most of *Tomb of Dracula*'s seventy-issue run—a Dracula who, in his darkest, most honest moments, realizes that, as a creature of evil, he is powerless against the superior might of heaven and foredoomed to defeat in that final moment when goodness will ultimately triumph.[62] And it turns out to have been an unsuccessful step at that, for *Blade* folded after its tenth issue, before the "collapse" of the Montesi Formula and the consequent return of Dracula could even be explained. This seems to confirm what Wolfman and Colan had intuited by *Tomb of Dracula*'s tenth issue: that a character with the perverse allure and potential for complexity of Dracula, who has survived and thrived in the mass culture for over a century now, can support a comic-book vehicle only when portrayed as a complex, humanized, sympathetic protagonist—but not when he is presented as a one-dimensional, unreservedly evil antagonist. Much of the deep appeal of Dracula is lost when he is cast solely as the Other, the external evil, for much of the character's attraction rests—as many other contemporary interpretations also suggest—on the fascinating tension inherent in the suggestion that he is *not* completely Other, but is a reflection of some somber aspect of ourselves, that we do indeed "relish the dark, sensual perversity" in ourselves that he represents. The unsophisticated audience of Wertham's imagination would have been satisfied with the simplified Dracula portrayed in *Blade*. But that audience doesn't exist. The real audience for contemporary comic books is considerably more sophisticated; this audience, which reveals its character at the cash register, prefers the multi-dimensional complexity of *Tomb of Dracula*'s humanized lord of vampires.

And this humanized Dracula is depicted through a wide variety of narrative strategies: portraying him as an historical figure who is the victim of a brutal vengeance and a gypsy curse, as a sympathetic underdog facing overwhelming odds, as a foil to the venal and foolish, and as a vehicle of poetic justice; emphasizing his possession of such positive character traits as cunning, courage, willpower, strength, and endurance; endowing him with such sympathetic human emotions as compassion, honor, perseverance, grief, pity, guilt, remorse, gratitude, and love; pitting him against such thoroughly unsympathetic antagonists as other vampires, supervillains, sadistic Nazis, degenerate nobility, terrorists, drug addicts, mass murderers, professional hit men, mafia dons, false priests, devil worshippers, and even Satan himself, among other supernatural horrors; allowing him to present his own point of view as a first-person narrator; and even having him revert temporarily to his original humanity and embrace explicitly Christian values. Yet the complexity of the Marvel Comics Dracula is far from unique: It is mirrored in the comparable complexity of such characters as the Silver Surfer, Adam Warlock, Spider-Man, and She-Hulk. Moreover, complexity of characterization is but one of the signal characteristics elite literature shares with contemporary comics, which also exhibit a corresponding complexity of plot structure, sophisticated use of mythical and archetypal material, and a reflexive resonance with the mass culture that can be demonstrated through detailed analyses of individual stories and titles (such as Gabilliet's of *Silver Surfer*) just as it is evident superficially in the vast number and inclusive breadth of the allusions they contain. As it has much in common with elite literature in its narrative aspect—and differs from such literature primarily in appearance only, as a consequence of being an essentially visual medium—the late-twentieth-century comic book does not merit the scorn with which it is still saddled.

NOTES

1. In addition to Fredric Wertham's *Seduction of the Innocent* (New York: Holt, Rinehart and Winston, 1954), the other highly critical midcentury studies of comic books are Gershon Legman's *Love and Death: A Study in Censorship* (New York: Breaking Point, 1949) and Geoffrey Wagner's "Popular Iconography in the U.S.A.," in *Parade of Pleasure* (New York: Library Publishers, 1955).

2. Dick Lupoff and Don Thompson, eds., *All in Color for a Dime* (New Rochelle, NY: Arlington House, 1970), 9.

3. Joseph Witek, *Comic Books as History: The Narrative Art of Jack Jackson, Art Spiegelman, and Harvey Pekar*, Studies in Popular Culture (Jackson: University Press of Mississippi, 1989), 11.

4. Ibid.

5. Jean-Paul Gabilliet, "Cultural and Mythical Aspects of a Superhero: The Silver Surfer 1968–70," *Journal of Popular Culture* 28, no. 2 (Fall 1994): 210.

6. Ibid., 203–4.

7. Ibid., 206–7.

8. Ibid., 207–10 passim.

9. Donald Palumbo, "Comics as Literature: Plot Structure, Foreshadowing, and Irony in the Marvel Comics' *Avengers* 'Cosmic Epic,'" *Extrapolation* 22, no. 4 (Winter 1981): 309.

10. Ibid., 309–22 passim.

11. Donald Palumbo, "The Marvel Comics Group's Spider-Man Is an Existentialist Super-Hero; or, 'Life Has No Meaning without My Latest Marvels!'" *Journal of Popular Culture* 17, no. 2 (Fall 1983): 68–69.

12. Ibid., 74.

13. Donald Palumbo, "Adam Warlock: Marvel Comics' Cosmic Christ Figure," *Extrapolation* 24, no. 1 (Spring 1983): 33.

14. Ibid.

15. Donald Palumbo, "The Pattern of Allusions in Marvel Comics," *Proteus: A Journal of Ideas* 6, no. 1 (Spring 1989): 61, 63–64.

16. Donald Palumbo, "Metafiction in the Comics: *The Sensational She-Hulk,*" *Journal of the Fantastic in the Arts* 8, no. 3 (December 1997): 310.

17. Ibid., 313.

18. Ibid., 329.

19. These events occur in *Tomb of Dracula* 1, nos. 1–3 (April, May, July 1972), nos. 6–8 (January, March, May 1973), and no. 10 (July 1973). These endnotes identify comic books by title, volume, and issue number; as is common in citing other periodical publications, the number following the issue number's date and separated from it by a colon is the page number. This is far clearer and less cumbersome than identification by author, or by writer/artist team, would be, for numerous writer/artist teams contribute to the various issues that comprise the run of a given title.

20. *Tomb of Dracula* 1, no. 3 (July 1972): 6.

21. *Tomb of Dracula* 1, no. 49 (October 1976): 26.

22. *Tomb of Dracula* 1, no. 9 (June 1973): 28.

23. The issues in which these characters first appear are as follows: Frank Drake, *Tomb of Dracula* 1, no. 1 (April 1972); Rachel Van Helsing and Taj, no. 3 (July 1972); Quincy Harker, no. 7 (March 1973); Blade, no. 10 (July 1973); Hannibal King, no. 25 (October 1974); and Harold Harold, no. 37 (October 1975).

24. These events occur in *Tomb of Dracula* 1, nos. 20 (May 1974), 31 (April 1975), 33 (June 1975), 12 (September 1973), 19 (April 1974), and 45 (June 1976).

25. *Tomb of Dracula* 1, no. 64 (May 1978): 15–16.

26. *Tomb of Dracula* 1, no. 43 (April 1976).

27. These events occur in *Tomb of Dracula* 1, nos. 51–53 (December 1976, January 1977, February 1977); *Doctor Strange* 1, no. 62 (April 1983); *Giant Size X-Men Annual* 1, no. 6 (November 1982); and *Tomb of Dracula* 1, no. 70 (August 1979).

28. These events occur in *Tomb of Dracula* 1, nos. 14 (November 1973) and 45 (June 1976).

29. *Tomb of Dracula* 1, no. 65 (July 1978): 14.

30. These events occur in "A Poison of the Blood," *Dracula Lives* 1, no. 1 (1973); "The Terror that Stalked Castle Dracula," *Dracula Lives* 1, no. 2 (1973); "This Blood Is Mine," *Dracula Lives* 1, no. 4 (January 1974); "Night Flight to Terror," *Dracula Lives* 2, no. 1 (March 1974); "The Death Man," *Dracula Lives* 1, no. 7 (July 1974); and "Black Hand . . . Black Death," *Dracula Lives* 1, no. 8 (September 1974).

31. Steve Gerber, "Lilith, Daughter of Dracula: The Blood Book," *Dracula Lives* 1, no. 10 (January 1975): 41–42.

32. Steve Gerber, "Nobody Anybody Knows," *Dracula Lives* 1, no. 11 (March 1975): 38, 36.

33. These events occur in "Lord of Death . . . Lord of Hell," *Dracula Lives* 1, no. 3 (October 1973); "Look Homeward, Vampire," *Dracula Lives* 1, no. 4 (January 1974); *Tomb of Dracula* 1, nos. 21 (June 1974), 22 (July 1974), and 67 (November 1978; *Defenders* 1, no. 95 (May 1981); and *Tomb of Dracula* 1, nos. 68–70 (February, April, August 1979).

34. *Tomb of Dracula* 1, no. 21 (June 1974): 17.

35. *Tomb of Dracula* 1, no. 37 (October 1975): 31.

36. The events described in this paragraph occur in *Tomb of Dracula* 1, nos. 21 (June 1974), 37–40 (October 1975, November 1975, December 1975, January 1976), and 42 (March 1976).

37. These events occur in *Tomb of Dracula* 1, nos. 47–59 (August 1976 through August 1977).

38. These events occur in *Tomb of Dracula* 1, nos. 59 (August 1977), 11 (August 1973), 69 (April 1979), 41 (February 1976), 32–33 (May, June 1973), 5 (November 1972), 19 (April 1974), 21 (June 1974), 42 (March 1976), and 54 (March 1977).

39. These events occur in *Tomb of Dracula* 1, nos. 62–64 (January, March, May 1978) and 68–69 (February, April 1979).

40. These events occur in *Tomb of Dracula* 1, nos. 65–66 (July, September 1978).

41. *Tomb of Dracula* 1, no. 61 (November 1977): 2–3.

42. *Tomb of Dracula* 1, no. 70 (August 1979): 46.

43. Marv Wolfman, "That Dracula May Live Again!" *Dracula Lives* 1, no. 2 (1973).

44. These events occur in *Tomb of Dracula* 1, no. 60 (September 1977); "To Walk Again in Daylight!" *Dracula Lives* 1, no. 1 (1973); and *Tomb of Dracula* 1, nos. 44 (May 1976), 61 (November 1977), and 68 (February 1979).

45. These events occur in *Tomb of Dracula* 1, nos. 15 (December 1973), 30 (March 1975), 34–35 (July, August 1975), 66 (September 1978), and 29 (February 1975).

46. In *Giant-Size Dracula* 1, no. 2 (September 1974); "Bloody Mary," *Dracula Lives* 1, no. 13 (July 1975); and *Tomb of Dracula* 1, no. 24 (September 1974).

47. In *Tomb of Dracula* 1, nos. 29–30 (February, March 1975).

48. In *Tomb of Dracula* 1, no. 46 (July 1976).

49. In *Tomb of Dracula* 1, no. 53 (February 1977).

50. In *Tomb of Dracula* 1, no. 50 (November 1976).

51. *Tomb of Dracula* 1, no. 55 (April 1977): 31.

52. In *Tomb of Dracula* 1, no. 60 (September 1977).

53. Doug Moench, "Parchments of the Damned," *Dracula Lives* 1, no. 12 (May 1975): 7.

54. For additional examples of Dracula as a first-person narrator, see also *Tomb of Dracula* 1, nos. 15 (December 1973), 23 (August 1974), 30 (March 1975), and 47 (August 1976).

55. These events occur in *Tomb of Dracula* 1, nos. 26–28 (November 1974, December 1974, January 1975), 31 (April 1975), and 47–59 (August 1976 through August 1977).

56. These events are related in *Thor* 1, nos. 332–333 (June, July 1983); *Doctor Strange* 1, nos. 59–61 (June, August, October 1983); and *Avengers* 1, nos. 186–187 (August, September 1979).

57. These events occur in *Thor* 1, nos. 332–333 (June, July 1983); *X-Men Annual* 1, no. 6 (November 1982); "A Death in the Chapel," *Dracula Lives* 1, no. 6 (May 1974); and *Doctor Strange* 1, nos. 60–62 (August, October, December 1983).

58. *Blade* 1, no. 4 (October 1994): 18.

59. *Blade* 1, no. 1 (July 1994): 23.
60. *Blade* 1, no. 2 (August 1994): 17.
61. Ibid., 10; see also *Blade* 1, no. 8 (February 1995): 5.
62. As in *Tomb of Dracula* 1, no. 60 (September 1977).

Chapter 5

"Blood in the Sky": The World War II-Era Boys Series of R. Sidney Bowen

M. Paul Holsinger

During the years of World War II, more than 200 juvenile novels filled with supposed wartime adventures poured off publishers' presses into the hands of America's youth. Though a few received plaudits,[1] the great majority, nearly all parts of multivolume series designed specifically for either boys or girls, got little more than scorn and derision from critics in such professional journals as the American Library Association's *Booklist*, *The Horn Book*, or even *Publishers' Weekly*. The volumes' clichéd storytelling, their hackneyed writing, their unrealistic or repetitive plots, the frequent mind-numbing violence, the constant bloodletting—especially in books written primarily for male readers—and even the comic-book quality of some of the books were cited as reasons for young readers, and their parents, to avoid them.

These accurate imprecations did little to sway the reading public. Young Americans believed that World War II was, to use the words of the contemporary oral historian Studs Terkel, a "good war," and they embraced any juvenile series book—some priced as low as thirty-nine cents—that constantly waved the flag and pictured bloody victories over the nation's enemies. The series' volumes patriotically reiterated that the American people were "a superior race," who could always be expected to "knock the stripes off any [enemy, and] what's more, do it with one hand tied behind [their] backs,"[2] and the result was that the books sold in ever-increasing numbers.

Young male readers had more than their share of such tales. There was an eight-volume series of so-called Yankee Flier stories penned by Al Avery, another eight written by Canfield Cook detailing the career of a young American pilot (Bob "Lucky" Terrell) in Great Britain's RAF, three Steve Knight Flying Stories by Ted Copp, eight volumes by the popular juvenile author Rutherford Montgomery, and, most numerous of all, twenty-three volumes—in two different series—by R. Sidney Bowen featuring three young American flying aces, Dave

Dawson, Red Randall, and Jimmy Joyce.[3] Girl stories were almost as plentiful. Louise Logan published fourteen excruciatingly awful volumes during the war years, each recounting a dramatic episode in the supposed life of Army *and* Navy nurse-spy Susan Merton as she single-handedly helped save both branches of service and a good number of their leaders as well. Elizabeth Lansing, using a number of pseudonyms, wrote fifteen novels with war themes, five about Navy nurse Ann Bartlett, six featuring Army nurse and sometime pilot Nancy Naylor, and four others whose heroines best spies at home and abroad. Another Army nurse, the soon-to-be-famous Cherry Ames, also appeared for the first time during the war years. Before author Helen Wells pictured the vivacious Cherry as a nurse in virtually every known medical setting, she gave readers four volumes highlighting various aspects of Cherry's career as an Army nurse.[4]

The idea of featuring supposedly invincible young Americans in juvenile war-related series books was not, of course, new. During the bloodiest days of the American Civil War, William Taylor Adams—Oliver Optic, as he dubbed his writing persona—had begun to publish his Army and Navy series novels about young boys fighting in that war and, for the next thirty-plus years, sixteen other books about sixteen- or seventeen-year-olds serving with either the Blue or the Gray continued to attract readers. At the end of the nineteenth century, Edward Stratemeyer used military events from the Spanish-American War, the Philippine Insurrection, and the Boxer Rebellion to launch what soon became the most successful syndicate of writers of children and young adult books in publishing history. At the same time, Joseph Altsheler, chosen by a national committee of public librarians in 1918 as the most popular boys' writer in the United States, began his illustrious writing career for juveniles by featuring a number of young men at war in settings as diverse as the Old Northwest during the American Revolution, the Trans-Mississippi West, or the Texas frontier.[5]

American publishers were also quick to capitalize on the horrors of World War I. Hundreds of volumes, nearly all featuring teenaged boys and girls directly involved with the war, poured from publishers' presses between 1915 and 1919. Young readers were inundated with often unbelievable war stories whose heroes, such as the ever-present "Boy Allies"—the Army's Hal Paine and Chester Crawford and the Navy's Jack Templeton and Frank Chadwick—or heroines like Grace Harlowe, Ruth Fielding, and a covey of "Red Cross Girls," always overcame great odds to help advance the Allied cause. Even after the bloodletting had officially ended, stories dealing with the war remained popular, and novels by such well-known authors for boys as Eustace L. Adams, Thompson Burtis, or Fredric Nelson Litten sold consistently.[6]

The power of these war-related books in the early years of the twentieth century—especially those written primarily with a youthful male audience in mind—has nowhere been better expressed than in Arthur Prager's *Rascals at Large, or The Clue in the Old Nostalgia*, an exceptionally clever, and always thoughtful, book about juvenile popular culture in the early years of the twentieth century:

Those of us who were born in the intermission between the two World Wars, were hawks in every sense of the word. A boy with dovish tendencies would have been drummed out of my gang in short order as would anyone who played with dolls or hated baseball. To us pacifism was equivalent to effeminacy [and we were] kept ... at a white heat of militarism that would have done credit to a Samurai ... [by] the juvenile literature sold to us. [7]

Though Prager looks only at war-related books focusing on World War I, his generalizations are no less true for the millions of boys and girls who came of age after 1941. Just as he and his friends understood how important World War I had been to their parents by pulling out of storage faded uniforms from the American Expeditionary Force of 1918, many slightly younger children knew where *their* fathers kept a treasured medal from Navy service in China in the mid-1920s, a Marine cartridge belt from Nicaragua, or Army accouterments from duty in Haiti or Santo Domingo.[8] They, too, learned about war's supposed superlatives, directly or indirectly, from their parents, and, consequently, they read the same kind of lurid prose as their predecessors. Such reading quickly led them, as it had their older acquaintances, into what Prager has accurately called "the treacherous minefields of the ten to fourteen year old no-man's land,"[9] but no one doubted that being in such metaphorical places would do anything but rekindle love for the nation and its heroes once again.

Of all the dozens of World War II series books that appeared after early 1941, none were more popular, or more representative of all those things despised by juvenile literary critics, than R. Sidney Bowen's numerous volumes of wartime adventure. The first of the author's "War Adventure Series" was published even before the United States was forced into the war. In April 1941, Bowen—a volunteer during World War I with the British Royal Flying Corps and, later, the editor in chief of such periodicals as *Aviation Magazine* and *Flying News*—and his publishers, Crown Books, introduced readers to Dave Dawson, a seventeen-year-old all-American track star at Boston Latin High School in Massachusetts.[10] Caught in Europe just as German forces begin their murderous *blitzkrieg* through the Low Countries and France in May 1940, Dave and Freddy Farmer, a sixteen-year-old English boy that the young American meets as he is trying to escape from the fighting, are able to help a number of British troops cut through the enemy's lines and make a successful escape at Dunkirk. Even though Dave knows that the United States is officially neutral, "a fierce anger at [the Nazis'] injustices ... sprung up" inside him. "He wanted to do something about it. What, he did not know. But today there had been born in him a blazing desire to do what he could do to spare Europe and perhaps the world from the bullets and bombs and the tyranny of the Nazi legions."[11] He tells his diplomat-father that he and Freddy, both apparently expert fliers at such a young age, want to join the RAF because "nothing else seems important now except trimming the pants off the Nazis."[12] With his father's blessing, Dave instantaneously becomes a pilot in the British ranks and is soon plunged headlong into the war.

By the time that the United States was forced into the war after December 7, 1941, Crown had already published five different Dave Dawson novels.[13] Four more were issued the following year. Each was as formulaic as any of the dozens of Stratemeyer Syndicate books of an earlier era: Assigned a dangerous mission against the Axis, Dave and Freddy are invariably captured by an enemy arch-villain with a name such as Baron von Peiplow or General Kashomia. Though it seems they will surely be killed, they always escape, steal one or often two enemy planes, drop enough bombs to blow up an entire airfield (a battleship, a rocket-launching facility, a secret laboratory, or what-have-you), and then, their victory complete, fly home to a much-deserved heroes' welcome—all in a neatly packaged 256 pages or less.[14] It was a formula for publishing and bookselling success. As an early *Publishers' Weekly* advertisement proclaimed: "You can recommend [these books] without reservation.... [They have] everything—flying, bombing, capture, escape, chases, [and] battles.... [M]illions of American boys will go for [them] in a big way."[15] Priced initially at only fifty cents,[16] the books, with their repeated episodes of derring-do and bloody excitement, followed the rule of thumb for all such low-priced juvenile volumes: Adolescent heroes never failed no matter how superhuman their exploits might be.

Though it is easy today to wonder why even the most gullible of junior readers, most of whom knew of families whose sons had died in the war, would be interested in unrealistic stories about boys who never lost and who hardly even received a scratch in the process,[17] each of the many newly issued Bowen-authored books rarely stayed on dealers' shelves for more than a week or two. Even after Crown worked out an agreement with the Saalfield Company of Akron, Ohio, to reproduce each volume from the original plates in a cheaper, less soundly bound edition for sale in the nation's many five-and-ten-cent stores, there were never enough copies to please the many eager male readers. In one city after another, stores had a difficult time keeping up with the demand. More than one disappointed boy during the war had to accept the fact that he (or his parents) simply would never be able to purchase a complete set of all the Dave Dawson stories no matter how hard they tried.[18]

R. Sidney Bowen's reputation as both the most popular and prolific writer of juvenile war-related novels during the early 1940s might have been cemented had he only written the fifteen "Dave Dawson" books,[19] but, beginning in April 1944, a second series, eventually eight books in length, began to appear under the imprimatur of Grosset & Dunlap, the nation's largest publisher of juvenile series books. *Red Randall at Pearl Harbor*, the first in the new collection,[20] featured eighteen-year-old Red, the son of a career Army Air Force officer stationed in Hawaii just before the Japanese attack, and his best friend, Jimmy Joyce. Like Dave Dawson, these two teens were both exceptionally talented aviators, and, after Jimmy's father, a naval officer assigned to the USS *Arizona,* is killed on December 7, 1941, the two boys pledge themselves to "make those dirty devils pay and pay."[21] Joining the Army Air Corps, the two have adventures fighting the Japanese from one side of the Pacific to the other. Though this new series never had the opportunity during its less than two years of publication to gain as wide an audience as the Dave Dawson War Adventure Series, it, too, was always popular and became one of Grosset's best sellers as the war rapidly came to a close.

Every Dave Dawson or Red Randall novel is filled with heavy doses of flag-waving, "For God and Country" patriotism. All of Bowen's three fictional American pilot-heroes are, indeed, the truest of true-blue patriots. After witnessing the fast-moving Nazi *blitzkrieg*, for instance, Dave Dawson finds "the fighting American spirit of Lexington and Concord" flaming up inside him,[22] and it remains there for the rest of the war. "The American spirit knows no such thing as defeat," a senior officer tells Dave on one occasion,[23] and the teenager agrees emphatically. "I hope and pray that before too long," the boy says, that American liberty "will extend around the world."[24] Red agrees. The United States, he says, is "a great nation that [will] fight to final and complete victory with everything in its power,"[25] and he pledges himself to do his part to make that come true.

All of Bowen's fictional heroes believe, unquestioningly, in the righteousness of the American cause. Theirs is a "my country, right or wrong, my country" approach that would have made the original author of that thought, the U.S. Navy's Stephen Decatur, proud. The boys never doubt, even for a second, the policies of their superiors nor wonder whether some of the nation's many leaders might perhaps be in the wrong. Douglas MacArthur was "the best darn soldier" in the Pacific and "one of the finest generals of all time." J. Edgar Hoover was the perfect head of the FBI. All of the nation's Allies are also worthy of the boys' praise. Joseph Stalin, for instance, is a brave Christian warrior; Chiang Kai-shek, "a splendid leader"; and Winston Churchill, incomparable "in real fighting ability."[26] Victory obviously came from absolute and unyielding loyalty and obedience to country no matter what one might be asked to do.

Besides being overtly patriotic, the three teens are nothing less than paragons of virtue—"high-flying, clean-living, hard fighting boys," to quote the dust jacket of several of the earliest volumes. None of them smokes, drinks anything stronger than Coca-Cola, or ever uses vulgar language. The most violent expletive Dave Dawson allows himself is an occasional "heck" or an even less frequent "nuts"; Red utters a "darn" from time to time. Surprisingly, the boys also seemingly have no interest—pure or otherwise—in girls. Dances, dating, romantic encounters between the sexes never intrude in a Bowen tale.[27] The glory of combat and the war's many "adventures" are the interrelated focal points of all the novels in Bowen's two series, and he never allows his readers to be sidetracked by extraneous romantic interludes—or anything else.

Though there was never any effort made to explain how it was possible for the four fictional teens to become instantly, without further training, fighter pilots, flying for either the British RAF in Dave's and Freddy's case[28] or the Army Air Corps in Red and Jimmy's, the stories soon took them to virtually every major battlefield of the early war years. Dave and Freddy are at Dunkirk, in occupied France, in Libya fighting Rommel's *Afrika Corps*, at Singapore, the Russian Front, Guadalcanal, or Casablanca. They fight with British commandos in France, the U.S. Fleet in the Pacific, General Claire Chennault's Flying Tigers in China, and the Eighth Air Force over occupied Europe. Not to be outdone, Red and Jimmy are at Pearl Harbor and Midway, on New Guinea, in the Aleutians, Burma, the Philippines, and even "over Tokyo." It soon becomes evident that without the three young Americans the fate of the free world would have been dramatically changed for the worse. Red and Jimmy, for instance, single-handedly save General Douglas MacArthur from sure death at the hands of the Japanese Navy that is rushing to intercept the PT boat taking him and his family from the beleaguered Philippines in early 1942.[29] Dave and his British pal Freddy not only keep President Franklin Delano Roosevelt and Prime Minister Winston Churchill from being blown to bits during the Casablanca conference early the next year but also prevent the extermination of most of the Allied air forces in England from German "liquid fire bombs."[30] Their commanders clearly appreciate such theatrical heroics. On one occasion, for instance, a general tells Dave that "the entire civilized world" is in his debt.[31] Similar sentiments are repeated in nearly every other volume in both series.

Saving the world, however, obviously required endless bloodshed, and Bowen made no attempt to hide such a fact from his readers. Whereas most of the other writers of juvenile male series fiction during World War II tried to bring their several heroes victory with a minimum of death and destruction,[32] Bowen left little to the imagination in any of his volumes. With garish chapter titles such as "The Dead Can't Breathe," "Vultures over Europe," "Sky Killers," "Satan Is Gleeful," or "Blood in the Sky," readers were clued in to expect constant mayhem and endless destruction—at least of the enemy.[33] Within each of the volumes in which they are featured, Dave and Freddy get to kill, on average, at least 250 enemy soldiers or sailors. If not quite so successful (or so bloody), Red and Jimmy are responsible for the deaths of no fewer than 150 in each of their eight books. Though there is no way to measure accurately the total number of deaths the three Americans (and one Briton) bring about, a figure of at least 4,000 enemy dead is not out-of-line.

This bloodletting is done with considerable relish. Jimmy Joyce, for instance, pledges himself to kill no fewer than "a million" Japanese.[34] Dave Dawson is no less sanguine, confessing happily to being "thrilled to the very depths of his soul to be able to . . . do his share and fight and fight and fight until the war thirsty dictators were no more."[35] On several occasions, he becomes obsessed with the "thought of hammering [the enemy] into the ground as long as his plane and guns . . . hold out."[36] Though, significantly, Freddy Farmer is on one occasion allowed to say: "Blast war . . . how I hate the whole rotten business,"[37] even the most cursory reading of any of the many novels reveals such a statement to be an anomaly. On the contrary, the boys clearly enjoy war and the bloodletting that goes with it. Dave admits to being consumed with "cold rage" and filled with "a wild, completely insane recklessness" as the guns on his plane cut down his enemies one by one.[38] Red's "joy is wild" as he blows apart a Japanese bomber over the Philippines and watches its crew plummet to their deaths.[39] He frequently notes that he hopes to shoot every "jap rat" from the skies, "and when there aren't any left in the air, smack all their heathen brethren on the ground and keep smacking until there aren't any of them left."[40]

Killing enemies, especially when they were German or Japanese, was justified, in Bowen's thinking, by their cruelty to others. Adolf Hitler, for example, is described as "the lowest form of life ever to be born,"[41] and the average Nazi is ruthless, barbaric, and insane.[42] Since it seemed clear that the Germans would eventually "be caught in the wheels of right and justice and be ground to a pulp,"[43] there seemed no reason why Dave and Freddy should not help the bloodshed along. Bowen's descriptions of such deaths are not only vindictive but also almost always turgid. Consider his account of the deaths of two young *Luftwaffe* aviators in the following passage from *Dave Dawson, Flight Lieutenant*:

[Dave's] guns yammered sound and death. The Messerschmidt took the whole works square in the cockpit. The plane leaped and bolted off to one side as though it had been sideswiped by an invisible express train. For a brief moment Dave saw the pilot and the gunner fighting desperately to shove the cockpit's hood wide open and bail out with their parachutes. Then they became lost to view as sheets of flame belched out from both the port and starboard engines and the whole plane became a raging ball of fire that went tumbling over and over down toward the ground. "Another one you won't be using any more, Goering!" Dave grunted as he pulled [his plane] out of its howling dive.[44]

The same thing was true with regard to the Japanese "monkey-men of the Far East." "Savages," "heathen," and "butchers," they had gone to war with "decent people" and their "strutting around" was a "sight to make any Christian's heart weep blood." To exterminate them as quickly as possible was an absolute necessity, Bowen had his heroes aver.[45] "If I get my wish," Red Randall says on one occasion, "a thousand Jap rats" will die for every American they kill.[46] Since the Japanese were "beasts and fiends who knew no rules" and persons "who would slay [their] own mother[s] just for the thrill of it," killing them was clearly not the same as making war on civilized men.[47] Red, on one occasion, guns down dozens of those "slant-eyed fools" on the ground and later compares it to "shooting fish in a barrel."[48]

This overt racism, though hardly unique for its day,[49] runs rampant through the pages of every Bowen book centered in the Pacific Theater. Though all the nation's enemies were evil and deserved to be totally defeated, it was the Japanese who received the most violent and unremitting hatred. Red Randall, for instance, expresses a "blind rage at everything Japanese," a rage that shakes him "with fury from head to foot."[50] The Japanese were "slow-thinking" and "in countless things ... unquestionably the stupidest people on the face of the earth."[51] Even their language was little more than "singsong jabbering" that sounded at best like "somebody putting sheets of tin to a buzz saw blade."[52] If Nazis were often "cunning and fiendish clever beyond words," the Japanese were simply "dirty killing skunks" who had "not one speck of decency in [their] whole race."[53] Men like that deserved to die. A minor character in *Red Randall over Tokyo*, without even a trace of irony, seemingly expresses what everyone in the series feels: Thousands are dying every year in Japan "but they [are] Japs ... so that [is] good. All Japs [are] better dead."[54]

In many ways, Bowen's Dave Dawson and Red Randall novels were little different from the hundreds of contemporary comic book (and strip) versions of combat that also were so popular with young (mostly male) readers during the war years but so despised by nearly every serious critic of "good" literature. *Wings Comics,* for instance, was "dedicated to American flying men who are carrying the Stars and Stripes to the sky so that freedom may prevail." Heroes such as Captain Wings, Jimmy Jones, and Suicide Smith took on and destroyed endless German and Japanese foes. *Barney Baxter* and his constant companion, Gopher Gus, went to war in 1942 and fought the Japanese for the next several years in some of the goriest stories to be found in American comics during the war. *Buz Sawyer* and the irrepressible *Captain Easy* also did their share as well in hundreds of daily and Sunday newspapers. Terry Lee and his pal Hotshot Charlie kept readers on the edge of their seats in Milton Caniff's famous *Terry and the Pirates,* and the always successful Airboy, the star of Hillman Periodicals' *Air Fighters Comics,* killed the enemy without remorse.[55] Violence was endemic in nearly every characterization. As one contemporary young reader said at the time, most comic-book wartime plots were little more than "routine slaughter-the-Japs-and-Huns stories."[56]

It was an easy jump from reading such comics to becoming a fan of R. Sidney Bowen's heroes. Like those of all the comic-book stars, Dave's, Red's, and Jimmy's guns "hammer . . . out made-in-America doom" to all their country's enemies with almost no harm coming to any of them in return.[57] Though the boys clearly were neither superheroes like Superman, Captain Marvel, or the newly created Captain America, they seemed nearly as immune to physical harm as any of those dominant patriots. Red Randall, for instance, is knocked out occasionally when he is forced to crash-land his plane, and Jimmy Joyce and Freddy Farmer also suffer a few cuts and bruises but little else. Dave Dawson is, perhaps, roughed up the most, but even he receives no more than a few minor concussions, considerable scratches, a broken left arm, and a severely wrenched leg—the latter two coming only after he crashes his fighter plane into that of an enemy spy at more than 300 miles an hour. In contrast, it is the rare novel in which one or more of the teens does not kill or badly wound several dozen enemy in the first 100 or so pages.

Though the series' publishers did issue several additional volumes after the official end of the war, stories about the three young American heroes came to a screeching halt in mid-1946. None of the boys was given a chance to try to make the adjustment to civilian life in postwar America. It was probably just as well. It is hard to imagine, for example, the now twenty-two-year-old Dave Dawson, heavily decorated for bravery and, according to Bowen's many plots, responsible for perhaps 2,500 enemy deaths, suddenly trying to cope with college life for the first time. It was one thing for loyal readers to enjoy the intrepid protagonist killing another "funny," "dopey," or "incredibly stupid" Nazi or Japanese soldier. But Dave and some sweet "Betty Coed" at a sock hop in a school gymnasium? Not even Bowen wanted to think about those possibilities.[58]

Bowen's books, and, to some degree all the many other war-related boys' series books of the era, for all their popularity, left a cruel legacy to their naïve young readers in the years ahead. Unlike the hundreds of books from World War I or even earlier wars—all coated with a patina of innocence and slightly silly heroics—Bowen's stories, filled as they were with accurate descriptions of airplanes and modern technology, seemed all too believable. If Dave, Red, and Jimmy could overcome the astronomical odds that their author had set for them—odds that rarely were less than one million to one and, on one occasion, even one billion to one—why, it was reasoned, couldn't they? There seemed little reason to think that wars might not always bring out the best in each of us. The United States had just overwhelmingly crushed two of the greatest powers in world history and done so because, in Bowen's words, American boys, with a "clear light in [their] eyes" and "good old U.S.A. rosiness in [their] cheeks,"[59] always won. We had now become, the many books averred, the leaders of the modern world, the only people capable of bringing the world "happiness,"[60] and we had a duty never to waver in that commitment until everyone was truly free. There seemed no one who could possibly stand in our way. Everyone learned differently in the bloody fields and rice paddies of Korea and Vietnam.

The scorn heaped upon the large number of cheaply priced juvenile series, especially upon the twenty-plus volumes written by R. Sidney Bowen, was well deserved even if unheeded. In retrospect, it is easy to wish that all of us had been wise enough at the time to pay attention to those critics who tried to tell us that daily doses of death, bloodshed, and constant gore coupled with unremitting racism and bigotry were the wrong prescriptions for the future. Like Arthur Prager's "gang" in an earlier era, however, we all knew better—or thought we did. Dave, Red, Jimmy, and their pals showed us the way we thought all young Americans ought to take. We were wrong.

NOTES

1. See, for example, Philip Harkins, *Bomber Pilot* (New York: Harcourt, Brace, 1944), a novel about the young men who flew B-17s for the U.S. Eighth Air Force over occupied Europe. Gregor Felsen, *Some Follow the Sea* (New York: E.P. Dutton, 1944), a taut and often exciting tale of the many dangers that faced merchant seamen bringing convoys of supplies to Great Britain or the Soviet Union during the height of the war, was also touted. Few books written predominantly for young feminine readers were praised though Janet Lambert's several books about Army life on the home front—*Star-Spangled Summer* (1941), *Dreams of Glory* (1942), *Glory Be* (1943), *Candy Kane* (1943), and *Whoa, Matilda* (1944)—all published by E.P. Dutton, were well received. So, too, was Phyllis Crawford's *Second Shift* (New York: Henry Holt, 1943), a story about a young "Rosie the Riveter" in a defense plant. Praiseworthy reviews of all these volumes are plentiful but see, for instance, the reviews for Harkins' *Bomber Pilot*: "a story that boys have been waiting for since the war began" (*Saturday Review of Literature* 27 [November 11, 1944]: 44), and "excitement, adventure, courage and fortitude—and a vivid picture of what it takes to become an Army Air pilot" (*Kirkus Review* 12 [August 1, 1944]: 344), or those for Phyllis Crawford's *Second Shift*: "it is hard to stop reading . . . [an] unsentimental, honest [story] told truly" (*Weekly Book Review*

[November 28, 1943]: 6) and "a completely honest picture . . . there isn't a single phony paragraph in [this novel]" (*Book Week* [February 20, 1944]: 11).

2. R. Sidney Bowen, *Dave Dawson, Flight Lieutenant* (New York: Crown, 1941), 197, 162.

3. For a list of most of the hundreds of hardcover series books written explicitly for a young male audience from the days of the Civil War on, including the 100 or more juvenile combat-related books designed especially for boys during World War II, see E. Christian Mattson and Thomas B. Davis, *A Collector's Guide to Hardcover Boys' Series Books, or Tracing the Trail of Harry Hudson* (Newark, DE: Mad Dog Books, 1997). During the early 1940s, the Whitman Publishing Company of Racine, Wisconsin, also produced a number of juvenile war-related novels in their "Better Little Books" series of cardboard-covered volumes. A complete listing can be found in William Borden and Steve Posner, *The Big Book of Big Little Books* (San Francisco: Chronicle Books, 1997). Full annotations of more than 750 juvenile works of fiction dealing with World War II written before 1994 can be found in M. Paul Holsinger, *The Ways of War: The Era of World War II in Children's and Young Adult Fiction* (Methuchen, NJ: The Scarecrow Press, 1995). Also see: M. Paul Holsinger, "Thirty-Nine Cent Americanism: The Fighters for Freedom Series," *Newsboy: The Official Publication of the Horatio Alger Society*, XXX (November–December 1992): 16–23, and M. Paul Holsinger, "World War Combat in American Juvenile and Paperback Series Books," *Pioneers, Passionate Ladies and Private Eyes: The Library of Congress Symposium on Dime Novels, Series Books and Paperbacks*, eds. Larry E. Sullivan and Lydia Cushman Schurman (New York: Haworth Press, 1997), 147–62.

4. For a complete list of these and many other World War II-related juvenile novels for girls, see *Girls' Series Books: A Checklist of Titles Published 1840–1991* (Minneapolis: Children's Literature Research Collections, University of Minnesota Libraries, 1992). An excellent study about the Cherry Ames novels is Sally E. Parry, "'You Are Needed, Desperately Needed': Cherry Ames in World War II," *Nancy Drew and Company: Culture, Gender, and Girls' Series*, ed. Sherrie A. Innes (Bowling Green, OH: Bowling Green State University Popular Press, 1997), 129–144. Nothing has as yet been published about the long-forgotten Nurse Merton books but M. Paul Holsinger, "Developing a Popular Fictional Heroine for World War II America: Louise Logan's 'Susan Merton'," an unpublished paper presented at the annual meeting of the Popular Culture Association in the South, Jacksonville, Florida, October 7, 1989, is available on request from the author.

5. An excellent bibliography of the works of William Adams is Dolores Blythe Jones, comp., *An "Oliver Optic" Checklist* (Westport, CT: Greenwood Press, 1985). The definitive list of the many Stratemeyer books including those with war-related themes is Deidre Johnson, ed., *Stratemeyer Pseudonyms and Series Books: An Annotated Checklist of Stratemeyer and Stratemeyer Syndicate Publications* (Westport, CT: Greenwood Press, 1982). Johnson's *Edward Stratemeyer and the Stratemeyer Syndicate* (New York: Twayne, 1993) provides much detail about the author's work. Sadly, there are no equivalent works for the popular Joseph Altsheler though a simple listing of his many different juvenile novels can be found in George Kelley, "Altsheler, Joseph A(lexander)," *Twentieth Century Children's Writers* (Chicago: St. James, 1989), 23–24.

6. A complete and thoughtfully annotated bibliographic listing of the hundreds of juvenile novels dealing with World War I published both during and after that conflict can be found in Philip E. Hagler and Desmond Taylor, *The Novels of World War I: An Annotated Bibliography* (New York: Garland Press, 1981), 313–449. Also see M. Paul Holsinger, "Down with the Kaiser and Up with the Flag, or How the Boy Scouts of

America Won the First World War," *Dime Novel Roundup* 58 (3) (June 1989): 34–42, and David K. Vaughan, "Hap Arnold's Bill Bruce Boys Series," *Dime Novel Roundup* 58 (5) (October 1989): 66–72.

7. Arthur Prager, *Rascals at Large, or The Clue in the Old Nostalgia* (Garden City, NY: Doubleday & Co., 1971), 169–70. Anyone interested in this subject should take a close look at Prager's further insights in that volume's chapter six, "Beating the Boche," pp. 167–213.

8. I was no different. My father, as a member of the U.S. Marine Corps, had fought in Nicaragua during the first Sandinista revolt before 1933, and he took great pride in his long-outgrown uniform, especially after he was rejected for re-enlistment because of his age in the days after Pearl Harbor. It never occurred to me or, I suspect, any of my friends that war was not the best way to settle international disputes. This attitude changed slightly after some of the young men from our neighborhood were killed in Europe or the Pacific but never enough to keep us from eagerly buying and reading every war novel, no matter how similar it might be to all the others, that we could find. We hurried each day to our nearby railroad tracks to wave happily to the numerous troop trains filled with boys heading for European battlefields while endlessly fighting mock battles, taking turns playing the country's German or Italian enemies—no one was willing to take the part of the supposedly far more despicable Japanese—and we died, dutifully every time, in a hail of bullets from the guns of those neighborhood youngsters who were lucky enough to become that particular battle's American GIs.

9. Prager, 10.

10. Some critics have wondered whether Dave Dawson was intended to be Bowen's alter ego. Like his fictional counterpart, Bowen, a native of suburban Boston, also volunteered to fight the Germans at the age of seventeen. Though it seems clear that he never "shot down a number of German planes and balloons" as his publisher later claimed on many of the early dust jackets of the War Adventure series books, he did fly for the British not only throughout Europe but also in Egypt, India, and East Africa just as young Dawson found himself doing many years later.

11. Bowen, *Dave Dawson at Dunkirk* (New York: Crown, 1941), 71–72.

12. Ibid., 249.

13. A complete chronological listing of the War Adventure Series or, as it eventually became known officially, "The Dave Dawson War Adventure Series," can be found in the Appendix.

14. The fifteen Dave Dawson books invariably range from a low of 247 to a high of 255 pages. Most have either 17, 18, or 19 chapters, each almost always between 12 and 14 pages in length. Later, after 1944, when Bowen authored a second series of war-related books for Grosset & Dunlap, the limited supply of paper available to commercial publishers limited him to no more than 214 pages per volume even though the general formula remained the same.

15. Advertisement, Crown Books, *Publishers' Weekly* 139 (April 26, 1941): 1706.

16. After 1943, the books' price rose to sixty cents. At a time when many other juvenile volumes were approaching or, in some cases, had already surpassed the two-dollar mark, Bowen's books were always a bargain.

17. None of the many boys who eagerly rushed to buy Bowen's books at the time, I suspect, ever considered that the "Dave Dawson War Adventure Series" or the "Air Combat Series" that featured Red Randall and Jimmy Joyce were anything but realistic. I certainly did not. It was not until I sat down and reread the entire two series several years ago that I finally realized how hopelessly stereotyped each of the many books was or why

teachers, librarians, and other reviewers at the time had refused to recommend them but willingly praised a book like Esther Forbes' Newbery Medal-winning *Johnny Tremain*.

18. As a youngster, I faced, more than once, such disappointment in Collingdale, Pennsylvania, one of Philadelphia's many suburbs. Today, I frequently encounter other "sixty-somethings" whose experiences were identical, no matter where they lived during the war years.

19. There was a sixteenth volume, *Dave Dawson over Berlin*, quoted at the conclusion of volume #15, *Dave Dawson at Truk* (New York: Crown, 1946), which was apparently never released.

20. See the Appendix for a chronological listing of the eight Red Randall volumes.

21. R. Sidney Bowen, *Red Randall at Pearl Harbor* (New York: Grosset & Dunlap, 1944), 215.

22. Bowen, *Dave Dawson at Dunkirk*, 125.

23. Bowen, *Dave Dawson on the Russian Front* (New York: Crown, 1943), 40.

24. Bowen, *Dave Dawson with the Pacific Fleet* (New York: Crown, 1942), 14.

25. Bowen, *Red Randall at Pearl Harbor*, 214.

26. Bowen, *Red Randall on Active Duty* (New York: Grosset & Dunlap, 1944), 129; *Dave Dawson with the Flying Tigers* (New York: Crown, 1943), 152; *Dave Dawson at Casablanca* (New York: Crown, 1944), 40; *Dave Dawson on the Russian Front*, 129–43; *Dave Dawson with the Flying Tigers*, 23; and *Dave Dawson at Dunkirk*, 238.

27. Only once do Dave and Freddy show any interest in a young woman. Senior Lieutenant Nasha Petrovski of Soviet Intelligence is beautiful and, perhaps, alluring, but what appeals to both boys is not her femininity but her ruthlessness at gunning down Germans without a second thought (Bowen, *Dave Dawson on the Russian Front*). Such was not the case in the various juvenile girls' series books. Nurses Nancy Naylor and Ann Bartlett, for instance, are both engaged to Air Force pilots, and they spend endless hours longingly looking forward to the few moments they can be alone with their future husbands. Cherry Ames always has a host of suitors vying for her hand, as does nearly every other featured young heroine during the war years.

28. Since Bowen's first several novels in the War Adventure Series were published before American entry into the war, it was necessary to have Dave and Freddy fly for the RAF. After the Japanese attack on Pearl Harbor, however, beginning with 1942's *Dave Dawson with the Pacific Fleet*, both boys join the forces of the United States and fight with them for the rest of the war. It never seems to matter what branch of the service they may have been in during an earlier adventure; somehow or other, the two boys switch from the Army to the Navy, and then back again, at the proverbial drop of a hat, serving in whichever branch of the military is necessary to the story line at the time.

29. Bowen, *Red Randall on Active Duty*.

30. Bowen, *Dave Dawson at Casablanca* and *Dave Dawson with the Eighth Air Force* (New York: Crown, 1944).

31. Bowen, *Dave Dawson on Convoy Patrol* (New York: Crown, 1941), 246.

32. Al Avery's Stan Wilson, the Yankee Flier, and his mates shoot down lots of enemy planes but usually with few of the graphic descriptions of burning cabins or enemy pilots spiraling through space after their parachutes have failed to open that are so prevalent in Bowen's stories. Canfield Cook's Bob "Lucky" Terrill also has to kill significant numbers of Japanese (and a handful of Germans as well) but he, too, seems to do so with only a few written examples of the actual gore of war in the air.

33. Bowen, *Dave Dawson with the Eighth Air Force*, 37–51; *Dave Dawson Flight Lieutenant*, 114–30; *Red Randall over Tokyo* (New York: Grosset & Dunlap, 1944),

63–77; *Dave Dawson on the Russian Front*, 199–211; *Dave Dawson with the Flying Tigers*, 168–79.

34. Bowen, *Red Randall at Pearl Harbor*, 215.

35. Bowen, *Dave Dawson with the R.A.F.* (New York: Crown, 1941), 65.

36. Bowen, *Dave Dawson with the Flying Tigers*, 218.

37. Bowen, *Dave Dawson with the Air Corps* (New York: Crown, 1942), 33.

38. Bowen, *Dave Dawson at Casablanca*, 154; Bowen, *Dave Dawson with the Air Corps*, 104, 222.

39. Bowen, *Red Randall on Active Duty*, 21.

40. Ibid., 7.

41. Bowen, *Dave Dawson with the Eighth Air Force*, 52.

42. Bowen, *Dave Dawson with the R.A.F.*, 91; *Dave Dawson on the Russian Front*, 33.

43. Bowen, *Dave Dawson with the Pacific Fleet*, 132–33.

44. Bowen, *Dave Dawson Flight Lieutenant*, 35.

45. Bowen, *Red Randall on Active Duty*, 110; *Red Randall at Pearl Harbor*, 115; *Red Randall in the Aleutians* (New York: Grosset & Dunlap, 1945), 163; *Dave Dawson with the Pacific Fleet*, 229; *Dave Dawson with the Flying Tigers*, 39.

46. Bowen, *Red Randall over Tokyo*, 73.

47. Ibid., 145; Bowen, *Red Randall at Pearl Harbor*, 47.

48. Bowen, *Red Randall over Tokyo*, 101.

49. It was quite usual throughout the United States during World War II to see such vicious appellations as "jap rats" or "buck-toothed monkey men" used to describe this nation's Japanese enemies. In today's world with its aura of "political correctness" such terms seem out of line, but they unquestionably reflected the often-held beliefs of a great majority of Americans at the time.

50. Bowen, *Red Randall in Burma* (New York: Grosset & Dunlap, 1946), 187.

51. Bowen, *Dave Dawson with the Flying Tigers*, 200; and *Dave Dawson at Singapore* (New York: Crown, 1942), 98.

52. Bowen, *Dave Dawson with the Flying Tigers*, 171; and *Dave Dawson on Guadalcanal* (New York: Crown, 1943), 171.

53. Bowen, *Dave Dawson with the R.A.F.*, 91; *Red Randall on New Guinea* (New York: Grosset & Dunlap, 1944), 41; and *Red Randall's One Man War* (New York: Grosset & Dunlap, 1946), 169.

54. Bowen, *Red Randall over Tokyo*, 179.

55. There have been dozens of attempts in recent years to analyze the many World War II comic book and strip heroes and heroines. Among the better are Don Thompson, "OK, Axis, Here We Come!" in *All in Color for a Dime*, Dick Lupoff and Don Thompson, eds. (New York: Ace Books, 1970), 121–43; Ron Goulart, "Wartime," in *The Funnies: 100 Years of American Comic Strips* (Holbrook, MA: Adams Publishing, 1995), 143–66; and Dick Lupoff, "The Propwash Patrol" and "The Propwash Patrol Flies Again," in *The Comic Book Book*, Don Thompson and Dick Lupoff, eds. (New Rochelle, NY: Arlington House, 1973), 62–86 and 174–204.

56. Lupoff, "The Propwash Patrol Flies Again," 190.

57. Bowen, *Dave Dawson with the Commandos* (New York: Crown, 1942), 77.

58. Bowen, *Dave Dawson, Flight Lieutenant*, 236; Bowen, *Dave Dawson on Convoy Patrol*, 127.

59. Bowen, *Dave Dawson with the Eighth Air Force*, 56.

60. Bowen, *Dave Dawson with the Flying Tigers*, 20.

APPENDIX

THE "DAVE DAWSON WAR ADVENTURE SERIES" AND THE "RED RANDALL AIR COMBAT STORIES"

The "Dave Dawson War Adventure Series"

1. *Dave Dawson at Dunkirk* (New York: Crown, 1941).
2. *Dave Dawson with the R.A.F.* (New York: Crown, 1941).
3. *Dave Dawson in Libya* (New York: Crown, 1941).
4. *Dave Dawson on Convoy Patrol* (New York: Crown, 1941).
5. *Dave Dawson, Flight Lieutenant* (New York: Crown, 1941).
6. *Dave Dawson at Singapore* (New York: Crown, 1942).
7. *Dave Dawson with the Pacific Fleet* (New York: Crown, 1942).
8. *Dave Dawson with the Air Corps* (New York: Crown, 1942).
9. *Dave Dawson with the Commandos* (New York: Crown, 1942).
10. *Dave Dawson on the Russian Front* (New York: Crown, 1943).
11. *Dave Dawson with the Flying Tigers* (New York: Crown, 1943).
12. *Dave Dawson on Guadalcanal* (New York: Crown, 1943).
13. *Dave Dawson at Casablanca* (New York: Crown, 1944).
14. *Dave Dawson with the Eighth Air Force* (New York: Crown, 1944).
15. *Dave Dawson at Truk* (New York: Crown, 1946).
16. *Dave Dawson over Berlin* [quoted in #15 but never issued].

The "Red Randall Air Combat Stories"

1. *Red Randall at Pearl Harbor* (New York: Grosset & Dunlap, 1944).
2. *Red Randall on Active Duty* (New York: Grosset & Dunlap, 1944).
3. *Red Randall over Tokyo* (New York: Grosset & Dunlap, 1944).
4. *Red Randall at Midway* (New York: Grosset & Dunlap, 1944).
5. *Red Randall on New Guinea* (New York: Grosset & Dunlap, 1944).
6. *Red Randall in the Aleutians* (New York: Grosset & Dunlap, 1945).
7. *Red Randall in Burma* (New York: Grosset & Dunlap, 1946).
8. *Red Randall's One-Man War* (New York: Grosset & Dunlap, 1946).

Chapter 6

"It is a pity it is no better": The Story Paper and Its Critics in Nineteenth-Century America

Dawn Fisk Thomsen

For the better part of the nineteenth century, the story paper, a weekly periodical that contained mostly fiction, provided much of the American reading public with light literature for their leisure reading.[1] Affordable, easily available, and full of interest, the most popular story papers claimed circulation in the hundreds of thousands, reaching almost as many—and sometimes more—readers than many of the century's best-selling books.[2] At the same time that the story paper enjoyed this success, it also was scorned by intellectuals, religious authorities, social critics, and literary pundits, who found this genre of popular literature disturbing.[3] The specifics of their complaints varied over the years, but the attitudes that underlay their scorn shared ideas about class, democratic principles, intergenerational hegemony, and cultural power. This essay provides a brief overview of the American story paper, its audience, and its content; it examines the nature of scorn levied against the story paper as well as some of the strategies publishers used to counter these attacks.

HISTORY

The history of the story paper in America spans nearly a hundred years. Its development most closely resembles a bell curve that begins in the early 1830s, peaks in the 1870s, and ends in the 1920s.[4] Like other forms of cheap literature, the story paper benefited from the universal literacy movement, increased time for leisure after 1830, technological innovations in printing, improved transportation systems, and favorable postal regulations. Intended for mass consumption—publishers frequently said it was "for the million"[5]—the story paper typically sold for five cents and was distributed nationally by means of railroads, waterways, freight wagons, and the post, and was made available for sale by retail establishments, newsstands, newsboys, and peddlers as well as by subscription. Story papers were published most often in Boston, Philadelphia, and New York City, although firms in smaller cities around the country, such as Chicago, San Francisco, and Richmond, also issued them.

The story paper began when antebellum publications turned to fiction as their major product and expanded from local to national markets. Two seminal story papers, both originating in Boston, were the short-lived *Brother Jonathan*, which began in July 1839, and *Flag of Our Union*, which started in 1846 and ran until 1870. Described as "an elegant, moral and Miscellaneous Family Journal, devoted to polite literature, wit and humor, prose and poetic gems, and original tales,"[6] the *Flag* proved extremely successful, reaching a circulation of about 100,000 copies in the 1850s.[7] While *Brother Jonathan* and similar papers contained some elements of the genre, story-paper historian Mary Noel explains that *Flag of Our Union* "had all the qualifications of a full-fledged family story paper. It was cheap, and weekly. It was dependent for its earnings on circulation rather than on advertising. Almost all its matter was 'original' and paid for. It avoided politics and sectarianism. It was boasting of its high moral tone and appealing to the entire family, young and old. It was devoted entirely to entertainment, or in the words of the publisher, 'to Domestic and Foreign Literature, News, Science, the Arts and Amusement.'"[8]

Numerous story papers emerged after the appearance of *Brother Jonathan* and *Flag of Our Union*. Among the most prominent in terms of circulation and longevity were Cauldwell, Southworth and Whitney's *New York Mercury* (1838–70), Robert Bonner's *New York Ledger* (1855–98), Street and Smith's *New York Weekly* (1855–1915), James Elverson's *Saturday Night* (1865–1901), George Munro's *Fireside Companion* (1867–1903), and Beadle and Adams's *Saturday Journal* (1870–82). Their success inspired others and "the time of the great story-paper flood" occurred in the 1870s.[9] Also during this time, beginning after the Civil War, some publishers added boys' and girls' story papers, further expanding the market—but also laying the foundation for future problems with critics and custodians of culture. The period from the mid-1860s to the mid-1880s can be considered the "heyday" of the story paper, when successful papers boasted high circulation and publishers eagerly tried new offerings in the genre.[10] By the end of the 1880s, however, the family story paper's popularity had begun to wane; the juvenile papers soon followed suit.[11]

CONTENT AND READERS

The story paper published short and long fiction almost exclusively, for it was intended to entertain and enlighten.[12] Most commonly the story paper appeared as an eight-page weekly periodical that resembled a newspaper in format while offering the kind of miscellany found in monthly literary magazines. Like a newspaper, the story paper was printed on pulp paper, usually ran four to seven columns wide, and carried a masthead at the top of the first page. This page typically contained an installment of a serial novel, which would be continued on the inside pages, an illustration for the story, and frequently a short poem printed at the top left under the masthead. Again like a newspaper, the story paper included one page of opinions and articles, usually found on page four, which had a correspondent's column, notes from the publisher, short human-interest items, advice columns, or humor and opinion pieces. The rest of the paper printed stories with settings ranging from cities to Western frontiers and from the home to gambling halls. This fiction, frequently sensational, featured a range of characters including working girls, street urchins, immigrants, and romantic heroes; it also depicted criminals, spies, drunkards, gamblers, and confidence men. Nearly always the tales highlighted adventure or romance and were chosen to capture reader interest. Novelist and Yale professor W.H. Bishop, surveying the story paper phenomenon in an article for the *Atlantic Monthly* in 1879, called story paper literature "the greatest literary movement, in bulk, of the age, and worthy of very serious consideration for itself." He observed, "Disdained as it may be by the highly cultivated for its character, the phenomenon of its existence cannot be overlooked."[13]

Story paper readers formed a significant portion of the nineteenth-century reading public. Initially, the story paper, frequently referred to as the *family* story paper, typically targeted the entire family unit of women, men, and children, and publishers made certain that the content of each issue contained something to appeal to every age and interest. According to Madeleine Stern, historian of nineteenth-century publishing, "There were papers for children and for the ladies, there were scandal sheets and news sheets, story papers and joke papers, papers to satisfy every appetite."[14] Sales were ubiquitous: in New York City, Bishop found the story paper at commercial stationers' shops and newsstands everywhere, in neighborhoods as far removed from each other socially and economically as the notorious Five Points[15] and prosperous "up-town avenues," as well as in East Side tenements which housed poor immigrants. Readership crossed economic, social, age, and gender lines. Bishop observed "a shop-girl on her way home from work; a servant from one of the good houses, come on her own account, or possibly for a school-girl mistress;" and "a middle-aged woman, with a shawl over her head and a half peck of potatoes in a basket."[16] Yet "the most ardent class of patrons," he concluded, were boys, among them elevator boys, "boys from the streets," and school-lads.[17] Indeed, years later, William Lyon Phelps of Yale University disclosed that as a child he "used to read regularly the *Fireside Companion,* whenever it was left at the front door,"[18] and a collection of reminiscences solicited by Edmund Pearson contains several other men's memories of boyhood reading of juvenile and family story papers.[19]

Perhaps to appeal to a wide readership, most story papers professed a very high moral tone as did the *Flag of Our Union* in 1856 when it described itself as a "moral and Miscellaneous Family Journal."[20] The *New York Mercury,* for example, wrapped itself in a moral cloak, claiming in 1859 that "The *Mercury* is the peculiar glory of every respectable fireside, and a fountain of intellectual pleasure, on account of the *pure and moral tone* of its Tales and Sketches. Not a word or a sentiment is allowed to appear in it that would prove distasteful to the fastidious moralist, or wound the feelings of any class of readers."[21] As the *Flag* noted in 1856, "The influence exerted by a good family paper in a home circle is almost incalculable. . . . such a paper, various in its contents, and strictly moral in its tone, is a welcome and reliable addition—we will not say to home luxuries, but, to home comforts and necessities."[22] And Robert Bonner, proprietor of the *New York Ledger* (considered by many to be the finest of the story papers), insisted that the standard of his story paper should meet with the approval of "the most pious old lady in a Presbyterian Church" and instructed his editors that "any word or phrase, innuendo or expression, that she would want to skip if she were reading a *Ledger* story to her grandchild, strike out."[23] Claims such as these were common throughout the story paper industry as publishers attempted to present their businesses in an approving light.

Although most story paper publishers maintained a moral tone, the lure of sensation as a means of attracting readers consistently pulled at them and some capitulated. Primary among them was Norman Munro. His *New Sensation*, published in New York City from 1873 to 1875, presented "a lively picture of pleasure-seeking life in New York" that was unlike its competitors. According to story paper historian Ross Craufurd, "what set the *New Sensation* apart from its competition in the beginning was its frankness. Instead of priding itself on its 'moral tone' as did the *New York Ledger, New York Weekly* and *Fireside Companion,* its approach was more that of the broad wink and the leer."[24] Publishers of juvenile papers faced a similar dilemma. Some also opted for the sensational, in the form of "blood and thunder" tales,[25] while others, such as James Elverson, publisher of *Golden Days*, hewed to more respectable fare.[26] These sensational papers and "blood and thunder" stories made it easier for critics to attack the story paper despite the claims of high moral tone made by many publishers. Perhaps the variety found in the genre expressed the commercial nature of story paper publishing, for publishers were in business to sell papers "to the million."[27]

CRITICS' SCORN

Publishers' commercial emphasis, in fact, laid the groundwork for criticism and censure, for the commercial nature of the writing brought scorn upon both writer and publication. The hack writer was required to produce fiction on demand in order to fit a commercial publishing schedule. As one wrote in 1895, "Hack writers are merely job workers who are paid by the piece like mill-hands and itinerant scissors-grinders. . . . [A hack's] pen is expected ever to be ready at a penny a word to do his master's bidding in his master's way."[28] The story papers' success, as measured in terms of circulation, was also a progenitor of the scorn levied against it. In one article, "Use and Abuse of Reading," popularity itself was brought under attack: "Needing to be always on the popular side, the press not only plants itself on the lowest general average of intelligence and virtue, but it tends constantly to lower that general average and hence becomes low and debasing in its influence."[29]

Scorn for the content of the story paper readily spread to its format. As one critic commented, the story paper "consists of eight shabby diminutive pages of typography inscribed on a square of rubbishing paper about the size of half a page of the *Times* newspaper. In quality the paper is perhaps a little superior to that in which the grocer ties up his parcels of tea; in all probability it would not be so good only that a picture goes with every penny weekly installment of the story, and it is necessary that this should be made to appear as bold and striking as possible."[30]

Mostly, critics scorned the story paper for its mainstay, the stories, leveling charges about their lack of style and their immorality. Even Bishop, devoting an entire essay to the significance of the genre, could not commend the story papers' content; the best he could muster was a lukewarm comment that "the legitimate charge against them is not that they are so bad, but only that they are not better." As did others who suggested that reading the story papers was better than not reading at all, Bishop found reading preferable even though it was "nourished on no better food than story papers." He added, however, "But it is a pity it is no better."[31]

Other critics vehemently attacked the story paper for its inferior literary content and the poor quality of the writing, its immoral tone, and its influence and potential effect on readers. An 1868 article, "Pen-Poison," asserted the stories "differ[ed] one from the other so little, that the authors themselves could scarcely tell which was which," and the characters were little more than "puppets" and "machinery" to advance the plot.[32] Ten years later, another article also denigrated the writing style, remarking, "The dialogue is short, sharp, and continuous. It is broken by the minimum of description and by no preaching. It is almost entirely in slang of the most exaggerated kind, and of every variety."[33] And an 1889 essay referred to "[g]rossly improbable and sensational incidents ... described in vulgar English, plentifully besprinkled with coarse and slangy expressions."[34]

Even Noel evinces a certain disdain for the publication and its reader: In *Villains Galore,* she refers to the story paper's "little influence, for good or for bad"; comments that "the literary deficiencies of the story paper are too obvious for discussion"; and remarks that what the young girls and housewives who read the story paper "need in their bored simplicity is a stimulus. What they get is a drug, which in the end only wearies them the more."[35] Noel concludes, "When social judgment is passed upon the story paper ... Indulgence and human understanding are required. To millions of poor, hard-working, monotony-ridden lives, the story papers were a wide new world of high escape ... The authors were not literary men—they were professional entertainers."[36]

Critics also deplored the immoral tone of the story papers' fiction, feeling criminals were portrayed in the stories as "objects of high admiration ... [set] up for worship and emulation."[37] The lesson taught in these stories, one anonymous author asserted, was that "the law is a tyrant and none so brave and bold as those who defy it."[38] The greatest complaints, however, were against content. "What Our Boys Are Reading" charged that "[t]he literary material is either intensely stupid, or spiced to the highest degree with sensation. The stories are about hunting, Indian warfare, California desperado life, pirates, wild sea adventure, highwaymen, crimes and horrible accidents, horrors (tortures and snake stories), gamblers, practical jokes, the life of vagabond boys, and the wild behavior of dissipated boys in great cities. . . . There are no other stories."[39] Even story paper publishers occasionally expressed concern about content—their rivals', of course, not their own. In 1873, the *New York Weekly* piously lamented that other papers were allowed to "disseminate their filthy trash" and spoke out strongly against the "many professed 'family papers' which are filled with romances of a most pernicious character."[40]

Concern about the effects of such reading took many forms. In "The School Library a Factor in Education," a paper read to the New York State Teachers' Association, George Hardy spoke of "the vast and villainous aggregation of the so-called 'libraries' and story papers" and "the irreparable damage wrought every day by these publications which first prostitute and then pander to the natural taste of young people for excitement"; he went on to quote "an eminent educator['s]" assertion that "[n]othing is more fatal to intellectual and moral growth."[41] Bishop advised caution when assessing the influence of periodicals like the story paper: "They are by no means needed to account for an adventurous spirit in human nature" that might lead a boy to run away to sea, he wrote for the *Atlantic Monthly,* "But they certainly foment it to the utmost."

Others feared such reading would lead to a life of crime. One critic, writing for *Scribner's Monthly* in 1878, conceded that "[p]robably many boys outgrow them and come to see [their] folly and falsehood," but felt it was "impossible, however, that so much corruption should be afloat and not exert some influence."[42] Given the romanticized portrayal of criminals in the story paper and the relative inexperience of the boys reading them, another writer argued, crime and sin could be played out for readers by trying lesser misdeeds than those read of in the papers: "There is no reason why you should not become a very expert and successful rogue in a more modest way. There are tills to be robbed, and pockets to be picked, and the cash-boxes and drawers of masters and parents to be pilfered." [43]

The battleground of cultural authority was moral tone. Cultural authorities feared the influence of fiction, believing that what was portrayed in fiction might be repeated in life. They also feared the influence of places where the story paper was sold, for the proprietor of such an emporium typically sold tobacco and had a back room "where men smoked and played pool," and some worried "that boys who bought books in the front of the shop might some day be led into the dissipations which were rampant in the rear of it."[44] From the unscrupulous, ne'er-do-well characters that critics believed these stories put forth as heroes to "the views of life which these stories inculcate and the code of morals and manners which they teach," the story paper challenged traditional values of parents, teachers, and religious authorities.[45] According to the 1878 article "What Our Boys Are Reading," "The persons who are held up to admiration are the heroes and heroines of bar-rooms, concert saloons, variety theaters, and negro [*sic*] minstrel troupes. . . . The heroes are either swaggering, vulgar swells, of the rowdy style, or they are in the vagabond mass below the rowdy swells . . . low people who live by their wits."[46]

The most extended criticism of the story paper may have been that of the New York Society for the Suppression of Vice and its secretary, Anthony Comstock. They conducted a prolonged campaign in the 1870s and 1880s against the story paper,[47] especially the boys' papers, in an effort to suppress them as "evil reading."[48]   The Society charged that boys' papers were "pregnant with mischief" and a "fruitful source of evil among the young."   To them the stories in the boys' papers created juvenile criminals by instructing impressionistic young readers in the mechanics of crime, presenting the life of crime as fun, and glorifying criminals. "The fearful increase of youthful criminals in our cities in recent years," the Society insisted, "should be traced very largely to this source."[49] In 1880, the Society clearly stated its rationale for the campaign: "The Board are deeply impressed with the importance of guarding the youthful mind from the debasing influence of what are called Boy's Papers."[50] The Society charged that story papers printed "stories of criminal life," and, in so doing, encouraged readers to commit crimes. "What is the result?" the Society demanded: "The knife, the dagger and the bludgeon [which are] used in the sinks of iniquity, and by hardened criminals, are also found in the school-room, the house and the playground of tender youth.   Our Court rooms are thronged with infant criminals—with baby felons."[51]

The New York State legislature was also certain of the negative influence of story papers and similar periodicals, especially when it came to crime fiction. In June 1884, in a move to curtail the distribution of these papers to boys, the New York State legislature passed a bill that outlawed the sale to minors of story papers and other publications that contained crime stories. In its final form Chapter 380 of the Laws of 1884, as reported in the Eleventh Annual Report of the Society for the Suppression of Vice, prohibited "all persons [from] selling to minor children any paper, magazine or newspaper, 'principally made up of criminal news, police reports, or accounts of criminal deeds, or pictures and stories of deeds of bloodshed, lust or crime.'"[52]   Over the next several years, other states enacted similar legislation.[53]

PUBLISHERS REACT

In response to the scorn engendered by their story papers, publishers directly defended reading fiction against attacks that ranged from scorn to censorship. One tool they used to counter indirectly the effects of scorn was to advise their readers about reading through articles printed on the opinion pages of their papers. These articles endeavored to elevate the status of story paper reading and constructed an image of the story paper reader as an intelligent, educated, discriminating individual. One such article discusses the physiological aspects of reading, giving advice on the best light, body position, and time of day for reading.[54] Still others discuss what one should read, what public library records show was being read, and why one should read. Many specifically address the reading of popular fiction, which was the mainstay of the story papers. Additional articles assess the influence of English publishing upon reading in the United States, provide a historical view of language, urge the development of particular reading habits, or explain the benefits of reading "cheap literature." Others address the book trade, public libraries, novel reading, and the readers' influence on supply and demand in the marketplace.

These articles countered scorn in three ways: first, in a persuasive mode, by informing readers that reading fiction was a beneficial activity; second, in a technical mode, by advising readers on the physical requirements of reading, what reading habits to develop, and how to approach their reading for education and recreation; and third, in a prescriptive mode, by telling readers what to read.

Their first assertion that reading was beneficial was certainly in the best interests of the story paper publishers, who, after all, were in business to make a profit and could do so by increasing sales. Consequently, the articles stressed the importance of light reading—such as romances, tales, or sketches. According to an article in the *New York Mercury* in 1859, "The reading of fictitious matter is . . . necessary to the wear and tear of mind that life naturally incurs."[55] An article from 1873 contended that reading of fiction was a step toward reading "higher" literature and a positive alternative for boys who might otherwise get into mischief.[56] "Light Literature," published in 1874, boldly claimed that these "periodical publications, cheap books and reprints . . . are calculated to invigorate the intellect without fatiguing it."[57] "Cheap Libraries," from 1879, asserted the long-term effect of reading is to "stimulate the minds and educate the tastes of the people, and eventually increase the demand for solid works," concluding that cheap libraries were "beneficial to the people, and far-reaching in their consequences."[58] Articles in the story papers also expanded on the beneficent effects of reading by emphasizing it was good for the country as well as for the individual. According to "Popular Reading," published in 1872 by the *Saturday Journal,* "It is evidence of American prosperity and intelligence that so great a proportion of the population is given to reading. No country on the earth supplies so many readers, in proportion to its population, as the United States, north of a given line, and it is fair to assert that no country on the globe is so intelligent, free and happy."[59]

Second, story paper publishers reinforced reading as a serious activity by borrowing from the prestige of contemporary science and technology to make their point. A typical article published in the *Saturday Journal* in 1872 contains advice from physicians regarding proper light, reading small print, the reader's relationship to the light source, and the best time of day for reading.[60] Another article relating reading to science and technology argued that the age of steam enabled a "rapidity of movement" that placed new emphasis on the expenditure of time involved in any activity. The demand, therefore, is for "weekly journals, cheap volumes, magazines, reviews, [and] articles which have the cream of literature on the surface, and may be easily skimmed."[61]

Third, the story paper publishers countered scorn by advising their readers what to read. In doing so, they conveyed confidence in the story paper reader's judgment and good sense. An 1874 article from the *Saturday Journal* informed parents that the content of a good home library included standard works of fiction, poetry, biographies, travel books, and histories, as well as "magazines and papers of the better class, for daily and hourly association."[62] (The publishers, of course, undoubtedly considered themselves part of the better class of papers.) "Unwholesome Literature," published in the *New York Weekly* in 1877, also touches on what one should read, even going so far as to encourage support for the efforts of the Society for the Suppression of Vice.[63]

Thus, in a complex relationship between publisher and reader, these articles addressed the audience directly as readers, and, as such, they delivered a positive message about the story paper that was communicated without intercession from the scorn of critics. The publishers' direct appeal to their readers helped maintain the popularity of the story paper despite the criticism and scorn of traditional authorities. Noel suggests that publishers thought readers of their story paper "must be flattered into thinking that they were reading literature," with a capital "L," when in fact they were not.[64] She hastens to add, however, that "[f]or fifty years the editors and storytellers of the new weeklies never forgot to appeal to the dignity and the self-esteem of the people they entertained."[65] The publishers' appeal to their audience, whether flattering or sincere, constructs the reader as independent, intelligent, and in control. "[N]ot to be a reader," as one article stated, "is a sign of dire ignorance."[66]

Representations of the story paper made by its publishers and images of the story paper created by those who scorned, criticized, and censored it seem like two alien worlds coexisting in alternate realities. To the publishers, the working class was a vast market for their wares; to the cultural critics, the working class was a "mob" without judgment or taste. To the publishers, the reader was disciplined and discerning; to the critics, the reader was unskilled and uneducated, easily manipulated to the publishers' own ends. To the publishers, the story paper offered the public entertaining fiction; to the cultural critic, the story paper enticed young people to lead immoral lives, defying traditional authority of home, school, and church. A look at the cultural work of each of these disparate forces, however, suggests the values that underlay their coexistence in nineteenth-century American society.

NOTES

1. The origin of the term *story paper* is unknown. The term was used by story paper publishers in the 1870s and possibly earlier, and it may be they who coined the phrase. Few of its critics used the term, preferring instead to call it "cheap literature" or "boys' papers." The only example found of its use by critics was "Story Paper Literature," the title of an article that was published in the *Atlantic Monthly* in 1879.

2. The most popular story papers claimed sales of hundreds of thousands of copies of each issue. *Flag of Our Union*, for example, claimed a circulation of 100,000 before the Civil War when the average of all periodicals in 1860 averaged a circulation of less than 12,000 copies; the *New York Ledger*, one of the most popular story papers, claimed sales at its height of nearly 400,000 copies weekly (Frank Luther Mott, *A History of*

American Magazines, 5 vols. [Cambridge, MA: Harvard University Press, 1938–68], vol. 2, 473). Dime novels typically printed original editions of 60,000 (Henry Nash Smith, *Virgin Land: The American West as Symbol and Myth* [1950; reprint, with a new preface, Cambridge, MA: Harvard University Press, 1970], 90–91); clothbound books typically ran in editions of less than 10,000.

3. For the purposes of this article, the term *genre* is used in its less common meaning of "kind" or "sort." The story paper was a publication of distinct characteristics and may be referred to in a manner similar to a magazine, journal, or newspaper, but the term *story paper* was also used synonymously with its content, which Bishop referred to in 1879 as *story paper literature*. The use of *genre* in this article is not meant to suggest that the story paper or its literature was a genre in its more common meaning of a type of literary composition with distinctive form, style, and content.

4. Mary Noel's *Villains Galore: The Heyday of the Popular Story Weekly* (New York: Macmillan, 1954) provides the most complete history of the story paper in America. Other sources for its history include Albert Johannsen's *The House of Beadle and Adams and Its Dime and Nickel Novels: The Story of a Vanished Literature*, vols. 1–2 (Norman: University of Oklahoma Press, 1950), which documents the history of the Beadle story papers; Frank Luther Mott intermittently references individual story papers in *A History of American Magazines* and included a section on the *New York Ledger* in volume 2, 356–63; Quentin Reynolds discusses the story papers of Street and Smith in his history of the firm, *The Fiction Factory: Or From Pulp Row to Quality Street* (New York: Random House, 1955). A number of excellent articles appear in *Dime Novel Round-Up*, "a magazine devoted to the collecting, preservation and study of old-time dime and nickel novels, popular story papers, series books, and pulp magazines" (masthead).

5. "The Flag of Our Union," advertisement, *Flag of Our Union*, 4 March 1854, 8.

6. "A Happy New Year," editorial, *Flag of Our Union*, 5 January 1856, 4.

7. Mott, vol. 2, 10, 35.

8. Noel, 32.

9. Ibid., 133.

10. Robert Bonner's *New York Ledger* peaked at 377,000 in 1869, Street and Smith's *New York Weekly* claimed 350,000 in 1877, and George Munro's *Fireside Companion* reported 280,000 in 1885. Noel, 138.

11. Edward T. LeBlanc, "900 Series Titles for The Dime Novel Publishing World Research Guide." Unpublished paper.

12. Mary Noel identified the story paper through five characteristics that distinguished it from other types of periodicals. For Noel, the story paper (1) had a national distribution, (2) contained no advertising, (3) consisted of eight pages, (4) sold inexpensively, and (5) printed mostly fiction. Noel, 32. Few story papers met these criteria completely, and none met them unequivocally; what is considered a story paper from a historical viewpoint, therefore, is open to interpretation. No definitive list of story papers exists, although *Villains Galore* might come closest to forming one.

13. W.H. Bishop, "Story Paper Literature," *Atlantic Monthly*, September 1879, 383.

14. Madeleine B. Stern, *Imprints on History: Book Publishers and American Frontiers* (Bloomington: Indiana University Press, 1956), 222.

15. The Five Points was one of New York City's most crime-ridden and poverty-stricken neighborhoods. For a discussion of the Five Points and crime see Herbert Asbury, *The Gangs of New York: An Informal History of the Underworld* (1928; reprint, New York: Marboro Books Corporation, Dorset Press, 1989).

16. The absence of adult men in Bishop's record, while suggestive, does not necessarily mean that men did not buy or read the story paper. They may have purchased it from other places, such as at a newsstand or from a newsboy, and may well have read it at home. Story paper publishers frequently referred to their readers as men and women, and many writers in this genre were men.

17. His list of boys who purchased the story paper included those school-lads who probably came from economically stable families and boys who had no family at all. The boys from the streets, many of whom were homeless or orphaned, may have gotten the story paper from their work as newsboys who hawked the papers on the streets, or they may have earned enough money to buy a story paper working as bootblacks, selling chestnuts from their own sidewalk stands, or making pinwheels to sell to storekeepers. Charles D. Shanley, "The Small Arabs of New York," *Atlantic Monthly*, March 1869, 283.

18. Edmund Pearson, *Dime Novels; or, Following an Old Trail in Popular Literature* (Boston: Little, Brown, & Company, 1929), 247.

19. Ibid., 247–52.

20. "A Happy," 4.

21. "Proclivior! *The New York Mercury* for 1860," *New York Mercury*, 10 December 1859, 8.

22. "Worthy of Consideration," *Flag of Our Union*, 2 January 1856, 13.

23. Matthew Hale Smith, *Sunshine and Shadow in New York* (Hartford: J.B. Burr & Company, 1868), 613.

24. Ross Craufurd, *Bibliographic Listing: "The New Sensation" and "The Sporting New Yorker"* (Fall River, MA: Edward T. LeBlanc, 1976), 3. *New Sensation*, for example, illustrated one of its stories with a drawing of a group of women in low-cut dresses who were merrily drinking in a private room while two men looked on from a partly opened doorway. See *New Sensation*, 1 November 1873, 1.

25. W.M. Burns writes that at about age fifteen or sixteen he was given a batch of story papers including *Happy Days, Young Men of America, Banner Weekly, Golden Days*, and others; while he liked *Happy Days, Young Men of America*, and *Banner Weekly*, "After reading 'blood and thunder' for years, this run of 'Golden Days' just simply did not appeal to [him]"; he "pass[ed] them up as a 'namby-pamby' story paper . . . [because he was] more interested in the 'blood-and-thunder' type of story paper." W.M. Burns, "Our Old Story Papers: 'Golden Days,'" *Reckless Ralph's Dime Novel Round-Up* 16 (February 1948), 9.

26. Harry Castlemon, quoted in Jacob Blanck [comp.], *Harry Castlemon: Boys' Own Author* (New York: R.R. Bowker, 1941), 131. In an 1882 letter to his book publisher (reprinted in Blanck), boys' author Harry Castlemon (pseud. of Charles A. Fosdick) wrote that Street & Smith had offered him $1,000 for a story for the *New York Weekly*, but Castlemon refused, preferring to write for Elverson instead, noting "*Golden Days* is a respectable paper."

27. "The Flag," 8.

28. "The Literary Hack and His Critics," *Forum*, December 1895, 512.

29. "Use and Abuse of Reading," *Catholic World*, July 1866, 464.

30. "Pen-Poison," *Hours at Home*, February 1868, 292.

31. Bishop, 393.

32. "Pen-Poison," 294–96.

33. "What Our Boys Are Reading," *Scribner's Monthly*, March 1878, 681.

34. George E. Hardy, "The School Library a Factor in Education," *Library Journal* 14 (August 1889), 343.

35. Noel, 306–7.

36. Ibid., 307.

37. "Pen-Poison, 296.

38. Ibid.

39. "What Our Boys," 681.

40. "A Sensible Librarian," *New York Weekly*, 17 November 1873, 4.

41. Hardy, 344.

42. "What Our Boys," 684–85.

43. "Pen-Poison," 294–96.

44. Pearson, 90.

45. "What Our Boys," 684.

46. Ibid.

47. Robert Bremner, in his introduction to the 1967 reprint of Comstock's *Traps for the Young*, documented Comstock's reading of two story papers, the *Fireside Companion* and the *Family Story Paper*. Indeed, he found that "[a]s early as 1872 Comstock arrested the editor of *Fireside Companion*, whom he called 'one of the worse sneaks in the business,' for publishing obscene matter." Robert Bremner, Editor's Introduction to *Traps for the Young*, by Anthony Comstock (Cambridge, MA: Harvard University Press, Belknap Press, 1967), xx–xxiv.

48. Anthony Comstock, *Traps for the Young* (1883; reprint, with an Editor's Introduction by Robert Bremner, Cambridge, MA: Harvard University Press, Belknap Press, 1967), 5. For a detailed example of Comstock's attack on the story paper see Chapter 3, "Half-Dime Novels and Story Papers" in *Traps for the Young*, 20–42.

49. New York Society for the Suppression of Vice, "Fourth Annual Report," in *Annual Reports of the New York Society for the Suppression of Vice* (New York: The Society, n.d.), 7; New York Society for the Suppression of Vice, "Eighth Annual Report," in *Annual Reports of the New York Society for the Suppression of Vice* (New York: The Society, n.d.), 9; and New York Society for the Suppression of Vice, "Tenth Annual Report," in *Annual Reports of the New York Society for the Suppression of Vice* (New York: The Society, n.d.), 8.

50. New York Society for the Suppression of Vice, "Sixth Annual Report," in *Annual Reports of the New York Society for the Suppression of Vice* (New York: The Society, n.d.), 6.

51. Ibid., 6–7.

52. New York Society for the Suppression of Vice, "Eleventh Annual Report," in *Annual Reports of the New York Society for the Suppression of Vice* (New York: The Society, n.d.), 8. This legislation was introduced by Senator Gilbert at the urging of the New York Society for the Prevention of Cruelty to Children (7–8).

53. Lawrence M. Friedman, *Crime and Punishment in American History* (New York: HarperCollins, Basic, 1993), 135.

54. "Don't Abuse the Eyes," *Saturday Journal*, 21 December 1872, 4.

55. "Reading," *New York Mercury*, 16 April 1859, 4.

56. "A Sensible Librarian," 4.

57. "Light Literature," *Family Story Paper*, 27 April 1874, 4.

58. "Cheap Libraries," *Fireside Companion*, 18 August 1879, 4.

59. "Our Arm Chair—Popular Reading," *Saturday Journal*, 12 October 1872, 4.

60. "Don't Abuse the Eyes," 4.

61. "Light Literature," 4.

62. Jennie Davis Burton, "What Shall We Read?" *Saturday Journal*, 10 January 1874, 4.

63. "Unwholesome Literature," *New York Weekly*, 13 August 1877, 4.
64. Noel, 287.
65. Ibid., 288.
66. "Our Arm Chair—Popular Reading," 4.

Chapter 7

The Effect of Nineteenth-Century "Libraries" on the American Book Trade

Lydia Cushman Schurman

INTRODUCTION

"Book?" repeated Corey, while she [Irene] reddened with disappointment. "Oh yes. *Middlemarch*. Did you like it?"

. . .

"Yes; I liked it immensely. But it's several years since I read it."

"I didn't know it was so old. It's just got into the Seaside Library," she urged, with a little sense of injury in her tone.

"Oh, it hasn't been out such a very great while," said Corey politely. "It came out a little before *Daniel Deronda*."[1]

In this conversation from *The Rise of Silas Lapham* (1885) by William Dean Howells, Irene Lapham and Tom Corey discuss one of the most popular inexpensive paper-covered publications of the latter nineteenth century—George Munro's *Seaside Library*. So famous was this series that Howells, then called "the Dean of American Letters," knew his readers would readily recognize the reference to it. Publisher George Munro had reprinted in various editions George Eliot's *Middlemarch* and *Daniel Deronda*, selling them each in two parts, each part for twenty or twenty-five cents.[2]

The *Seaside Library* was one of nearly 500 such inexpensive popular reprint publications known as libraries. They were issued by 150 publishing firms, predominantly located in New York City, but which spanned the country from Maine to Minnesota. Also called "series," the paperback libraries appeared in editions ranging from 5,000 to 60,000,[3] thus greatly outnumbering story papers and dime novels issued during the same period.[4] Originally the libraries appeared in small newspaper format, known as quartos; they measured 8 by 5 inches to 13 by 10 inches and had black-and-white pictorial drawings on the cover. Later they appeared as paper-covered books.

Libraries were a boon to the general reading public. Ranging in price from five to twenty-five cents, each volume contained a complete book (unless it was a long work, in which case it was issued in two parts or two numbers). A single issue customarily cost ten cents, a double one twenty cents. At such low prices, working-class readers could purchase not only George Eliot's works but also other classics such as Jonathan Swift's *Gulliver's Travels*, Charles Dickens' *David Copperfield*, Miguel de Saavedra Cervantes' *Don Quixote*, Alexander Dumas' *Les Miserables*, and Homer's *Iliad* and *Odyssey*.[5] Less often, the libraries featured standard American works, albeit usually those upon which copyrights had expired. Libraries issued by publishers of dime novels and story papers often had reprints of popular contemporary tales as well.

Nevertheless, although popular, libraries were among the most scorned publications during the last three decades of the nineteenth and early twentieth centuries.[6] Indeed, one might ask, "If the libraries made good literature affordable for the masses, why would there be reason to scorn them?" This essay endeavors to answer that question by tracing the history of the libraries during this period and analyzing the major effects they had on the American book trade. The onslaught of the libraries jolted the trade into a painful awareness of books as mass-produced commodities rather than as aesthetic artifacts. Consequently, regular publishers bitterly scorned the libraries from their inception to their demise. The trade repudiated the piratical tactics of cheap library publishers, criticized the library format, deplored the commodification of the book, took retaliatory actions, chastised library readers, and denounced the reliance of libraries on foreign literature and their effect on American authors.

HISTORY OF THE LIBRARIES

The library movement began in earnest in 1874 when Donnelley, Loyd and Company of Chicago started to reprint noncopyrighted literary classics in the *Lakeside Library*, a small newspaper-type format or quarto.[7] It soon became the prototype for numerous series of inexpensive paper-covered reprints of primarily foreign novels. So popular were the libraries by 1876 that bookseller August Brentano remarked: "No matter how cheap the cloth edition of a book may be, in order for it to succeed (provided it is a novel) it must be issued in pamphlet form. . . . As soon as a cloth novel is shown to a customer, and if he takes ever so great or little fancy to it, in two cases out of three the first question is 'Have you not got this in paper?'"[8] The *Lakeside Library* resembled the earlier *New York Tribune Novels*, which had started as "novel extras" in 1873 and sold for ten cents.

George Munro's *Seaside Library*, Ordinary Edition, first published on May 20, 1877, was the first and most successful follower of the *Lakeside Library* and soon "dominated the market."[9] Regular publishers observed with acute displeasure the ascendancy of the successful piratical reprinter "Seaside Munro." "Oh! for international copyright!" *Publishers' Weekly* had exclaimed even then.[10] Much to the trade's astonishment, Munro scored a literary coup with the publication of the Revised version of the New Testament in 1881. This work had been published on May 20 in England, in a project that had been zealously guarded during several years of scholarly labor.[11] The following day Munro issued the first of two parts in the *Seaside Library*; he published the second part two days later.[12] Ill will fomented further when a contemporary journal praised Munro's speed in publication as "probably the most notable instance on record of rapid work in the production of books" and described George Munro's imprint "as the most familiar in the United States."[13] Remarked J. Henry Harper archly, neither the *Lakeside Library* nor the *Seaside Library* was "handicapped by payments to authors or by regard to decency of paper and print."[14]

Munro was not the only publisher to understand the success of the library format. Among others who started libraries that same year were his brother Norman, who simply "appropriated" the name "Riverside" from Houghton Mifflin and began the *Riverside Library* (1877–circa 1879);[15] Beadle and Adams, who originated both the *Fireside Library of Popular Reading* (1877–82) and *Sunnyside Library* (1877); Frank Leslie, with *Frank Leslie's Home Library* (1877); and Harper & Brothers, who issued *Harper's Half Hour Series* (1877).[16] *Publishers' Weekly* counted fourteen different library publications by September 1877.[17] Remarked publishing historian Raymond Howard Shove, "The outstanding phenomenon in publishing during the year 1877, however, was the very general success suddenly attained in the reprinting of standard novels in the ten cent quartos."[18] In 1880 *Publishers' Weekly* reported approximately 2,500,000 issues of the libraries had been sold.[19]

"Who is this Munro?" a reporter asked one of the Scribners of Charles Scribner's Sons, shortly after George Munro's first *Seaside Library* appeared. "He's an intrusive and impudent meddler," was the reply, "fooling with things he doesn't understand."[20] However, George Munro understood the business only too well. In March 1879, he bought the *Lakeside Library* from Donnelly, Gasette, and Loyd, thereby greatly increasing his store of plates.[21] Munro absorbed the *Lakeside* into the *Seaside Library*, which became "the most flourishing" of all the cheap libraries, rivaled primarily only by Harper's *Franklin Square Library*.[22] In addition to the Ordinary Edition of the *Seaside Library* (1877–86), which ran for 2,081 issues, the other most important libraries were Harper & Brothers' *Franklin Square Library* (1878–93), which lasted for 758 issues; John Lovell's *Lovell's Library* (1882–89), which appeared for approximately 1,470 issues; and Norman Munro's *Munro's Library*, Pocket Edition (1883–88), which ran for about 849 issues.[23] By 1882, the *New York Evening Express* reported that many libraries were selling editions of 50,000: "Taking the low figure of 10,000 as the average sale," it commented, "we have 650,000 as the circulation of the 'Franklin Square,' and 5,500,000 as the circulation of the 'Seaside.' Such figures are almost appalling, yet they are probably far below the actual sales of the two libraries."[24]

REGULAR TRADE SCORNED LIBRARIES' PIRACY

Standard publishers accused library publishers of pirating their foreign books, thereby totally ignoring the rules of trade courtesy, a gentlemen's agreement by which publishers honored each other's claims to a foreign work. Under this informal system, if one paid royalties for advance sheets, then he became the American publisher. Although *Publishers' Weekly* as early as 1875 reported that this custom had "degenerated" and "floats 'in a sea of doubts,'"[25] standard publishers such as Appleton, Harper, Holt, Lippincott, Peterson, and Ticknor and Fields honored the system. J.B. Lippincott explained, "Before the advent of the Seaside, and kindred 'Libraries,' when what are known as the 'trade courtesy rules' (still in force with all reputable publishers but ignored by the 'pirates') gave the authorized American publisher some protection in his ventures, we were enabled to pay large sums for the advance sheets of foreign books."[26]

They watched in astonishment as library publishers pirated texts from their expensive cloth or hardback editions, as well as their less expensive paper-covered publications. They observed the pirates charge a dime for cheap reprints of a $1.50 book or twenty cents for a $4 book.[27] Bitterly they listened to remarks such as John Lovell made when he claimed in 1879, "As a young publisher I look back at the early beginnings of the larger houses, and I find no such thing as this so-called 'courtesy of the trade.' In olden times it was 'every man for himself,' and only after firmly established businesses had been built up, largely through reprinting foreign works, it was found a matter of policy by certain houses not to infringe upon each other . . . Go in heartily for the 'courtesy of the trade' and—starve," he warned others.[28]

Regular publishers saw pirates issue libraries within twenty-four hours bearing the same titles for which royalties had been paid.[29] The trade's scorn turned to rage as Harper & Brothers reported paying £1,700 for *Daniel Deronda* only to have it pirated and sold in a library for twenty cents, and the works of Wilkie Collins, for which the firm had paid royalties amounting to almost £6,000, met the same fate.[30] In 1879, editorializing about the outlook for spring, *Publishers' Weekly* expressed the trade's opinion when it blamed the libraries for having "very nearly killed the sale of paper novels in better style."[31] Publishers suffered intense competition from pirates like George and Norman Munro, who, in the 1880s, each owned multistoried buildings, where they manufactured their libraries under one roof: typesetting, presswork, and binding all done by machines, so libraries could be produced in as few as ten hours.[32] In 1884, when a reporter visited George Munro's office, he marveled that "[t]he building is, I believe, the largest printing establishment in the world except Harper's. One entire floor is filled with Burr type-setting and distributing machines, each of which does the work of ten compositors. In the two press rooms web presses feed-off from their large rolls 25,000 Seaside sheets an hour."[33]

Regular publishers were joined in their contempt of the pirates by authors who were pirated. Two English novelists registered their complaints in the *London Times*, explaining the disastrous impact library publishers had upon them:

[B]ut a number of firms have recently sprung up in Chicago and other American cities who seize upon the book as soon as it appears in the States, and . . . in three or four days flood the market with cheap editions at 15¢ and even less. Within a few days after its completion in England, every prominent work of fiction is sold all over the United States. . . . This system of piracy has completely ruined the chance of the English author . . . and the respectable firms are deferred from producing editions more expensive than those piratically issued.[34]

The prominent author Ouida also wrote the *London Times* to express her outrage:

Until lately a sort of payment was made by American firms for "advanced sheets." Messrs. Lippincott & Co., of Philadelphia, gave me always £300 sterling for each work of which I sent them the proofs. Now even this slender *honorarium* is done away with under the wholesale piracies of every new work by [George] Munro & Co. in cheap and villainously printed paper copies. Lippincotts often informed me that they would give thousands where they gave hundreds if there were a copyright law. Now even their hundreds are not forthcoming, since Munro instantly pirates their publications . . . I can protect my horse, my rings, the saucepans my cook uses, the spade my gardener works with; I cannot protect that work of my own brain, which without me could never have taken shape or seen the light, and must be more intrinsically and utterly mine than anything on earth.[35]

Again in 1883 she wrote the *Times* reiterating her message, adding wryly that George Munro had only once sent her "conscience money," proof that he "was perfectly conscious that piracy is not altogether the perfectly enjoyable thing. "[36]

Standard publishers in Canada found the situation no better than did their colleagues across the border, despite the fact that Canada had a copyright law that protected republication rights of British writers. Protesting to the *London Times*, two authors reported, "The book trade has been completely demoralized here, and the plan now adopted by the United States publishers of issuing at 10¢, 15¢, 20¢, and 25¢ works formerly published at $1 and $1.50 has ruined the little market we had . . . The cheap American editions come in, in spite of everything."[37]

FORMAT

In addition to scorning piratical practices of library publishers, the standard trade disdainfully regarded the mass-produced library quarto format because it represented an aesthetic decline in book publishing. Flimsy and ephemeral, the library featured cheap printing, close typography, and paper covers. In both appearance and cost, the format offered the book as a throwaway product. Contemptuously, the trade observed the library's three closely printed columns of small type to a page, a practice which, at times, allowed library publishers to reduce a complete novel to as few as a dozen pages.[38] "The [library] publishers are vieing with each other in producing books which cost next to nothing," reported the *Evening Mail*.[39] "It is a question whether this has not resulted in lowering the dignity of literature in the general estimation. When a book cost money, it was something to be preserved with care, and guarded and cherished as a thing of value. . . . At present, books, even of sterling value, are read and thrown away . . . The publication which may be bought for a few pence, however worthy its contents, is likely to be regarded like a newspaper, as something to be skimmed over and forgotten." In 1881, *Publishers' Weekly* reported that the "plague" of libraries with their tightly packed, three-columned pages and "variety-shop gaudiness" not only discouraged regular publishers from investing in the tasteful production of books but also made them "fight shy of substantial ventures."[40] The journal characterized the "swarm of cheap reprints" as a major cause of the dull book trade market. Exclaimed the periodical three years later, "In the rage for cheapness we have sacrificed everything for slop and a dainty bit of bookmaking is like a jewel in the swines' snout."[41]

Standard trade publishers also deplored the eagerness with which piratical library publishers transformed books into periodicals in order to guarantee their cheaper delivery through the mails at substantial government subsidy. According to the Postal Act of March 3, 1879, all a publisher had to do to have a publication classified as a periodical—hence eligible for distribution at lower mailing costs in the second-class bulk rate—was to print something in paper covers; issue it regularly, at least four times a year, from a known office of publication; stamp on it the date of issue; number it consecutively to indicate it was one issue in a particular series or library; and indicate it had a subscription rate verifiable by a list of subscribers.[42] Publishers who followed these instructions could distribute their publications through the mails for two cents a pound from 1879 to 1885 and one cent a pound from 1885 to 1904.[43] During this period, regular publishers paid third-class rates of eight cents a pound to mail their books, an amount initially four times higher—then after 1885 eight times higher—than the second-class postal rate library publishers paid to mail periodicals. While standard publishers had been accustomed to distributing their magazines like *Harper's, Lippincott's*, and *Putnam's* at the bulk rate since 1875, they challenged the eligibility of the cheap libraries as periodicals. In 1877, the mailing of the *Lakeside Library* became a test case. The attorney general decided the library was entitled to second-class rates,[44] and his decision stood for a quarter of a century.

In April 1882 when John Lovell introduced *Lovell's Library* in a new library format, a small paperback book,[45] regular publishers viewed with dismay how rapidly the smaller-sized library format became popular among readers. The demand for it forced other piratical publishers to adopt it, an action they took unwillingly because its profit margin was lower than on the quarto.[46] The regular trade was incensed as the libraries—now even shaped like books[47]—continued to enjoy second-class mail rates. Cheap publishers also began to issue diverse kinds of libraries: standard works on medicine, law, science, history, and religion—even the Bible and the dictionary became periodicals.[48] Argued a member of Congress, "This law . . . has been so distorted and warped . . . we now have a condition prevailing whereby any publication under our American sun, even to the advertisement of a private business, a dime novel, or a side show of a circus is admitted as second-class matter."[49] Library publishers rushed foreign novels through their printing presses regardless of merit or market. The libraries soon reached flood proportions and glutted the market.

COMMODIFICATION

Above all—and integrally intertwined with other aspects of scorn—regular publishers held library pirates accountable for the commodification of the book. The trade charged that pirates had transformed the book into an economic object, far from its rightful place as an intellectual or aesthetic work of art. Standard publishers believed the distribution of the libraries emphasized the portrayal of books as articles of commerce, a concept enhanced by the fact that most were packaged like newspapers and shipped to booksellers and newsdealers across the country by the American News Company. J. Henry Harper even attributed the prosperity of the libraries directly to this giant distribution company "without whose encouragement," he said, "they would have been short-lived."[50] Also emphasizing the idea of book as object, when competition grew fiercest, George Munro gave away cakes of soap with his libraries.[51] "The books which are given away with cakes of soap are the old flat libraries of George Munro," explained the *American Bookseller*, "and in the present state of the trade, it is about the best disposition that could be made of them; they will prove their usefulness on wash days and warm many a kettle full of suds."[52] The combination became so popular a soap manufacturer gave away a new novel with fifteen-cent cakes of soap.[53] Books and soap went so well together that by 1889 one manufacturer issued an entirely new trademarked product called "Book Soap." Other dealers offered sets of paperback books with fifty-cent purchases of patent medicine.[54] Editorialized the *American Bookseller*, "We have no doubt that the fierce competition among the publishers of Libraries, which has cut the wholesale price of twenty-five cent books to eight cents, has contributed to this result somewhat. It is now totally clear to the meanest capacity that the book trade is not analagous [*sic*] to the trade in hams and sugar, and that an effort to make it so is simply destructive to the trade altogether."[55] Nevertheless, in the frequent linking of libraries with products, the idea of book as object continuously presented itself to the public.

DEPARTMENT STORE WARES

The trade also found distasteful the way some library publishers not only made arrangements with department stores to publish libraries for them bearing the stores' imprints but also allowed department stores to sell libraries just like other goods. In 1900, after the failures of Harper & Brothers and D. Appleton Company, an editorial in the *New York Commercial* argued, "The book business of the big department stores has a good deal to do with the troubles of the old publishing houses. The growth of this branch of the department stores has been enormous, and while it has undoubtedly increased the production of books the old publishing houses have not profited by this increase, because they are not the producers of the bulk of the books sold in dry goods stores, whereas they have suffered by the cheapening of prices."[56]   Norman Munro had an arrangement with Macy's whereby he published about fifty-nine issues of *Macy's Popular Star Novels* in the early 1890s.[57]   In 1891, *Life* magazine commented cynically: "Mr. Norman Munro is as fond of fast steam yachts as Mr. Bonner is of fast trotting horses. There is no harm in stating that when Mr. Munro gets blown up, LIFE intends to derive what solace it can from recollecting that he was the first to instigate the sale of books in dry-goods stores."[58]   The department store chain Jordan Marsh of Chicago published three libraries: *J.M. & Co.'s Popular Standard Novels*, a small-sized edition of the same title in the 1890s, and another *Seaside Library*, 1900–10.[59]

One of the biggest commodifiers of the cheap libraries was John Wanamaker, who described books as "the quietest of merchandise."[60]   Regular publishers noted ominously that by 1887 Wanamaker conducted "the largest retail book business in the United States."[61]   Although he criticized the cheap libraries during his tenure as postmaster general from 1889 to 1892, he had an arrangement with John Lovell in the 1890s and early 1910s whereby Lovell published 550 issues of the *Keystone Library* with "Sold by John Wanamaker, Philadelphia, Pa." on the cover.[62]   Wanamaker then sold the library at cut rates in his dry goods store. "The Wanamaker way is to handle books like any other goods," boasted the publisher's blurb. "We have done what no other bookseller has done," Wanamaker bragged: "We have applied to bookselling the principle that has given us the lead in other merchandise."[63]   A writer to the *Critic* depicted the results of commodification: "The only thing that abounds is the pirated novel, which, like a rank weed in a garden, is surely choking all fiction of native growth. 'All regular twenty-five cent editions marked down to seven cents,' is a sign in the windows of a large dry-goods house in this city. . . . The competition among the pirates is closer than ever. . . . Rather than sell them [the libraries] for waste paper, which is all they otherwise would be good for, the publisher then takes the lot to some dry-goods house, and offers to put new covers on them with the imprint of the purchasers, if the latter will buy a certain number of thousands at five cents a copy. It is thus that they can be sold with flannel, laces, underwear, and scented soap, for seven cents a copy." [64]

REGULAR TRADE PUBLISHERS REACT

Standard publishers, knowing their scorn would be an insufficient deterrent to the pirates, also took action. Due to ubiquitous sales of the cheap libraries, the trade experienced fierce competition in selling its more expensive books. J. Henry Harper recalled that "frequently within twenty-four hours after publication a piratical edition would appear on the market, making it necessary to reduce the retail price of the authorized work so low that there would be little if any profit accruing therefrom."[65]   Reluctantly, publishers lowered prices and issued inexpensive libraries of their own. Harper's *Library of Select Novels* fell from 20 to 40 percent. Holt dropped the cost on its linen-covered *Leisure Hour Series* from $1.25 to $1.00.[66] D. Appleton & Company issued seven libraries, Harper & Brothers and G.P. Putnam's Sons four; Rand McNally and J.B. Lippincott three each; Houghton Mifflin two; and P.F. Collier, Henry Holt, T.B. Peterson & Brothers, and Ticknor each issued one.[67] The trade, however, generally paid royalties and charged more for their series than the cheap library publishers did.[68] J.B. Lippincott maintained in 1882, despite the flood of cheap reprints on the market and the low profit margins on sales of authorized editions, "[W]e always pay the author something."[69] Among the trade's series enumerated above, half were more expensive than the cheap libraries, and nine of these cost fifty cents or more. Both the Harper firm and Houghton Mifflin frankly admitted their purpose in issuing their inexpensive series. Explained J. Henry Harper: "Our idea, therefore, in starting the Franklin Square Library was to stop the profit at least on some of their [the pirates'] issues. We determined that they should not share our profits, because we intended that there should be no profit for a division. We began to print on ourselves [reprint from their other editions]."[70] A spokesman for Houghton Mifflin, which initiated its fifty-cent *Riverside Paper Series* in 1889, observed: "One purpose of the undertaking was to secure at least some of the readers being developed by the cheap reprints in George Munro's *Seaside Library*, Norman Munro's *Riverside Library*, Donnelley & Lloyd's [sic] *Lakeside Library*, Frank Leslie's *Home and Fireside Libraries*, John W. Lovell's Library, the *Harper Franklin Square Library*, and the tawdry productions of the American Book Exchange."[71]

Like their rivals, regular publishers called attention to the physical appearance and utility of their series, highlighting both size and convenience.[72] *Harper's Handy Series* quoted Dr. Johnson on its front cover, "Books you may hold readily in your hand are the most useful after all." One publisher noted that books were "sewed in the back, so each book will open flat"; *Ticknor's Paper Series of Choice Reading* emphasized the series contained "Choice Copyright Reading" for "leisure-hour and railroad reading." *Appleton's New Handy-Volume Series* stressed each volume could be read "within the compass of a single reading," and that it could be "carried in the pocket, ready for use on the train, on the steamboat, in the horse-cart, at moments snatched at twilight or bedtime, while sitting on the seashore or rambling in the woods, at all periods of rest or leisure, whether in town or country." In this regard the trade simply echoed the practical aspects to which piratical publishers also called attention.

HARPER'S FRANKLIN SQUARE LIBRARY

Of all the regular publishers who competed with the cheap library publishers, Harper's was the one firm that most vigorously challenged the pirates with its *Franklin Square Library*. Although Harper's lost money on it[73] and was criticized for publishing it, the firm kept issuing the series because the company wanted to maintain its reputation as a first-rate publishing house that brought inexpensive literature to the people. *Publishers' Weekly* described it as "Harper's cheap line of light reading for the millions."[74] Nevertheless, retailers bitterly faulted Harper's for joining the library movement. In 1879, publisher A.D.F. Randolph expressed this frustration:

Every time that I see an announcement of a new number of The Franklin Square Library, I cannot but heave a sigh and ask how long that business is to go on . . . The public has got into its head the idea that books are too dear, and every $2.50 book put into a fifteen-cent pamphlet strengthens that idea amazingly. . . . [M]y chief regret is to be found in the fact that your adoption of the Library has dignified the whole business—given it a respectability it would not otherwise have obtained.[75]

Booksellers had initially shunned the cheap libraries, declining to sell them because of their low profit margin of only three cents a copy.[76] However, so prestigious was the Harper imprint that they could no longer afford to disdain the libraries and, grudgingly, began to sell them. In 1884, *Publishers' Weekly* reflected their continued frustration: "to all the people who frequent bookstores 'libraries' are non existent . . . People who buy 'libraries' are the people who read the *New York Ledger*—utterly unknown to bookstores . . . The gross return on a hundred copies of 'John Inglesant' in cloth is $100. In the *Seaside* it would have been $20. Harper's, by putting their best books in the *Franklin Square Library*, are not doing themselves justice, and the trade is starved by the reduction of the volume of business."[77] Defending the firm, Harper insisted: "It is proper to observe here that we print no new books in our Franklin Square Library without paying some honorarium to the British author, and we strictly maintain our adherence to the rules of trade courtesy, by abstaining from printing on [pirating the text of] our neighbors."[78]

The key words in the Harper statement were that royalties were paid for "new books." According to company records, in cases where Harper's paid royalties for works that appeared in *Harper's Weekly* or *Harper's Bazaar*, the firm usually explained to its English publisher: "Should we deem it necessary, for the protection of our (library) edition of the work, to publish a cheap edition in our *Franklin Square Library*, we would not pay royalty upon copies sold of that edition."[79] Harper's did pay royalties, however, on some works reprinted in the series. It paid, for instance, 12 1/2 percent of the retail price of all copies sold of editions of William Dean Howells' *The Quality of Mercy*, *An Imperative Duty*, *April Hopes*, *A Shadow of a Dream*, and *A Hazard of New Fortune*.[80] When the firm paid W.S. Gilbert ten pounds for reprinting his "Original Comic Operas," however, an insulted Gilbert gave the money to charity.[81]

REGULAR TRADE PROTESTS

Although many regular publishers issued libraries themselves and used low second-class bulk postage rates to distribute them as periodicals, they believed their cloth and hardback books should also be allowed to go through the mails at the same price. Why, they demanded, were poorly printed books in flimsy paper covers more privileged than cloth or hardback books? A representative of T.B. Peterson & Brothers, Philadelphia, maintained that the disparity in postal rates between the libraries and books had "for a long time operated to the serious damage of legitimate trade" and insisted that adoption of a uniform postal rate for the two "involves the prosperity, if not the very existence, of the whole legitimate publishing trade of the country."[82] He observed, "How a complete book becomes a serial, even if dated, numbered, and issued at a stated period, is not clear." He added that a subscriber to a library was an "anomaly," someone who "cannot be found," and characterized the subscription rate as "merely a blind to preserve the low rate of postage." So strongly did members of the Peterson firm repudiate the cheap libraries that, at considerable cost to themselves, they insisted their series of inexpensive paper-covered books were not periodicals.[83] Consequently, the firm paid $3.64[84] a pound to mail *Peterson's Twenty-Five Cent Series* in third class as a book[85] instead of mailing it as a periodical for forty-five cents per hundred copies.[86]

As the book rate controversy expanded, Ainsworth Rand Spofford, the Librarian of Congress and spokesman for the American Library Association, argued before a Senate committee that books borrowed from a lending library should also be eligible for second-class postal rates.[87] "We never heard of a book as a periodical until after this law [the Postal Act of March 3, 1879] was passed," he insisted.[88] "Does it make it [a book] any more a periodical to reprint it with a fresh date? Why should you [the U.S. Government] carry through the mails at a loss a whole ton of Dickens' *Oliver Twist*, published in 1837, or two tons of Miss Austen's novels first published in 1812 on the plea that they are periodicals issued in this year of our Lord? Are these tons of novels, first issued before we were born, periodicals?"[89] He asserted that "from 85 to 95 per cent, of the editions of books thus favored are novels. In Lovell's Library, out of 1,142 publications issued, 1,031 are works of fiction, and only 111 are miscellaneous books. In the Franklin Square Library there are 510 works of fiction and 109 of history, biography, poetry, and other miscellaneous literature. In the Seaside Library a still greater proportion of fiction is found."[90]

In order to illustrate the unfairness in the postal rates, Spofford gave the committee an "object-lesson" to demonstrate the cost differential in mailing books versus libraries.[91] Holding up *A New Astronomy*, a recent book by S.P. Langley, then Secretary of the Smithsonian Institution, Spofford stated that the book weighed three and a half pounds, and, that, if he wished to mail it to New York City, the postage would be twenty-eight cents. He then held up a dozen numbers of the *Seaside Library*, which also weighed three and a half pounds; all of them, he said, could be mailed anywhere in the country for three and a half cents.

Despite such arguments, Congress failed to enact legislation to resolve the postal inequities, and, in July 1901, the Post Office Department took matters into its own hands. The Postmaster-General issued orders to exclude periodicals "having the characteristics of books" from second-class mail.[92] With reference to the libraries, exulted the *Philadelphia Public Ledger*, "At length the Postmaster General found courage to make the startling and revolutionary ruling—that a book was a book, and not a periodical."[93] Finally, after much agitation and further legal battles, the Supreme Court decided in 1904 that "the publications were books and not periodical publications within the meaning of the act of March 3, 1879."[94]

REGULAR TRADE BLAMES LIBRARY READERS

In addition to charging the government with inequities in its second- and third-class postal rates, the regular trade also blamed library readers for causing a decline in book sales.

Publishers had watched anxiously as readers became eager consumers of the libraries. Initially regular publishers scorned readers of the cheap libraries, dismissively saying the piratical reprints appealed solely to the lowest class. *Publishers' Weekly* characterized their attitude when it described the readers as shop boys and counter girls, members of the working class who fancied story papers and dime novels—"a large numerical but low intellectual body of readers," who, the journal hoped, might "ultimately" be educated "into a higher class of reading."[95] A correspondent to the *Atlantic Monthly* reaffirmed this view, describing readers as the "Texas Jack" dime novel kind.[96] This initial assumption proved misleading, however, as regular readers were soon discovered buying handfuls of libraries for fifty cents or fifteen ten-cent libraries for the price of one clothbound book.

As the 1870s ended, it was impossible for the standard trade to ignore the variety and number of library readers. "Middle-aged book-keepers, well-to-do artisans, cashiers of good standing, young married women whose principal occupation is shopping, and the like, keep these books in the market," explained a newsdealer to an inquiring bystander at the Brooklyn ferry waiting room.[97] A traveling correspondent reported to *Publishers' Weekly* an even wealthier class of readers: "On the trains I have met well-dressed men and women, whose external appearance gives evidence of intelligence and pecuniary possessions . . . At the hotels, the signs of abundance and of elegance are many: the ladies gorgeously apparelled; the men in the finest of cloth, smoking the best of cigars . . . Time was when among such travellers one would see here and there a delicate jewelled hand holding a *bound* book, or a 50-cent copy of the Library of Select Novels. Alas! no such vision has been mine on this journey. But I have seen the *Sea Side* [sic] and the *Franklin Square Library* everywhere."[98]

When it became clear that libraries appealed to all classes, regular publishers blamed the libraries for the declines in both book buying and reading. Publisher A.D.F. Randolph bemoaned the fact that even owners of mansions bought libraries instead of purchasing well-made books.

The paper-covered book has brought us to a time when in thousands and thousands of refined homes there is no longer any accumulation of books. They have ceased to be a necessity . . . India rugs lie upon the polished floors. Sumptuous hangings divide the rooms. Elegant curtains drape the plate-glass windows. On the walls are etchings and beautiful prints . . . in corners or on mantel are bits of rare china and costly *bric-a-brac*. . . . [A]nd on an antique table of the period of Louis XIV, (purchased, it may be, at a great price) lies, ready to your hand, the masterpiece of the great English novelist, reprinted in the *Seaside* or *Franklin Square* "library"—price, twenty cents! And should you suggest a better edition of such a book, the owner of the mansion may answer, "What do I need more when I have all the text in this?"[99]

Henry Holt concurred:

Ten years ago there was a book-buying habit . . . Now most of those book-stores no longer exist, at least as book-stores. They are toy-shops and ice-cream saloons with files of *Seaside Libraries* in one corner, and the substantial citizen, instead of taking home an occasional volume of Irving or Emerson or Macaulay . . . takes home a toy, or a pound of candy or pamphlet copy of, the chances are even, some minor English author. . . .

The result of all this, I claim, has been a great diminution, outside of this trash, in the reading habit.[100]

LIBRARIES UNFAIR TO AMERICAN AUTHORS

Regular publishers argued that the cheap libraries not only exposed the American reading public to predominantly foreign literature and ideas but also placed the American author—to whom royalties must be paid—in an unfair position; others concurred with their complaint. The trade pointed out that although American copyright law protected authors from piracy in their native land (they were pirated abroad), the high number of cheap foreign reprints issued in America caused them great harm. J. Henry Harper termed the situation a "disastrous discrimination."[101] He explained, "A novel, say by Dickens or Thackeray, would retail here at from ten cents to a dollar, whereas the price of a romance by Hawthorne or Irving would be at least a dollar and a half." A spokesman for the publishing firm of Belford, Clarke and Company argued that since the libraries were primarily composed of works by foreign authors, the favored position of the libraries in the postal rate system was a cruel inequity to American authors whose copyrighted works also appeared in other paperbound books.[102] To members of the Senate, Spofford stressed that libraries educated their readers "in foreign ideas instead of American ones," in concepts of "aristocracy in place of republican democracy."[103] He deplored the plight of American authors deluged by the onslaught of pirated reprints and blasted the low postal rates by which they were distributed at the "cheap rate about ninety foreign books to ten American books. That is about the proportion of American books these libraries send out," he exclaimed.[104] "Out of the 2,080 Seaside Library publications there are less than 75 American books among them. The Franklin Square Library embraces in its lists 599 foreign and only 20 American books. The Lovell Library gives 228 American books to 913 books by foreign writers."

The press also took up the cause, and American authors addressed it as well. The *Boston Globe* cautioned, "The extent to which the 'Seaside,' the 'Franklin Square,' and other popular series are steeping our people in English thoughts, English views, English customs, is considered with apprehension in many quarters."[105] A writer to the *Critic* admonished, "A customer going to the seaside or to the country will buy ten or a dozen copies [of libraries]; and meanwhile the copyrighted book of the native author, with its tasteful binding and creditable typography, lies neglected on the booksellers' counters."[106] Another writer succinctly summarized the situation to members of Congress when he testified: "Authors of the United States have had and are having a hard time of it. This Government may be paternal to the press, to pig-iron, and other material interests, but it is the hardest of step-parents to its brain workers."[107] So greatly did the regular trade and American authors suffer at the hands of the cheap library publishers, the *American Bookseller* editorialized in 1890, "[t]hat the present system of reprinting foreign works is responsible for much, if not all, of the demoralization of the book trade is unquestionable."[108]

LIBRARIES AND COPYRIGHT

Most regular publishers had opposed international copyright until the cheap libraries became popular, believing they could control publications of foreign authors through the practice of gentleman's agreements. As the piratical reprinting business became vicious, however, the trade's attitude began to change; by 1880, most publishers agreed that an international copyright law was essential.[109] George Haven Putnam spoke for his fellow publishers when he commented: "These pamphlet series have, however, done a most important service in pointing out the absurdity of the present condition of literary property, and in emphasizing the needs of an international copyright law."[110]

By 1884, a survey conducted by *Publishers' Weekly* showed that only three out of fifty-five publishers opposed international copyright.[111] J. Henry Harper, citing the plethora of foreign novels published in the cheap libraries and their resultant unfairness to American authors, claimed the situation simply "did not tend to enourage literary production in the United States, and was one of the main reasons for the strenuous efforts made by American authors and publishers to procure international copyright."[112] Even the piratical publishers realized their heyday was coming to an end. After newsdealers returned 1,200,000 unsold copies of the *Seaside Library* to George Munro in 1883,[113] *Lovell's Library*, *Munro's Library*, and *Harper's Franklin Square Library* gave Munro "a good run for his money."[114] As competition among the cheap publishers grew even fiercer, Munro halved prices on the *Seaside Library*, hoping increased sales would follow, but they did not. In 1886 news and book dealers, who also had the privilege of returning at the low second-class periodical rate, unsold, unwanted libraries to publishers after six months, added an additional 1,500 titles to the already over-long list of libraries published.[115]

That year *Publishers' Weekly* reported: "The literary pirates of New York have so savagely cut one another's throats that the loss of blood seems likely to kill most of them . . . Every foreign novel, no matter whether there was a reasonable chance or not that it would have any sale, has been grabbed at the earliest possible moment by three to six of the 'Library' publishing firms. . . . Now rumors are afloat of insolvencies and impending bankruptcies."[116] So over-burdened was the market that Charles Dudley Warner, writing in *Harper's*, remarked: "For the price of a box of strawberries or a banana, you can buy the immortal works of the greatest genius of all time in fiction, poetry, philosophy, or science."[117]

Two years later *Forum* reported that once again "some million copies" of the *Seaside Library* had been returned to George Munro.[118] Although Munro had once maintained that "foreign authors were a greedy lot and undeserving of payment for their writings," he now "conveniently" hoped for copyright legislation.[119] "There is no money any longer in publishing cheap reprints unless the publisher owns the copyright," Munro asserted. "Our own interests demand a copyright bill. And I can say that my ideas are shared by all the cheap reprint houses of this city."[120]

In 1888, the final and decisive push for international copyright legislation began. Members of the clergy, including the Reverend Henry Van Dyke, pastor of the old Brick Presbyterian Church on New York's fashionable Fifth Avenue, added their voices in support of the movement. Addressing his congregation on "The National Sin of Literary Piracy," Van Dyke argued that piracy had the same effect "upon the moral sense of the Nation . . . as that produced upon the moral sense of the boy if his father told him, 'My son, it is a sin to steal a pin, but it is not a sin to steal a book from an Englishman.'"[121] By the year's end, the *American Bookseller*, citing an array of publishers who had recently attended a dinner at Delmonico's at the invitation of the Authors' Copyright League, reported that American publishers "are practically a unit on the question of International Copyright."[122] Always one who enjoyed adding a final word, John Lovell insisted righteously in 1890, "As the publisher or controlling the principal series of reprints and copyright works . . . I am in a position to state that whatever opposition has been developed against the Copyright bill, does not come from the publishers of the cheap reprints of foreign books."[123]

LOVELL'S BOOK TRUST

Lovell was certainly by then the spokesman for library publishers. He had, in fact, either rented their book plates or bought most of them out by 1890. In a final effort to end the cutthroat price slashing that threatened to decimate the library business, Lovell had started two years earlier to organize a book trust, a gigantic organization of publishers of cheap paperbook reprints. He purchased *Munro's Library* from Norman Munro in 1888. The following year Lovell and George Munro agreed that Munro would rent the *Seaside Library* plates to Lovell for $50,000 a year, giving Lovell the option to buy them for a million dollars within three years.[124] Then Lovell grabbed up the plates of Pollard and Moss for $51,000. Like the rest of the trade, Holt, Peterson, Rand McNally, and Harper were invited to join the trust, but they declined.[125] Undaunted, Lovell persevered and secured the plates of uncopyrighted works—by either renting or buying them—from fifteen other companies. Lovell and his supporters "have gone tooth and nail to capture the business," the press reported.[126]

Once in control of the plates for cheap reprint editions from eighteen publishing firms, Lovell realized he needed more capital in order to dominate the cheap book publishing business on a national scale. His next step was to transform his own publishing company into a new one, the United States Book Company, which was incorporated under New Jersey law on July 8, 1890, with a reported capital of about three and a half million dollars.[127] After years of throat cutting, explained the *New York Herald*, "A book publishers' trust is the latest thing on deck . . . small men tremble lest they be wiped from the face of the earth. Every one of the publishers of English reprints with a capital less than $1,000,000 is hesitating between fight and capitulation."[128]

Gradually, other publishers who reprinted books cheaply and who had earlier declined to listen to Lovell's scheme to raise and to standardize prices instead of killing each other off, began to accept his offer to turn over to him their stock and book plates of their cheap reprint editions.[129] A short time after the new trust organized, Lovell made arrangements with several more cheap reprinters to cease for a. time publishing certain lines of their noncopyright books.[130] By March 1890, Lovell reported he controlled over three-fourths of the annual production of paperback books. The regular trade generally regarded the book trust favorably throughout the year. *Publishers' Weekly* reflected the optimism, characterizing the trust as "one of the best things that has happened to the book trade in years—provided the combination *does* as fairly as it talks and can hold out long enough."[131] Others, however, referred to it cynically. The press inquired, "Shall there be no more cakes and ale, now that these rapacious publishers have become virtuous?"

The libraries continued for a few years, but when the Platt-Simmonds Act of 1891, the international copyright decision in the United States that governed American publishers, became effective, it sounded their death knell. Lovell's book trust went bankrupt by the end of 1893. Although *Publishers' Weekly* faulted Lovell for its failure, others disagreed.[132] Lovell, one admirer reasoned, was "a regular Svengali in business," "a genius of finance," one to whom "the loss of a million or two of other people's money is merely an episode in his career."[133] To the delight of the regular trade, *Publishers' Weekly* reported "an almost entire cessation of the cheap and undesirable fiction—French and English—appropriated by piratical publishers and printed in villainous typography on worse paper in ten, fifteen, and twenty-five cent 'libraries.'"[134] Despite favorable words in support of international copyright, the actions of publishers like the Munros and Lovell, who kept stealing foreign works to reprint, had helped bring the law into effect. The *Dictionary of American Biography* observed of Munro, "Though his reprints undoubtedly brought to the masses cheap and, at the same time, good reading material, they also hastened the passage of the international copyright law, when the more dignified publishers at last arrayed themselves in favor of the copyright side."[135]

At long last, gone forever were the days when regular publishers confronted the pirates only to hear their attorneys seriously exclaim: "But we deny the stealing in toto. The words of Homer, Virgil, Dante, Cervantes, Moliere, Goethe, Shakespeare, Milton, Spenser, and all the other immortal thinkers of the past, are the free inheritance of the world, in which we have an equal share. As well charge us with theft of sunshine when we appropriate it, because it has first flooded the eastern hemisphere with its effulgence before it has lightened our land, as with the theft of literature because we avail ourselves of its beneficial influence under existing laws."[136]

CONCLUSION

The cheap library movement—scorned though it was—changed the publishing trade in significant ways. As a result of it, regular publishers recognized the book as an economic commodity, they redefined production to accomodate different class markets, and they established popular literature as a distinct market category. In 1886 the *American Bookseller* aptly described this new direction for publishers:

Popular literature in the true sense of the word, as literature intended for the people and bought by the people, must of necessity be cheap in the first place, and, in the second place, must be formed of books which appeal to the largest possible number of readers. The publisher of such literature cannot rely on wealthy bibliophiles with a craze for tall copies, uncut edges, and splendid bindings, nor on collectors of special libraries, nor on any single class of purchasers; he must produce what the great public will read. As this great public desires to read chiefly for amusement, the works such a publisher issues are almost all tales and stories, with a few religious works, and possibly a cook-book or two. In the tales there is considerable mixture, from works of world-wide reputation to stories that are never heard of in fashionable society; but in all there is plenty of action, lots of mystery, and the end invariably is that virtue is rewarded and vice punished. The popular taste demands, in all cases, poetical justice.[137]

The regular trade's struggle with the piratical reprint publishers had been long and hard, the scorning deep and divisive, yet out of the upheaval emerged this fuller understanding of the people's need for cheap and popular books.

NOTES

The author expresses appreciation to Kathleen Chamberlain for her discerning comments and questions on an early draft of this paper and to Deidre Johnson for her invaluable insights, painstaking editing, and stimulating critiques throughout its writing.

1. William Dean Howells, *The Rise of Silas Lapham* (New York: The New American Library of World Literature, Inc., 1963), 103.

2. According to the bibliographic listings by Edward T. LeBlanc, the three editions of the *Seaside Library* published by George Munro were: the Ordinary edition, quarto format, (1877–86), 2,081 issues; and two paperbook formats: the Pocket Edition, (1883–1905), 2,544 issues; and the Twenty-Five Cent edition, (1885–90s), 400 issues. *Middlemarch* was published in the Ordinary Edition, no. 70, 1877, in the Pocket Edition, no. 31, 1883, and in the Twenty-Five Cent edition, no. 180, circa 1887. *Daniel Deronda* appeared in the Ordinary Edition, no. 80, 1877, and in the Pocket Edition, no. 34, 1883. A double number of the Ordinary Edition cost twenty cents; in the paperbook formats, the novels appeared in two parts, each costing twenty or twenty-five cents. All the bibliographic listings by Edward T. LeBlanc cited in this chapter are photocopied.

3. Frank E. Comparato, *Books for the Millions* (Harrisburg, PA: The Stackpole Company, 1971), 124.

4. Edward T. LeBlanc to the author, September 15, 1992. According to LeBlanc, there were approximately 450 different libraries, as opposed to approximately 80 story papers, and about 360 series of dime novels during the period under study. Publishers such as Arthur Westbrook and Street and Smith reissued earlier series in the 1920s and early 1930s.

5. According to the bibliographic listings by Edward T. LeBlanc for the following libraries, the works mentioned appeared in these publications: *Gulliver's Travels*, *Lovell's Library*, no. 68; *David Copperfield*, *Munro's Library*, no. 38; *Don Quixote*, *Seaside Library*, no. 691, and *Lovell's Library*, no. 417; *Les Miserables*, *Seaside Library*, nos. 262–65; *The Iliad*, *Seaside Library*, no. 1649; the *Odyssey*, *Seaside Library*, no. 1670, and *Lovell's Library*, no. 391. Citations from the *Seaside Library* refer to George Munro's Ordinary Edition, and those from *Munro's Library* refer to Norman Munro's Pocket Edition.

6. With the exception of one mention of a "lending library," the words "library" and "libraries" throughout this essay refer to the paper-covered publications that are the topic of this chapter.

7. The 1874 date has been accepted here because in a letter to *Publishers' Weekly*, dated July 2, 1877, Donnelley, Loyd and Company state, "[T]he *Lakeside Library* was carried [in the mails] for three years as a regular periodical." See Donnelley, Loyd and Company to *Publishers' Weekly* in "Post-Office Perplexities," *Publishers' Weekly* 11 (1877): 74.

8. Raymond Howard Shove, *Cheap Book Production in the United States, 1870 to 1891* (Urbana: University of Illinois Library, 1937), 6.

9. John Tebbel, *The Expansion of an Industry, 1815–1919*, vol. 2 in *A History of Book Publishing in the United States* (New York: R.R. Bowker Co., 1972–81), 489. All references to Tebbel in this chapter refer to volume 2.

10. *Publishers' Weekly* 11 (1877): 426.

11. "George Munro," *Biographer* 1 (May 1883): 20–21.

12. According to LeBlanc's bibliographic listing of "The Seaside Library, Ordinary Edition," *The Revised New Testament* appeared in two parts of no. 1000 of the *Seaside Library*, issued on May 21 and May 23, 1881.

13. *Biographer* 1 (May 1883): 21 and 19, respectively.

14. J. Henry Harper, *The House of Harper: A Century of Publishing in Franklin Square* (New York and London: Harper & Brothers, 1912), 447.

15. Tebbel, 491.

16. Edward T. LeBlanc, "900 Series Titles for the Dime Novel Publishing World Research Guide," May 1996, photocopy.

17. *Publishers' Weekly* 12 (1877): 363–64.

18. Shove, 5.

19. Shove, 7.

20. "A Virtuous Old Pirate,"*Journalist* 1 (1884): 2.

21. Shove, 74. Although Shove spells the company name "Donnelley Lloyd and Company," the firm used "Loyd" on its masthead of the *Lakeside Library* and in its correspondence to *Publishers' Weekly*.

22. Shove, 10.

23. LeBlanc's bibliographic listing of "Harper's Franklin Square Library" reports Harper's changed the series' name to *Harper's Franklin Square Library* on November 25, 1881, with number 215. All dates and number of issues known, are reported in LeBlanc's bibliographic listings for "Harper's Franklin Square Library," "Seaside Library," Ordinary Edition," "Lovell's Library," and "Munro's Library, Pocket Edition."

24. "Cheap Libraries," *Seaside* 1 (1882): 35; quoting *New York Evening Express*, n.d.

25. *Publishers' Weekly* 7 (1875): 56.

26. "International Copyright. The Copyright Controversy," *Publishers' Weekly* 22 (1882): 867.

27. Eugene Exman, *The House of Harper* (New York: Harper & Row, 1967), 50.

28. John W. Lovell, Letter to the Editor, *Publishers' Weekly* 15 (1879): 471.

29. "The Cheap Libraries,"*Publishers' Weekly* 12 (1877): 397.

30. Harper, 446.

31. "The Spring Outlook,"*Publishers' Weekly* 15 (1879): 342.

32. Comparato, 124; "Troubles of Literary Pirates," *Publishers' Weekly* 30 (1886): 555–56.

33. "A Virtuous Old Pirate," *Journalist* 1 (1884): 2.

34. "The Chicago Pirates," "Letter to the Editor of the *London Times*, by Two English Novelists," *Publishers' Weekly* 18 (1880): 265.

35. "'Ouida' on Anglo-American Copyright," *American Bookseller* 11 (1881): 199.

36. "International Copyright," *Publishers' Weekly* 24 (1883): 165.

37. "The Chicago Pirates,"*Publishers' Weekly* 18 (1880): 265.

38. "A Shabby Piracy," *Publishers' Weekly* 12 (1877): 490.

39. "Cheap Books," *Publishers' Weekly* 17 (1880): 561. The lines next quoted are also from this source.

40. "The Spring Outlook," *Publishers' Weekly* 19 (1881): 335; the next quotation is also from this source.

41. Shove, 21.

42. "The Postal Bill as Passed," *Publishers' Weekly* 15 (1879): 280–81.

43. "Periodicals vs. Books," *Publishers' Weekly* 27 (1885): 711. See also Lydia C. Schurman, "Those Famous American Periodicals—The Bible, *The Odyssey* and *Paradise Lost*—or, the Great Second-Class Mail Swindle," *Publishing History* (40) 1996: 33–52.

44. Charles Devens to David M. Key, dated July 28, 1877, *Official Opinions of the Attorneys-General of the United States* (Washington: W.H. & O.H. Morrison, 1880) 15 (1877): 346.

45. These were called twelvemos or duodecimos. While the original library format had been the quarto, made up of printers' sheets that measured around 9 by 12 inches and were folded into four leaves or eight pages, the twelvemos measured approximately 5 by 7 1/2 inches, and the printers' sheets were folded into twelve leaves.

46. Shove, 13.

47. "Second-Class Postage on Books," *Publishers' Weekly* 38 (1890): 126.

48. According to the bibliographic listing of Edward T. LeBlanc for *Harper's Franklin Square Library*, the Bible appeared in *The Revised Version of the Old Testament* in four parts: numbers 472, 474, 476, and 478. LeBlanc's bibliographic listing of the *Seaside Library*, Ordinary Edition, indicates the *Revised New Testament*, appeared in number 1000. *Stormonth's English Dictionary—Pronouncing, Etymological, and Explanatory—Embracing Scientific, Familiar, and Other Terms, and Many Old English Words* by James Stormonth was published in *Harper's Franklin Square Library*, numbers 393, 395, 397, 399, 401, 403, 405, 407, 410, 413, 417, 419, 424, 426, 428, 431, 432, 434, 437, 439, 441, 443, and 445.

49. Eugene H. Loud, "Second-Class Matter," dated February 5, 1896, to the Committee of the Whole House [of Representatives], Report No. 260: 4, 54th Congress, 1st Session.

50. Harper & Brothers to A.D.F. Randolph, undated, [February 1879] in J. Henry Harper, 446.

51. Tebbel, 506.

52. "Trade Notes,"*American Bookseller* 27 (1890): 106.

53. Shove, 41; Tebbel, 487.

54. Tebbel, 487.

55. "International Copyright," *American Bookseller* 23 (1888): 6.

56. "Why Publishers Fail," *New York Commercial*, n.p. n.d., in Adolph Growoll, *American Book Trade History*, original scrapbook, vol.1: 83.

57. Edward T. LeBlanc, bibliographic listing "Macy's Popular Star Novels."

58. *Life,* 18 (10 September 1891):130.

59. Information on the Jordan Marsh department store publications is from Edward T. LeBlanc's bibliographical listings "J.M. & Co's Popular Standard Novels," and "Seaside Library." The latter was a publication similar to Munro's *Seaside Library*, Twenty-Five Cent edition, and possibly was published through some arrangement with George Munro & Sons.

60. *Publishers' Weekly* 27 (1885): 8; the article, "Mr. Wanamaker's Book Business," is reprinted from a signed article by John Wanamaker in the advertising columns of the *Philadelphia Press*, 27 December 1884: n.p.

61. Herbert Adams Gibbons, *John Wanamaker* (New York: Harper & Brothers, 1926), vol.1, 202.

62. Edward T. LeBlanc, bibliographical listing "Keystone Library." Although the *Keystone Library* appeared without the name of a publisher, the words "Sold by John Wanamaker, Philadelphia," Le Blanc says, indicate Wanamaker was responsible for the library's publication. The next quotation from the publisher's blurb is also from this source.

63. "Mr. Wanamaker's Book Business," *Publishers' Weekly* 27 (1885): 8.

64. "The Tribulations of the Pirate," *Publishers' Weekly* 32 (1887): 196.

65. Harper, 113.

66. Shove, 7.

67. See Appendix for listing of their libraries.

68. Although their series prices ranged from ten cents to a dollar, most often they ranged from thirty-five to sixty cents. Standard publishers also issued series in cloth-bound editions that usually cost $1.75.

69. "International Copyright," *Publishers' Weekly* 22 (1882): 867.

70. Harper, 447.

71. Ellen B. Ballou, *The Building of the House: Houghton Mifflin's Formative Years* (Boston: Houghton Mifflin, 1970): 320.

72. Publishers' comments in the remainder of the paragraph may be found in the order referred to: T.W. Speight, *A Barren Title, Harper's Handy Series*, no. 38, November 27, 1885; R.D. Blackmore, *Cripps the Carrier*, no. 121, *Manhattan Library*, no. 121, back cover, August 3, 1895, A.L. Burt, publisher; Mary Hallock Foote, *The Led-Horse Claim, Ticknor's Paper Series of Choice Reading*, no. 32, April 7, 1888; Julian Hawthorne, *Mrs. Gainsborough's Diamonds, Appleton's New Handy-Volume Series*, no. 14, 1878, inside front cover; Robert Louis Stevenson and Fanny Van De Grit Stevenson, *The Dynamiter, Seaside Library*, Pocket Edition, no. 855, September 13, 1886, advertisement section at the end of the book; Lord Bulwer Lytton, *Leila or the Siege of Granada, Lovell's Library*, no. 12, June 15, 1882, inside page.

73. "International Copyright: Pros and Cons," *Publishers' Weekly* 33 (1888): 45.

74. "Literary and Trade Notes," *Publishers' Weekly* 14 (1878): 124.

75. Harper, 445.

76. *Publishers' Weekly* 15 (1879): 340.

77. "Starving the Book-Trade," *Publishers' Weekly* 26 (1884): 643.

78. Harper, 447.

79. Letter from Harper & Brothers to William Blackwood and Sons, August 21, 1883, Reel 2, A 5: 303–4, Microfilm of the Archives of Harper & Brothers, 1817–1914.

80. Harper & Brothers to William Dean Howells, August 3, 1892, Reel 2, A 6: 483, Microfilm of the Archives of Harper & Brothers, 1817–1914. The numbers of Howells' novels and their price when they appeared in the *Franklin Square Library* are as follows: *The Quality of Mercy*, no. 726, 75¢; *An Imperative Duty*, no. 732, 50¢; *April Hopes*, no. 699, 75¢; *A Shadow of a Dream*, no. 672, 50¢; and *A Hazard of New Fortune*, no. 661, 75¢, and no. 693, $1.00.

81. "Harper and Brothers' Reply to Mr. Gilbert," dated 15 February 1886, *Publishers' Weekly* 29 (1886): 360.

82. T.B. Peterson & Brothers to the Editor of *Publishers' Weekly*, "The Postal Rate on Books," *Publishers' Weekly* 33 (1888): 422. The quotations in the next sentence are also from this source.

83. *Publishers' Weekly* 38 (1890): 132–33.

84. "Petersons' and Pound Rates," *Newsdealer* 1 (September 1890): 188.

85. See, for example, entry for *Peterson's Twenty-Five Cent Series* in "Wholesale Price and Returnable List of Periodicals Commonly Handled by Newsdealers," *Book and News-Dealer* 4 (1892): 377.

86. In contrast to T.B. Peterson and G. Putnam's Sons, other regular publishers who mailed some of their paper-covered publications at low second-class rates included: D. Appleton & Company, Harper & Brothers, Henry Holt, Houghton Mifflin, and J.B. Lippincott.

87. Remarks of A.R. Spofford, Librarian of Congress, in "Cheap Literature in the Mails, Statements before the Senate Committee on Post-Offices and Post-Roads in Regard to the Privileges Accorded the Publishers of Cheap Literature," Monday, April 9, 1888, 6. See also the author's essay, "The Librarian of Congress Argues against Cheap Novels Getting Low Postal Rates," in *Pioneers, Passionate Ladies, and Private Eyes: Dime Novels, Series Books, and Paperbacks*, eds. Larry E. Sullivan and Lydia Cushman Schurman (New York and London: The Haworth Press, 1997), 59–71.

88. Spofford, 9.

89. Spofford, 7.

90. Spofford, 9–10.

91. Spofford, 8.

92. "Second-Class Mail Matter," *Publishers' Weekly* 60 (1901): 87.

93. "Communications in Favor of Excluding Libraries from Second-Class Mail Privileges," *Publishers' Weekly* 65 (1904): 1256; quoting the *Philadelphia Public Ledger*, n.d.

94. *The Washington Law Reporter* 32 (1904): 241.

95. "The Cheap Libraries. "*Publishers' Weekly* 12 (1877): 396.

96. Shove 9; quoting the *Atlantic Monthly* 42 (1878): 370–71.

97. "What New Yorkers Read," *Publishers' Weekly* 22 (1882): 142.

98. Communications, "The Mission of the 'Cheap' Libraries," Letter from "Traveller," from Atlantic City, dated 14 May 1879, *Publishers' Weekly* 15 (1879): 564.

99. "The Typothetae at Dinner," *Publishers' Weekly* 31 (1887): 92.

100. Henry Holt to the Editor, "On the Decline of the Book-Buying Habit," *Publishers' Weekly* 32 (1887): 18–19.

101. Harper, 115. The next quotation is also from this source.

102. "Another View of the Postal Rates," *American Bookseller* 23 (1888): 165.

103. Spofford, 10.

104. Spofford, 9; the next quotation is also from this source.

105. "Cheap Books," *Publishers' Weekly* 23 (1883): 522.

106. "The Tribulations of the Pirate," *Publishers' Weekly* 32 (1887): 196.

107. Donn Piatt, "Cheap Literature in the Mails," 4.

108. "Trade Syndicates," *American Bookseller* 27 (1890): 138.

109. Shove, 12.

110. Shove, 11.

111. Tebbel, 506.

112. Harper, 115.

113. Shove, 16.

114. Shove, 62.

115. Tebbel, 485.

116. "Troubles of Literary Pirates," *Publishers' Weekly* 30 (1886): 555–56.

117. *Harper's Magazine* 73 (1886): 807.

118. Shove, 63.

119. Shove, 37.

120. Shove, 63.

121. "International Copyright in the Pulpit," *Publishers' Weekly* 33 (1888): 182–83.

122. "International Copyright," *American Bookseller* 23 (1888): 6.

123. J.W. Lovell on International Copyright and the Book Trust," *American Bookseller* 27 (1890): 240.

124. "Library Publishers at Work on a Trust," *New York Herald*, 7 February 1890: 3.

125. "The 'Library' Publishers' 'Combine.'" *Publishers' Weekly* 37 (1890): 275; also *Publishers' Weekly* 37 (1890): 557.

126. *New York Herald*, 7 February 1890: 3.

127. Shove, 102.

128. *New York Herald*, 7 February 1890: 3.

129. Shove, 45.

130. "The 'Library' Publishers' Combination," *Publishers' Weekly* 37 (1890): 354 and Shove, 103.

131. Shove, 103. The following quotation is also from this citation.

132. Shove, 105.

133. Adolph Growoll, *American Book Trade History*, original scrapbook, vol.12: 56.

134. *Publishers' Weekly* 44 (1893): 1063–64.

135. Oliver W. Holmes, "George Munro," in the *Dictionary of American Biography*, 1934, ed. Dumas Malone (New York: Charles Scribner's Sons, 1928–[58]), vol. 13: 332.

136. "International Copyright," *American Bookseller* 27 (1890): 234.

137. "Contributions to Trade History. No. 31. J.S. Ogilvie & Co." *American Bookseller* 19 (1886): 305.

APPENDIX

LIBRARIES PUBLISHED BY SOME REPRESENTATIVE REGULAR TRADE PUBLISHERS

All information in this Appendix is based on the bibliographical listings by Edward T. LeBlanc for each series listed. The Issues column means the highest number of a particular series seen or advertised.

Publisher *Library*	Date	Issues	Price

D. Appleton & Co.

	Date	Issues	Price
Appleton's Illustrated Library of Romance	1877	23	$1
Appleton's Library of American Fiction	1878	19	50¢–$1
Appleton's New Handy-Volume Series	1878–80	69	15¢–60¢
Appleton's Town and Country Library	1888–1901	312	50¢
Collection of Foreign Authors	1878	10	50¢-60¢
Library of Choice Novels	1875–77	57	50¢–$1.25
New Twenty-Five Cent Series	1887	1	25¢

P.F. Collier

	Date	Issues	Price
Once a Week Library	1889–94	298	20¢–50¢

Harper & Brothers

	Date	Issues	Price
Harper's Franklin Square Library	1878–93	736	10¢–20¢
Harper's Half-Hour Series	1877	67	15¢–25¢
Harper's Handy Series	1885	45	25¢
Harper's Select Fiction	1900	1	50¢

Henry Holt

Leisure Moments Series	1883	54	30¢

Houghton Mifflin

Riverside Literature Series	1886–1904	278	15¢–50¢
Riverside Paper Series	1889–97	78	15¢–50¢

J.B. Lippincott

American Novels	1880s	ca12	Unknown
Lippincott's Magazine Series of American Copyright Novels	1880s–90	264	25¢
Lippincott's Series of Select Novels	1885–1902	248	25¢–50¢

T.B. Peterson & Brothers

Peterson's Series of Choice Fiction [Also titled and advertised as *Peterson's 25 Cent Series* and later as *Peterson's New 25¢ Series*]	ca1875–88	ca52	25¢

G.P. Putnam's Sons

Hudson Library	1895–96	14	50¢
Knickerbocker Novels	1878	15	50¢
TransAtlantic Novels	1880–82	20	60¢
University Series	ca1886	ca4	50¢

Rand McNally

Globe Library	1886–02	391	$7 per year
Oriental Library	1899–1904	ca82	25¢
Rialto Series	ca1890–98	ca84	50¢

Ticknor and Field

Ticknor's Paper Series of Choice Reading	1887–89	58	50¢

   D. Appleton & Company had issued three earlier paper-covered series, and Harper and Lippincott had each issued one from 1867 to 1870 before the *Lakeside Library* appeared. These earlier publications were distinct from the later libraries, however, because they varied in size and were never distributed in the low second-class mail rates (which became effective in 1879). According to the bibliographical listings by Edward T. LeBlanc for the series listed below, these early series were:

D. Appleton & Co.

Appleton's Edition of the Waverly Novels	1868–69	25	25¢
Appleton's Works of Charles Dickens	1868–69	17	15¢–35¢
Popular Edition of Dickens [This series was the same as *Appleton's Works of Charles Dickens* except it had 18 instead of 17 issues.]	1869	18	15¢–35¢

Harper & Brothers

Library of Select Novels	1843–85	611	20¢–90¢

J.B. Lippincott

Good Words	1867–70	35	25¢

"The ragtag and bobtail of the fiction parade": Pulp Magazines and the Literary Marketplace

Erin A. Smith

In 1936, *American Mercury* ran an article by an anonymous writer for pulp magazines called "A Penny a Word," an exposé of this literary underworld for *American Mercury*'s upscale readers. This pulp writer had little to say in defense of his profession, his readers, or the venues in which his fiction appeared. He characterized pulp magazines as a blatantly commercial aesthetic wasteland that catered to an audience of the lowest sort. His heartfelt confession of complicity was at the center of the article: "I myself have become a dependable purveyor to those 5 million morons who pay a few nickels each month for their mechanized dreams. I am one of the camp followers of the pulp-writing profession, the ragtag and bobtail of the fiction parade, who, for bare subsistence, scavage [*sic*] in the garbage heaps of literature."[1] Although many pulp writers and editors protested the denigration of their magazines, their readers, and their craft, this attitude was nonetheless a cultural commonplace. Pulp magazines—named for the untrimmed, rough wood-pulp paper on which they were printed—were unambiguously "trash," cheaply produced periodicals whose pages often fell apart after a reading or two.[2] Roughly 200 pulp titles crowded newsstands during their heyday in the 1920s, 1930s, and 1940s, their garish covers competing for the attention of their ten to twenty million regular readers.[3] Although their lurid covers often featured scenes of sex or violence, these seven-by-ten-inch magazines were remarkably unassuming on the inside. They consisted largely of column after column of uninterrupted, densely packed print, punctuated only by a rare pen-and-ink line drawing and a few pages of ads clustered at the front and back. From their origin in 1896 to their demise in 1953, pulp magazines provided roughly 130 pages of stories for between five and twenty-five cents, a great deal of fiction for the money.

The pulps were direct descendants of nineteenth-century dime novels published for the urban working classes between the 1860s and World War I by companies like Beadle & Adams and Street & Smith. Frank Munsey's *Argosy,* the first pulp magazine, competed for this same audience until changes in postal regulations made it prohibitively expensive to distribute dime novels through the mail. As a consequence, many dime novel publishers simply repackaged their cheap fiction as pulp magazines, continuing to feature favorite series characters like Nick Carter or Buffalo Bill.[4] Street & Smith, the largest dime novel publisher, switched over to pulp format in 1915. The pulp magazine business boomed between the wars, driven by expanding levels of literacy and the falling production costs. There were twenty to twenty-five pulp magazines in circulation before World War I, but well over 100 by the 1930s.[5] *Black Mask,* perhaps the best known of the pulps, was founded in 1920 during this phenomenal period of growth. Well into the twentieth century, pulp magazines eschewed heavy use of advertising and subscription sales, continuing to rely on low production costs and newsstand sales to stay in business.[6]

"Respectable" magazines like *American Mercury* were printed on the more expensive "slick" paper necessary for quality reproduction of images for their handsome illustrations and glossy ads. Until the late nineteenth century, only genteel, well-educated readers bought magazines, learning about art, literature, European travel, and manners from *Century, Harper's,* and *Scribner's*—whose twenty-five- or thirty-five-cent cover price placed them beyond the means of most Americans. In 1893, Frank Munsey inaugurated the "magazine revolution" by slashing the price of *Munsey's Magazine* from twenty-five cents to ten cents. The low price attracted a new mass audience large enough to interest advertisers, who—in turn—subsidized the substantial costs of production.[7] Munsey's new strategy—low price, large circulation, lots of advertising—served a whole generation of media entrepreneurs including S.S. McClure, John Brisben Walker, George Horace Lorimer, Cyrus H.K. Curtis, and Edward Bok. By cutting prices and tailoring editorial content for a general audience, *McClure's, Cosmopolitan, Munsey's, Ladies' Home Journal,* and *Saturday Evening Post* achieved unprecedented levels of circulation, most of it through subscription.[8]

The pulps were completely untouched by this "magazine revolution," remaining the same cheaply produced, comparatively ad-free, small-circulation magazines they had always been. Why would this residual form of mass culture have motivated such persistent scorn? How was it related to the dominance of slick-paper magazines that targeted middle-class readers? How did pulp writers, editors, and readers negotiate the cultural hierarchy that placed their livelihood and leisure definitively outside the mainstream?

PRODUCING PULP FICTION

Pulp fiction was scorned in part because the pulps' notion of authorship differed from the the liberal model prevailing in more self-consciously literary circles. While modernist writers imagined themselves as lone artists creating expressions of their individual talent, pulp writers saw themselves as manufacturers, paid for making a product (prose) in much the same way workers in factories and on assembly lines were.[9] Pulp writer Erle Stanley Gardner called himself "a fiction factory," explaining that he was willing to do endless revisions to get his stories ("merchandise") to his editor's ("wholesaler's") specifications.[10] Such production metaphors fill his letters. He urged his editor at *Argosy,* "Let me know what you want and I'll try to manufacture something right to order."[11]

Pulp writers were piece workers, paid for the quantity of prose they produced rather than for completed works of literature. Rates ranged from one to five cents a word, which required steady, rapid production to make a decent living. "You had to keep them coming all the time . . . otherwise you'd starve," claimed veteran pulp writer Richard Sale.[12] Pulp writers did generate prose at astonishingly fast rates—an average of 3,000 to 5,000 words per day, although the stars did twice as much.[13] Walter Gibson, writing under the pseudonym "Maxwell Grant," churned out two 40,000-word novels a month for Street & Smith's pulp *The Shadow.*[14] Erle Stanley Gardner's diaries have little to say about the aesthetics of his fiction, but he concludes each day's entry by recording how many words he wrote and how much money it earned him.[15]

Moreover, pulp magazines often owned authors' names, requiring several authors to write under a single pseudonym or a single author to write under several names. Pulp writer Steve Fisher's stories appeared in Street & Smith's *Clues* and *The Shadow* with bylines crediting Steve Fisher, Stephen Gould, Grant Lane, and William Bogart. If several stories by an author appeared in a single issue, one or more usually appeared under a pen name. In extreme cases a lone writer cranked out an entire issue but used a different author's name for each story.[16]

Most pulp writers also lacked the university training of more self-consciously literary writers. Although some pulp magazine editors and writers were graduates of prestigious colleges, those who made their living writing for the pulps—a core of several hundred writers responsible for a disproportionately large percentage of the output—did not have this kind of education.[17] Pulp writer Frank Gruber recalled that few of his colleagues had college degrees at all, much less majors in English or journalism common for writers in mass-market magazines.[18] The pulps were clearly cast as subordinate to mainstream publishing. Many editors saw the pulps as an entry-level job in the publishing industry, a way to prove themselves before moving on to more lucrative positions with book publishers or mass-market magazines. Pulp editor Frederick Clayton defended his magazines from a 1935 attack in the *New York Times* by calling the pulps a "proving ground" for new talent, which had no chance whatsoever against the established writers preferred by the slicks.[19]

Pulp writers themselves talked about writing as work rather than an inspired form of artistic production that depended on innate talent or genius. One author, asked to discuss his work in pulp magazine *Black Mask*'s writers' column, queried, "I wonder how many writers have reached the conclusion that authorship is made up of 90% desire and tenacity, 10% imagination and 0% genius?" Another added, "I've long ago lost the twin foolish ideas that fiction is done by inspiration and that it isn't work."[20] Authors did not talk about their muses, but instead about the anxious pacing, talking to themselves, chewing their nails, and locking themselves up at the typewriter six to ten hours a day that the writing life required.[21] Writer Paul Ernst told Street & Smith's *Clues* about his efforts to dream stories in his sleep after a bad bout of writer's block (which could threaten a pulp writer with bankruptcy in no time at all). This form of inspiration was so physically destructive (Ernst lost over twenty pounds in a very short time) that he began to ignore the dreams in hopes of returning to his old, workman-like ways of writing.[22] The advertisements in pulp magazines also offered a model of cultural production that called attention to its craftsman-like nature. Ads offering training in journalism and drawing emphasized that no special "gift," "talent," or "genius" was necessary; most writers and illustrators were relative unknowns whose skills were all acquired through practice.[23] One writer summed it up in the *Black Mask* column "Our Readers' Private Corner": "How do I work at my fiction generally? Simply go at it every morning like any man at his work."[24] Clearly, the pulps made no distinction between cultural production and any other kind of production, between the realms of art and life. That is to say that pulp writers refused the distinction between the aesthetic and the everyday that Pierre Bourdieu argues is at the center of the bourgeois world-view.[25]

Pulp editors were consummate market researchers, behaving as though producing fiction for a mass public was little different than producing soap or razor blades. They were forever surveying their readership about their likes and dislikes in order to create a more marketable product.[26] Almost all of the pulps had columns of reader letters, ran periodic surveys of readers, or included coupons readers could return ranking their favorite stories and authors in each issue. To encourage readers to take part, the company often offered free issues of its other pulps for each response. In 1924, pulp editor Phil Cody published a "Notice to Our Readers" in which he made all of *Black Mask*'s readers associate editors. Telling them they had approximately 125 pages to dispose of as they saw fit, he urged them to mail in a proposal for their ideal edition of *Black Mask*—favorite authors, stories, types of stories, departments, ideal length of features, favorite magazines they would like *Black Mask* to resemble, and so on. He concluded this invitation: "This is your magazine; you are on its editorial staff; get on the job!"[27] In 1930, his successor at the editorial helm, Joseph Thompson Shaw, began a column in which readers and writers could exchange ideas, a department that grew out of reader demands made in letters over the years. At the end of the first column, Shaw asked, "Does she get the gas or does she get the brake? . . . It's up to you . . . Just say what you want . . . We want only to please."[28]

Street & Smith's *Crime Busters* took its market research even further. Each month it dedicated two to four pages to analyzing reader rankings of stories in the previous month's issue. The editors used text and graphics to demonstrate how they had learned from consumer feedback to increase the number of satisfied readers with each successive issue. Moreover, readers did not just exercise their rights through selection; *Crime Busters* tried to encourage its writers to tailor their stories to reader specifications: "We give each of our authors complete returns on the ballots, and every one gets all remarks and comments on his own story in detail, as well as a general summary of all other remarks and suggestions. We have created a keen rivalry among the authors, all seeking to land on the top when the ballots are counted. That all means that they strive to give you the very best they've got."[29]

Crime Busters even surveyed readers on the advertising that best met their needs. Readers would receive a free magazine in exchange for answering questions about their age, occupation, sex, marital status, weekly salary, family members' ages, and a variety of consumer data. *Crime Busters* wanted to know if readers owned or rented their homes, what kind of cars they drove, the brands of toothpaste, razor blades, shaving cream, and hair tonic they used, and the kinds of cigarettes, scotch, beer, or whiskey they preferred.[30]

Some writers conducted their own market research. Erle Stanley Gardner employed a disabled veteran in a VA hospital to record comments from fellow residents about stories in the pulp magazines they regularly read.[31] Gardner believed letters from readers were "about the best opportunity, both an editor and an author have, of checking up on the popularity of a story."[32] He repeatedly asked Joseph Thompson Shaw, the editor of *Black Mask,* to run mail-in ballots for readers to vote on favorite authors and stories.[33] The lack of reliable data on reader desires was, in fact, an endless source of frustration for him: "sitting out here in the sticks all I can do is get hunches, and sometimes put two and two together and make six . . . And it irritates me, for the thing that I love above all things is getting data and analyzing sales possibilities. I wish I could get more of a slant on the situation."[34]

Not only was pulp fiction conceived of as a commodity, its flow through the large companies that published it was dictated almost entirely by the laws of supply and demand. Although there were many pulp magazines with relatively small circulations, few companies published only one title. Most owned a line of magazines and quickly killed off any that became unprofitable. Pulp titles had a lower profit per issue than slick titles, so pulp publishers tended to have long lists of titles in order to earn a respectable income.[35] Street & Smith, the largest company, had approximately thirty-five pulp titles at any given time; Popular Publications, twenty to twenty-five titles. Other major players were Munsey's, Dell, Fiction House, Standard, Warner, Culture Publications, and Clayton Magazines.[36] Many editors edited as many as eight or ten pulps at a time, and the companies often shifted editors around from pulp to pulp.[37] In addition, a story purchased for one pulp quite often was transferred to another in the last-minute scramble to fill the pages of every magazine every week or month. Street & Smith regularly swapped stories back and forth from *Clues* to *Detective Story* to *Crime Busters* to *The Shadow.*[38] Publishers frequently sold advertising space in all of their pulps as a package, reporting combined circulation figures.[39]

This mass production system, in part, gave the pulps their reputation for featuring low-quality fiction. A *New York Times* editorial titled "Fiction by Volume" summed up the common interpretation: "Millions of words are written every month for the pulps. . . . A pulp editor will get [out] as many as half a dozen magazines a month. The result of this production system is inevitably an emphasis on quantity rather than quality."[40]

READING PULP FICTION

Another reason the pulps commanded so little respect was that their readers were widely held to be socially and economically marginal. They were working-class, young, poorly educated, and often immigrants.[41] Although pulp publisher Harold Hersey claimed there were pulp readers in all social strata, he did concede that the majority were probably manual laborers, miners, ranchers, soldiers, dockworkers, office or factory girls. One survey by Popular Publications found that the typical reader of their pulps was "a young, married man in a manual job who had limited resources and lived in an industrial town."[42] Research from the University of Chicago library school in the 1930s confirmed these class-based reading patterns.[43] One study concluded that 55 percent of the pulp magazine audience had only a grade school education, 29 percent had a high school education, 7 percent had some college, and 9 percent had college degrees. Detective and adventure pulps were read roughly ten times more often by residents of working-class neighborhoods than by middle-class suburbanites.[44] In fact, Depression-era cultural commentators lamented that workers read little else besides pulp magazines,[45] and many demoralized left-wing intellectuals—noting the abysmal sales of proletarian novels—maintained that the *real* proletarian literature was the pulp Westerns and romances huge numbers of workers actually did read.[46] In 1934 the Marxist periodical *Pen & Hammer Bulletin* went so far as to suggest that the "ideological weakness" of American workers could be attributed to their vociferous reading of pulp magazines and their slick-paper competitors.[47]

"Respectable" (middle-class) citizens had nothing good to say about this trashy reading material that captivated the lower classes. A 1935 study of reading habits of residents of a Queens, New York, neighborhood elicited all sorts of scorn for the pulps from the patrons of the public library. Very few reported reading pulp magazines, but many took the opportunity to write comments in the margin of their survey: "This trash has no place in the public library" and "God forbid."[48] Researchers in library schools of the period inevitably lamented the preponderance of pulp magazines in the reading their research subjects did, and identified the improvement of their literary tastes as a major policy goal.[49]

One of the reasons pulp magazines were so popular among the working classes was that their language was accessible to readers with little formal education. Librarians, adult educators, and reading researchers during the Depression estimated that because of restricted diffusion of advanced literacy, approximately half of American readers found books on topics that interested them too difficult in style or vocabulary.[50] This might explain why many workers reported finding the complicated prose of most proletarian novels "hard-going," preferring pulp magazines and Sunday supplements to fill their leisure hours.[51] Most readability formulas combined three variables: sentence length, word length, and word familiarity.[52] Recent assessment of the difficulty of prose in newspapers and magazines from 1920 found that *Argosy*, an all-story pulp magazine, was considerably more readable than most newspapers and elite and middlebrow magazines of the period.[53] In Gray and Leary's *What Makes a Book Readable* (1935), the authors ranked all of the pulp magazines in their sample in the "easy" category based on a readability index derived from sentence length, proportion of monosyllables, variety of vocabulary, and number of simple sentences. They even went so far as to urge authors attempting to write more accessible prose to study cheap wood-pulp magazines and second- and third-grade textbooks as models.[54]

Ads in pulp magazines also targeted working-class readers, offering them education and job training by correspondence, ways to supplement their incomes by working at home, body building programs, etiquette manuals, patent medicines, and guides to speaking and writing proper English.[55] Ads for the International Correspondence School (ICS) were representative. Harold Hersey, the publisher of dozens of pulps, claimed that ICS ad copy was "as familiar as the fiction sheets themselves."[56] Some of these ads included long testimonials from bosses about ICS training—telling how few ICS men were out of a job in spite of the Depression, how a man who spent his lunch break learning more about his job was bound to rise into executive ranks.[57] One ICS hero explained how awkward it was to be promoted over his foreman because of his correspondence training.[58] Other ads addressed workers as providers for their families: "Was this part of your marriage contract? Did you tell her that she would have to do the washing? That she would have to wear last year's clothes?"[59] Another man who had noticed that all the recent promotions at his company were ICS students made a resolution to his wife: "I've thought it out, Grace. I'm as good a man as any one of them. All I need is special training—and *I'm going to get it*. If the I.C.S. can raise other men's salaries, it can raise *mine*. If it can bring a better home with more comforts to Jim and his family, it can do it for *us*. See this coupon? It means *my* start toward a better job."[60] The ad concluded by urging the reader to join the large and growing numbers of ICS students preparing themselves for better jobs through correspondence study. The mail-in coupon at the bottom of the page listed occupations for which ICS could provide training—electricity, railways, wiring, machine shop practice, builder, draftsman, sheet metal worker, and a variety of other unambiguously working-class occupations.

Many pulps courted working-class readers by displaying the union label on their covers.[61] "This magazine produced entirely by union labor" blazed across the front cover of Street & Smith's *The Shadow* in the early 1930s. The title page of Clayton's *Clues* appealed not only to workers engaged in manufacturing, but also to the small businessmen, clerks, farmers, and professionals who were linked to them in an unstable class alliance commentators of the period called the "producing classes."[62] The "Clayton Standard" guaranteed: "That the stories therein are clean, interesting, vivid; by leading writers of the day and purchased under conditions approved by the Authors' League of America; That such magazines are manufactured in Union shops by American workmen; That each newsdealer and agent is insured a fair profit; That an intelligent censorship guards their advertising pages."[63] "Clean" stories and "intelligent censorship" were particularly important for the pulps' youngest readers. Harold Hersey characterized pulp readers as "juvenile anywhere from sixteen to sixty," and young readers were widely held to be a significant part of the pulps' audience.[64] It was also easy for librarians and cultural commentators to cast the workers, immigrants, and poorly educated readers of the pulps as metaphoric children in need of their guidance. Pulp publishers repeatedly invoked words like "clean" and "wholesome" in describing their fiction, a defense against the common charge that pulp magazines were violent, sensational, and immoral. Many pulp editors felt a special responsibility for young readers, and one went so far as to ask Erle Stanley Gardner to change the ending of a story so as not to corrupt *Black Mask*'s adolescent readers.[65]

Pulp magazines did attract some wealthier, better-educated readers. *Black Mask*, for example, published letters from doctors, lawyers, and other professional men, anxiously asserting that not *all* of their readers were marginal. Editor Shaw distinguished his "regular letter writing readers" from what he called some "darned big men around town"—bankers, professors, important businessmen—whose approval of *Black Mask*'s stories mattered more to him than the opinions of ordinary readers.[66] However, the stigma attached to reading pulp magazines in educated circles could be formidable.[67] *Vanity Fair* snidely referred to pulp readers as "those who move their lips when they read."[68] Harold Hersey maintained that college graduates "would not be caught dead" with anything as "lowbrow" as a pulp magazine.[69] Erle Stanley Gardner ran across a group of wealthy golfers who "confessed" to being readers of *Black Mask*, relating that they were often so embarrassed to ask for it at the newsstand that they whispered the request.[70] The paucity of information about pulp readers is itself evidence of their marginal economic and social position. Mass-market magazines during this period collected all sorts of data about middle-class consumers. The failure of pulp magazines to research the buying habits of their readers suggests that publishers thought pulp readers' incomes were too small to make them attractive targets for national brand advertising.

Pulp fiction, authored by hack writers paid piece rates, may have had particular appeal for working-class readers, whose own world-views were determined in part by the daily grind of production work. Authors' social and institutional situations profoundly shape their narratives, and pulp writers were no exception. The pride in hard work, speed, and productivity that a life pounding the typewriter for a few cents a word required left traces in pulp fiction, traces that would have had resonance for readers with similar experiences.[71] Because writers' lives and readers' lives resembled each other in these ways, there was a good fit between working-class world-views and the pulp fiction forms workers appropriated to express and reinforce their ways of being in the world.

THE GENDERED MARKET FOR PULPS

Pulp publisher Harold Hersey explained the appeal of the pulps to male readers this way: "One is not afflicted in the fiction magazines with an infinite variety of copy relating to female complaints and perplexities."[72] Such copy *did* afflict readers of slick-paper magazines. Because mass-market magazine publishers made their profits by selling advertising space, most slicks targeted white, middle-class women as purchasing agents for their families.[73] Pulp writers expressed similar sentiments. Frank Gruber dismissed slick-paper magazine stories, because "[m]ost of them were terribly effeminate . . . and I was more at home with the virile, masculine type of story."[74] Raymond Chandler read the pulps because they were cheap and "because I never had any taste at any time for the kind of thing which is known as women's magazines."[75]

The idea that women read slicks and men read pulps was an oversimplification. Some mass-market magazines (e.g., the *Saturday Evening Post*) did target male readers. Moreover, although pulp titles were overwhelmingly action and adventure magazines targeting men, every major pulp publisher had at least one romance pulp for women. Although there were fewer romance titles, their circulations were among the highest. As a consequence, although there were more men's pulps than women's, the numbers of male and female readers were probably equal.[76] Moreover, slick-paper magazines of the period were as likely to ridicule the female readers of pulp magazines—"girls in Pennsylvania hosiery mills and Kansas City ten-cent stores"—as the male readers—"Chicago soda-jerkers living in tenements with their mothers and three snivelling little sisters."[77]

The first pulps were general fiction magazines, but by the 1920s and 1930s there were roughly two hundred titles on highly specialized topics: gangsters, Westerns, aviation, detective stories, romance, pirates, railroads, boxing, war, football, science fiction, sea stories. Pulps were niche marketed. Street & Smith explained their marketing strategy to news dealers in a 1930 trade publication. *Detective Story* was intended for "men in all walks of life"; *Top-Notch* targeted "the up-and-coming young man"; *Wild West Weekly* was "a young chap's magazine."[78] Gender was clearly the most important demographic category. Romances were for women; the endless variety of adventure pulps, for men. *Argosy All-Story,* title aside, made it clear to contributors that the "stories of nearly any type" they solicited had to have "strong masculine appeal." "Slushy romances" were to be sent elsewhere.[79]

The evolution of the pulp *Black Mask* is representative.[80] It was one of three pulps started in 1920 by H.L. Mencken and George Jean Nathan to subsidize their *real* concern, the highbrow periodical *Smart Set.* The early issues, in fact, featured fiction from *Smart Set*'s reject pile, a clear illustration of the pulps' position as what Lee Server calls "publishing's poor, ill-bred step-child."[81] It began with the subtitle "An Illustrated Magazine of Detective, Mystery, Adventure, Romance and Spiritualism," presenting itself as offering the best stories every month in each of these categories. However, it rapidly became focused on more masculine genres. By 1926, it featured Westerns, detective stories, and general adventure, and by 1927, it was subtitled "The He-Man's Magazine." Westerns figured prominently throughout the 1920s, but in 1932 *Black Mask* went all detective. The tough-talking private eye was created in the pages of *Black Mask* in the 1920s and 1930s by writers like Carroll John Daly, Dashiell Hammett, Erle Stanley Gardner, and Raymond Chandler. *Black Mask* became the most important publishing outlet for hard-boiled detective fiction between the wars, although its most successful writers left for better-paying jobs writing for slick magazines, book publishers, and Hollywood studios.

Black Mask editorials in the 1920s and 1930s made the increasing masculinization of the magazine clear. Phil Cody, the second editor of *Black Mask,* told readers in a 1926 editorial that circulation was continuing to climb, because "*Black Mask* gives its readers more real, honest-to-jasper, he-man stuff . . . than any other magazine."[82] "He-man" is an important term, salient for its redundant gendering. Along with Cody's emphasis on the authenticity of this masculine fare—it is both "real" and "honest"—the term suggests an undercurrent of anxiety about the integrity of manliness during this period, an anxiety the all-male communities called into being by action and adventure pulps assuaged.

Captain Joseph Thompson Shaw, the editor at the helm while *Black Mask* consolidated and built its reputation for featuring the best tough-guy mysteries around, published an editorial in 1933 in which he described the ideal *Black Mask* reader with a series of phallic images: "He is vigorous-minded, hard . . . responsive to the thrill of danger, the stirring exhilaration of clean, swift, hard action . . . [he is] a man who . . . knows the song of a bullet. The soft, slithering hiss of a swift-thrown knife, the feel of hard fists, the call of courage."[83] For the modern reader, the manly editorial copy in *Black Mask* does seem anxiously overdone. *Black Mask* regularly informed readers about the manly exploits of its writers as soldiers, airmen, police officers, athletes, and adventurers. Offering further evidence that its writers were not she-men, one "Behind the Mask" column listed all the *Black Mask* writers over six feet tall, a column that irritated the 5'8" Erle Stanley Gardner no end.[84] In a society that valued men's concerns more highly than women's, *Black Mask*'s he-manliness gave it some cultural legitimacy. This legitimacy was hard for *Black Mask* to come by, since scorn for pulp magazines in general was ubiquitous.

Black Mask accommodated women as writers, editors, and readers, but not without a great deal of uneasiness. F.M. Osborne, the first editor, appeared on the masthead in the drag of her initials in order "to project a masculine image."[85] When Fanny Ellsworth, editor of the more profitable *Ranch Romances,* replaced Shaw as editor of *Black Mask* in 1936, her initials also replaced her given name on the masthead. Ellsworth's editorship was scandalous. Writer Frank Gruber explained: "A shock ran through the publishing world. A woman at the helm of *Black Mask!*"[86] Although she was good at her job, Gruber does argue that "you would have thought she would be more at home with a magazine like *Vogue* or *Harper's*"[87]—that is, a slick-paper magazine that targeted women readers.

Women were also writing for *Black Mask* during this period, although their fiction usually featured male heroes and they often published under men's names.[88] One extraordinary "Behind the Mask" column in 1942 unmasked writer

Alan Farley as Mrs. Lee Harrington of Kansas City.   From 1926 to 1936, two women writers were frequent contributors—Erika Zastrow and Katherine Brocklebank—but they were seldom featured in writers' columns or blurbs for the next month's issue the way male contributors were.   Outside of romance pulps, women writers tended to be paid for writing filler or brief contributions for regular departments rather than for fiction.[89]

Women readers of *Black Mask* fared little better.   Roughly 20 to 25 percent of the *Black Mask* contest winners or runners-up in the 1930s and 1940s were women, but the editors never seemed to become accustomed to their female audience.   Most letters from women were marked as anomalous with headlines "From the Ladies" or "A mere woman."[90]   Moreover, these female readers clearly felt a little out of place. "Is it permissible for a mere woman to express a few comments?" asked one by way of an introduction.[91]   Another wrote: "Although this is not my first letter to *Black Mask*, being a woman, I hated to express my opinion."[92]

Even "feminine" material made *Black Mask*'s editor uncomfortable.   Shaw wanted someone to write stories about a woman detective for *Black Mask* in the late 1920s.   After a number of readers wrote to praise one of Erle Stanley Gardner's stories, Shaw decided Gardner was his man, the one with the "feminine touch" necessary to write about a woman detective.   However, Shaw sounded more than a little ambivalent about the whole undertaking. "I do not want too much femininity," he admonished Gardner's agent, "rather a masculine treatment of a female character."   Shaw thought Gardner could plunk an initially hostile woman detective into the adventures of his regular detective, Ed Jenkins, who would win her over by repeatedly coming to her rescue.   Shaw thought his plan would offer "a touch of feminine interest that would not let down our he-man readers and would at the same time bring in a swarm of new ones of both genders."   Gardner declined the offer, but he did suggest they contact Nell Martin, a female pulp writer who might be willing to do it for them.[93]   The specter of feminine copy reappeared in 1934 when Shaw decided it was time to add sympathetic characters, "glamour," and "a touch of romantic appeal" to the customary he-manly fiction.   Shaw ended an exchange with Gardner on the topic by declaring that "this magazine is by no manner going to be feminine," and promising to reread the correspondence to see what had given Gardner this (mistaken) impression.[94]

The all-male imagined communities of readers called into being by detective, Western, and adventure pulps compensated for the disappearance of all-male work and leisure spaces in working-class communities.[95]   Once women could vote in 1920, partisan politics ceased to be a boys' club.[96]   Between 1880 and 1930, the number of women engaged in paid work outside the home increased twice as fast as the female population.   By 1930, half of all single women were in the paid workforce.   Moreover, the number of women employed in domestic service in private homes ("invisible" working women) declined while those employed (often alongside men) in offices, stores, and other public places increased.[97]   In addition, working-class leisure became less segregated by gender between 1880 and 1920. The center of working-class communities moved from the men-only saloon to the heterosocial world of commercial leisure—the movies, amusement parks, dance halls.[98]

The world of action and adventure pulps, then, functioned as a homosocial imagined community that addressed some of the needs once met on the shop floor, in the voting booth, or in the saloon. The *"Black Mask* boys," as those in the industry called its stable of writers, were one such all-male community.[99] Erle Stanley Gardner invited most of the *Black Mask* crowd to visit his ranch in California, and many of them came to hunt, camp, fish, ride horses, and argue about literature and politics late into the night. They exchanged gifts at Christmas, sent each other souvenirs from their travels, and mailed dirty limericks back and forth. Shaw asked Gardner to mentor some of the younger writers, to share his impressions of other writers, and to give Dashiell Hammett a pep talk when his productivity lagged. The annual reunion lunch in New York was well attended, and those who had to miss it asked for a report of it in their letters. "I've always regarded the Black Mask bunch as . . . a baseball team in which each one had his work to do, and I've tried my darndest to do my share," Gardner explained, invoking team sports to describe the male camaraderie he had found at *Black Mask*. As he prepared to leave the magazine in 1929–30, he told Shaw that "the personal visits with the Black Mask gang meant a hell of a lot to me."[100]

If the hard-boiled writers at *Black Mask* were typical, men's action and adventure pulps were concerned with creating all-male imagined communities at a historical moment when all-male work and leisure spaces were eroding. For some, reading pulp fiction was also a refusal to read slick magazines, which trafficked in genteel, feminine fare and placed consuming women at the center of American life. Men's pulps were a nostalgic recreation of an era when working men's supremacy in the workplace and centrality to working-class life were unchallenged.

THE PULPS AND THE SLICKS: GENDER, CLASS, AND CULTURAL HIERARCHY

Artisanal, masculine pulp magazines and genteel, feminine slick-paper magazines waged a war of words in the 1920s and 1930s over which magazines would represent average Americans, that mass audience left untapped by elite publications like *Atlantic Monthly* and *Scribner's*. The *New York Times* 1935 editorial "Fiction by Volume" came down definitively on the side of the slicks. Describing the pulps as "another publishing world little known and certainly officially unrecognized," it maintained that the emphasis on volume over quality robbed pulp writers of their artistic integrity: "If he began his writing life with any feeling for style, it is washed out of him by the flood of words in a few years."[101] Pulp editors did not take such criticism lying down. A.A. Wyn, who described himself proudly as "the publisher of approximately ten western, detective, flying, spy, and mystery magazines," wrote a letter to the editor pointing out that with ten million regular buyers and thirty million regular readers, the pulps were hardly "unknown" except to "that small coterie" of condescending intellectuals at the *New York Times*. Fueled by pride and populism, he continued: "You may laugh at the stories we use; you may laugh at the paper we use . . . But you can't quite laugh off the 10 million Americans who plunk down their hard-earned cash each month for their favorite magazine."[102] Wyn did suggest that pulp readers included those from the professional classes and that he would leave the verdict on the pulps' aesthetic quality to future historians, but his primary purpose was to characterize himself as much too busy pleasing the American reading public to waste much time with the *New York Times*: "But I should be the last one to think about the verdict of the future. I've got a western pulp, a detective pulp, and a mystery pulp all going to press. There is a foot and a half of manuscript to be read with a bang-bang and rat-tat-tat and corpses galore."[103] Frederick Clayton, editor of *Argosy,* wrote in with his rebuttal several days later. He provided an impressive list of well-known writers who got their start in the pulps, pointing out that many continued to write for pulp magazines long after their fame made it unnecessary.[104]

Margaret MacMullen of *Harper's Monthly Magazine* fired off another salvo in 1937. After immersing herself in pulp magazines, she developed a "composite picture of shop-girls, factory girls, mechanics, bell-hops, farm wives and taxi-drivers" targeted by the pulps. "It is not a happy picture," she dryly noted. Although she did concede that long hours of boring, mechanized work and bad living and working conditions played a part in the poor literary taste of the working classes, she could not hide her disgust for what she found: "It is not pleasant to think of the immature minds and mature appetites that feed on such stuff as their staple fodder, but there is no ducking the fact that sensationalism is the age-old need of the uneducated. The steady reader of this kind of fiction is interested in and stirred by the same things that would interest and stir a savage."[105]

Joseph Thompson Shaw, the most prominent editor of *Black Mask,* had a particular bone to pick with *Vanity Fair.* Its 1933 article "The Pulps: day dreams for the masses" maligned pulp writers as ignorant hacks, denigrated pulp readers as (at best) marginal literates, and deemed the pulps themselves "gaudy, blatant, banal," representative of "the incursion of the Machine Age into the art of tale-telling."[106] Shaw was so offended by this unwarranted attack that he wrote a rebuttal and published it in the next editor's column in *Black Mask.* Shaw did discuss the high quality of *Black Mask* fiction and the professional standards of his writers, but he also saved a little space to ridicule the average reader of *Vanity Fair*—"the society matron who considers it smart to have on her table the so-called class magazine with its illustrations regardless of its text."[107] Pulp fiction, Shaw implied, was good enough to sell itself without the pretty pictures necessary to make slick-paper fiction appealing to its status-seeking, effeminate audience.

Black Mask's positioning vis-à-vis slick-paper magazines was a great deal more complex than this column would indicate. Although full of sneering disdain for handsomely illustrated "class" magazines read by society women, *Black*

Mask endlessly rehearsed the successes of its writers who were discovered by the slicks. When Frederick Nebel, a *Black Mask* regular, had a story accepted by the *Saturday Evening Post,* an entire "Behind the Mask" writers' column commemorated the event: "This accomplishment puts upon Fred Nebel the hallmark of approval and acceptability of the smooth paper brethren and 'sistern' and further confirms what we have always maintained, that he is among the very best in the field."[108] Another column marked the storming of the slick-paper gates by Erle Stanley Gardner, Frederick Nebel, and Dashiell Hammett, who had been published in *Liberty, Collier's,* and *Redbook,* respectively.[109] Many 1930s and 1940s "Behind the Mask" columns catalogued the slick-paper magazine, book, film, stage, screen, and radio credits of its writers, and reproduced highbrow praise for their work from newspapers and mass-market magazines.[110]

Shaw accepted the slicks/pulps hierarchy that shaped interwar publishing. His rhetorical strategy for dealing with scorn for the pulps was to maintain that *Black Mask* was the exception that proved the rule. In this account, the existence of a pulp magazine that featured high-quality fiction did not challenge the cultural devaluation of the pulps, but merely gave *Black Mask* honorary slick-paper status. The publishing world largely followed Shaw's lead. Even some of the slick-paper indictments of the worthless fiction in which pulp magazines trafficked deigned to cite *Black Mask* as the exception.

However, *Black Mask's* self-congratulation did not conceal its ambivalence about having its writers hired away by the "respectable" publishing establishment, who paid them far better. "Take a Laugh" was the title of one editor's column explaining how critics were just now "discovering" the new type of detective story that *Black Mask* had pioneered long ago: "For all the 'new type' stories, which on their appearance in book form the critics are becoming so enthusiastic about, you read first in *Black Mask—*Hammett's *Red Harvest, The Dain Curse, The Maltese Falcon,* and *The Glass Key,* Raoul Whitfield's *Green Ice* and *Death in a Bowl.* Pick up any of the Sunday literary reviews and read about the 'discovery' of a 'new school of detective fiction writing' and have a laugh."[111]

The contradictory mix of disdain and desire for cultural legitimacy was fairly typical. Although readers were supposed to sneer at the slick-paper magazines for their tardy discovery of hard-boiled detective fiction, they were also expected to take the slicks' (belated) notice as evidence of *Black Mask's* value. Shaw's vision invoked a single hierarchy of cultural value—there were good stories, and there were bad ones. In his radically democratic vision, worthy work, although initially appearing in trashy magazines, could rise on its own merits to an appropriate cultural venue. Moreover, whether rich or poor, highly educated or barely schooled, readers would all eventually agree on which stories displayed aesthetic excellence.

Some writers and readers did not accept Shaw's single cultural hierarchy. Erle Stanley Gardner heaped invective on Shaw in the early 1930s because of Shaw's "arty" tastes, his fawning attention to the slicks' aesthetic judgments, and the privileged treatment he gave Dashiell Hammett, the slicks' favorite son. In one particularly heated exchange, he berated Shaw: "I have said before, and I am going to keep yelling it until somebody stops me, that if a man wants to get *Saturday Evening Post* type of fiction or *Liberty* type of fiction, he buys the *Post* or *Liberty* at five cents and saves exactly fifteen cents on the transaction. If he wants to buy *Black Mask* type of fiction he has got to pay fifteen cents more to get it. Therefore, at least as far as that man is concerned, the *Black Mask* type of fiction is superior to the *Saturday Evening Post-Liberty* type of fiction."[112] As a consequence, the exasperated Gardner continued, the editor of *Black Mask* ought to stop wasting *Black Mask*'s pages reprinting slick-paper magazine praise and spend his columns talking about *Black Mask* instead.

This little tantrum made clear that Gardner's aesthetics were more pluralistic and conditional than Shaw's.[113] In compulsively cataloguing his writers' publications in more "respectable" media, Shaw implicitly accepted the superiority of slick-paper fiction. Gardner maintained that slick-paper fiction and pulp fiction were different and incomparable types of prose. If a man wanted to read "arty" stories, he bought the *Post* or *Collier's*. If he wanted action, adventure, and escape, he bought *Black Mask*. Neither one was better, he argued; they were just good for different things. Gardner also made clear that trying to sell "arty" fiction like Hammett's to people who were seeking pulp fiction pleasures was the first step on the road to bankruptcy. "You have lost the sales viewpoint and gone arty," Gardner accused the executives at Warner publications, claiming the red ink in *Black Mask*'s account books could be explained by Shaw's preference for Hammett's more "literary" fiction over his own "plain honest-to-God wood pulp" writing that ranked higher in reader preference polls.[114] Some pulp readers shared Gardner's sentiments. In a 1938 letter in *Clues,* one reader asked: "Am I supposed to think because a writer appears sometimes in *Collier's,* or *Post,* or the *Bar, Grill, and Tavern Weekly* that he is any better than my old friends who have been writing for me for years, and whom I enjoy? To heck with that. Don't go highbrow. Give us lots of shooting duels and other peril."[115]

The vast majority of pulp fiction never did go highbrow. The case of hard-boiled detective fiction is representative. Although pulp writers like Dashiell Hammett and Raymond Chandler did achieve tenuous literary respectability, few modern readers remember their colleagues Carroll John Daly, Paul Cain, Dwight W. Babcock, Norbert Davis, Lester Dent, William Brandon, Roger Torrey, and Theodore Tinsley, who remained hack writers paid by the word. Hammett, Chandler, Frederick Nebel, and George Harmon Coxe—all *Black Mask* regulars—were published in expensive hardback editions in Alfred Knopf's quality Borzoi line of mysteries.[116] The prestigious Modern Library line of literary classics published Hammett's *The Maltese Falcon* in 1934, the first detective novel to be honored in this way.[117]

However, the pulp origins of Hammett and Chandler continued to shape their works' reception long after they left the pulps for greener pastures. Hard-boiled fiction remains uneasily situated in the cultural hierarchy.[118] Because of its lowly origins, many reviewers in the 1930s and 1940s addressed hard-boiled fiction's "respectability" explicitly. Some recognized the dual position of the books: Hammett is the "darling of brows both high and low."[119] Other reviewers felt the need to reassure privileged readers that this was legitimate literature: "To be caught with a Raymond Chandler whodunit in hand is a fate no highbrow reader need dread."[120] Some critics preferred it when this fiction retained a whiff of ill-repute: "Now that Dashiell Hammett is beginning to be taken seriously by the highbrows, my first enthusiasm for him is beginning to cool a little."[121] Some of the appeal of this fiction for highbrows, then, was the slumming it enabled and the forbidden pleasures of being a tourist on the wrong side of the cultural tracks. Even the few pulp writers who were accorded some measure of literary legitimacy were granted it because of their lowbrow origins. The appeal of this fiction for educated readers was, in part, that it came out of worlds that did not include people like them.

The scorn most mainstream publications and cultural commentators expressed for pulp magazines was intimately enmeshed with class and gender. Mass-market magazines and newspapers targeting middle-class consumers repeatedly placed pulp writers and readers outside mainstream American culture, denigrating pulp fiction as utterly lacking aesthetic value. Pulp magazines, in turn, had nothing but disdain for the society ladies who read mass-market magazines, reputedly drawn more by their expensive illustrations than the quality of the editorial copy. While advertising-supported publications were at work placing consumption and the white, middle-class women who did most of it at the center of American life, pulp magazines provided a residual publishing world that continued to focus on working-class men and the production work in which they engaged. The war of words between the pulps and the slicks was a contest about who would represent the American mass public, and whether the consumer society they inhabited would be most profoundly shaped by the concerns of men or women, producers or consumers.

NOTES

1. Anonymous, "A Penny a Word," *American Mercury* 1936, quoted in Robert Lesser, *Pulp Art: Original Cover Paintings for the Great American Pulp Magazines* (New York: Gramercy, 1997), 17.

2. On the history of pulp magazines, see Lee Server, *Danger Is My Business: An Illustrated History of the Fabulous Pulp Magazines* (San Francisco: Chronicle, 1993); William F. Nolan, *The Black Mask Boys: Masters in the Hard-Boiled School of Detective Fiction* (New York: Morrow, 1985); Tony Goodstone, ed., *The Pulps: Fifty Years of American Pop Culture* (New York: Chelsea House, 1970); Frank Gruber, *The Pulp Jungle* (Los Angeles: Sherbourne, 1967); Harold Hersey, *Pulpwood Editor: The Fabulous World of Thriller Magazines Revealed by a Veteran Editor and Publisher* (New York: Stokes, 1937); Ron Goulart, *Dime Detectives* (New York: Mysterious, 1988) and *Cheap Thrills: An Informal History of Pulp Magazines* (New Rochelle, NY: Arlington House, 1972). General histories of magazines include John Tebbel and Mary Ellen Zuckerman, *The Magazine in America, 1741–1990* (New York: Oxford University Press, 1991) and Theodore Peterson, *Magazines in the Twentieth Century* (Urbana: University of Illinois Press, 1956), although neither treats pulp magazines at length.

3. The figures are based on a survey by A.A. Wyn, a pulp publisher (Peterson, 309).

4. On the production and distribution of dime novels, see Michael Denning, *Mechanic Accents: Dime Novels and Working-Class Culture in America* (New York: Verso, 1987), chap. 2; and Christine Bold, *Selling the Wild West: Popular Western Fiction, 1860–1960* (Bloomington: Indiana University Press, 1987), chap. 1.

5. Peterson, 309.

6. On pulp magazines as business enterprises, see Hersey, 11–28; Peterson, 69; Tebbel and Zuckerman, 341.

7. On price-cutting and circulation increases around the turn of the century, see Peterson, 2–14, 21–29, 223–24; Tebbel and Zuckerman, 66–68.

8. Peterson, chap. 1.

9. The notion of authorship predominant in Hollywood screenwriting circles resembled that of pulp writing in selected ways. Self-consciously literary writers were frustrated when they discovered that screenwriting was a collective labor for which they often received no screen credit; that they were employees of a studio that owned their creative output rather than proprietors of their own work; and that their new profession lacked the prestige accorded to novelists and writers of plays in New York. The lack of protest in pulp-writing circles about similar working conditions is evidence that pulp writers felt themselves to be engaged in an enterprise that was fundamentally different from more self-consciously literary writing. On writers in Hollywood, see Richard Fine, *West of Eden: Writers in Hollywood, 1928–1940* (Washington, D.C.: Smithsonian, 1993).

10. See Erle Stanley Gardner, letter to Joseph Thompson Shaw, 23 August 1926; Erle Stanley Gardner, letter to Don Moore, 28 September 1932; Erle Stanley Gardner, letter to Phil Cody, 27 March 1925; Erle Stanley Gardner, letter to Joseph Thompson Shaw, 6 August 1925; Erle Stanley Gardner Papers, Harry Ransom Humanities Research Center (HRC), University of Texas, Austin.

11. Erle Stanley Gardner, letter to A.H. Bittner, 21 June 1928. See also Erle Stanley Gardner, letter to H.C. North, 27 March 1925; Erle Stanley Gardner, letter to Phil Cody, 6 August 1925, Erle Stanley Gardner Papers, HRC.

12. Quoted in Server, 15.

13. Gruber, 23; Server, 19.

14. Although not the customary arrangement, regulars were sometimes commissioned to write for a given pulp and paid a monthly salary or guaranteed highest word-rates for their submissions, whose acceptance was guaranteed. Erle Stanley Gardner negotiated an annual contract with *Black Mask* to accept one story a month from him without revision at their highest word rates in the early 1930s (see Erle Stanley Gardner, letter to Joseph Thompson Shaw, 23 February 1931, Erle Stanley Gardner Papers, HRC). Several writers for Street & Smith pulps, including Gibson, were paid a fixed salary for their regular monthly contributions (Editorial Files, Box 27, Street & Smith Collection, Syracuse University Library Special Collections).

15. See Day Books, Box 11, Erle Stanley Gardner Papers, HRC.

16. See, for example, Editorial Files, Boxes 6 and 27, Street & Smith Collection, Syracuse; Server, 19.

17. Leroy Lad Panek, *An Introduction to the Detective Story* (Bowling Green, OH: Bowling Green State University Popular Press, 1987), 159.

18. Gruber, 105.

19. Frederick Clayton, letter, *New York Times,* 7 September 1935, 14.

20. *Black Mask* VI, no. 15 (1 November 1923): 126; *Black Mask* VI, no. 7 (1 July 1923): 126. The most complete collection of mystery pulps, including *Black Mask*, is at the Department of Special Collections, University of California, Los Angeles.

21. See, for example, *Black Mask* XXIII, no. 1 (April 1940): 97.

22. *Clues* XLI, no. 2 (February 1939): 125–27.

23. *Black Mask* XXII, no. 8 (November 1939): 112; *Black Mask* VI, no. 2 (15 April 1923): 3.

24. *Black Mask* VII, no. 5 (July 1924): 127.

25. Pierre Bourdieu, *Distinction: A Social Critique of the Judgement of Taste*, trans. Richard Nice (Cambridge: Harvard University Press, 1984), 4, 11–18.

26. See especially, Christopher Wilson, "Rhetoric of Consumption: Mass-Market Magazines and the Demise of the Gentle Reader, 1880–1920," *The Culture of Consumption*, ed. Richard Wightman Fox and T. J. Jackson Lears (New York: Pantheon, 1983), 42. Editors of western pulp magazines also regularly requested reader feedback on their stories (Bold, chap. 1; Tebbel and Zuckerman, 198).

27. *Black Mask* VII, no. 5 (July 1924): 4.

28. *Black Mask* XIII, no. 3 (May 1930): 120.

29. *Crime Busters* II, no. 2 (June 1938): 25.

30. *Crime Busters* II, no. 6 (October 1938): 115–16.

31. Erle Stanley Gardner, letter to Don Moore, 2 February 1931, Erle Stanley Gardner Papers, HRC.

32. Erle Stanley Gardner, letter to Don Moore, 11 February 1931, Erle Stanley Gardner Papers, HRC.

33. See, for example, Erle Stanley Gardner, letter to Joseph Thompson Shaw, 3 May 1929; Erle Stanley Gardner, letter to Joseph Thompson Shaw, 23 December 1929; Erle Stanley Gardner, letter to Joseph Thompson Shaw, 1 December 1929, Erle Stanley Gardner Papers, HRC.

34. Erle Stanley Gardner, letter to Phil Cody, 1 May 1928, Erle Stanley Gardner Papers, HRC.

35. In the 1930s, the net profit on 100,000 copies of a pulp magazine was $460 to $730. In order to make a living, a publisher had to carry a great many different titles (Peterson, 73).

36. For a thumbnail sketch of "The Establishment" of pulp publishing as of July 1934, see Gruber, 20–22. See also Server, 14.

37. Gruber, 20.

38. Editorial Files, Box 41, Street & Smith Collection, Syracuse.

39. Peterson, 57. In the early 1920s, *Black Mask* carried ads for the "newsstand group," a string of 10 pulp publications (including *Black Mask*) whose combined circulation was over a million copies a month (*Black Mask* V, no. 5, (December 1922). By the mid-1920s, the ad pages had "Newsstand Group—men's list" printed across the bottom of each page.

40. "Fiction by Volume," editorial, *New York Times,* 28 August 1935, 16.

41. On pulp readership, see Hersey, chap. 1; Frank Schick, *The Paperbound Book in America: The History of Paperbacks and Their European Background* (New York: Bowker, 1958), 56; Panek, 159–60; Goodstone, xii; Nolan, 29; William S. Gray and Ruth Munroe, *The Reading Interests and Habits of Adults: A Preliminary Report* (New York: Macmillan, 1929), 84, 150, 206–7; William Frank Rasche, *The Reading Interests of Young Workers* (Chicago: University of Chicago Press, 1937), 10, 12; Louis Adamic, "What the Proletariat Reads: Conclusions Based on a Year's Study among Hundreds of

Workers throughout the United States," *The Saturday Review of Literature* XI, no. 20 (1 December 1934): 321–22.

42. Hersey, 7–9; Bold, 7–8.

43. The best summary and analysis of this material is Stephen Karetzky, *Reading Research and Librarianship: A History and Analysis* (Westport, CT: Greenwood Press, 1982). Those studies that focused on the reading of factory workers specifically include Gray and Monroe; Rasche; and Hazel Ormsbee, *The Young Employed Girl* (New York: Woman's Press, 1927), 75–95.

44. Gray and Monroe, 149; Douglas Waples, *People and Print: Social Aspects of Reading in the Depression* (Chicago: University of Chicago Press, 1938), 150–52.

45. This claim was commonplace in both the popular press and the scholarly work of librarians and adult educators of the period. For examples from library research, see Gray and Munroe, 84, 150, 206–7; and Rasche, 10, 12. For an example from the popular press, see Adamic. Adamic's findings are challenged by Robert Cantwell, "What the Working Class Reads," *The New Republic* 17 July 1935: 274–76. Cantwell argues that most of the readers checking Twain, Shaw, Hardy, and the Greek classics out of the public library were working class.

46. Barbara Foley, *Radical Representations: Politics and Form in U.S. Proletarian Fiction, 1929–1941* (Durham: Duke University Press, 1993) 101–3.

47. "The Pulps and Shinies," *Pen & Hammer Bulletin* 2 (5 April 1934): 117–18, reprinted in Jon Christian Suggs, ed., *Dictionary of Literary Biography Documentary Series*, vol. 11, "American Proletarian Culture: The Twenties and the Thirties" (Detroit: Gale, 1993): 219–21.

48. Quoted in Helen Damon-Moore and Carl F. Kaestle, "Surveying American Readers," *Literacy in the United States: Readers and Reading since 1880*, ed. Carl F. Kaestle et al. (New Haven: Yale University Press, 1991): 199–200.

49. See, for example, Gray and Munroe: "Inquiries made of children and parents reveal the fact that a surprisingly large number of the cheap, sensational types of magazines are subscribed for regularly or purchased at the newsstand. The prominence of these magazines on the home library table suggests the urgent need of campaigns among adults to elevate their tastes and to stimulate interest in magazines of a better class" (266).

50. See William S. Gray and Bernice E. Leary, *What Makes a Book Readable* (Chicago: University of Chicago Press, 1935), v; Karetzky, 325.

51. See Adamic. Although Adamic is concerned with proletarian literature here, he limits his discussion to books that are experimental in form, a characteristic of modernist literature written from any number of political positions. His failure to discuss more "realistic" (and more accessible) works is surprising, since a substantial number of writers on the left (most notably Max Eastman) argued that proletarian writers must reject modernist bourgeois experiments with form and invent an authentically proletarian form based on reportage. For a good introduction to proletarian literature and the debates over its accessibility and aesthetics, see Part II, "Tradition on the Left" in Marcus Klein, *Foreigners: The Making of American Literature, 1900–1940* (Chicago: University of Chicago Press, 1981). My argument here is concerned here with Adamic's findings regarding workers' reactions to formal experimentation rather than with this literature as specifically proletarian.

52. William Vance Trollinger, Jr. and Carl F. Kaestle, "Highbrow and Middlebrow Magazines in 1920," *Literacy in the United States*, 207. This is not to say that these structural features were the most important variables related to readability, only the ones most easily measured and quantified. Other variables—level of reader interest,

familiarity of topic, concreteness or abstractness of concepts, purpose for reading, organization, or format, for example—may have been equally or more important, but were too difficult to study systematically (see Gray and Leary, 6–9).

53. Trollinger and Kaestle, 209.

54. Gray and Leary, 176, 291–92.

55. On pulp magazine advertising, see Erin A. Smith, *Hard-Boiled: Working-Class Readers and Pulp Magazines* (Philadelphia: Temple University Press, 2000), chap. 2.

56. Hersey, 68–69.

57. *Black Mask* XIV, no. 1 (March 1931): viii; *Black Mask* II, no. 1 (October 1920).

58. *Black Mask* II, no. 6 (March 1921): 125.

59. *Black Mask* VII, no. 8 (October 1924): 7.

60. *Black Mask* III, no. 3 (June 1921): 125.

61. On the union label, see chap. 6, "Producers as Consumers," in Lawrence B. Glickman, *A Living Wage: American Workers and the Making of Consumer Society* (Ithaca: Cornell University Press, 1997).

62. On the use of this term in the nineteenth century, see Denning, 45–46.

63. See, for example, *Clues* XLI, no. 1 (1 December 1938).

64. Hersey maintained that the largest portion of pulp magazine readers were children or adolescents (5). Erle Stanley Gardner thought high school students were some of the biggest readers of the pulps (Erle Stanley Gardner, letter to Phil Cody, 1 December 1929). See also Joseph Thompson Shaw, letter to Erle Stanley Gardner, 28 March 1927, Erle Stanley Gardner Papers, HRC.

65. H.C. North, letter to Erle Stanley Gardner, 7 July 1924, Erle Stanley Gardner Papers, HRC.

66. Joseph Thompson Shaw, letter to Erle Stanley Gardner, 17 March 1927, Erle Stanley Gardner Papers, HRC.

67. For a discussion from reading research of the period, see Douglas Waples, Bernard Berelson, and Franklyn R. Bradshaw, *What Reading Does to People: A Summary of Evidence on the Social Effects of Reading and a Statement of Problems for Research* (Chicago: University of Chicago Press, 1940), 94.

68. Marcus Duffield, "The Pulps: day dreams for the masses," *Vanity Fair* 40. 4 (June 1933): 26.

69. Hersey, 8.

70. Erle Stanley Gardner, letter to Joseph Thompson Shaw, 4 March 1927; Erle Stanley Gardner, letter to Joseph Thompson Shaw, 27 October 1927, Erle Stanley Gardner Papers, HRC.

71. Pierre Bourdieu argues that the "quasi-miraculous correspondence" between the tastes of audiences and the products offered for sale is a result of homologies between the logic of the field of production and the logic of the field of consumption (232). Pulp fiction writers (piecework prose producers) and working-class readers (piecework goods producers) occupied homologous positions in the fields of production and consumption, thus explaining the affinity of working-class readers for this fiction.

72. Hersey, 85.

73. See Helen Damon-Moore and Carl F. Kaestle, "Gender, Advertising, and Mass-Circulation Magazines," *Literacy in the United States*, 245–71, for a more detailed examination of how the needs of advertisers determined the specific ways middlebrow magazines were gendered.

74. Gruber, 150.

75. Raymond Chandler, letter to Hamish Hamilton, 10 November 1950, *Selected Letters of Raymond Chandler*, ed. Frank MacShane (New York: Columbia University Press, 1981), 236.

76. Hersey, 1.

77. Duffield, 26.

78. "Street & Smith News Trade Bulletin, June 1930," Editorial Files, Box 41, Street & Smith Collection, Syracuse.

79. A.H. Bittner, letter to Erle Stanley Gardner, 6 July 1928, Erle Stanley Gardner Papers, HRC.

80. The best publishing history of *Black Mask* is William Nolan, "History of a Pulp: The Life and Times of *Black Mask*," *The Black Mask Boys*, 19–34. My narrative here is informed by Nolan's account.

81. Server, 15.

82. *Black Mask* VIII, no. 11 (January 1926).

83. *Black Mask* XVI, no. 2 (April 1933): 7.

84. See *Black Mask* XIV, no. 12 (February 1932): 120.

85. Nolan, 20.

86. Gruber, 98.

87. Gruber, 77. On women hard-boiled writers in general, see Bill Pronzini and Jack Adrian, eds., *Hard-Boiled: An Anthology of American Crime Stories* (New York: Oxford University Press, 1995), 163, 348.

88. *Black Mask* XXV, no. 7 (November 1942): 8.

89. See Editorial Records, Box 7, Street & Smith Collection, Syracuse.

90. *Black Mask* VI, no. 4 (15 May 1923): 127; *Black Mask* VI, no. 20 (15 January 1924): 128. See also *Black Mask* VI, no. 8 (15 July 1923): 127.

91. *Black Mask* VI, no. 8 (15 July 1923): 127.

92. *Black Mask* VI, no. 20 (15 January 1924): 128.

93. Joseph Thompson Shaw, letter to Robert Thomas Hardy, 23 August 1926; Joseph Thompson Shaw, letter to Erle Stanley Gardner, 31 August 1926; Erle Stanley Gardner, letter to Joseph Thompson Shaw, 27 October 1927, Erle Stanley Gardner Papers, HRC. Martin had a whole series running in Street & Smith's *Top-Notch,* told from the angle of the secretary who always saved her boss, a lawyer, from his repeated screwups (see Erle Stanley Gardner, letter to Joseph Thompson Shaw, 24 October 1932, Erle Stanley Gardner Papers, HRC). Theodore Tinsley, a *Black Mask* regular, wrote about his Carrie Cashin, woman private detective, for Street & Smith's *Mystery* (see, for example, *Mystery* VII, no. 6 [January 1942]).

94. Joseph Thompson Shaw, letter to Erle Stanley Gardner, 17 April 1934; Joseph Thompson Shaw, letter to Erle Stanley Gardner, 1 May 1934, Erle Stanley Gardner Papers, HRC.

95. On "imagined communities" fostered by print capitalism and their role in constituting nationalism and other forms of community not characterized by face-to-face interactions, see Benedict Anderson, *Imagined Communities: Reflections on the Origin and Spread of Nationalism,* 2d ed. (New York: Verso, 1991).

96. Paula Baker, "The Domestication of Politics: Women and American Political Society, 1780–1920," in *Unequal Sisters: A Multi-Cultural Reader in U.S. Women's History,* 2d ed., ed. Vicki L. Ruiz and Ellen Carol DuBois (New York: Routledge, 1994), 85–110.

97. On women as wage earners, see Joanne J. Meyerowitz, *Women Adrift: Independent Wage Earners in Chicago, 1880–1930* (Chicago: University of Chicago Press, 1988), esp. xvii, 5.

98. Kathy Peiss, *Cheap Amusements: Leisure in Turn-of-the-Century New York* (Philadelphia: Temple University Press, 1986), introduction.

99. The second-class citizenship of the women who wrote for *Black Mask* is readily apparent in this term. Although they wrote—some quite frequently—for the magazine, women did not count as members of the stable of writers, who were always known as "boys."

100. Erle Stanley Gardner, letter to Joseph Thompson Shaw, 13 October 1929; Erle Stanley Gardner, letter to Phil Cody, 31 March 1930, Erle Stanley Gardner Papers, HRC.

101. "Fiction by Volume," 16.

102. A.A. Wyn, letter, *New York Times* 4 September 1935, 18.

103. Ibid.

104. Clayton, 14.

105. Margaret MacMullen, "Pulps and Confessions," *Harper's Monthly Magazine* 175 (June 1937): 98.

106. Duffield, 26–27.

107. *Black Mask* X, no. 7 (September 1933): 5.

108. *Black Mask* XV, no.4 (June 1932): 123.

109. *Black Mask* XVII, no. 1 (March 1934): 9.

110. See, for example, *Black Mask* XIII, no. 4 (June 1930): 119–20; *Black Mask* XIII, no. 11 (January 1931): 9; *Black Mask* XV, no. 6 (August 1932): 126; *Black Mask* XVI, no. 1 (March 1933): 124–25; *Black Mask* XVI, no. 7 (September 1933): 126; *Black Mask* XIV, no. 7 (September 1931): 7.

111. *Black Mask* XIV, no. 5 (July 1931): 5.

112. Erle Stanley Gardner, letter to Joseph Thompson Shaw, 23 April 1934, Erle Stanley Gardner Papers, HRC.

113. Gardner's nonhierarchical categorization of different *kinds* of stories resonates with the editorial practices at the Book-of-the-Month Club, founded in 1926. See Janice A. Radway, "The Book-of-the-Month Club and the General Reader: The Uses of 'Serious' Fiction," in *Reading in America: Literature and Social History,* ed. Cathy N. Davidson (Baltimore: Johns Hopkins University Press, 1989), 259–84.

114. Erle Stanley Gardner, letter to Phil Cody, 5 April 1930; Erle Stanley Gardner, letter to A.H. Bittner, 9 April 1930, Erle Stanley Gardner Papers, HRC.

115. *Clues* XLI, no. 1 (December 1938).

116. Most hardback books cost $2 to $2.50 during the Depression. On Knopf's reputation for producing high-quality books and the "literariness" of the Borzoi line specifically, see John Tebbel, *Between Covers: The Rise and Transformation of Book Publishing in America* (New York: Oxford University Press, 1987), 229–233.

117. Richard Layman, *Shadow Man: The Life of Dashiell Hammett* (New York: Harcourt, 1981), 107.

118. For a brilliant analysis of the way these writers' uneasy positioning in the publishing world is inscribed in their texts as tensions between the criminal classes (the trashy world of pulps) and the authorities (highbrow literary gatekeepers), see Sean McCann, "A Roughneck Reaching for Higher Things: The Vagaries of Pulp Populism," *Radical History Review* 61 (1995): 4–34. See also Sean McCann, *Gumshoe America: Hard-Boiled Crime Fiction and the Rise and Fall of New Deal Liberalism* (Durham, NC: Duke University Press, 2000).

119. Will Cuppy, "Mystery and Adventure," review of *The Thin Man,* by Dashiell Hammett, *New York Herald Tribune Books* 10 (7 January 1934): 11. See also Walter R. Brooks, "Behind the Blurbs," review of *The Glass Key,* by Dashiell Hammett, *Outlook and Independent* 157 (29 April 1931): 601.

120. "Murder at the Old Stand," review of *The Little Sister*, by Raymond Chandler, *Time* 54 (3 October 1949): 82.

121. T.S. Matthews, "Mr. Hammett Goes Coasting," review of *The Thin Man*, by Dashiell Hammett, *New Republic* 77 (24 January 1934): 316.

Chapter 9

From Abbott to Animorphs, from Godly Books to Goosebumps: The Nineteenth-Century Origins of Modern Series

Deidre Johnson

For over 160 years, series books have delighted American children and elicited varying responses—sanction, silence, or scorn—from adults. Like other forms of children's fiction, series books have continually evolved to reflect current ideas and publishing practices, and yet, in some ways, they have also remained much the same, so that twentieth-century series really rest firmly on a nineteenth-century foundation. Contemporary series draw on organizing patterns, categories of series, and promotional strategies derived from writers and models that emerged and flourished during the previous century, when series first began. Although the characters and content of recent series may reflect twentieth-century perspectives, most of the strategies used for developing series, even within the last two decades, owe a debt to those introduced and popularized by a number of innovative authors during the middle third of the nineteenth century. Even some of the stances—either scornful or supportive—adopted by librarians and critics toward modern series echo those voiced a century before. This paper provides an overview of the origins and development of series fiction. It analyzes some of the major connections among nineteenth-century and modern series as well as the reception series encountered, and it demonstrates the powerful influence of earlier series on the design and marketing of some of this century's most popular juvenile fiction.

In *Behold the Child: American Children and Their Books 1621–1922*, Gillian Avery notes that series books,[1] or "this marketing of books in named series," was a "particularly American phenomenon."[2] The first series book for children was published in America in 1835—though it apparently was not labeled as such until 1839. Jacob Abbott, who has been called the "father of the story series,"[3] anonymously published *The Little Scholar Learning to Talk: A Picture Book for Rollo* and a second volume, *Rollo Learning to Read*, both in 1835. He added two more volumes in 1837, *Rollo at Work* and *Rollo at Play*. Although the title pages of the 1837 volumes mentioned the previous books, they made no effort to link the works. But in 1839, when another book by Abbott appeared, the title page stated it was "by the author of 'the Rollo books.'" This marks the first time the Rollo stories were classified as a group, and by 1841 books by Abbott generally bore that notation.[4] Soon the books also carried a complete list of titles in the series—a marketing strategy that probably contributed to Abbott's success and one that has been employed for promoting series ever since.

The Rollo books told of the daily doings of a little boy named Rollo, who was about five years old when the series began. Like contemporaneous children's books, the series had a strong moral and educational slant—basically, Rollo learns about the world and proper behavior within it—but the books also contained touches of humor, and Abbott possessed a flair for making everyday adventures seem special. Rollo's stories succeeded for at least some of the same reasons contemporary series do: they were exciting reading, often more exciting than many of the existing books for children. One commentator remarked that "the Rollo books added liveliness and warmth to the severely ethical juvenile literature which preceded them,"[5] and another study of the series notes that Rollo "is a very real boy,"[6] quoting one of the more charming passages from *Rollo at Play* as an example. In it, Rollo and his cousin James have been trying to establish which is taller. Rollo can hold his hand higher, but then:

James determined not to be outdone, so he took up a stick, and reached it up in the air as high as he could, and said, "I can reach up as high as that."

Then Rollo took up a stone, and tossed it up into the air, saying, "And I can reach as high as that."

Now, when boys throw stones into the air, they ought to consider where they will come down, but unfortunately, Rollo did not . . . and the stone fell directly upon James's head.[7]

Abbott thus treats the reader to humorous glimpses of boyish behavior (as well as a practical example of why one should not throw stones into the air). As this excerpt also shows, Abbott deals with the ordinary rather than the extraordinary, describing a cozy, generally safe world, where a child learns through trial and error and through the guidance of his parents and other wise mentors.

Like many subsequent series authors, Abbott was quite prolific. He wrote 180 books and edited or cowrote thirty-one others.[8] He was also a master of marketing strategies. In 1839, while the Rollo series was still in progress and selling well, Abbott published a book called *Jonas's Stories: Related to Rollo and Lucy*. This was the first of four books about a young farmhand named Jonas, already a regular character in the Rollo books. The title highlighted the connection, thus simultaneously attracting readers already familiar with Rollo and further publicizing the Rollo series. Jonas, an older boy, was typical of the mentor figure in much of Abbott's fiction,[9] overseeing the younger children and proving himself well able to meet all challenges. The second book in the Jonas series was even titled *Jonas, a Judge; or, Law among the Boys*, wherein, according to Abbott, Jonas "[settles] the questions and disputes which arise between

Rollo and his companions."[10]   As one reviewer noted, "Jonas is an admirable creation . . . steady, sensible, sagacious . . . His little barn-chamber is always neat; his tools are always sharp; if he makes a box, it holds together; if he digs a ditch, there the water flows. He attends lyceum lectures, and experimentalizes on his slate at evening touching the abstruse properties of the number nine."[11]

Although the Jonas books were well received and Abbott wasn't faulted for bestowing an unusual degree of wisdom and maturity on Jonas—indeed, the entire series still appeared on recommended reading lists forty years after its inception[12]—Jonas's character nonetheless introduced a type that would later earn series fiction much criticism: the "adolescent *übermenschen*," or ultracapable child, wise beyond his years. The Hardy Boys, Nancy Drew, and similar characters, managing adeptly in all circumstances and admired by all their companions, are essentially Jonases without the overt moral teachings—and frequently fared far worse at the hands of critics than Jonas did.[13]   The next century would find librarians shunning many series, citing as one reason that "no popular character of history or legend was ever more wise, more brave, more resourceful than some of these up-to-the minute boy heroes" and speaking disparagingly of "the superhuman exploits of adolescent heroes."[14]

In 1841, two years after starting the Jonas series, Abbott again displayed his talent for creating successful series and capitalizing on existing ones. This time, Rollo's cousin Lucy, a frequent visitor in both the Rollo and Jonas tales, received *her* own series—more cross-pollination that promoted further sales. Like Rollo, Lucy experienced innocent adventures and mishaps, generously laced with moral and educational material. The Lucy series enjoyed the same favorable reception as its predecessors and, decades later, continued to be included on lists of recommended books for the young.[15] In addition to being the first girls' series, the Lucy books also introduced another trend that would continue in series fiction for the next century: the idea of modeling a girls' series on a successful formula that had been used for boys. This trend was especially prevalent among Stratemeyer Syndicate series in the 1910s and 1920s: the Motor Boys begat the Motor Girls; the Moving Picture Boys spawned the Moving Picture Girls; the Radio Boys inspired the Radio Girls; and so forth.

Abbott's marketing genius didn't stop there, however. In 1843, after writing fourteen volumes in the Rollo series, he must have felt he had exhausted topics for his character—Rollo had progressed from learning to read through studying philosophy and the natural sciences—and so the series ended. But, ten years later, a new series, Rollo's Tour in Europe, resurrected a slightly older Rollo, taking him and his Uncle George on the grand tour. The pair usually visited one country per book, providing readers with a combination story and travel guide, replete with European history and geography plus useful travel tips. With Rollo's Tour in Europe, Abbott thus introduced the travelogue series—a genre that would flourish later in the century—and the concept of using established characters to begin a new series. The latter technique is still evident in modern works like Francine Pascal's 1990s Sweet Valley University, the sequel to her 1980s Sweet Valley High series. (The original series, Sweet Valley High, centered on the social activities and romances of twin sisters, Jessica and Elizabeth Wakefield, and their clique in high school; the sequel portrays their experiences at college.)

Abbott's works were enormously popular—the forty volumes comprising the Rollo, Jonas, and Lucy series sold 1,250,000 copies in only twenty-five years—this at a time when the entire population of the United States was only about 20,000,000.[16] However, despite Abbott's success, it took some time for other authors to try the format. The only two series that began in the 1840s were both by Abbott, as were three of the twelve series that started in the 1850s. The situation changed in the next decade when approximately fifty new series emerged, and a similar number originated in the 1870s.[17] By then, so pervasive was the practice of issuing books in series or boxed sets that one journal carried a query asking plaintively, "When in the world is the present rage for series of books to die out?"[18]

Although many of the series appearing from the 1840s to the 1870s differed from modern ones in some aspects of their publication patterns and content, even amid these differences, there were similarities. One key difference was that authors or publishers often predetermined the length, usually four or six volumes.[19] The initial volume might announce forthcoming titles or the intended focus, and, in some cases, the entire series would be completed in only one or two years, with volumes sold individually or available as a boxed set.[20] Today's authors rarely restrict themselves to a set number of volumes, and the length and ongoing nature of current series generally preclude the use of boxed sets for an entire series; however, many series still begin with an initial release of three or more titles (thereby presenting readers with a ready-made series). The last few decades have witnessed a variation on the idea of boxed sets: boxed "gift sets" of three to five sequential volumes in a long-running series, such as the Hardy Boys Casefiles or Nancy Drew Files.

Other publishing and advertising techniques popular during this early period have continued into the present. Publishers issued—and sometimes reissued—all volumes in a series in a uniform edition, an effective way of distinguishing titles in a particular series; most publishers still practice this tactic. Authors sometimes promoted future volumes in a series by referring to the title or subject matter of the next book in the current volume's final paragraph. Joanna H. Mathews's *Bessie and Her Friends* from 1868, for example, concludes by telling young readers, "And if you are not tired of Maggie and Bessie, you may some time learn how they spent their summer in the mountains."[21] (Needless to say, *Bessie among the Mountains* appeared the following year.) A number of modern series books also end by advertising the title and contents of the next volume: some, like Nancy Drew Files, devote the final pages (after the story's conclusion) to a teaser synopsis; others, like Ann Martin's Baby-Sitters Club, print the opening paragraphs of the next volume. A few authors even modify Mathews's direct address to the reader by introducing a subplot to be resolved in the next story and conclude with tantalizing questions. For example, in the first Sweet Valley High title, *Double Love*, the Wakefield twins' friend,

Enid, makes several oblique references to her past, which is brought up again in the final paragraphs of the story; the book ends with a separate paragraph asking, "What is the dark mystery in Enid's past, and how does Jessica [Wakefield] use it to her own advantage? Find out in Sweet Valley High #2, *SECRETS*."[22]

Since books on child rearing still promoted reading as a means of moral and practical edification and since Sunday School libraries constituted another market for fiction, many early-nineteenth-century series had a distinctly religious tone. Such series dealt with the moral or spiritual reform of the child, with the dire and doleful consequences of wrongdoing, or with children who were already practically perfect and thus served as pious exemplars. Often clergymen or their wives pseudonymously penned these works. One early author in this field was Harriette Newell Woods Baker, daughter of a theologian and wife of a Congregationalist minister.[23] In the space of twelve years, from 1860 to 1872, Baker turned out ninety-four children's books in sixteen different series. Most were published anonymously or under the pseudonyms Aunt Hattie or Mrs. Madeline Leslie; all, like Baker herself, are now virtually forgotten and absent from histories of children's literature. Nevertheless, her Robin Redbreast series was the first anthropomorphic series, beginning a tradition continued in the twentieth century by authors like Thornton Burgess.

Baker's real interest, however, wasn't the frolics of her feathered family: as she explained in the preface to *The Robin's Nest*, she'd studied the works of Audubon and other naturalists, but her true aim was "to present to [young readers] in the history of Mr. Robin and his family, the dispositions and traits, both lovely and unlovely, the virtues and the vices, of little children, in such a manner to persuade them . . . to cultivate the one and avoid the other."[24]

Other of Baker's series, such as Little Frankie, adopt a more overtly religious tone, doling out Christian precepts and behavioral guidance: in *Little Frankie at His Plays*, when Frankie misbehaves, his "good Christian mother" prays with him, "[asking] God to take away his wicked heart and give him a good one";[25] Frankie not only modifies his actions and attitudes—"blow[ing] Satan away"[26] when he is tempted to lose his temper or pout—but also regales his friends with Biblical stories and, in later volumes, worries about other children's souls.

Religious series may have enjoyed a moderately long life in Sunday School libraries, but apparently received little attention almost everywhere else. The concept of Christian series and their place as a regularly overlooked subgenre of series fiction are two trends that continue into the twentieth century, as seen in series such as Danny Orlis, Elizabeth Gail, and Mandie, all of which combine traditional series adventures with Christian protagonists who refer to the Lord or ask His guidance during the course of the story. These series are published by religious presses, are sold almost exclusively in Christian bookstores, and, until very recently, were virtually ignored by children's book reviewers and most series book researchers.[27] Indeed, when a mainstream publisher issued Laura Peyton Roberts's Clearwater Crossing series in 1998, one reviewer noted, "For decades . . . no subject has been out of bounds—except the ordinary, everyday presence of religion in American life," later remarking that "the Clearwater Crossing books, in their portrayals of the many facets of the adolescent search for a God, are taboo-breaking on the part of [the publisher]."[28]

Although most series books—religious or secular—relied on a central character or characters as their unifying device, a few authors experimented with other methods for connecting titles in a series. Rather than following the adventures of one main character through multiple volumes, a few authors linked volumes geographically or thematically. In some cases, the volumes also shared common characters but with the protagonist of one book appearing only as a secondary character in other titles. The ever-innovative Jacob Abbott had pioneered the geographical techinque in 1850 with the Franconia Stories, ten volumes telling of a group of children who live in the village of Franconia. A modern variant of this occurs in the Baby-Sitters Club, where a group of friends join forces to create a combination club and baby-sitting business; each member of the club is featured in a continuing rotation as the main character of a story. Katherine Applegate's recent Animorphs series employs a similar technique.

Thematic series linked individual volumes through a shared concept rather than a particular location. Sometimes the unifying thread was religious. A title list at the beginning of Julia Mathews's six-volume Golden Ladder series from 1867, for example, follows each title with a segment of the Lord's Prayer. *Nettie's Mission*, the initial volume, carries the phrase "Our father which art in heaven, hallowed be thy name"; the second volume, *Little Margery*, continues the theme with "Thy kingdom come." Each volume relates a story of everyday life—albeit usually a melodramatic one—loosely based on its particular phrase.[29] Thematic series were less common than other types of series—although it may also be that they are harder to identify from title lists and cataloging records. They never disappeared completely, and their best-known modern incarnation is undoubtedly R.L. Stine's Goosebumps books, in which the unifying thread is light horror. A similar technique, loosely combining thematic series with a pseudogeographical connection, occurs in Jordan Cray's danger.com series from 1997: as series ads explain, the books feature "Different people in different places. The one thing they have in common is a new address on the Internet: danger.com. Where all your fears come true."

By the 1860s and 1870s, series fiction exhibited considerable diversity. One extremely popular type was the travelogue, a variation on Abbott's Rollo's Tour in Europe. Like Abbott's series, the travelogues catered to the taste for educational reading matter since the story remained clearly secondary to the descriptions and historical information. While Abbott had contented himself with Europe, however, the new breed of travelers enjoyed wider horizons: no accessible corner of the globe was overlooked.[30] For example, the fifteen volumes of Thomas Knox's Boy Travellers series began in 1879 by bringing two boys to the Far East. The pair travel through Japan and China in the first book, Siam and Java in the second, and continue in subsequent volumes through Ceylon, India, Africa, most of South America, Russia, Australasia, and all of Europe, ending in the Levant in 1894. Others followed similarly adventurous routes: the full title of one volume in Elizabeth Champney's Three Vassar Girls series from the 1880s is *The Three Vassar Girls in South America: A Holiday Trip of Three College Girls through the Southern Continent, up the Amazon, down the Madeira, across the Andes, and up the Pacific Coast to Panama.*

Travel series started to proliferate in the 1860s in a standard series format—like Oliver Optic's Young America Abroad series, which modified Abbott's formula by introducing the idea of a school ship taking a group of boys through Europe. This strategy allowed more adventures and interplay among characters, and by the 1870s most travel series featured groups instead of single protagonists. However, most travelogues from the 1870s through the 1890s differed from earlier series in that they were designed as visual feasts and issued in quarto format—oversize and lavishly illustrated, frequently with at least one picture on every two-page spread—the nineteenth-century equivalent of a coffee table book. *The Boy Travellers: Central Africa*, a typical offering in the genre, contains no fewer than 308 illustrations in its 479 pages—not counting the color frontispiece or the maps on the endpages.[31]

One of the more unusual aspects of these series is the way they were written. Because the illustrations were so important and expensive, publishers would buy engravings from various sources and then require authors to write the story around these illustrations.[32] This process resulted in an eclectic mix, in both pictorial style and content—and occasionally led to some strange inclusions in the text. For example, as the central characters in the Hales' Family Flight series are boarding a ship to begin their journey, one of the boys is sent in search of his brother. He questions an assortment of newsboys, bootblacks, flower sellers, and the like—all so that the publisher could insert spot drawings of the various pedlars and street urchins. When the boy returns, although the travelers' destination is Europe, a character suddenly waxes rhapsodic on the beauties of New York's Trinity Church—just in time to accompany a full-page illustration of same.[33]

Although many of these books received favorable reviews, the reviewers were aware of the publishers' practice—one even referred to the illustrations as "veterans in service"; another keen-eyed critic noticed the same picture had been used in two different series to depict two different locations.[34] Ironically, while a number of the travelogue series ended up in libraries—and indeed can still be found in circulating collections at some universities—one of the reasons librarians later cited for scorning series fiction by organizations like the Stratemeyer Syndicate was that ghostwriters worked from prefabricated outlines.[35] Apparently, in the case of the travelogues the value of the information outweighed the dubious method of production.

Gradually, the fad for travelogues died down, although the idea of using fictional series to educate children about other lands persisted into the 1920s, 1930s, and 1940s, with series such as the Children of Many Lands and Lucy Fitch Perkins's Twins of the World. These were actually a combination of thematic and travelogue series, since each volume was set in a different country and described the activity of a child native to that land. After that, fictional series about children of other lands faded out, and in recent years they seem to have been supplanted by nonfiction series like Cultures of the World.

In the 1860s and the 1870s, some series began to break away from the moral and educational tone, instead showing children either in realistic daily adventures or else striving for action and adventure for boys and domestic or sentimental stories, often evolving into romance, for girls. One author instrumental in demonstrating the market potential of tots' series (series aimed at younger children)—building, of course, on the foundations laid by Jacob Abbott's Rollo and Lucy books—was Rebecca Clarke, better known under the pseudonym Sophie May. Beginning in 1863 with the publication of *Little Prudy*, the first volume of the eponymous series, May gradually fashioned several series affectionately recounting the adventures of a bevy of alliteratively named little girls: Prudy Parlin, Dotty Dimple, Flaxie Frizzle, and Flyaway (Katie Clifford). Although some librarians would later view these books with scorn, criticizing May's use of childish mispronunciations and ungrammatical speech patterns, May's series initially proved a phenomenal success with critics and readers. In an 1866 commentary on children's books for the *North American Review*, Thomas Wentworth Higginson wrote, "Genius comes in with 'Little Prudy.' Compared to her, all other book-children are cold creations of literature only . . . All the quaintness of childhood, its originality, its tenderness and its teasing . . . all these waited for dear Little Prudy to embody them. . . . The rare gift of delineating childhood is [Sophie May's]. "[36]

By 1871, only eight years after May began her series, sales were estimated to have reached 300,000 copies.[37] In *Lee & Shepard: Publishers for the People*, Raymond Kilgour summarizes two articles that appeared in 1884 and 1885 surveying Lee & Shepard's offerings: in the first, the author "opined that Sophie May's books were the most popular juvenile books published in the United States at the time of his writing"; the second commentator was even more effusive in his praise of May's work, feeling that "*Little Prudy* had achieved a reputation not surpassed . . . by *Little Women*."[38]

May's approach was a simple one: like Abbott, she focused on the simple activities of children at home and on visits to relatives, and she favored characters who matured gradually during the course of the series; unlike Abbott, she eschewed educational information and instruction except for the occasional bit of moralizing and focused her stories primarily on young girls.[39] Her series frequently commenced when the protagonist was very young—sometimes, as with Little Prudy's Flyaway, only three years old—and invariably followed that character, her siblings, and cousins for six books. Each series ended after the sixth volume and a new series—usually centering on the title character of the final book in the finished set—began. Thus, the Little Prudy series concluded with *Dotty Dimple*, a volume about Prudy's younger sister, and the Dotty Dimple series was launched the same year. Then, two years after the Dotty Dimple series wrapped up with *Dotty Dimple's Flyaway*, about Dotty and Prudy's cousin, the Little Prudy's Flyaway series appeared—presumably to a ready-made audience already anticipating future tales. The favorable publicity and high sales of

May's series probably prompted others (including May's cousin, Sarah Jones Clarke, who wrote as Penn Shirley) to try creating similar episodic adventures for the young; indeed, the longest-lived and most famous tots' series, the Bobbsey Twins, premiered only three years after May published her last book. May's use of childish speech patterns and mispronunciations was also echoed in the dialogue of four-year-old Flossie and Freddie Bobbsey in the early volumes of their series; more recently, Barbara Park, the author of the 1990s series about an impish kindergartener, Junie B. Jones, has adopted a similar childlike voice for her young narrator. Additionally, May's strategy of creating spinoff series about the younger siblings of popular characters presaged such offerings as the 1980s Baby-Sitters Little Sister.[40]

The 1880s also witnessed the emergence of another type of informational series—historical fiction. These books may have derived from the travelogues, which had begun to include volumes where travelers toured historic sites in the United States and recalled incidents from America's past. Another influence may have been the work of William Taylor Adams, "the great maker of books in series,"[41] who published under the pseudonym Oliver Optic. One of the era's best-selling boys' authors, Optic wrote 123 books, many of them series fiction, and enjoyed sales as high as 100,000 copies annually, achieving an estimated total of 2,000,000 copies sold during his lifetime.[42] During the Civil War, Optic created the Army and Navy series telling of the ongoing conflict. Using the war as a setting enabled Optic to incorporate more sensational adventures than were commonly found in series, yet keep the books acceptable to most adults because ostensibly they contained educational material. Indeed, publisher's advertisements for the series touted both its sensational and educational aspects. One ad read: "This series of six volumes recounts the adventures of two brothers, Tom and Jack Somers, one in the army, the other in the navy, in the great civil war. The romantic narratives of the fortunes and exploits of the brothers are *thrilling in the extreme. Historical accuracy* in the recital of the great events of that period is *strictly followed*, and the result is not only a library of *entertaining* volumes, but also the *best history of the civil war* for young people ever written."[43] Optic also employed a clever narrative strategy by alternating volumes between the brothers' adventures; this meant that the characters could take part in different facets of the conflict, providing multiple perspectives while still keeping the series unified.

Only two series about the Civil War appeared during the 1860s—and, technically, it could be argued that these weren't historical fiction, but topical series chronicling current events. It took another twenty years before many series authors began setting stories in the past. Optic was again one of the first, with The Blue and the Gray Afloat series in 1888, also about the Civil War. By the 1890s, several other authors had recognized the possiblities inherent in the genre and emulated his approach, setting their books amid famous battles or frontier skirmishes to take advantage of the marketable combination of adventure and information. Wars remained the most popular setting, typified by series such as Everett Tomlinson's seven-volume War of 1812 series or Edward Stratemeyer and James Otis's twelve-volume Minute Boys (junior versions of the Minute Men). A number of boys' authors also followed Optic's lead by creating series set during ongoing conflicts, resulting in a spate of topical series during the Spanish-American War and World Wars I and II. Perhaps the most unusual modern variant of this strategy appears in the phenomenally successful Animorphs series from the mid-1990s, which is not historical fiction, but science fiction. Lacking a current war with American involvement to use as background, the author has instead postulated that aliens with the power to possess humans are trying to conquer the earth, and the series concentrates on a group of children (with the ability to "morph" into animal form) who are fighting this invasion.

One effect of Optic's pioneering efforts in historical fiction series was to help shift series fiction toward a more adventurous—some would say sensational—tone, thereby unwittingly laying the groundwork for some of the more severe criticisms of the genre. Although Optic believed his fiction had a high moral tone and lacked sensationalism—and many initial reviewers of his fiction concurred—not everyone agreed with this sanguine assessment. Among his early critics was Louisa May Alcott, who incorporated a now-famous attack on Optic's works into the pages of *Eight Cousins*. Reports on children's fiction in *Library Journal* from the 1870s through the 1890s found librarians and other interested adults divided on the issue, with Optic's books frequently cited as examples during the debates: some stated that "this sensational . . . trash-gratis" did not belong in free libraries and believed such fiction could harm a boy's character, intellect, or reading ability.[44] As William Atkinson explained, "I don't think it is the really clever boys who are much addicted to Oliver Opticism, and on the limp mind of the ordinary boy I think it has a mischievous influence. He settles down into it and does not rise above it; it is well if he does not sink below it. I don't believe the assertion . . . that a taste for better reading is fostered by unlimited supplies of [such fiction]. One might as well say that the youthful digestion was strengthened by unlimited supplies of cheap confectionary."[45] Others took an opposing stance and argued that Optic and writers like him fed a boy's "love of adventure," lured him to the library, or whetted his taste for reading.[46] One librarian stated, "I put Oliver Optic into the library freely. . . . [Works by Optic and similar writers] will attract young readers when better books will fail. If they do not go from these to better reading, they have at least not been harmed by the brief time spent reading these little tales; and if they do drop them for better, we can score a point gained."[47]

These divergent positions foreshadowed viewpoints that would be voiced by concerned adults in debates about series fiction for the next century. For example, in the 1990s, the popularity of horror series such as R.L. Stine's Goosebumps and Fear Street series elicited criticisms that the series were "'total titillation' with 'no character development'"[48] and triggered a 1997 complaint by a parent who "found the books gory" and "knew in [her] heart it wasn't something [her daughter] should read."[49] Others defended the series' inclusion in libraries, explaining, "Goosebumps can teach children that books have something to offer them . . . They appeal to boys . . . who may not have been turned on to books."[50]

During the nineteenth century, fewer historical fiction series were published for girls than boys, and, predictably, they were considerably less violent. While some girls' authors still chose wars as settings, characters' involvement was usually limited to expressing patriotic sentiments or carrying messages to historical figures. Most girls' authors favored a thematic approach coupled with a broader scope than that found in boys' series: rather than concentrating on the adventures of one or two characters for an entire series, they would use a different protagonist and location in each volume and describe the domestic activities of girls in historic cities and settlements. Amanda Douglas's Little Girl series, published at the turn of the century, covers the life of a pioneer girl in Old Pittsburg in one book, a Quaker girl in Old Philadelphia in another, with other volumes set in such diverse cities as San Francisco, New Orleans, and Chicago. Currently, the Dear America series, with volumes penned by different authors, follows Douglas's approach, with each title set in a different place and historical period and the series continuity established through a diary format. The popular American Girls series uses a modification of Douglas and Optic's approaches: it features multiple protagonists and settings—including three different war eras—for a broad scope, but it also follows each main character for several books and tries to present different perspectives on similar events as a unifying device.[51]

Just as there were fewer historical series for girls than for boys, so, too, were there fewer series in general for them. The one that has received the most attention—almost invariably negative—is Elsie Dinsmore. Elsie was the product of a time when the sentimental novel flourished, when readers would cheerfully weep their way through stories of misunderstood, persecuted heroines who endeavored only to do right and help others. Elsie was a classic example of the form.[52] The series begins when Elsie is eight years old, a fervently Christian child living with her father's secular family, all of whom dislike and mistreat her; it ends when she is a much-loved grandmother, overseeing the trials and tribulations of her children and grandchildren. Critics panned the books for their sentimentality and unbelievable plots and characters: a reviewer in *The Nation* remarked of the sixth volume, *Elsie's Children*, that "the story flows on unimpeded by any hindering deference to human nature,"[53] while an 1896 article from *Scribner's* observed "nothing can be more dreary than the recital of Elsie's sorrows and persecutions. Every page is drenched with tears."[54] Decades later, librarians and educators still scorned the series: a 1935 text on children's literature dismissed the books as "poorly written, foolishly sentimental and consequently unwholesome for the preadolescent girl for whom they were meant," and a 1948 essay on nineteenth-century children's fiction referred to Elsie as a "tiresome prig."[55]

Although literary adults deplored the Elsie books, children apparently adored them. The apocryphal story behind the series is that while the author, Martha Finley, "was bedridden and dependent upon her [relatives] for support . . . [she] prayed for the ability to write a book" that would provide her with some income.[56] The result was *Elsie Dinsmore*, the series's first volume, which is estimated to have sold close to 300,000 copies during the decade it was published and launched a twenty-eight-volume series that ran from 1867 to 1905. The series ultimately sold over 5,000,000 copies and stayed in print in the United States and England for over seventy-five years, earning its author approximately a quarter of a million dollars.[57] (This may be one reason Finley's character is such a fervent believer in the power of prayer.)   Although modern readers tend to sneer at the saintly Elsie—just as her unfeeling relatives did—the patterns she established lingered long after the demise of the series. Elsie was one of the earliest series heroines to come from an affluent, single-parent family and enjoy a close relationship with her father, a pattern most successfully repeated in the twentieth century with Nancy Drew.[58] Unlike Nancy—but like a number of other series heroines—Elsie starts out beleaguered and alone, but, after weathering ostracism and emotional duress, she eventually wins the love and admiration of those around her. This is, essentially, the Cinderella story, which was replayed in some of the most successful series from the turn of the century,[59] most notably Pollyanna and Anne of Green Gables—which, like Elsie, also follow their heroines into marriage and then go on to chronicle events in their children's lives as part of the same series. Vestiges of Elsie can also be seen in some early volumes of the Sweet Valley High and Sweet Valley Twins series, where the near-saintly Elizabeth Wakefield contends with her more ruthless and self-centered sister Jessica.

By the time the Elsie Dinsmore series ended in 1905, series fiction was well established as part of the reading diet of American children. The writer from the 1870s who complained about the proliferation of series could not have imagined what lay ahead. Between 1900 and 1909, approximately 160 new series began; this figure is exclusive of older series still in progress or those that had ended but were still in print. The number more than tripled during the following two decades, with over 490 new series published,[60] much to the dismay of librarians and educators, many of whom feared such reading would destroy a child's taste for good literature. Accordingly, attacks on series books gradually increased; one study of such criticisms suggests that the growing number of professionally trained children's librarians, their attitudes about protecting children, and the disappearance of the dime novel (which previously had drawn the worst attacks) account for much of the hostility.[61]   From the 1930s to the late 1960s, librarians often criticized the books' unrealistic plots and characters and the series' method of production, fearing that series fiction kept children from enjoying more literary works.   As one librarian explained, "[S]eries of mediocre and worthless books . . . help to form a taste for the mediocre and the melodramatic . . . [and] vitiate our children's taste to give them false and vulgar ideas."[62] Although it seems unlikely that librarians' campaigns dissuaded many prospective purchasers—the Elsie Dinsmore series had been roundly denounced practically since its inception with no appreciable effect on sales—the series' popularity gradually waned from the 1930s until the early 1980s.

By the 1970s, attitudes about series fiction were beginning to change; the books were now seen as a way to lure children back to reading and combat declining circulation in libraries.[63] In the 1980s, the genre enjoyed a renaissance resulting in a tidal wave of new series: a chronological list of girls' and tots' series in one bibliography shows over 210 series premiering from 1980 to 1989.[64] Moreover, sales totals for a few series have reached unprecedented heights: R.L. Stine's Goosebumps, which began in 1992, sold approximately 100,000,000 copies during the first four years of its run.[65] Currently, though series books still receive some criticism over their content, quality, or effect on children, overall, they exist in a more hospitable climate than they have enjoyed since the final decades of the nineteenth century. By the 1990s, continued concerns about children's reading—perhaps combined with the American Library Association's position against censorship and restricting children's freedom to read—meant that more and more libraries carried series books. One 1990s survey of librarians in the Chicago suburbs found that more than 95 percent of the respondents worked in libraries that purchased series fiction,[66] and a number of recent articles either have advocated the use of series to promote interest in library use or have suggested that, far from discouraging a taste for books, series books may actually help nurture readers[67]—attitudes reminiscent of the debates over sensational and sentimental series a century ago.

Thus, although the authors of most contemporary series are probably unaware of the history and controversies surrounding the genre, many of their basic formulas and marketing strategies derive from their nineteenth-century forebears, most of whose works are now long forgotten and out of print, their names consigned to brief mentions in histories of children's literature. Nonetheless, the traditions they established live on in contemporary series. The contents and packaging of today's series may be geared to modern readers, but their true origin dates back to the period when American children's books were coming into their own. From the foundations built by Jacob Abbott spring the permutations found in today's Animorphs—and thus the series tradition lives on.

NOTES

1. Although definitions vary, for purposes of this discussion, the term "series" is defined as three or more fictional works above picture book level that were advertised or marketed as a named group and that have a deliberate textual or thematic link among volumes. While numerous picture story books feature continuing characters, the study of series fiction has traditionally excluded them, perhaps initially because they were not of interest to series book collectors (who were responsible for most of the seminal research in the field), and later because much series research evolved from those early studies and, consciously or unconsciously, echoed those decisions. Additionally, unlike other children's books, which are intended to be read *by* children, many picture story books are designed to be read by adults *to* young children (and, accordingly, to be purchased by adults, often for a preliterate audience); since a number of the debates about series fiction centered on children's choices and children's book purchases, picture story books were not mentioned presumably because adults controlled access to the text. Since it is not the intent of this study to redefine the genre, I also exclude them.

2. Gillian Avery, *Behold the Child: American Children and Their Books 1621–1922* (London: The Bodley Head, 1994), 190.

3. Alice M. Jordan, *From Rollo to Tom Sawyer and Other Papers* (Boston: The Horn Book, 1948), 78.

4. A descriptive bibliography appears in Rollo G. Silver, "Rollo on Rollo," *The Colophon*, new graphic series, no. 2 (1939), n.p.

5. Silver, 6.

6. Carol Gay, "Jacob Abbott," *Dictionary of Literary Biography* 42 (Detroit: Gale Research Co., 1985), 7.

7. Quoted in Gay, 7.

8. Avery, 87.

9. Avery, 89.

10. Jacob Abbott, "Preface," *Jonas a Judge; or, Law among the Boys* (1840; reprint, New York: Clark, Austin, & Smith, 1853), n.p.

11. [Thomas Wentworth Higginson], "Children's Books of the Year," *North American Review* 102 (Jan. 1866), 246. Quoted in Jordan, 75. The article was unsigned; Raymond L. Kilgour, *Lee and Shepard: Publishers for the People* (n.p.: The Shoe String Press, 1965) identifies the author, 42–43.

12. C[aroline] M. Hewins, *Books for the Young: A Guide for Parents and Children* (New York: F. Leypoldt, 1882) includes all the volumes in the Jonas series, 35.

13. The phrase "adolescent *übermenschen*" appears in "For It Was Indeed He," *Fortune* (April 1934), 86. The article described the rising popularity of series books, as well as the assembly-line method of production the Stratemeyer Syndicate—producers of the most popular series—employed (ghostwriters worked from outlines prepared by the heads of the Stratemeyer Syndicate). In *Series Books and the Media; or, This Isn't All! An Annotated Bibliography of Secondary Sources* (Rheem Valley, CA: SynSine Press, 1996), Ilana Nash and David Farah state that the *Fortune* article "is the single most influential article of the 20th century on series books . . . More articles trace their information back to this source than to any other. . . . It is likely that any article about series books which uses the terms 'tripe' 'Übermenschen,' or 'hack' (in reference to Syndicate ghostwriters) used the *Fortune* article, or one that derived from it, as a source." 24, 26.

After the *Fortune* piece appeared, librarians began to publish more criticisms of the series. For a discussion of the far-reaching effects of this article, see John T. Dizer, "*Fortune* and the Syndicate," in *Tom Swift and Company* (Jefferson, NC: McFarland, 1982), 15–29.

14. Franklin K. Mathiews, "Blowing Out the Boys' Brains," *The Outlook* 108 (18 November 1914), 652; [Janie Smith], "*Bobbsey Twins* History Told," *Kansas Library Bulletin* 30 (December 1961), 15.

15. Hewins, 35. During her tenure as a librarian, Hewins campaigned against many series books but firmly approved of Abbott's work.

16. Frank Luther Mott, *Golden Multitudes: The Story of Best Sellers in the United States* (New York: The Macmillan Company, 1947), 98, 306–7.

17. Information on the number of series published from 1830 to 1870 is based on the chronological listing in *Girls' Series Books, 1841–1991* (Minneapolis: Children's Literature Research Collections, University of Minnesota Libraries, 1992) and the author's own research. The number of series from the 1860s and 1870s series may be slightly inflated due to some publishers' practice of repackaging unrelated volumes in boxed sets and giving them a title such as "Little Agnes Library"; whenever it was possible to identify such pseudoseries, they have been omitted from the count.

18. "Notes." *Independent* 28 (26 October 1876), 9. Richard L. Darling, *The Rise of Children's Book Reviewing in America, 1865–1881* (New York: R.R. Bowker Company, 1968) cites a similar lament in *Independent* the following year, 28.

19. Darling, 28.

20. Kilgour notes that in a number of cases, these "series" consisted of previously published, sometimes unrelated, books, 35–36.

21. Joanna H. Mathews, *Bessie and Her Friends* (New York: H.M. Caldwell, 1868), 366.

22. Kate William, *Double Love* (New York: Bantam, 1983), 182, vol. 1 in the Sweet Valley High series created by Francine Pascal. For brief descriptions of the concepts and contents of most twentieth-century girls' series, see Society of Phantom Friends, *The Girls' Series Book Companion 1994* (n.p.: n.p., 1994).

23. "Baker, Harriette Newell Woods," *National Cyclopedia of American Biography* 14 (1910; reprint, Ann Arbor: University Microfilms, 1967), 154.

24. Harriette Newell Woods Baker [Mrs. Madeline Leslie, pseud.], *The Robin's Nest* (1860; reprint, Boston: Woolworth, Ainsworth, & Co., 1870), 11–12.

25. Harriette Newell Woods Baker [Mrs. Madeline Leslie, pseud.], *Little Frankie at His Plays* (1860; reprint, Boston: Woolworth, Ainsworth, & Co., 1870), 39, 45.

26. Ibid., 53.

27. Until the mid-1990s, the entire genre of Christian fiction was given scant attention, at best, in standard review journals. In November 1994, *Library Journal* finally began a quarterly column reviewing Christian fiction. The first column, by Henry Carrigan, Jr., "Christian Fiction," *Library Journal* 119 (1 November. 1994) noted that "Until recently . . . librarians had little guidance other than patron requests and an occasional article . . . in selecting Christian fiction," 64. The only article cited in that column had been published three years earlier; it was Jonathan D. Lauer's "Popular Fiction for the Faithful," *Library Journal* 116 (1 November 1991), and its opening paragraph asked, "Who are these people [writing Christian fiction] and why do so few [librarians] know anything about them?" and then went on to note that most "Christian fiction lines . . . [are] sold almost exclusively through Christian bookstores. . . . [and] underrepresented in libraries," 65.

28. Patty Campbell, "Mainstreaming the Last Taboo," *Horn Book Magazine* 74 (May/June 1998), 379; Patty Campbell, letter, *Horn Book Magazine* 74 (July/August 1998), 406.

29. Although the Golden Ladder series is thematic, it also employs some common characters, albeit in a method apparently unique to religious fiction. Margery, the protagonist of the second and third volumes, first appears in a minor role in *Nettie's Mission*, the first volume; at the conclusion of the third volume, *Margery's City Home*, she dies joyfully and piously. Although she is gone, she is not forgotten: the protagonists of the remaining three books regularly recall her preachings and remember her affectionately.

30. For a detailed discussion of the different travelogue series and their approaches, see Virginia Haviland, "The Travelogue Storybook of the Nineteenth Century," in *The Hewins Lectures 1947–1962*, ed. by Siri Andrews (Boston: The Horn Book, 1963), 25–63.

31. Thomas Knox, *Adventures of Two Youths in a Journey through Africa*, Part 5 of *The Boy Travellers in the Far East* (New York: Harper & Brothers, 1883). The cover title reads *Boy Travellers: Central Africa*, and the series is usually referred to as the Boy Travellers series.

32. Darling, 26–27; Kilgour, 191–92.

33. E[dward] E[verett] Hale and Susan Hale, *A Family Flight through France, Germany, Norway and Switzerland* (Boston: D. Lothrop & Company, 1881), 16–23.

34. The "veterans in service" comment is from a review in *Lippincott's Magazine* 25 (January 1880), 25, and is quoted in Darling, 27. Darling also noticed and identified

the reused illustrations: "an identical picture appeared in Horace Scudder's *Mr. Bodley Abroad* on page 157 with the caption 'Climbing the Alps in Imagination,' and in [Hezekiah] Butterworth's *Zigzag Journeys in Classic Lands* as the frontispiece with the caption 'Climbing Parnassus,'" 27.

35. Again, the *Fortune* article "For It Was Indeed He" spawned much of this criticism. See also note 13.

It is also worth noting that almost a century later a picture still had the power to influence the content of a book. At the "Small Group Session," Eighty Years of Juvenile Series Fiction conference, University of Wisconsin–LaCrosse, 23 June 1984, Sam and Beryl Epstein, authors of the Ken Holt series, mentioned that they had shown their publisher an outline for a forthcoming title. Afterward, they decided they did not like one of the scenes they had planned and removed it from the book—then learned that the publisher had used that scene as the basis for the dust jacket art. As Sam Epstein explained, "Well, they are not going to throw out $1000 worth of plates, so we put the scene back in"; Beryl Epstein added wryly, "Not by [Sam's] choice, you understand, but this is what the publisher suggested might be a good idea."

36. [Higginson], "Children's Books of the Year," 243. Quoted in Kilgour, 43.

37. Carol Doll, "The Children of Sophie May," in *Research about Nineteenth-Century Children and Books*, ed. Selma K. Richardson, Monograph—University of Illinois Graduate School of Library Science, no. 17 (Urbana–Champaign: University of Illinois, 1980), 97.

38. Kilgour, 235, 237.

39. Although the stories centered on little girls, this focus did not prevent boys from reading them; a charming commentary on the series appears in Robert Morss Lovett's essay "A Boy's Reading Fifty Years Ago," *The New Republic* (Nov. 10, 1926), "I bribed my sister to go . . . and borrow *Little Susie's* [*sic*] *Captain Horace* . . . And once drawn in I read the whole lot [of May's series] . . . and I fell for them all, all the heroines I mean—sedate Susie, and patient Prudy and dashing Dotty Dimple—my first love. It was probably my own heart interest that engraved these stories on my memory as nothing else in my long course of reading." 334–35.

40. The use of younger siblings to begin a series was a way of continuing to reach a young audience when the original series protagonists had become too old for adventures appropriate to the interests of their readers. An interesting variant on this technique from the late 1980s and 1990s, for which no parallel in nineteenth-century series has yet been found, is that of creating a new series based on favorite characters' earlier years, presumably to build an audience among younger readers, who then graduate to the original series. Francine Pascal was apparently the first to try this: her Sweet Valley Kids, which began in 1989, showed the childhood of the Wakefield twins, the protagonists of her enormously popular Sweet Valley High series. More recently, the Nancy Drew Notebooks and the Clues Brothers series were created to depict the childhoods of Nancy Drew and the Hardy Boys, respectively.

41. Kilgour, 270. Kilgour credits Optic with popularizing series fiction, remarking that he "was certainly the great initiator of this method of mass production of books for children," 270.

42. Dolores Blythe Jones, comp., *An "Oliver Optic" Checklist: An Annotated Catalog-Index to the Series, Nonseries Stories, and Magazine Publications of William Taylor Adams*, (Westport, CT: Greenwood Press, 1985), xvi. Jones adds that this "estimated" total of 2,000,000 was "more than that of any other author living at the time," xvi. Kilgour gives a somewhat lower estimate—"far over a million copies," 269.

43. The Lee & Shepard ad is quoted in Jones, 99; emphasis added. Contents of the series are also described, via excerpts from reviews, in Jones, 22–23, 25–27, 99.

44. Charles Frances Adams, Jr., "Fiction in Public Libraries and Educational Catalogues," *Library Journal* 4 (September–October 1879), 331. Adams felt such fiction "destroys the intelligent reading power," 334.

45. William P. Atkinson, "Address," *Library Journal* 4 (September–October 1879), 361.

46. T.W. Higginson, "Address," *Library Journal* 4 (September–October 1879), 357.

47. C.H. Garland, letter printed in Mrs. Minerva A. Sanders, "Report on Reading for the Young," Fabyan House Conference Proceedings, *Library Journal* 15 (1890), 61. Others who defended Optic included W.H. Brett, in "Books for Youth," *Library Journal* 10 (June 1885): "Even the much-criticized 'Oliver Optic' is vastly better than 'Jack Harkaway', and a boy who reads 'Oliver Optic' can be easily induced to read [better fare]," 128.

48. Q & Q, "The Horror, the Horror: The Pros and Cons of Series Fiction Take on a New Dimension with the Advent of Young-Adult Horror," *Quill & Quire* 60.5 (1994), 34–35; quoted in Catherine Sheldrick Ross, "'If They Read Nancy Drew, So What?': Series Book Readers Talk Back," *Library & Information Science Research* 17 (Spring 1995), 206.

49. Theresa Monsour, "'Goosebumps' Raises Questions," *St. Paul Pioneer Press*, 12 January 1997: 4B.

50. Ibid.

51. As of this writing, the American Girls series follows the adventures of six different girls and uses a developmental pattern reminiscent of preplanned nineteenth-century series. Each character appears in six books; rather than creating new stories about an existing character, the series grows by adding new characters for additional six-book sets. Each set uses identical titles, except for the character's name (i.e., the first book is always *Meet* [character's name]; the second, —— *Learns a Lesson*, etc.), thus underscoring the combination of variety and similarity. The general series description found on the back cover of the books reinforces these dual concepts, noting, "Some things about growing up have changed, while others, like families, friendships, and feelings—haven't changed at all. These are the things that American girls will always share."

52. For a discussion of the three "most read, most reread, most influential ladies-of-the-pen in the nineteenth century" (Susan Warner, Maria Cummins, and Martha Finley), authors "linked together for all times by a surfeit of sentiment and sensibility . . . [who] made books out of emotion when emotion was in style," see Jane Manthorne, "The Lachrymose Ladies," 3 parts, *Horn Book* 43 (June, August, October 1967), 375–84, 501–13, 622–31; quoted material from 376, 629. See also Nina Baym, *Woman's Fiction: A Guide to Novels by and about Women in America, 1820–1870* (Ithaca, NY: Cornell University Press, 1978) for parallels in adult fiction.

53. "Children's Holiday Books," *The Nation* 25 (November 15, 1877), 304. For examples of unfavorable reviews of early volumes in the series, see Darling, 108, 195. Some of the librarians who criticized Optic also disliked Finley's work.

54. Agnes Repplier, "Little Pharisees in Fiction," *Scribner's Monthly* 20 (December 1896), 722.

55. Blanche E. Weekes, *Literature and the Child* (New York: Silver, Burdett & Company, 1935), 71; Jordan, 35.

56. Janet Elder Brown, "The Saga of Elsie Dinsmore," *University of Buffalo Studies* 17 (1945), 79.

57. Ibid., 80.

58. For a comparison of Elsie Dinsmore and Nancy Drew, see Deidre Johnson, "Nancy Drew—A Modern Elsie Dinsmore?" *The Lion and the Unicorn* 18 (1994), 13–24.

59. Carol Billman refers to the Cinderella formula in relation to the Ruth Fielding series and its prototypes in *The Secret of the Stratemeyer Syndicate: Nancy Drew, the Hardy Boys, and the Million Dollar Fiction Factory* (New York: Unger, 1986), 69–70. Although Billman feels that, unlike her predecessors, Ruth Fielding was not a Cinderella figure, in "Patterns in Early Stratemeyer Syndicate Series for Girls," a paper given at the Popular Culture/American Culture Association Conference, Louisville, Kentucky, 21 March 1992, I suggest that Ruth Fielding—and the protagonists of several other popular Stratemeyer Syndicate girls' series—do, indeed, fit the formula. Although we disagree on Ruth Fielding, Billman's comments were instrumental in suggesting the idea of the Cinderella pattern.

60. Figures are based on the chronological lists in *Girls' Series Books 1840–1991*, 327–32, and compiled from series dates provided in *American Boys' Series Books 1900 to 1980* (Tampa: University of South Florida Library Associates, 1987) and *American Anthropomorphic Animal Series Books 1900–1987* (Tampa: University of South Florida Library Associates, 1988).

61. Mark I. West, "The Response of Children's Librarians to Dime Novels and Series Books," *Children, Culture and Controversy* (Hamden, CT: Archon Book/Shoe String Press, 1988), 20–30.

62. Elizabeth Wisdom, "The Development of Good Taste in Little Children's Reading," *Library Journal* 49 (15 October 1924), 875.

63. See Ernest J. Gaines, "Viewpoint: Closed Circuit Children's Books," *Library Journal* 95 (April 1970), 1455, for an argument in favor of placing series books in libraries. This was one of the first articles signaling a change in attitudes.

64. *Girls' Series Books 1840–1991*, 338–43.

65. An article on Goosebumps from May 1996 estimated sales at between 80,000,000 and 90,000,000 copies; an October article placed them at 130,000,000. Murray Dubin, "The Stephen King of Preteen Readers: R.L. Stine Knows How to Give Kids Goosebumps," *Philadelphia Inquirer* (12 May 1996), D1; Joyce M. Rosenberg, "Goosebumps: So Successful It's Scary," *San Diego Daily Transcript* (22 October 1996), San Diego Source, <http://www.sddt.com>.

66. Penny Blubaugh and Sharon S. Ball, "The Series Controversy and How It Grew," *Public Libraries* 37, no. 1 (January/February 1998), 49–50.

67. Ross, 217, 233. See Ross, 201–36, for an overview of the controversies surrounding series books, past and present; a study of series book readers and their adult reading habits; and an analysis of the way series books can help children become more successful—and thus more enthusiastic—readers. For other defenses of the series book, studies of the potential of series books to develop reading skills, or the use of series to lure children to the library, see Dorine Geeslin and Anita Dishman Sanders, "Children's Book Choices in the Eighties," *Delta Kappa Gamma Bulletin* 48 (Winter 1982), 51–58; Margaret Mackey, "Filling the Gaps: The *Baby-Sitters Club*, the Series Book, and the Learning Reader," *Language Arts* 67 (September 1990), 484–89; Adele A. Greenlee, Dianne L. Monson, and Barbara M. Taylor, "The Lure of Series Books: Does It Affect Appreciation for Recommended Literature?" *Reading Teacher* 50, no. 3 (November 1996), 216–25; Barbara Black, "Using Series as Bait in the Public Library," in *Rediscovering Nancy Drew*, eds. Carolyn Stewart Dyer and Nancy Tillman Romalov (Iowa City:

University of Iowa Press, 1995), 121–23. For an opposing view, see Judith Saltman, "Groaning under the Weight of Series Books," *Emergency Librarian* (May–June 1997), 23–25.

Chapter 10

Poisoning Children's Culture: Comics and Their Critics

Amy Kiste Nyberg

The modern comic book appeared on newsstands in the mid-1930s. Although reprints of comic strips had been published periodically since the comic strip was established in newspapers around the turn of the century, this marked the first time the comic book appeared as a monthly publication in the familiar half-tabloid format used today. Almost from the beginning, educators and librarians categorized the comic book as a form of children's literature and condemned it as undesirable reading material. Some attacked both the content and form of comics, while others saw nothing inherently wrong with the medium, provided that the comics offered content intended to educate and enlighten. This early categorization and criticism has had a lasting impact on the comic book, because by and large, the perception of comic books as a form of subliterature intended for children persists today. This essay will briefly trace the development of the modern American comic book, analyze the criticism generated by comic books in the years before and during World War II, and discuss the impact that early criticism of comics has had on the contemporary comic book.

THE DEVELOPMENT OF THE MODERN COMIC BOOK

Eastern Color Printing Company published the first modern comic book to appear on the newsstands, *Famous Funnies*. Many comic book historians attribute the birth of the comic book to two Eastern employees, Harry Wildenberg and Max Gaines. They initially conceived the comic book as a premium giveaway and convinced Procter & Gamble to offer comic books to customers who sent in coupons from the company's products. That collection, titled *Funnies on Parade*, was so popular that its entire press run of 10,000 was distributed in weeks. Eastern's owner, Harold A. Moore, soon realized he had a potentially profitable idea. After a couple of false starts and initial distribution difficulties, Moore published *Famous Funnies*, which appeared in May 1934, and sold nearly all of its 200,000 copies. By the end of its first year, the comic was generating $30,000 a month.[1]

Despite the success of *Famous Funnies*, other publishers were slow to embrace the new medium. The supply of comic strips for reprint was rapidly exhausted, and the handful of publishers producing comics scrambled to find contributors who could generate original material. There were only about twenty titles on newsstands in 1937. But that was to change in mid-1938, the year Superman made his debut. The now-familiar superhero proved tremendously popular after his first appearance in a comic titled *Action Comics*, and his success spawned numerous imitations. Between 1938 and the time America entered World War II in 1941, the comic-book publishing industry took off in a big way. A newsstand survey in December 1941 found nearly 150 different titles with a combined circulation of fifteen million.[2] The period of growth in the comics industry from 1938 until 1945 is labeled the "Golden Age" of comics by historians of the medium.

The appearance of Superman did more than spur interest on the part of comic-book publishers; it created a genre that would become closely associated with comic books, which have introduced more than 1,000 major and minor superhero characters over the past fifty years.[3] The concept of the superhero was developed and refined during the Golden Age of comics, although the term "superhero" was not in common use until sometime in the mid-1940s. The artists and writers producing early comics simply called them costumed heroes, or more irreverently, "union suit" or "long underwear" heroes. The flashy costume quickly became a convention of the genre. Other conventions included the creation of a "super power" for the hero and the need for a secret identity. The colorful medium, with its crude drawing, proved to be the ideal showcase for superheroes and their incredible feats. Until the advent of sophisticated special effects, film and television simply could not duplicate the fantastic adventures of the superhero in a convincing manner.[4]

Adult response to the introduction and subsequent popularity of the superhero ranged from benevolent spoofing to the suggestion that the characters were a sinister reflection of world events. In a *New Yorker* piece, E.J. Kahn, Jr. wrote that while he was willing to believe that Superman could fly and shed bullets like raindrops, the one stumbling block to embracing the concept was the matter of clothes—just what happened to Superman's civilian clothes when he transformed from Clark Kent into Superman?[5] Others saw in Superman and his ilk the glorification of a breed of hero that was presented as an alternative to the justice system, an "omnipotent and infallible strong man beyond all law, the nihilistic man of the totalitarian ideology."[6] Even the publisher of *Action Comics* initially thought that the Superman character was too fantastic and banned further appearances on the cover. He would change his tune, however, when an informal newsstand study showed that children were asking for the comic "with Superman in it."[7]

Readership studies supported the conclusions of publishers that children were a major audience for comics and that they preferred the superhero comic over other genres. In the early 1940s, about 90 percent of all children aged six to seventeen, both boys and girls, were regularly reading comics, establishing comic-book reading as the dominant leisure activity for youth. The most popular titles for all age groups were *Superman* and *Batman*.[8] Although marketing studies also found that up to 40 percent of adults reported reading comic books, publishers concentrated on the juvenile market, where there was little competition. Despite the fact that children's publishing emerged as a distinct field in the 1920s, and new developments in printing made large-format picture books widely available beginning in the 1930s, the primary market for children's books was libraries. Even magazines targeting children relied more on subscriptions than newsstands sales and targeted adult purchasers.[9] Comic books, on the other hand, were selected and purchased by children themselves, often without the direct supervision of adults. Pass-along readership ensured that most children had easy access to comic books, even in homes where such reading material was discouraged or banned.

In the years following World War II, there was a decline in interest in the superheroes, and publishers turned to other genres. Two that proved successful were crime comics and horror comics. However, the graphic violence in many of these comics titles, depicted in a real-world setting rather than in the fantastic world of superheroes battling supervillains, stirred new concerns about comic books and children. This shift in comic-book content coincided with increased public attention to the problem of juvenile delinquency in postwar America. One explanation that was widely circulated and accepted on a commonsense level was that modern mass culture, particularly radio, the movies, and comic books, was turning children into juvenile delinquents.[10] Critics attacked media violence, and comic books were the most vulnerable to criticism for two reasons: first, other media, notably television and film, had codes in place that regulated content, and producers could point to that code in response to their critics; and second, comic books were perceived as a medium primarily for children.

Fredric Wertham, a noted child psychiatrist, led a national campaign against comic books, culminating in the 1954 publication of his scathing attack on comics, *Seduction of the Innocent*.[11] In response to increasing public pressure to act, Congress scheduled hearings on the comic-book industry as part of its ongoing investigation into juvenile delinquency. The Senate Subcommittee on Juvenile Delinquency called a number of expert witnesses, as well as representatives of the comic-book industry, to testify. The hearings, held in New York City over two days in April and continued for one day in June, attracted wide media coverage. Especially damaging to the case of the comic-book publishers was the testimony of William Gaines, publisher of EC Comics, under fire for his popular crime and horror titles. When he was asked if it did children any good to read such stories, Gaines replied: "I don't think it does them a bit of good, but I don't think it does them a bit of harm, either."[12] Gaines added that he was guided by "good taste" in judging the content of his comics. Senator Estes Kefauver then held up a cover of a comic book from *Crime Suspenstories*, remarking: "This seems to be a man with a bloody ax holding a woman's head up which has been severed from her body. Do you think that is in good taste?" Gaines had little choice but to answer: "Yes, sir, I do, for the cover of a horror comic." The *New York Times* played that testimony on its front page the next day.

The comic-book publishers, eager to counter the bad publicity the hearings had generated and to stave off any possible legislative action, formed a trade association, the Comics Magazine Association of America. That association, supported by most of the major comic-book publishers, adopted a regulatory code, modeled closely on the film code, that banned horror comics altogether and set down specific guidelines on the portrayal of crime and sex. The adoption of the code, with its accompanying "Seal of Approval," meant that all comic books that wished to carry the seal had to be suitable for the child reader. Many titles could not continue publication under the new regulations, and publishers searched for substitutes. They turned to the tried-and-true genre of the superhero, revamping the Golden Age characters for a new generation of readers and launching what comics historians identify as the Silver Age of comics.

The dominance of the superhero genre, combined with publishers' concentration on the juvenile market for comic books, were the two key factors in establishing comic books as juvenile literature. It is interesting that comic books, unlike most other mass media, were and are still perceived as exclusively juvenile entertainment. Newspaper strips have no such stigma; they are enjoyed by young and old alike. Radio, film, and television all offer fare that appeals to all age groups. Comics, however, were categorized almost immediately as a form of entertainment geared almost exclusively to children. The perception of comic books today, by and large, has changed little. Despite the creation of the graphic novel and the critical acclaim for *Maus*, the holocaust narrative that has become the best known of the so-called adult comics, there remains in the minds of the American public the perception that comics are for children.

There are several possible explanations. First, as suggested earlier, the popularity of the superhero in American comics and the predominance of this genre through much of the seventy-year history of the comic book mean that the content of comics holds little appeal for a more generalized adult reading audience. Second, the imposition of the comics code in 1954 severely restricted the material comic-book publishers could offer. The code's strict regulation on depiction of violence and sex and its insistence on content appropriate for even the youngest reader stifled any development of more adult-oriented fare. Although those restrictions have eased somewhat and not all publishers are bound by them today, the majority of comic books are still censored by the comics publishing industry. Third, the distribution and sale of comic books, which shifted from newsstands and mom-and-pop groceries to specialized comic-book shops in the 1970s, fail to reach beyond the existing niche market for comics.

While almost all of comic books' critics and supporters alike in the 1940s and 1950s seemed to accept without question the categorization of comic books as juvenile literature, one provocative essay by Sidonie Gruenberg of the Child

Study Association of America challenged that notion. Gruenberg was invited to contribute to a special issue of *Journal of Educational Sociology* edited by a staunch supporter of comics in the classroom, New York University professor Harvey Zorbaugh. But rather than focus on the educational value of comic books, Gruenberg instead suggested that the medium was still in its infancy, and, like film and radio before, comic books would gradually improve in order to make themselves "acceptable and approved." She acknowledged that "[a]s art, many of the comics are crude. As literature, they are extremely elementary." However, she pointed out that writers and artists had "barely begun" to show what was possible with the medium. She separated form from content: "The instrument itself need no longer be judged as good or bad . . . We have to judge only the uses to which it is put."[13] Hers was a minority view, however, as will be discussed in the next section.

THE EARLY DEBATE OVER COMICS

The popularity of comic-book reading among children in the 1940s and 1950s is analogous to television's place in the leisure time of children today. Children's attention to and fascination with comic books became a topic of concern partly because of the ubiquitous nature of the medium. Hundreds of articles about comics were published in trade, academic, professional, and popular periodicals. During the early years of comic-book publishing, the primary critics of comics were teachers and librarians, and the focus of their attack was not effects on behavior but the impact on children's culture. While the discourse on comic books found in the professional journals did not present a unified position, the dominant view was that comic-book reading was an undesirable activity.

Three basic types of articles appeared in these professional journals. One type was the article written by a teacher or librarian sharing personal observations and anecdotal information regarding comic books. Often, it was a description of some experience with or activity involving comics tried in the classroom or the local library. The second type of article was the essay, or opinion piece, expressing the author's beliefs about comics but not usually supported with any firsthand experience or research. The final type was a more formal presentation of research on comic books, often written by an education professor at a college or university. This distinction is important, because while the first and second categories of articles tended to be largely negative, research often did not support the assumptions made about comic books.

The most widely publicized early attack on comics came from literary critic Sterling North, who wrote an editorial published in the *Chicago Daily News* on May 8, 1940, titled "A National Disgrace."[14] Although it appeared in a newspaper, not in a professional journal, it is significant because it was tremendously influential in setting the agenda for the discussion of comics. In countless articles that followed North's editorial, teachers and librarians echoed his attitudes about comics, often couched in the same language.

North noted with alarm that almost every child in America was reading comic books, accounting for sales of ten million comics a month, paid for directly out of the pockets of children. Curious to discover what attraction comics held, he examined more than 100 comics and concluded that 70 percent of them contained material that would not pass muster at a "respectable newspaper." He characterized the comics as "badly drawn, badly written and badly printed—a strain on young eyes and young nervous systems . . . [that] spoil a child's natural sense of color, their hypodermic injection of sex and murder make the child impatient with better, though quieter stories." North placed the blame for comic books squarely on the shoulders of parents, calling on them to become more aware of what their children were reading and to provide substitutes for this undesirable new reading material. He wrote that "the antidote to the 'comic' magazine poison can be found in any library or good bookstore. The parent who does not acquire that antidote for his child is guilty of criminal negligence."

The newspaper was deluged with requests for reprints of the editorial, and a number of other publications carried part or all of the editorial. It also established a starting point for a dialogue about comics in the journals that served educators and librarians, those most concerned about the growing threat of comic-book reading. Two important themes emerge from this brief editorial. First, comic books are seen as a threat to children, and North reinforces that with metaphors of contagion, disease, and addiction. Second, the solution to the problem of comic-book reading was to substitute "good" children's literature as an "antidote" to the comic-book poison.

Two examples illustrate the influence of North's editorial. An article in *Elementary English Review* carried the headline "The Plague of the Comics," drawn from the author's assertion in the article that comics reading "has developed into a serious, wide-spread plague" that will leave behind "horrible desolation, grief and putrefaction." Continuing with the metaphor of disease, the author wrote that once the problem is diagnosed, the "treatment" consists of finding the proper "antidote" for "comicitis" in the school and town library.[15] The staff of the public library in Toledo, Ohio, noted that "there seemed to be a contagious attraction" about the comics "that spread like wildfire" as soon as one child was seen reading a comic book. Arguing that "comics were a serious problem in the schools as well as in the home," the authors suggested that only through exposure to good books could children be "protected" from the comics.[16]

What harm did educators find in comic books? An analysis of the criticism leveled against comics shows that educators and librarians believed allowing children to read comics was harmful in two ways. First, educators argued that comic-book reading hampered the development of reading skills and language use. Second, they believed that children who read comics would find it difficult to appreciate better literature. Each of these arguments will be considered in more detail.

The combination of words and pictures in comic books led teachers to assume that students often followed the story simply by looking at the panels and not by reading the word balloons and text that accompanied the artwork. Thus, "reading" comics did not lead to the development of reading skills, since very little reading comprehension was necessary to understand the story. One researcher at Columbia Teachers College concluded after a survey of comics readers that children were getting the story in picture form with only a small amount of reading.[17] She noted that students mentioned comics "are easier to read than books" and that "they do not require much concentration," accepting the children's perceptions that comics were easy to read and assuming that such responses necessarily indicated children were relying largely on the pictures in their reading.

One essay observed that even poor readers were able to read comics "and can supplement their grasp of the words by reading the pictures."[18] A teacher who had his remedial English students read comics to him reported that when these youngsters were asked to read comics, they made a number of reading errors, ranging from nonrecognition of a word to substitution of a word with a word with similar meaning. He concluded, "It appears doubtful that the majority of remedial reading pupils *read* the comics." In fact, he found the badly retarded readers simply created their own tales based on the pictures.[19] Noting that "comic books are the cheapest, most inartistic, worthless form of literature in existence today," one essay on comics published in the *Wilson Library Bulletin* argued that the short, episodic nature of the abbreviated text accompanying the pictures meant that only limited ideas could be expressed. The author concluded, "It cannot lead to skill in reading thoroughly well-written material."[20] In addition, educators condemned the comics because they believed that the slang and the simplicity of the language did little to improve vocabulary, and, in some cases, actually corrupted the spoken and written language of children. One teacher wrote that the impact of comics on the vocabulary of the children she taught was "potent." She continued, "They consider the faulty English humorous . . . and make use of stars, exclamation points and dashes to express their feelings in the same way that the professional artists circumvent censors."[21]

The assumption about vocabulary in comics was not borne out by research. One teacher categorized comics as "mental dynamite," finding their slang objectionable and arguing they contributed "nothing permanent to the mental development of the reader." Then, challenged by one of his students actually to *read* a comic book, he picked up a Superman comic. He conceded that the vocabulary ·was on a high level and comic books encouraged reading and increased reading speed.[22] Formal research supported his conclusion. An education professor studied the vocabulary used in popular comic books, concluding that the bulk of the language in comics was standard English rather than slang. Comics averaged about 10,000 words of reading material, refuting the assumption that comics were all pictures and very little text. The reading difficulty was at a fifth- or sixth-grade level. The researcher concluded that comic books provided a substantial amount of reading material at a level appropriate for a child in upper elementary grades.[23] Another study of vocabulary found that comic books were written at about a sixth-grade level. The researcher added: "It has been shown, however, that they include many words in advance of this level, and therefore, increase the reading vocabulary."[24] One experiment divided fifth-grade children into two groups, one that used comics as part of their reading lesson and one that did not. After several weeks, the researcher measured the vocabulary growth and reading comprehension of the two groups. She found no difference between the two groups, and concluded the use of comics in school "had no appreciable effect upon growth in vocabulary and reading comprehension."[25]

Publication of these studies, however, had little effect on educators' attitudes about comic books and reading skills. Articles in the professional journals continued to condemn comic books for their undesirable effects on reading and vocabulary. The authors either ignored the research or were unaware that their widely held beliefs had not been supported by scholarly investigation. One group that did embrace the findings, however, was comic-book publishers. They invited education professors to sit on advisory boards and provide advice about the content of comics. When criticized, publishers pointed to the inclusion of prestigious scholars from major universities on these editorial boards as evidence of their desire to improve their comics.

Even more pervasive in the education and library journals than the belief that comic books hampered the development of reading skills was the conviction that comic books prevented children from developing an appreciation for better literature. Critics argued that comic books were purely escapist fantasy that failed to provide readers with the same sort of "spiritual uplift" that better literature offered. Such critics argued that populated by one-dimensional heroes and villains, comic books presented a simplistic, black-and-white view of the world. They believed the action-adventure genre preferred by children was too sensationalistic and overstimulating, that once a child grew accustomed to a diet of comic books, his taste was ruined for other types of reading.

The editor of the *Wilson Library Bulletin* saw no relationship between reading a book and reading a comic: in fact, comic book reading "damages" children for "the more serene pleasures of the imagination."[26] A committee called upon to evaluate comic books in one school district studied 100 comics and concurred.[27] After acknowledging that there might be some positive aspects to comic-book reading, such as providing emotional release and appealing to children's desire for slapstick comedy, the committee concluded that children's interest in comics should be redirected, or "there will be a decline in artistic appreciation, a development of a taste for shoddy, distorted presentations, and perhaps permanent injury to the child's emotional and social development." Additionally, an essay in *National Parent-Teacher* called comic books "a narcotic of North American children." The author continued, "A child whose reading habits have been conditioned and corrupted by these ungrammatical scraps of narrative and conversation loses the sustained endeavor necessary for reading a full-length novel."[28]

Much of the blame for children's interest in comic book reading was placed squarely on the shoulders of those teachers, librarians, and parents who failed to expose children to more desirable reading material. Children's publishers, too, came under attack for not providing better-quality, lower-cost juvenile books that could replace comic books in children's reading diets. An assistant librarian wrote that her article represented "an S.O.S. cry to librarians, as well as to all lovers of literature."[29] The solution to the problem of comics reading is to encourage parents to put comics out of reach of children. And librarians, she argued, must offer children an alternative to comics reading that is equally attractive and exciting. "Three comic books are on tables in our living room," began an article in *Wilson Library Bulletin*.[30] The author recounted her dismay when her seven-year-old daughter went out for ice cream and instead came home with a Disney comic. When questioned about why she read comics, when library books were nicer, the child replied that she didn't have to return the comics, and she could read the comic book all by herself. The author placed the blame for such incidents on children's rooms at libraries, where librarians were too overworked to assist children in selecting books.

While educators had little control over comic-book content and could not directly address their complaint about comic books and reading skills, they could act on their belief that comic-book reading was undesirable and that children should be directed toward better reading materials. The professional journals were swamped with suggestions and strategies for weaning children from their comics. This goal was often presented as a "challenge" for teachers, or more dramatically, a "battle" or an out-and-out "war." Educators' solutions to the comic-book problem fell into two general categories: first, teachers and librarians needed to understand what attracted children to comic books and then find better literature that appealed to those same needs; and second, they needed to teach children the difference between comic books and literature so they would understand why their preference for comic books was unacceptable and why they needed to develop a taste for better literature.

In his column, the editor of *Wilson Library Bulletin* reported on letters received from two librarians, one distressed because she was being forced to provide comics in the children's reading room, and "another, more fortunate" librarian who was "waging an unspectacular and simple, but successful, campaign against the highly colored enemy" by steering children toward books that have the same appeal as comics, such as tales of Robin Hood.[31] A junior high librarian in Los Angeles placed comic books popular with children alongside children's books that seemed to be similar in theme.[32] She noted that gradually, a "bridge" was constructed between comic books and library books, and children were crossing over. The school found their experiment to stimulate reading was valuable enough to adopt as a regular procedure in the library. A freshman English teacher asked students to bring their favorite comic books to class. After a discussion on why they read comics, she encouraged the class to identify other material that had the same appeal as comics, "but which, at the same time, is more acceptable." After compiling a list, she noted that since the suggestions came directly from the students, they would be helpful in a "gradual substitution" of such literature for comics and that the process "will prove much more effective than enforced prohibition."[33]   A two-part article in *Elementary English*, "Substitutes for the Comic Books," offered criteria for selecting books as substitutes for comics and emphasized that the books should be illustrated and should be quick reading, enabling children to finish them in one sitting.[34] Included on the list were the perennial favorites such as the Dr. Seuss books, the adventures of Mary Poppins, and the children's classic, Dr. Dolittle.

Many comic-book critics concluded that the main reason children read comic books is that they had yet to develop the ability to discriminate among types of reading materials. Several educators experimented in the classroom with methods designed to teach children why comic books were not good literature. For example, a fifth-grade teacher had her pupils bring to school the comics they read.[35] In discussing their selection, she used a food metaphor—just as they should select food that is nutritious and good for them, so should they select this "food for the mind" with care. She classified their selections into three groups: informational, such as *True Comics* and *Bible Stories*, which she rated relatively wholesome; amusing, such as the Disney comics, which she saw as largely harmless; and unwholesome, which included many of the action-adventure comics such as *Action Comics* and *Captain Marvel*, which she classified as "definitely bad mental food for children." She encouraged the reading of the "better" comics by asking students to prepare oral reports based on an informational comic. At the end of the program, she distributed lists of these good comics. Her purpose was to create "a demand in the community for the *better* comics." The responsibility, she asserted, ultimately falls to the parent: "Until they discriminate, and to some extent *guide*, the unwholesome type of comic will continue to tempt children."

In many cases, such experiments were a failure—children happily critiqued the comics, but they continued to read them. A high school teacher in Chicago developed a unit on comic strips and another on comic books in teaching her freshman English classes.[36] In the unit on comic strips, students studied the use of humor. It was with some disappointment that the teacher wrote comic books were still read with avidity and Batman and Superman were still admired even after completion of the unit intended to develop students' critical abilities. In her unit on comic books, the teacher asked students to develop a rating sheet for magazines, including comics, to be included in the classroom library. She noted: "They observed that comic books, even the better ones that were devoted to biography and the retelling of the classics, did not offer provocative materials for class discussions and reports." After preparing and teaching the two units, the teacher concluded that comic books were escape literature preferred by the immature students; that comic books gave superficial treatment of subjects, and reports prepared from them were inferior; that the emphasis on pictures in comics failed to provide a "spiritual lift" that comes from fine writing; and that children needed to be taught standards by which to judge what they read.

Research on the effects of comic-book reading provided little support for educators' fears. Paul Witty at Northwestern University established himself as the leading researcher in this area, publishing a number of studies in the 1940s and early 1950s before moving on to the topic of children and television. In a study published in *Journal of Experimental Education*, Witty compared heavy and light readers of comic books to test the validity of the assumption that comic-book reading was harmful and should be discouraged.[37] He compared the two groups in terms of intelligence, academic achievement, and social adjustment. He discovered that there were no significant differences between the two groups in any of the three categories. Examination of the two groups' reading patterns also revealed comics reading had little impact on other types of reading. In fact, some of the heaviest readers of comic books had reading programs that were "varied, rich and generally commendable," while light readers had reading programs that Witty categorized as "inadequate."

Interestingly, despite the fact that his research did not support fears about the effects of comic books on children's reading, Witty was not prepared to defend comic-book reading.[38] He downplayed the results of his research, writing that while his studies found no immediate effects from reading comic books, it would be a mistake to assume comic-book reading was harmless. He believed that children were developing undesirable tastes in reading, and comic books led to a decline in "artistic appreciation" and a tolerance for shoddy storytelling. He maintained the "rehabilitation" of comic-book readers could be accomplished by providing them with good books.

One other aspect of comic-book criticism worth mentioning, because it, too, appeared frequently in the education and library journals, was the notion that comic-book reading, aside from its harmful aspects, was simply a waste of time that could better be spent elsewhere. This attitude about comics reading arises from the puzzlement adults felt over the attraction of something they saw as crude and without merit. Most adults simply could not understand why children *wanted* to read comics. Typical of this view was an essay in *Scholastic* that noted on the whole, comics are "crude, absurd, over-stimulating, and take time which could well be spent on something better."[39] One survey of comic-book content suggested the evaluation of comics needed to be done within the "limitations of the medium," arguing that comics should not be held to the literary and artistic standards of other types of reading. The criticism that comics are a waste of time, the authors wrote, is valid "only if we believe that children's hours must all be spent in ways which will be educationally and culturally profitable." The implication, of course, is there was nothing worthwhile to be gained from comic-book reading.[40] The most extreme attack on comics came in an essay titled "The Viciousness of the Comic Book," which portrayed comic-book reading as an activity that subverts American values. The author wrote that comics are "immoral and vicious" because they turn children into day-dreamers and loafers at school and "dead weights" at home, presumably because they would rather read comic books than do their schoolwork or chores. Encouraging that behavior, he asserted, will "diminish the power of a great democracy."[41]

Even those who did profess to understand children's fascination with comics stopped short of endorsing comic-book reading. Two librarians who surveyed children about their interest in the comics found that children expressed "a normal love of excitement, adventure and hero worship" that was largely missing from other reading material available to them, since children's books are "written down to childish levels, and strive to be correct, innocuous and entertaining all at the same time." Nonetheless, the authors were not willing to recommend comic-book reading because comics "represent that large mass of literature which, while not harmful, is not particularly distinctive."[42] Concluded one defender of comics: "As literature, I think they are terrible."[43]

THE IMPACT OF THE CRITICS

Comic-book publishers were not immune to this early criticism. One of the more direct responses to attacks on comics was the introduction of the educational comic book. The publishers of *Parents' Magazine* announced in 1941 the creation of *True Comics*, offering biographies of "real life heroes" such as Winston Churchill. That same year, a competitor, *Classic Comics* (renamed *Classics Illustrated* in 1947), entered the market with comic-book adaptations of novels. The success of these ventures encouraged other publishers to add educational titles to their offerings.

The publishers of *Parents' Magazine* quoted from Sterling North's editorial, then added: "It was widely reprinted. But nothing really happened. Now, however, the publishers of *Parents' Magazine* are doing something about it." The magazine's editor, Clara Savage Littledale, wrote that she expected teachers and parents to embrace the new comic because of its educational value, while "children will be delighted with it because the pictures and stories are truly exciting and more interesting because they are true."[44]

The publishers of *True Comics* argued that children liked comic books because they were colorful and easy to read. In addition, the stories focused on adventure and the daring exploits of heroes. Since trying to substitute good children's books doesn't work—children read the books, but keep right on reading comics, too, they concluded—the answer was to substitute reading material that offered all of the features of a comic book but substituted desirable content. To add respectability, the magazine appointed a junior advisory board of child movie stars and a senior advisory board of well-known individuals, such as George H. Gallup of the Institute of Public Opinion, and academics supportive of educational comics.

The first issue sold 300,000 copies ten days after its publication in early March, and the Canadian version, titled *True Picture Magazine*, also was a sellout. Extra copies were printed for both American and Canadian distribution. The comic, scheduled to come out every two months, was quickly shifted to a monthly publication schedule. Publisher George Hecht hosted a luncheon during Children's Book Week in October 1941, telling his audience that while a bestselling children's book might sell 5,000 copies, his comic book was reaching fifteen million a month, adding up to 180 million a year.[45]

Classic Comics made their debut in fall 1941, and by 1946, publisher Albert Kanter had produced twenty-eight titles and sold about 100 million copies. More than 20,000 schools reported using the comics, which adapted literary classics into a comic-book format.[46] In 1942, Max Gaines, who edited the All-American

Comics line for National Comics, brought out *Picture Stories from the Bible*, which won Catholic sanction and approval from an advisory board of Protestants and Jews. Each story was prefaced with appropriate citations for finding it in the Old Testament.[47]   Also in 1942, a comic book designed for distribution in Catholic schools, *Topix Comics*, was published; it featured stories about the pope and about Catholic saints, as well as stories from the Bible.[48]

The introduction of educational material in comic-book form added a new dimension to the debate over comics. While most educators agreed that their goal should be to wean children away from comics by introducing them to better literature, they were divided over whether comic books with educational content were an acceptable compromise. Some objected because they disapproved of both the content and the form. An editorial in *Wilson Library Bulletin* observed that "fighting comics with comics" was not an improvement on the crudeness of the medium, with its bad taste in color and design. The author also was skeptical about whether children would be taken in by this attempt to convert their favorite leisure activity to an educational one: "The reaction of children of my own acquaintance to *True Comics*," he wrote, "is that it is a pale imitation of 'the real thing.'"[49] One essay called *True Comics* a remarkable experiment but expressed hope the publisher would keep the informational content and the cheap price, then gradually drop the "imitation-comics approach."[50] Others, however, approved of the new venture. One editorial praised the efforts of *Parents' Magazine's* publishers, noting the comic "will be a boon to people of all classes who crave general information on public men and public issues, reaching back into the past, surveying the present—and all neatly packaged into a nutshell."[51] Another editorial suggested that in a society that has been conditioned by motion pictures to acquire information visually, the comic book could serve an educational function.[52]

Although educational comic books might have been popular with parents, teachers, and librarians who saw in them an answer to some of their objections to comics, children did not desert *Superman* and *Batman* for the real-life heroes touted in *True Comics* or the easy-to-read versions of classic literature presented in *Classic Comics*. However, the argument over the value of these so-called educational comics would take a backseat to new concerns about comics—their effect on children's behavior. As noted earlier, criticism of comics shifted in postwar America, when comic-book reading became linked with a rise in juvenile delinquency. In the late 1940s, the growing popularity of crime comic books sparked concern that children were imitating the crime and violence they saw in the pages of their comics. Newspaper articles were full of anecdotal evidence of children who had assaulted and even killed other children and who turned out to be heavy readers of this type of comic book. The introduction of EC Comics' popular horror comics—with titles like *The Crypt of Terror* and *The Vault of Horror*—spawned many imitators and also horrified adults with their realistic violence, albeit often committed by fantastic creatures such as vampires or ghouls.

Much of the public outcry over comic books in the late 1940s can be traced to two influential articles about psychiatrist Frederic Wertham's work: Judith's Crist's "Horror in the Nursery," published in *Collier's* in March 1948, and a follow-up article written by Wertham himself, titled "The Comics—Very Funny," published in *Saturday Review of Literature* two months later.[53] Various communities passed ordinances banning crime comics from newsstands, the New York Legislature appointed a special committee to consider state legislation to control comics, and various church and civic groups undertook "decency crusades" in their communities to force objectionable comic books off the shelves. The publishers responded by forming a trade association, the Association of Comics Magazine Publishers (ACMP), and adopting a code to regulate the content of comics. However, some of the major publishers refused to join and others refused to support the code as written, so the prepublication review process fell by the wayside.

Although legal remedies proved unconstitutional and were dropped, decency crusades were effective in removing offensive material in the short term, and the formation of the ACMP made it seem as if the industry was being responsive to public demands to clean up comics. For these reasons, the controversy over comics died down for awhile, to be rekindled again by Wertham with the publication of his book *Seduction of the Innocent* in 1954, excerpted in November 1953 in *Ladies' Home Journal*.[54] The renewed outcry led to hearings on the comic-book industry in the spring of 1954 by the Senate Subcommittee to Investigate Juvenile Delinquency. In its report issued in November, the committee concluded that while the evidence linking comic books to juvenile delinquency was inconclusive and more research was needed, the nation could not afford to take a wait-and-see approach. Instead, the committee pressed the industry to regulate itself, suggesting as a model the production code adopted by the film industry in the 1930s.[55]

Even before the committee issued its report, however, the comic-book publishers formed a new trade association called the Comics Magazine Association of America to take the place of the largely defunct ACMP; adopted a regulatory code specifically targeting the crime and horror comics and more generally addressing content attacked by critics; and hired a judge to oversee implementation of its new regulations, beginning in October 1954. Unlike the earlier code, this industry regulation was supported by most of the major publishers, and it had an enforcement mechanism—newsstand distributors refused to carry any comics unless they carried the code's "Seal of Approval." The impetus for the code was the outcry against the graphic content of comic books, but the earlier criticism of their quality was not forgotten in crafting the code. The code could not dictate that comic books become better literature, but publishers were encouraged to improve the writing. One clause read as follows: "Although slang and colloquialism are acceptable, excessive use should be discouraged and wherever possible good grammar shall be employed." That provision remained intact when the code was revised in 1971. It was modified slightly when a new code was adopted in 1989: "The language in a comic book will be appropriate for a mass audience that includes children. Good grammar and spelling will be encouraged."

More important, however, was the code's impact on what comic books could *not* be: anything other than children's reading material. In his book *Adult Comics*, Roger Sabin concludes that "the code left the way open for juvenile and teen-oriented material to flourish."[56] Comics scholar Joseph Witek is harsher in his assessment of the code's effects, noting that "the reactionary restrictions of the comic-book industry's self-censoring body, the Comics Code Authority, led to the thematic stagnation of the sequential art medium for several decades."[57] Largely as a result of the code, Witek argues, "the bland and tedious comic books it mandated are a literary stigma from which the medium has been hard-pressed to recover."

Two challenges to mainstream comics would surface briefly: the underground comics that emerged in the 1960s, and the so-called "independent" comics published by small, upstart companies in the late 1970s and early 1980s. Both the undergrounds and the independents were important because they provided an alternative to the juvenile fare offered by the mainstream publishers, allowed a new group of artists and writers unprecedented creative freedom, and demonstrated to their readers the possibilities of the medium.

The youth culture of the 1960s gave birth to comics that escaped the corporate control of the medium. These are known as underground comics (or, as they are often referred to in order to distinguish them from their mainstream counterparts, "comix"). Witek writes that the cheaply and independently published black-and-white comics served as "outlets for the graphic fantasies and social protests of the youth counterculture." The mainstay of these comics was sex and drugs, two topics banned by the code. Sabin describes their content: "The code stipulated 'no sex,' so the comix reveled in every kind of sex imaginable; the code stipulated 'no violence,' so the underground took bloodshed to extremes; above all, the Code stipulated 'no social relevance,' yet here were comics that were positively revolutionary."[58] As Witek and others have noted, one of the appeals for comix artists was the subversion of a medium the public perceived as children's entertainment. Witek argues the movement was "a crucial phase in the development of sequential art as a means of artistic expression," but underground comix were a short-lived phenomenon, lasting barely a decade. He cites the closure of drug paraphernalia shops, the distribution outlet for undergrounds, unfavorable court decisions concerning obscenity, and the loss of the counterculture's political and artistic energy as reasons for the decline of comix.[59] Although artists still work in the underground format, Witek believes the surviving undergrounds retain "only a shadow of their former vitality and transgressive force."

The second challenge to mainstream comics publishers was the emergence of the independent publishers in the late 1970s and early 1980s, spurred by a change in the distribution system for comics.[60] Under the old system, which is still in place and accounts for about one-quarter of all comic-book distribution, comic books are distributed by companies that also handle other periodicals and are sold at retail outlets offering a variety of magazines. Retailers return unsold copies to the publisher for credit. Under the direct market system, distributors who specialize in comics and comics-related merchandise solicit orders for upcoming titles and sell comic books directly to retailers on a nonreturn basis. Their primary customers are comic-book specialty shops, which benefit from direct market distribution because of a more timely delivery schedule and a deeper discount made possible by the nonreturn policy.

The new system reduced the risks associated with comics publishing in two ways. First, the comics are sold on a nonreturnable basis, which shifts the risk from the publisher to the retailer. And second, because orders are placed in advance, companies know how many copies of a title to print. Reducing the risk associated with publishing led to a boom in smaller, independent publishers. These independents distribute comics only through the direct-market system, bypassing the newsstand distribution, the enforcement mechanism for the comics code. Freed from the constraints of industry self-regulation, the independent publishers produced adult-oriented titles, some of which broke away from the traditional superhero genre. The independents found a market for their titles, and sales of independent comics were inflated by speculators who gambled on the value of comics as collectibles. However, their success was short-lived. Sales dropped as speculators deserted comic books, and an upheaval in the direct-market distribution system, which left only one major distributor and drove a large number of retail outlets out of business, led to a slump in the comic-book market. Independent publishers folded or were purchased by one of the larger publishers.

The demise of the independents left comic-book publishing firmly in control of two major publishers, Marvel Comics and DC Comics, which was a setback for those who had hoped comic books would finally escape their juvenile constraints. Both Marvel and DC Comics are members of the Comics Magazine Association of America and subscribe to the comics code, which means their code-approved comics are still aimed at a general audience. Since all of Marvel's titles and the majority of DC Comics' titles are code-approved, most comic books on the market today are still children's fare. One impact that the independents had on mainstream comics was that DC Comics now offers comics suggested for mature audiences under separate imprints, such as their Vertigo line. However, they are only a small portion of comics on the market. In addition, media economics dictate that publishers remain with the tried-and-true formulas that currently sell comics. Experimenting with genres other than superhero and making an effort to reach noncomics readers are risky economic ventures, and the two major publishers have little incentive to do so. In addition, there has been little interest in investing in the type of market research that would be a necessary antecedent to any successful efforts to expand the audience for comics.

CONCLUSION

Comic books today attract little of the criticism that dominated the professional journals of the 1940s and the larger public debate over comics and juvenile delinquency in postwar America. Occasionally, a comic book judged inappropriate for juvenile readers will spark an outcry, such as that by Joe Queenan's "Drawing on the Dark Side" published in *New York Times Magazine* in 1989.[61] The main reason there has been little sustained criticism of comic books since the 1950s is their popularity with children has waned. Competition for children's leisure time has increased dramatically, and comic-book circulation suffered as a result. A second, and related reason, is the shifting demographics of comic-book readership. While nearly all children reported reading comics in the surveys done in the 1940s and 1950s, the readership for comic books today is young adult males. And finally, the shift from newsstand distribution to specialty shops has largely removed the comic book from the public eye. However, the early criticism from teachers and librarians who first noticed and objected to comic books has had a lasting effect. From the beginning, these critics defined the comic book as juvenile literature, reinforcing in the minds of the public that comic books are strictly for children. There is nothing inherent in the medium to make it so—comics in Japan and France, for instance, find wide readership.

What will it take to raise the status of the comic book and give it the legitimacy of other literary and artistic endeavors? One possibility lies in expanding the distribution of comic books. Publishers have had limited success with placing comics, particularly graphic novels—large-format, book-length comics usually published in hardcover—in bookstores. A reversal of the depressed market also could stimulate another challenge to mainstream comics publishing from independent publishers who are willing to give creators the freedom to explore the medium's possibilities. Finally, the increasing attention from academics, with their investigation of the formal properties of comics, their treatment of comics as literary texts worthy of analysis, and their scholarly research into comic-book history, may move the comic book in that direction. Similar scholarly attention to film and television has elevated those media from "mere entertainment" to cultural forms meriting such academic scrutiny. For the foreseeable future, however, it is likely that comic books will remain "scorned literature."

NOTES

1. Mike Benton, *The Comic Book in America: An Illustrated History* (Dallas, TX: Taylor Publishing Co., 1988), 15–17; John R. Vosburgh, "How the Comic Book Started," *The Commonweal*, 20 May 1948, 146–47; Nathan Abelson, "Comics Are a Serious Business," *Advertising and Selling*, July 1946, 42; Ron Goulart, *Over 50 Years of American Comic Books* (Lincolnwood, IL: Publications International, Ltd. 1991), 29.

2. "Superman Scores," *Business Week*, 18 April 1942, 54.

3. Benton, *Comic Book in America*, 174.

4. Mike Benton, *Superhero Comics of the Golden Age: An Illustrated History* (Dallas, TX: Taylor Publishing Co., 1992), 5.

5. E.J. Kahn Jr., "Why I Don't Believe in Superman," *The New Yorker*, 29 June 1940, 56–58.

6. James Frank Vlamos, "The Sad Case of the Funnies," *The American Mercury*, April 1941, 414.

7. Benton, *Golden Age*, 23.

8. Nathan Abelson, "Comics Are a Serious Business: Part II of a Study of Comic Magazines," *Advertising and Selling*, August 1946, 80; "Survey Reveals High Readership," *Advertising Age*, 27 September 1943, 54; Paul Witty, "Children's Interest in Reading the Comics," *Journal of Experimental Education* 10 (December 1941): 100–4; Paul Witty, Ethel Smith, and Anne Coomer, "Reading the Comics in Grades VII and VIII," *Journal of Educational Psychology* 33 (March 1942): 173–82; Paul Witty and Anne Coomer, "Reading the Comics in Grades IX-XII," *Educational Administration and Supervision* 28 (May 1942): 344–53.

9. Judith Duke, *Children's Books and Magazines: A Market Study* (White Plains, NY: Knowledge Industry Publications, 1979), 13, 19.

10. James Gilbert, *Cycle of Outrage: America's Reaction to the Juvenile Delinquent in the 1950s* (New York: Oxford University Press, 1986), 12–14.

11. For a detailed history of postwar comics criticism and the comics code, see Amy Kiste Nyberg, *Seal of Approval: The History of the Comics Code* (Jackson: University of Mississippi Press, 1998).

12. U.S. Senate Subcommittee to Investigate Juvenile Delinquency, *Juvenile Delinquency (Comic Books)*, Hearings, April 21, 22 and June 4, 1954, 103.

13. Sidonie M. Gruenberg, "The Comics as a Social Force," *Journal of Educational Sociology* 18 (December 1944): 204–13.

14. Sterling North, "A National Disgrace," reprinted in *Childhood Education* 17 (October 1940): 56.

15. Franklyn M. Branley, "The Plague of the Comics," *Elementary English Review* 19 (May 1942): 181–82.

16. Ethel C. Wright, "A Public Library Experiments with the Comics," *Library Journal* 68 (October 15, 1943): 832–34.

17. Ruth Strange, "Why Children Read the Comics," *Elementary School Journal* 43 (January 1943): 336–42.

18. Jennie Milton, "Children and the Comics," *Childhood Education* 16 (October 1939): 62.

19. David Zamchick, "Comic Books?" *English Journal* 41 (December 1952): 95–96.

20. Elinor C. Saltus, "The Comics Aren't Good Enough," *Wilson Library Bulletin* 26 (January 1952): 382–83.

21. Florence Brumbaugh, "The Comics and Children's Vocabularies," *Elementary English Review*, 16 (February 1939): 64.

22. David T. Armstrong, "How Good Are the Comic Books?" *Elementary English Review* 21 (December 1944): 283–85.

23. Robert Thorndike, "Words and the Comics," *Journal of Experimental Education* 10 (1941): 110–13.

24. W.W.D. Sones, "Comic Books as Teaching Aids," *The Instructor* 51 (April 1942): 14.

25. Edith Sperzel, "The Effects of Comic Books on Vocabulary Growth and Reading Comprehension," *Elementary English* 25 (January 1948): 113.

26. "Libraries, to Arms!" The Roving Eye, Column, *Wilson Library Bulletin* 15 (April 1941): 670–71.

27. G.A. Noble, "The Comics." *The School* 34 (December 1945): 304–8.

28. Roderick Ronson, "The Comic Corruption," *National Parent-Teacher*, June 1950, 24.

29. Eva J. Anttonen, "On Behalf of Dragons," *Wilson Library Bulletin* 15 (March 1941): 567.

30. Helen Smith, "Comic Books in Our House!" *Wilson Library Bulletin* 20 (December 1945): 290.

31. "The Comic Menace," The Roving Eye, Column, *Wilson Library Bulletin* 15 (June 1941): 846–47.

32. Mardie Jay Bakjian, "Kern Ave. Junior High Uses Comics as a Bridge," *Library Journal* 70 (April 1, 1945): 291–92.

33. Fleda Cooper Kinneman, "The Comics and Their Appeal to the Youth of To-day," *English Journal* 32 (June 1943): 331–35.

34. Constance Carr, "Substitutes for the Comic Books I," *Elementary English* 28 (April 1951): 194–214; Constance Carr. "Substitutes for the Comic Books Part II," *Elementary English* 28 (May 1951): 276–85.

35. Lena Denecke, "Fifth Graders Study Comic Books," *Elementary English Review* 22 (January 1945): 6–8.

36. Harriet E. Lee, "Discrimination in Reading," Roundtable, *English Journal* 31 (November 1942): 677–79.

37. Paul Witty, "Reading the Comics—A Comparative Study," *Journal of Experimental Education* 10 (December 1941): 109.

38. Paul Witty, "Those Troublesome Comics," *National Parent-Teacher*, January 1942, 30.

39. Julian C. Aldrich, "'Comics' Are Serious Business," *Scholastic*, 10–15 November, 1941, p. T-1.

40. Josette Frank and Mrs. Hugh Grant Straus, "Looking at the Comics," *Child Study* 20 (Summer 1943): 112–18.

41. James D. Landsdowne, "The Viciousness of the Comic Book," *Journal of Education* 127 (January 1944): 14–15.

42. Gweneira Williams and Jane Wilson, "They Like It Rough: In Defense of Comics," *Library Journal* 67 (March 1, 1942): 204–6.

43. George R. Reynolds, "The Child's Slant on the Comics," *School Executive* 62 (September 1942): 17.

44. Clara Savage Littledale, "What to Do about the 'Comics,'" *Parents' Magazine*, March 1941, 26–27.

45. "Cartoon Magazine for Children a Big Success," *Publishers' Weekly*, 8 March 1941, 1127; "Book Week Audience Hears About Comics," *Publishers' Weekly*, 22 November 1941, 1953.

46. "Classic Comics Sell a Hundred Million," *Publishers' Weekly*, 23 March 1946, 17.

47. "Biblical Comic Book," *Newsweek*, 3 August 1942, 55.

48. Thomas F. Doyle, "What's Wrong with the 'Comics'?" *Catholic World*, February 1943, 548–57.

49. "Libraries, to Arms!" The Roving Eye, Column, *Wilson Library Bulletin* 8 (April 1941): 670.

50. Louise Seaman Bechtel, "The Comics and Children's Books," *The Horn Book*, July 1941, 296–303.

51. "'Tis True 'Tis Comic, and Comic 'Tis 'Tis True," *School and Society* 10 May 1941, 598.

52. "Our Comic Culture," *Educational Forum* 6 (November 1941): 84.

53. Judith Crist, "Horror in the Nursery," *Collier's*, 29 March 1948, 22–23; Frederic Wertham, "The Comics—Very Funny," *Saturday Review of Literature*, 29 May 1948, 6–7.

54. Frederic Wertham, *Seduction of the Innocent* (New York: Rinehart and Co.), 1954; Frederic Wertham, "What Parents Don't Know about Comics, *Ladies' Home Journal*, November 1953, 50–53.

55. U.S. Senate, *Comic Books and Juvenile Delinquency*, Interim report of the Committee on the Judiciary, Subcommittee of Juvenile Delinquency, 84th Cong., 1st sess., 1955.

56. Roger Sabin, *Adult Comics: An Introduction* (London: Routledge, 1993): 163.

57. Joseph Witek, *Comic Books as History: The Narrative Art of Jack Jackson, Art Spiegelman, and Harvey Pekar*, Studies in Popular Culture (Jackson: University Press of Mississippi, 1989): 7.

58. Sabin, *Adult Comics,* 171.

59. Witek, *Comic Books as History*, 50–52.

60. Nyberg, *Seal of Approval*, 144–46.

61. Joe Queenan, "Drawing on the Dark Side," *New York Times Magazine*, 30 April 1989, 32–34.

Chapter 11

"Wise Censorship": Cultural Authority and the Scorning of Juvenile Series Books, 1890–1940

Kathleen Chamberlain

In 1965, when I was nine years old, I asked our children's librarian for a Nancy Drew book. The librarian said pleasantly, "Nancy Drews aren't the kind of books we like to have in the library. But we have some other series you might enjoy." She offered me Maud Hart Lovelace's Betsy-Tacy stories and Laura Ingalls Wilder's Little House books. I spent many happy hours reading the books found in libraries; I spent just as many pleasurable hours reading the other kind of books, the sort that many librarians and educators did not "like to have in the library." As a child, I made no qualitative distinctions between the two types of books, but I realized that others did. It seemed natural to me that there should be separate standards for library books and for home books.

But, of course, the removal of such series as Nancy Drew from many American library and school shelves was not a "natural" phenomenon. The lengthy cultural process that turned such books into "scorned literature" is complex, encompassing a variety of social, moral, and political concerns. From the 1880s onward, and especially during the Progressive Era, those involved in children's education devoted a great deal of attention to the question of what children did and should read. As journalists, teachers, and children's librarians debated the merits and purposes of children's literature, they also revealed much about the ways in which childhood and adolescence were socially constructed, about the commodification of juvenile books, the establishment of intellectual authority, the politics of canon formation, the professionalization of librarianship and teaching, and the cultural and moral goals of American education. Thus by studying how and why certain series books came to be scorned, we can learn a great deal about the construction of American cultural identity during the Progressive Era, those crucial years when the country was grappling with the consequences of rapid industrialization, immigration, and capital expansion.

Hardcover series books—that is, books grouped under a common thematic title or, more typically, that featured the same characters in three or more volumes—appeared early among American juvenile literature. The first successful series began in 1834. By 1940, literally hundreds of different hardcover juvenile series had been published in the United States.

The accepted scholarly wisdom is that series books in general have been dismissed by most adults as mediocre time-wasters at best and harmful mind-warpers at worst. Although this view is not completely accurate, it does represent a typical critical response, especially toward those series perceived to be hastily written, mass-produced, or "sensational" and unrealistic. Anyone who has done even a moderate amount of research into critical appraisals of series has come across comments such as the following, by Franklin K. Mathiews, the chief librarian of the Boy Scouts. In his 1914 article "Blowing Out the Boys' Brains," Mathiews contended that "as some boys read such books, their imaginations are literally 'blown out,' and they go into life as terribly crippled as though by some material explosion they had lost a hand or foot."[1] Some librarians and educators believed that a steady diet of the improbable characters and events common to many popular series books would give a child a false understanding of life. In somewhat less inflammatory language than Mathiews', Lewis Terman and Margaret Lima, in their book *Children's Reading: A Guide for Parents and Teachers* (1926), argued that series "command a market only because they gratify the child's desire to find in his reading the fulfillment of his daydreams . . . when the exploits of the hero are too fantastic to admit of duplication in real life, the results may be extremely harmful."[2]

To judge from these and similar remarks alone, one might conclude that scorners of series books were united in their opinions and that they based their conclusions on consistent and widely accepted literary and moral standards. But, while children's professionals usually did talk in terms of the artistic merit and the moral and educational effects of children's literature, and while there were many similarities in their views, the debate was messier, more complex, and more culturally suggestive than is usually indicated. Series were not universally damned as a class; in fact, they engendered praise as well as balanced criticism that stopped far short of condemnation. It will be instructive to examine the general nature of critical responses and then to explore specific reactions.

First, the issue was rarely presented in the simple binary of series versus nonseries fiction. Most critics situated their discussions within larger categories: for instance, they would try to identify "good" or "wholesome" children's books and would judge both series and nonseries books by that particular standard. Second, although they tried, critics never settled on a fully defined standard of aesthetic excellence. Most comments on standards remained vague and abstract, with critics calling for books that were "pure" and "true"[3] or "healthy"[4] or that had "vitality."[5] Finally, critics were by no means uniformly opposed to series fiction in general nor did they all unite against the same series. Significantly, many did not seem to fear the sort of serious damage described so vividly by Mathiews or by Terman and Lima.

As early as 1879, no less a literary and cultural authority than Thomas Wentworth Higginson argued that reading Oliver Optic did not lead boys to depravity; instead, he suggested, these books promoted what he saw as desirable cultural attitudes: "It is not a bad impulse but a good one that makes the child seek the kind of reading you call sensational. The motive that sends him to Oliver Optic is just that love of adventure which has made the Anglo-American race spread itself across a continent."[6] Such books had a place in libraries, he concluded. Nor did he view series as automatically low in literary quality. At one point, he even placed a series author in the exalted company of Dickens. Of Sophie May's heroine Little Prudy, he wrote, "compared with her, all other children are cold creations of literature: she alone is the real thing."[7]

Series were often praised in review essays on children's literature. In her article "A Child's Garden of Books," which ran in *The Bookman* in 1913, Margaret Anderson treated series books in the same manner as she did other titles, without condemning them as a class or discussing them separately from nonseries volumes. She praised the Five Little Peppers series and even had kind words for Margaret Vandercook's Camp Fire Girls books, one of the sort of cheaply produced series that rarely received mainstream attention.[8] In its list of recommended Christmas gifts, the *Elementary School Journal* in 1919 suggested Lucy Fitch Perkins' Twins books and Joseph Altsheler's French and Indian War Series.[9] Even often-maligned series such as Elsie Dinsmore were sometimes mentioned with approval. In 1915, Grace Colbron noted in *The Bookman* that series such as Jack Harkaway, Nick Carter, and Elsie had "given honest, wholesome pleasure to many a boy and girl."[10]

Quite a few critics acknowledged literary deficiencies in many series, but they did not always believe that children should therefore be kept from reading them. Of series reading, Alice Chadwick wrote in 1897 that children have "an immense stowage capacity. There seems a necessity for a great amount of provision which shall become waste material—taken in and thrown off—somehow helping in the building, yet leaving no conscious trace. If we look at this fairly, we shall not incline to the dogmatism of discarding all literature which seems to be only temporary."[11] Other critics recognized that, whatever adult objections, series books offered elements that children valued. "Certainly in these series books the children are finding something which is profitable to *them*: excitement, escape from hampering restrictions of reality, perhaps, relief from the very effort involved in reading 'good literature,'" wrote Josette Frank in 1941.[12] In fact, only a minority of critics seemed actually to believe that series threatened children's mental and moral welfare. Few resorted to the tone of moral outrage that marks the most-often-quoted scorners of series books.

Even when there was general philosophical agreement that many mass-produced series had little literary value, critics could not always agree on which series deserved scorn. Time and changing literary fashions had a great deal to do with which series were criticized and when. In 1926, the influential *Winnetka Graded Book List* listed in a *Supplement* over 100 books that librarians had designated as "trashy." Included among the rubbish were the Oz books, Alice

Turner Curtis's Little Maid series, the Little Prudy books, the Little Colonel stories, and a host of series from the Stratemeyer Syndicate.[13] Yet Margaret Anderson, for instance, had earlier approved of the Oz books as well as the Little Colonel and Little Maid stories. Not even Edward Stratemeyer, perhaps the most thoroughly scorned series author, was completely condemned. Between 1901 and 1912, Montrose Moses wrote an annual review essay on children's books for the magazine *The Independent* in which he often cited historical tales written by Stratemeyer. In 1911, Moses included a volume of Stratemeyer's Dave Porter series in a list of the "best of the class" of boys' school stories.[14]

In addition to book lists, other evidence also suggests the complexity and contradictions of many professionals' attitudes toward series. For instance, many series, even scorned ones, found their way into libraries. During the 1892–93 school year, M.B.C. True, superintendent of schools in Tecumseh, Nebraska, charted the circulation of the 179 books in the library of the town's high school.[15] High on the list of the most popular titles were Sophie May's Little Prudy and Flaxie Frizzle series. Not only did the students clearly like these books, but the Tecumseh educators themselves approved, since the school system purchased several additional May titles during the survey year. And among the 3,330 books listed in the 1920 *Catalogue of Books in the Children's Department of the Carnegie Library of Pittsburgh* are quite a few series, including nine Five Little Peppers titles and four of Curtis's Little Maid books.[16]

One of the most significant groups that did not scorn series books was children themselves. Whatever the objections of children's professionals, young readers continued to number series titles among their favorite books. When surveyed about their preferences, children almost always reported reading and liking many of the scorned series. One survey, done of Pittsburgh junior high school pupils in 1930, discovered that "when the books read by pupils with high IQ s and by those with low IQ s were checked it was found that just about twice as many series were reported by the pupils with *greater* mental ability."[17]

All this evidence raises an important question: if series books were not, in fact, consistently regarded as harmful to children's education and character, and if they were widely enjoyed by children themselves (and at least tacitly approved by the parents and other adults who bought such books as gifts), then why and how did the views of those who did scorn the books gain authority to the extent that most series books were eventually excluded from public and school libraries, from classrooms, from lists of recommended books, and from the curricula of teacher-education programs? How did a relatively small group of mostly wage-earning middle-class people effectively censor a popular and profitable mass-market *genre*?

The answers involve a number of complex issues. First, the major scorners, who were primarily librarians and educators, had a great deal of cultural authority, especially during the Progressive Era. This authority developed historically both as a response to and an encourager of various public attitudes about the nature of childhood and about the moral and social importance of reading and education. Scorners and nonscorners, professionals and parents shared many of the same views about the effect of reading, particularly the widely held belief that what children read significantly shapes their minds and characters and that therefore children should read those works that will do them "good" of some kind. A prevailing nineteenth-century perspective held that even the slightest events could have an indelible effect on a child's moral development. Although the strictness of this belief waned with the post-Civil War decline in the influence of evangelical Protestantism, its fundamental premise remained in the commonly held opinion that what children read influenced, if not their entire moral character, then certainly *something* important: their vocabulary[18] or their taste[19] or their ability to recognize and appreciate "good" literature[20] or their sense of "worthy ideals of conduct" and their "appreciation of the beautiful."[21] In a 1921 article criticizing writers of juveniles whose tales glorified battle and encouraged American xenophobia and racism, *The Nation* commented, "Let us make the boys' books of a nation and we care not a rap who makes its laws or its songs either. Boyhood is the susceptible age of the race."[22] So was girlhood, in others' views. Such widespread attitudes help indicate why many parents and other members of the public were willing to accept (or at least not to challenge too strongly) the edicts of the professionals. Since children's literature was so widely seen as educative in so many senses, it is logical that authority for ascertaining that its power was properly used was given over to—and taken by—children's librarians and educators.

The recommendations of librarians and educators carried significant cultural weight in part because both libraries and schools were held to serve major civic functions. In the Progressive Era, and even before, schools and libraries came to be regarded, not merely as intellectual training grounds or repositories of knowledge, but as major agents of socialization and citizenship, places where both native-born and immigrant children could learn what it meant to be "American" and what would be expected of them as functioning citizens of a democracy. "Civic responsibility" was a common argument offered in support of children's libraries, as demonstrated by such articles as "Children's Libraries a Moral Force" and "The Civic Value of Library Work with Children." In the latter, Dr. Graham Taylor wrote, "Equally with the schools and playground, our library centers are essential to American democracy."[23] Schools were believed to have even greater civic power and duty. To many adults, then, "reading" represented much more than merely a basic skill; it was seen as one of the major avenues for achieving the social and civic goals of education. "The schooling which does not result in implanting a permanent taste for good reading has failed in the main end of democratic education," said Charles Eliot, the president of Harvard University and the National Education Association, in 1903.[24]

Certainly by 1900, librarians and educators were in a good position to assume their place as literary gatekeepers. The latter decades of the nineteenth century saw a rise in the "professionalization" of many activities that had previously been thought to require relatively minimal training. Included in the movement toward professionalization were teaching and librarianship. As entry into the professions came to require more and more training and expertise, the positions increased both in social and intellectual status and in cultural authority. In 1968, Talcott Parsons argued that "the professional complex . . . has already become the most important single component in the structure of modern societies."[25] To qualify as a profession, an occupation must require formal training and must devise some method of assuring that its members have adequately met the formal requirements. The training must also "lead to some order of mastery of a generalized cultural tradition" that features an "intellectual component." Finally, a "full-fledged profession must have some institutional means of making sure that such competence is put to socially responsible uses."[26] In the modern capitalist/industrial world, professionals serve as the definers and defenders of social and moral ideology. Everett Hughes, another major theorist of the professions, defined the power of professions as a "mandate." When the members of a given occupation are able, through such means as organized training, licensing boards, and moral suasion, to convince society that they alone have the knowledge and expertise to accomplish their tasks, then they have achieved a "mandate" to define both their work and public attitudes toward it.[27] As Robert Dingwall explains, "not only do professions presume to tell the rest of their society what is good and right for it: they can also set the very terms of thinking about problems which fall in their domain."[28]

Although the occupations of librarian and elementary/secondary teacher have not achieved the same level of social prestige and academic mystique as, for instance, law or medicine, they nonetheless meet the major definitions of professionalization.[29] As the market for children's books grew, so did the perceived need for children's-book experts. After the Civil War, both librarianship and teaching became more standardized and institutionalized, as the proliferation of training schools, professional organizations, and professional journals attests. The American Library Association was formed in 1876; the first professional library school opened at Columbia University in 1887.[30] Teacher-training schools began earlier, but before the Civil War, only twelve normal schools existed in the United States. By 1900, there were 345.[31]

Most libraries did not begin to cater to children until the end of the nineteenth century. The Children's Library Association was formed in 1890, yet specialized children's rooms grew only slowly during the 1890s. By 1910, however, libraries in many cities, large and small, had children's sections. As was typical of the process of professionalization, this new institution required specialists to help perpetuate it. The result was the new profession of "children's librarian," a person whose accepted expertise not only justified the existence of the children's section of a library but also ensured her own survival and the expansion of the children's book market in general. The first professional "Training School for Children's Librarians" opened in 1900; the same year saw the creation of a "Library Work with Children" section as part of the American Library Association.

Librarians and educators established what Parsons called the "socially responsible" focus of their professional and cultural mandate in a variety of ways, particularly through their public proselytizing in print. In 1882, Caroline

Hewins, a prominent librarian in Hartford, Connecticut, published one of the first guides to children's book selection, *Books for the Young: A Guide for Parents and Children*. Hewins' influence on juvenile literature was strong. *Books for the Young* set the pattern for the many children's lists to follow: it offered "rules" for teaching "the right use of books," quotations about children's books from other sources, and lists of recommended books divided into such categories as myths and fairy tales, poetry, and nonfiction. This basic structure—a section that explains the need for and goals of such a list and that provides some standards for judgment, followed by a categorized bibliography of titles—remains common in lists of juvenile books even today. Thus the book lists themselves, complete with pages of learned, specialized critique, are inseparable from the cultural authority of their expert compilers.

Hewins was one of the large number of librarians critical of many children's series. In Hartford, she eventually rid the shelves of what she called "The Immortal Four": Horatio Alger, Oliver Optic, Harry Castlemon, and Martha Finley.[32] In addition to her publications in professional library journals, she also wrote letters to newspapers, urging parents to monitor their children's reading. Other librarians were equally vocal, and their voices were widely heard in both scholarly and popular publications. In 1914, Clara Herbert, children's librarian for the Washington, DC, public library, called publicly for better books for girls. Though she found it "rather appalling" that many girls admired Elsie Dinsmore, she believed that they did so primarily because there were so few better works.[33] Frances Jenkins Olcott, who headed the children's department of the Carnegie Library in Pittsburgh, wrote an influential guide called *The Children's Reading*, published in 1912 and later updated. In it, she warns parents of the dangers, not only of dime novels, but also of the many hardcover books that contain stories of the same stamp.[34] By 1929, the dismissal of series books had become so widely accepted a tenet among librarians that Mary E.S. Root could publish, in a professional journal, a list of "books in series not circulated by standardized libraries."[35] This list, presented under the title "Not To Be Circulated," contained not a word of explanation or justification as to why the nearly 100 different series were kept off library shelves. Nor did it indicate how many libraries were involved, thus giving the impression that the judgments were universal. It is not clear whether the list was intended to be prescriptive or merely descriptive, but in either case, librarians by this time were obviously exercising their mandate over one important avenue of public access to children's books.

Librarians' personal characters also did much to help establish the mandate of their profession. The majority of librarians who early took an interest in children's literature were women who saw their work as a high moral calling and who communicated this attitude to the public through their writings. Many were active in settlement houses and in efforts to extend free libraries to immigrant and other poor children. In 1922, *The Independent* referred to children's librarians as "enlightened women" who were "conscious of their opportunity of catching the child young and giving him a taste for good books."[36] In all the books and articles I have examined from the period, librarians and teachers presented themselves as people who respected children and who worked in children's best interests by giving them the guidance they needed to make their reading healthy, instructive, and enjoyable. In his article on librarians' responses to serial literature, Mark I. West states that "the efforts of librarians to suppress dime novels and series books were tied to an attempt to make children view childhood in the same way that librarians did, that is, as a time of innocence, happiness, and contentment."[37] But this conclusion does not accurately reflect the complexity of most professionals' published views. While it is true that librarians and educators insisted that children needed adult direction in their reading and that many saw it as their duty to direct readers *away* from series books, they did not do so because they wanted to promote an idealized picture of childhood. (Had such been their goal, they would have been more likely to recommend, not scorn, such series as the Bobbsey Twins and Dorothy Dainty and Honey Bunch.)

Instead, the professionals tended to emphasize that childhood reading had important real-life implications—and they presented themselves as the people best suited to decide which works offered the most desirable lessons. In their published comments, children's professionals constructed themselves not only as caring and skilled experts concerned about young people's mental and moral development but also as believers in children's abilities and value as individuals. They trusted children to appreciate the original and the complex and often called for books that provided both. Margaret Anderson observed in 1913 that many books lacked "the matter of ideas."[38] In 1914, Clara Herbert complained because too many girls' books provided little that was "stimulating intellectually."[39]

Given the widespread cultural agreement about the civic value of reading and education, coupled with librarians' and educators' genuine concern for children, it is not surprising that the popular press also contributed to the acceptance of the mandate of children's professionals. In addition to its willingness to print librarians' and teachers' opinions, the press offered support through journalists' own columns, in which they often recommended experts' published assessments of children's books. In his 1912 essay on children's books, Montrose Moses (himself an "expert" as the author of *Children's Books and Reading*) called Frances Olcott's *The Children's Reading* "the treatise [that] all parents and teachers should have," with its list of the "best" books and its "sane and lucid" discussions.[40] An unsigned article in *The Independent* in 1922 praised both Olcott's and Moses' books along with *Roads to Childhood,* by Anne Carroll Moore of the New York Public Library.[41]

Journalists commended not only individual works, but also the general practice of consulting and heeding the experts. In *The Bookman*, Grace Colbron asserted in 1915 that "our modern parent takes the child's reading seriously, and is questioning libraries, literary journals, and other centres of interest in books as to which books every child should read, both for its enjoyment and for its best mental and spiritual development."[42] *The Independent* of 1922 noted that "the excuse which once may have existed for parents to neglect children's reading, exists no longer," because "there is scarcely a town or city library which lacks its room or section set aside for children" and its "librarian who has training or experience in this work."[43]

And, of course, the professionals themselves did much to perpetuate the view that only through their expertise could parents and children avoid the harm that would come from the "wrong" reading. In addition to disseminating their views through journals, magazines, books, and university and normal school curricula, they met challenges to their authority by reaffirming not only the superiority of their professional qualifications but also society's support of their mandate. A fascinating exchange in the *Wilson Bulletin*, a professional journal for librarians, typifies the process by which middle-class professionals were able to consolidate their power. After the *Bulletin* published Mary Root's "Not To Be Circulated" list, a bookstore owner named Ernest Ayres answered with a column that took issue both with the list and with the librarians' right to create it. His article opened with a direct attack on librarians' position as cultural gatekeepers. "Why worry about censorship," he asked with rhetorical flourish, "so long as we have librarians?" Calling library professionals "these worthy arbiters of our literary pabulum," he raised an important question: "Is it the place of any librarian, holding a position as trustee of public funds, to tell men and women who enjoyed those books when they were young, that their children shall not be allowed to read the same tales?"[44]

This reference to "public funds" introduces a significant issue in the construction of cultural authority and the canon of children's literature: the distribution of power. As Richard Ohmann argues, literary canon formation is "a process saturated with class values and interests, a process inseparable from the broader struggle for position and power in our society."[45] The debate over the place of series books is, of course, a canonical one, and, as Ayres' remarks show, the terms of such a debate are never solely aesthetic. In a capitalist society, wealth and ownership are also important forms of power and cultural authority. As a businessman, someone outside the authority of the professional guild, Ayres could not fully meet the librarians on their own ground. So he challenged the professional mandate by attempting to assert a different, stronger one—he would trump intellectual capital with financial capital, making the professionals not leaders, but workers who needed to follow the mandate of those who paid their salaries.

Such a view is a direct threat, not only to professionals' cultural authority, but to their survival. If librarians and teachers are merely following standards instead of shaping them, then their cultural status becomes a sham, their training a waste, their expertise unnecessary. So it is no wonder that professionals fought such attacks fiercely. Lillian Herron Mitchell, a librarian, responded to Ayres' comments in the next issue of *Wilson Bulletin* by reasserting the professional mandate, first in terms of librarians' superior training. "We librarians," she wrote, "just happen to have the nature *and education* to think 'different,' because we see the problem from all angles" (italics mine). The implication is that without similar study, people such as Ayres could not make legitimate judgments.[46]

To her statements about training Mitchell added intellect. She insisted, "The really intelligent man or woman who was raised on this series stuff doesn't want sonny to waste any time on it." Having claimed for the professionals superiority in mind and education, she then also included the authority of the marketplace by arguing that it is the very position of librarians as "trustee[s] of public funds" that justifies their assertion of their critical judgments over those of untrained people such as Ayres: "Is it the place of any librarian," she asked, echoing Ayres' words, "'holding a position as trustee of public funds,' to squander them on books which are worthless when there are so many good ones available?" By casting her argument of value in Ayres' financial terms, Mitchell thus conscripted his assertion of power as her own. She concluded her article by assimilating the entire capitalist system: "You pay the taxes to support this institution," she said to the Ayres of the world, "and to pay my pitiful salary; if you really want your boys and girls to have an opportunity to read and enjoy books which will entertain, build character, [and] educate in the broadest sense . . . then we will pledge ourselves to buy only those worth while things."[47] She has acknowledged the authority of the nonprofessionals as consumers, but has claimed for the professionals the same power and more, constructing librarians as both consumer *and* commodity broker. Taxpayers may indeed pay librarians, she says in effect, but what their money has bought is the very expertise and authority that Ayres is attempting to deny. To deny that authority is to eliminate the source of power that he himself offered as his justification for questioning the professional mandate. And if he chooses to retain his financial authority by continuing to pay librarians' "pitiful salaries," then his position as consumer/taxpayer—the same position from which he tried to argue against librarians' control—has in fact legitimated the professionals' power to assert their cultural authority. The nonprofessional argument espoused by Ayres, then, has been defeated by its own terms.

By now it is clear that a great deal of the cultural authority of educators and librarians derived from their status as professionals and from the fact that prevailing social ideology about the civic and moral importance of children's reading corresponded with the professionals' agenda. But as the Ayres-Mitchell exchange shows, if the authorities were to cement their power, they had to differentiate their knowledge from the commonsense understanding of the uninitiated. To this end, they reinforced and validated their cultural conclusions with a complex methodology unavailable to those outside the profession. The empiricism that dominated nineteenth- and twentieth-century epistemology formed the basis of the research, experimentation, and quantification through which the professionals attempted to make their conclusions, if not unassailable, then at least strongly convincing. In his book *The Culture of Professionalism*, Burton Bledstein contends that a large part of professional authority derived from the perceived complexity of the subject matter and the expert status of the practitioner: "Laymen were neither prepared to comprehend the mystery of the tasks which professionals performed, nor—more ominously—were they equipped to pass judgment upon special skills and technical competence. Hence the culture of professionalism required amateurs to 'trust' the integrity of trained persons."[48] This process of establishing "special skills and technical competence" shows clearly in the studies of children's reading that multiplied after World War I.

Although children's reading interests had been examined since at least the 1890s, the studies tended to be limited in scope. Most lists of recommended books were based on the authors' own criteria, the validity of which they justified by their professional qualifications and experience rather than through systematic experimentation. The result was that the most of the lists, to use the words of an editorialist in the *Peabody Journal of Education,* were "arbitrary, subjective concoction[s] spun out of the inner consciousness and the love of good books" of the lists' authors.[49] But in an article from 1926, Elizabeth White, the director of school libraries in Long Beach, asserted that professionals "had long wished for a scientific report by school people on children's reading."[50] They got their wish after 1920, when several studies appeared that claimed to investigate children's reading materials and interests using systematic, largely objective, "scientific" methods. Arthur Jordan, a professor of educational psychology at the University of North Carolina, published *Children's Interests in Reading* first in 1921 and then in a revised edition in 1926.[51] Willis Lemon Uhl produced his *Scientific Determination of the Content of the Elementary School Course in Reading* in 1921.[52] Lewis Terman's and Margaret Lima's *Children's Reading* first appeared in 1925; a revised edition followed in 1931. Edwin Starbuck and a host of researchers at the Institute of Character Research at the University of Iowa published *A Guide to Literature for Character Training* in 1930. The Henry Frick Educational Commission authorized a survey of the reading habits of Pittsburgh junior and senior high school students; the results were published in 1930 and 1931.

In their published versions, these studies followed similar patterns of establishing their authority and validity. The title pages noted each author's academic degrees, professional affiliations, or other publications. Each book contained elaborate explanations of the methodology employed, insisting on its statistical reliability. The authors were careful to provide exact numbers and to make clear the large scope of their work. The results of these surveys were presented in ways designed to emphasize their objectivity and their complexity. Tables and graphs abounded; formulas, percentages, calculations, and other numbers filled the pages. Appendices provided additional statistical data and explanations.

Most of the studies reached some version of the following conclusion: that although children often showed good taste in their reading choices, they also read much that was unsuitable and therefore needed substantial guidance if they were to develop both a love of reading and a discriminating critical judgment. That such a conclusion reaffirmed the need for children's professionals is not surprising. And not only did the studies thus offer "scientific" validation of what most librarians and educators already believed, but they also served as one of the means by which professionals could direct children to the "best" reading. Many agreed that knowing children's tastes was indispensable to the goal of improving those tastes. "Since we believe the reading interests of children to be one of the most important factors in education," wrote Danylu Belser, the state supervisor of primary education in Alabama, "it is essential that we study the life of the child so as to cultivate his natural, wholesome tendencies in this as well as other lines."[53]   Arthur Jordan explained, "If we could determine what the child's major [reading] interests are, be those interests good or bad, it would be possible to direct these forces along lines which are desirable."[54]

The most ambitious study of the period was *The Winnetka Graded Book List*, published in 1926. It is worth examining in detail because it serves as microcosm of the process both of the scorning of series books and of the establishing of cultural authority. The authors—widely known educator Carleton Washburne and Mabel Vogel, Winnetka's director of research—wrote that "the importance of finding what books are suitable to children . . . can scarcely be overemphasized . . . The formation of right reading habits is essential to all future academic work, as well as to vocational and avocational life after one leaves school."[55]

The survey itself was a massive undertaking. During the academic year 1924–25, 36,750 children filled out nearly 100,000 ballots reporting their responses to more than 9,000 different books. Of these books, 796 were mentioned by twenty-five or more readers and thus formed the basis of the final published list. Thirty-four different school systems in eighteen states participated. For each book they read, the children filled out a card that offered two columns of possible responses. One column presented four choices for the reader's overall opinion of the book: "one of the best books I ever read"; "a good book, I like it"; "not so very interesting"; and "I don't like it." The second column asked the children to gauge the reading level of the book; the choices were "too easy," "just about right," "a little hard," and "too hard." The last line asked readers to write comments on the back.[56] The resulting data were then subjected to a variety of tabulations and analyses. The analysts assigned numerical values to the children's responses in order to calculate an "interest value." They determined what they called a "popularity index" by "multiplying the number of children liking a book by the number of cities in which it was read."[57] They calculated the "reading grade" of each book and correlated the children's ages with their reading level.

A great deal of attention was also given to the question of "literary merit." As a check against children's judgments and to ensure that "really undesirable books" were eliminated, the researchers asked thirteen "expert" librarians to rank the list's 796 books by placing them in the following categories: (1) "of unquestionable literary merit"; (2) "valuable for the list, although not of high literary quality"; (3) "not recommended because of low literary value"; and (4) "not recommended because of subject content."[58] Although the researchers did not provide the respondents with any standards for determining "literary merit," they did offer examples of books that fit each category. Category One examples included *Tom Sawyer*, *Alice in Wonderland*, and *Little Black Sambo*. In Category Two were *Anne of Green Gables*, *Little Lord Fauntleroy*, and *The Puritan Twins*.

Category Three—low literary value—included the Bobbsey Twins and Honey Bunch series. Among Category Four books were *The Circular Staircase* and *The Hound of the Baskervilles.*

"The reports from the experts," reported Washburne and Vogel with apparently straight-faced understatement, "varied materially." But because the authors "wished to exclude from our list any books that are undoubtedly trashy or unsuitable for children," they "arbitrarily" decided that any books categorized as "3" or "4" by three-quarters of the librarians would not be placed in the final published list,[59] regardless of how many children read them or of what "interest value" they earned. The thirteen experts identified 110 books as "trashy or unsuitable." Among these 110 (all of which had been read by at least twenty-five children) were, of course, many series, including Honey Bunch and the Bobbsey Twins, whose designation as "trashy" Washburne and Vogel had virtually guaranteed by offering them as examples of "Category Three" books. Other series books labeled "trashy" were the Stratemeyer Syndicate's Tom Swift, Ruth Fielding, and Bunny Brown and His Sister Sue. Baum's *Land of Oz* appeared, as did volumes of the Elsie Dinsmore, Tarzan, Curlytops, and Polly Brewster series. Among the "scorned" were several series titles that had earlier been praised in articles in the popular press, including Alice Turner Curtis's Little Maid books, Carolyn Wells' *Patty Fairfield,* the Little Colonel series, and Thomas Wentworth Higginson's favorite, Little Prudy. For the most part, these books earned high marks on the "popularity index" and the scale of "interest value." An average of 98 percent of the children who read the seventeen cited Bobbsey Twins books reported liking them; some titles had been read by more than 100 children, boys and girls alike. Books such as *Pollyanna* and the Bobbsey Twins ranked in the top 5 percent for popularity.[60]

In its final form, the *Winnetka Graded Book List* exerted considerable cultural power for several reasons, not all of them directly related to its content. First, as with similar lists, its appearance supported its claims. Regardless of whether the methodology and statistical analyses were in fact valid, the presentation of the data certainly made them *look* as if they were. The more than fifty pages of technical apparatus that preceded the actual list contained impressive-looking charts and graphs as well as tables of correlations and percentages. Also included were detailed descriptions, identified by boldfaced headings, of such technical issues as how the ballot was devised, how the data were gathered, how the responses were evaluated, how the reading grade and difficulty were determined, and how gender differences were interpreted. Considerable space was spent explaining how the data overall were determined to be valid. The format of the lists themselves also encouraged readers to view the material as objective and reliable. Under the title of each book appeared a miniature table identifying the number of children who had read each title, the percentage of readers who liked it, the "interest value," the median age of the readers, their median reading ability, the median reading ability of the children who read and liked the book, the number of cities in which the title was read, and finally, the "popularity index." Also included for each book was a child's personal comment as written on one of the original ballots.

The physical format of the list also reinforced the experts' verdict about which books were to be scorned. The official *Winnetka Graded Book List* was published in substantial hardcover with professionally typeset pages, first by the American Library Association and later by the mainstream firm of Rand McNally. Significantly, the 110 books identified as "trashy or unsuitable" by the Winnetka researchers were not mentioned by name in the hardcover list. Instead, these books were relegated to a separate *Supplement to the Winnetka Graded Book List* that initially could be obtained only if readers of the published version wrote to the Winnetka research office.[61] This twenty-two-page, stapled pamphlet appears to have been duplicated rather than printed, and its contents were typewritten, not typeset. Such ephemeral packaging gave physical form to the idea that the books listed in the pamphlet were worthless. And the limited circulation of the *Supplement* even more effectively erased the scorned books from cultural institutions. Many libraries that purchased the hardcover book apparently did not bother with the *Supplement*, to judge from the difficulty of finding it. After requests from other professionals, Washburne and Vogel did print the contents of the *Supplement* in the *Elementary English Review* in 1927, but this professional journal would not have had wide popular circulation.

Another major source of authority for the *Winnetka Graded Book List* was its name and origins. Few educators and librarians in the 1920s could have been unfamiliar with the town of Winnetka, Illinois, or with the name of its superintendent of schools, Carleton Washburne. By 1926, the year the *Book List* was published, the name "Winnetka" was synonymous with progressive, innovative education. The town's fame was due almost entirely to the efforts of Washburne. Born in Chicago in 1889, Washburne earned an Ed.D. from Berkeley in 1918. In 1919, he was hired as the superintendent of Winnetka Public Schools, a position he retained until 1943. An educator in the Progressive tradition of John Dewey, Washburne was prolific in both educational practice and theory, validating his ideas by extensive experimentation and numerous research projects. He published over a dozen books and many articles ranging from arithmetic and spelling textbooks to programs for improving education worldwide. It was in Winnetka that he first had the freedom to work out his educational theories in practical terms. His design for individualized, creative instruction geared to a particular child's needs and abilities came to be known as "the Winnetka Plan" and was tried in many schools throughout the country. Washburne carefully cultivated the national attention that his work began to receive.

Thus even as early as 1926, Washburne was widely known. His prominence did not mean that his ideas were never challenged, but it did guarantee that when he produced a major work such as the *Graded Book List,* it would receive considerable attention. Unsurprisingly, the publication of the *List* generated a significant amount of professional interest and controversy. In 1926 and 1927, the *Elementary English Review* devoted no fewer than ten articles and editorials to discussion of the list, including as its lead article in one issue Washburne's and

Vogel's "Reply to Their Critics." Reviews appeared in *The Elementary School Journal*, the *Peabody Journal of Education*, the *Catholic Educational Review*, the *School Review*, the *Library Journal*, and the *Library Association Record*. Readers wrote letters to the editors of *Libraries* and the *Library Journal*. An "Open Forum," attended by Mabel Vogel, was held to discuss the list at the 1926 conference of the National Council of Teachers of English; a report on that forum appeared in the *Elementary English Review*. Commentary was so widespread that, when writing his letter to the editor of *Libraries*, Arthur Bostwick wryly noted that "I am apparently the only librarian who has omitted to criticize, or defend, or notice in some way, the new celebrated Winnetka list, and I am anxious not to continue to be an exception."[62]

The majority of the reviews praised or recommended the list. "The book is necessarily most valuable to parents, teachers, and librarians," said "E.G.H." in the *Library Association Record*, "but it should also be of interest to a much wider circle, as it affords a thoroughly up-to-date insight into child psychology."[63] Sterling Leonard wrote that the "study seems to me the first and only model for the construction of all reading lists in future."[64] Even those who saw limitations in the methodology, such as Francis J. Macelwane, praised the list overall. "No one who has to do with children's reading can well afford to overlook the interesting data offered in this book," Macelwane stated.[65]

Macelwane's concern with methodology reflects one of the main sources of the list's authority: its status as a "scientific" study. I have examined twenty contemporary reviews, letters, and articles about the *Winnetka Graded Book List*. Thirteen of these twenty refer, almost always approvingly, to the scientific approach taken by the list. (Of the remaining seven sources, three are very short mentions; one is a review that, while it does not use the word "scientific," does discuss the "statistical" elements of the list; and the other three focus on the issue of literary merit and the *Supplement* rather than on the list as whole.) Many reviewers judged the list to be useful primarily because it *was* "scientific," by which term people seemed to mean empirical and quantitative. One writer recommended the study both as a book list *and* as a model for educational research in general: "In the substitution of scientific evidence for personal opinion," wrote G.T. Buswell, "the authors have contributed not only a worthwhile book list but also an example of scientific procedure which is worth careful study by students of education."[66]

Those who criticized the list usually did so by questioning the validity of its particular methodology or individual conclusions; they did not object to its conceptual framework. They did not, in other words, question whether one should approach children's reading from a "scientific" or quantitative standpoint in the first place; they merely tried to demonstrate that the "science" that the list did employ was flawed. Elizabeth White wrote that the list "reminded us of a problem in arithmetic, worked according to theory, but with the wrong answer."[67] Frank Shuttleworth of Yale devoted an entire monograph to examining and correcting the data in the *Winnetka List*. Although he found errors in some of the statistical analyses, he agreed that the overall conclusions of the list were valid and in accord with the conclusions reached by the *Guide to Literature for Character Training*, to which he had contributed.[68]

The most extensive criticisms came from a self-identified "group of librarians," who published their objections in the *Elementary English Review* and the *Library Journal*. The librarians stated that since the book list was "widely heralded as a scientific study," they had submitted it to two unnamed "specialists in statistical and scientific survey." These specialists, the librarians reported, found that the list was "an interesting, but not convincing, attempt to apply the statistical method to the field of children's literature."[69] In their "Reply to the Critics," Carleton Washburne and Mabel Vogel answered the librarians point by point on the same statistical grounds.

The textual conversation between the authors and their critics offers insights into the means by which these educators and librarians both defined and asserted cultural and professional authority. In their definitions, the two groups accepted both the validity of personal experience and the power of what they saw as fully disinterested, objective data. Interestingly, however, they tended to attack one element and affirm the other depending on which would best support their own claims of authority. The "group of librarians," for instance, demanded statistical accuracy, but disagreed with the reading grades assigned to various books because the designations were "contrary to our experience."[70] Washburne and Vogel scoffed at this assertion of personal expertise, saying that "this involves the naive assumption that if the facts don't agree with the personal opinion of the critics, the facts must be at fault."[71] Yet, in reply to the librarians' claim that the list's statistical methods were flawed, Washburne and Vogel justified their results, not by a statistical argument, but by simply asserting the expertise and professional qualifications of their statisticians.[72] Although both the librarians and Washburne and Vogel made valid points, this exchange demonstrates not only the means by which professional authority was asserted, but also how the professionals were willing, however subconsciously, to manipulate the grounds on which their authority stood if that authority was threatened.

Since this rather esoteric textual debate took place in professional journals, it was not likely to endanger popular views of the professionals' authority or of the validity of their claims. And one area in which the experts did *not* disagree was with Washburne and Vogel's assessment of "trashy" books, meaning that this particular assertion of authority was likely to make its way intact to the general public. In "Notes on the Winnetka Supplement," Bertha Hatch and Annie Spencer Cutter of the Cleveland Public Library offered additional arguments that reinforced the conclusion that such books were best kept away from children. Echoing the typical professional arguments against series books, they condemned the stories' "poverty of interest" and their "flatness and monotony" of style.[73] Using another traditional professional view, they argued that children *will* prefer better books if only they are guided to those books. "Are we willing to accept the untutored judgment of the children as the sole criterion" for what they read? asked Hatch and Cutter rhetorically. The answer, clearly, was "no."

The need for professional guidance, at least according to the professionals, remained secure.

When professionals did express interest in the Winnetka *Supplement*, it was not because they wanted to challenge its conclusions. Rather, most hoped that the *Supplement* would provide insight into why children enjoyed "trash." Dr. Florence Bamburger suggested that the *Supplement* be published "for the purpose of discovering in what respects the books were trashy and furthermore, discovering why children liked them."[74] Such knowledge, others agreed, could be used to help turn children away from "trashy" reading. The *Elementary English Review* ran a full-page editorial, titled "Why Study the Winnetka Supplement?" that stressed the idea that if teachers did not know what their pupils actually read and why, they would have no means of assessing the children's needs and influencing their tastes.[75] Through their reaction to the *Supplement*, then, professionals reinforced society's need for their cultural authority (and also, by extension, for their salaried services).

Despite its critics, who in any case were far outnumbered by its supporters, the *Winnetka Graded Book List*, with its weight of "scientific" data and the exceptional professional authority of Carleton Washburne, achieved considerable cultural power in defining children's reading and in contributing to the scorning of series books. For a specialized text, it was fairly widely sold in the United States—3,800 copies by early 1927[76]—and was even used elsewhere in the world. The *Elementary English Review* noted that the "Institute of Out School Work" in Moscow found the book list to have "practical value" in comparing American and Russian children's reading.[77] Nor did the influence of the list fade for many years. In 1933, Carleton Washburne used the *Winnetka Graded Book List* as the basis for a new work called *The Right Book for the Right Child*. To the original data about children's preferences were added annotations prepared by a "committee of librarians." In this volume, the "trashy" books of 1926 were even more effectively erased from the public mind, since there was no mention of them or of the *Supplement* at all. *The Right Book* was updated in 1936 with a pamphlet that added new titles, and a full second edition was published in 1942.[78]

But however effectively the professionals presented their moral and intellectual credentials and however influential the scholarly artifacts they produced, the establishment of cultural authority is never monolithic. For all the scorners' success at sustaining their mandate and at keeping certain series books out of public libraries and schools, they faced challenges from competing social forces, particularly those of the marketplace. Working against the scorners' moral and psychological objections to series was the fact that series made money. A lot of money. For instance, Edward Stratemeyer's handwritten ledgers show that his Syndicate alone grossed $41,896.18 in 1919, and he accounted for only part of the juvenile series market.[79] George Dunlap of Grosset & Dunlap, the firm that published many of Stratemeyer's series, wrote that by 1936, the Tom Swift series had sold 6,566,464 copies, the Bobbsey Twins 5,619,129 copies, and the Rover Boys 2,421,909.[80] The pull of profit meant that publishers and retailers had strong incentive to disregard the intellectual mandate of the academic professionals. That the proliferation of series books was directly related to their status as marketable commodities was a fact that did not escape children's professionals. They fought this challenge to their power in a variety of ways.

First, as we have seen, they relied on the traditional arguments for their mandate: the idea that only through librarians' and teachers' earned expertise could parents and children hope to find those books that would improve readers' minds and characters. Second, instead of simply arguing against the profit motive, professionals worked to ally their cause with financial interests. One method was to join forces with publishers in the quest for "good" books. As Kay Vandergrift has noted, "In the early years of the twentieth century, this reciprocal relationship between librarianship and children's publishing ... was especially strong."[81] Caroline Hewins' 1882 list, *Books for the Young*, which was written at the behest of the editor of *Publishers' Weekly*, is an early example of this approach. Perhaps the most outstanding single instance of this method was the creation in 1919 of the annual Children's Book Week, a collaborative effort among librarians, publishers, book dealers, and journalists that not only allowed the professional and the business worlds to join interests, but also ensured that the merger was well publicized. Children's Book Week, which expanded its scope considerably over the years, continues to bring together schools, libraries, and bookstores to promote "good" books through readings, sales, classroom units, and other activities. The Week did not promote most mass-market series books.

If alliance with the market was one method of deflecting money-driven challenges to professional authority, another common method took exactly the opposite approach: constructing the market as yet another scourge against which only intellectual expertise could prevail. Some writers suggested that the market itself encouraged low-quality literature—such as series books. Frances Olcott noted that "an author may write one good book and then rapidly produce a number of poorly written and possibly harmful stories that sell on the reputation of his first work. This is especially true of long 'series' of stories."[82] Twenty years later, Terman and Lima similarly claimed that the market encouraged books of scant literary value: "this is an age of easy and lucrative authorship ... prolific writers turn out twenty or more stories all woven around the impossible, unreal adventures of a single character or group of characters."[83]

The actual cost of children's books also became a contested territory. For the most part, the juvenile series that were scorned were also inexpensive. One of the most successful marketing practices of series publishers was to sell the books at the low price of fifty cents each, a move that effectively put many series into the reach of working-class parents and of children themselves. To many professionals, no doubt a reflection of their own middle-class orientation, the cheap cost was synonymous with cheap literary quality. The numerous fifty-cent books epitomized the literary dangers of series books (predictable, formulaic, repetitive) as well as the power of the marketplace to subvert professional authority through sheer volume of sales. As Edna Yost reported in *Publishers'*

Weekly in 1932, "a top-notch seller in the fifty-cent juvenile line today means a series which, within a few years—four or five, possibly—sells hundreds of thousands of copies."[84] Montrose Moses noted as early as 1912 that "the enormous sales of the inferior 50-cent book loom threateningly."[85] Professionals met the fifty-cent threat with the same methods as they met other market-related challenges: either by joining forces with the market or by opposing it. In the *Winnetka Graded Book List*, for instance, Washburne and Vogel cited inexpensive as well as pricier editions of each book included in the published list, so that all prospective purchasers could have access to worthy books. They did not, however, offer any pricing information in the *Supplement* of scorned books. Thus they acknowledged the importance of cost to book selection and withheld cost information for books they did not want to see chosen.

Discussions of cost invariably included issues of class. The majority of the library and education professionals (as well as the children's book editors and even many publishers) who shaped the cultural definitions of literary merit were middle class, but more than that, they belonged to what has been called the "Professional-Managerial class." This class, as Richard Ohmann describes it, "emerged and grew up only with monopoly capitalism."[86] It shared an uneasy relationship with both the upper and working classes. Members of the Professional-Managerial group, wrote Ohmann, had a "conflicted relation to the ruling class"; they had an "equally mixed relation to the working class; [the professionals] dominated, supervised, taught, and planned for [the workers], but even in doing so . . . served and augmented capital."[87]

In their class-related arguments about series books and other marginal children's literature, the librarians and teachers demonstrated these attributes of the Professional-Managerial class. Their relationship to the working class, for instance, often took the form of an altruistic concern for lower-class welfare. According to Yost, some publishers justified printing fifty-cent books as a sort of class-related charity, arguing that the series were for "the underprivileged boy particularly, boys who must have inexpensive books if they are to acquire the reading habit at all."[88] But librarians and educators could counter publishers' justifications *and* reassert their own authority by removing the working-class individual's need to participate in the market at all: they did so by advocating free libraries. With free libraries, not only would "underprivileged" youths have access to books, but they would also have the "right" books, as defined by the professionals. Frances Olcott offered such an argument in 1912, one that also introduced issues of race and ethnicity. In discussing the community influence of library reading clubs, she reported that "a member of a 'reading club' of colored and foreign boys said to the library leader in charge, 'we boys would read better things than nickels [i.e., dime novels], but they come high.'"[89] The library, of course, would provide the "better things" for free, thus removing the children's need to resort to cheap reading matter.

This altruistic motivation, while genuine, nevertheless also allowed the librarians and educators to assume power and control over the working class and over the racial and ethnic members of this class. Free libraries might indeed have offered poorer children access to books they could not otherwise afford, but this access was limited to those books preselected by librarians. This point was made most tellingly by Anne Campbell Rinehart, in her report on *What Pittsburgh Junior High Pupils Read*. This 1930 study made a rare attempt to identify African-American children's reading preferences. Rinehart noted that black children do not "seem to be excessive readers of 'series'—public and school libraries do not contain these books and many negroes may be largely dependent on these sources for their books."[90]

But the black children in Rinehart's study did at least report reading and liking the Rover Boys series. This fact introduces another form of challenge to professional authority: children themselves. Regardless of librarians' and teachers' exhortations, children continued to buy and read series books. In their writings, the professionals expressed bafflement and even exasperation at this dogged insistence on reading books that, to the adults, seemed clearly unimaginative and implausible. Over the years, professionals offered a variety of explanations to account for such reading: some suggested that children who liked series simply had not been introduced to better books; others argued that children would always choose the easiest reading route if left to their own devices. Arthur Jordan presumed, wrongly, that most boys who read "Nick Carter" and other such series were probably "intellectually less alert and morally more obtuse" than children with better taste.[91] Occasionally someone would argue for giving the children a little more credit. Arthur Bostwick, for instance, suggested that children liked series because such books featured exciting, fun stories.[92] But for the most part, the professionals united in the view that experts (and through their influence, well-informed parents) should hold the power of directing children's reading tastes. "Wise censorship," Terman and Lima revealingly called such guidance.[93]

This power issue suggests another reason why children may have been so devoted to series: the books formed a way for children to assert their own power and authority by reading those works of which they knew many adults disapproved. (Also, children's series reading was often a communal exercise that built a sense of belonging, as children traded books and discussed their favorites.) Whatever the reasons that youngsters read series, professionals met the children's challenge to their authority by using methods similar to those that they employed with the marketplace. They sometimes offered direct opposition and sometimes attempted to coerce the children to the adults' way of thinking. Terman and Lima's "wise censorship" is one example of the coercion approach. "The wise censor," they wrote, "never rigidly forbids the undesirable; he puts something better in its place and lets the cheap and shoddy die a natural death."[94] The number of studies done on children's reading interests represents another example of coercion. On the one hand, their acknowledgment of the importance of children's preferences shows the respect that most Progressive Era educators had for children; on the other hand, their efforts to learn these preferences can be seen as a form of adult espionage, a way of making it easier for adults to maneuver children to their side. In the editorial "Why Study the Winnetka Supplement?" the editorialist presented his/her answers using both these methods. Teachers owe it to their students, the writer contended, to meet them on their own ground, to be "well-informed and sympathetic" to the children's interests. The main purpose of such sympathy, however, is to "gain the real confidence" of the children so that the teacher can wean them from the "trashy books."[95]

In this essay, I have, of course, oversimplified and schematized the cultural phenomena. Children's professionals and the children's book market, for instance, were not necessarily so diametrically opposed as the foregoing discussion might suggest. Many of the publishers and most of the editors involved in the market were as committed to literary excellence and to children's well-being as were librarians and teachers. And the reactions of children's professionals to children's tastes did not solely reflect adults' attempts to assert power over children. In their writings, librarians and educators most often exhibited a genuine concern for children's welfare and a trust in children's critical acumen, at least to a point. But clearly one motive may coexist with others; people can belong to different cultural groups simultaneously. I have tried to demonstrate the complex and overlapping cultural negotiations that underlie any assertion of literary standards or any relegation of a given category of writing to the limbo of the "scorned." Nor is the debate yet settled, because struggles over power and authority continue as long as there are human societies. At the start of the twenty-first century, librarians and teachers still raise the same questions that faced the professionals of the Progressive Era. Although many public libraries carry mass-market children's series, the various e-mail discussion lists devoted to children's literature still periodically erupt into impassioned arguments over whether children should read such books as Goosebumps and Animorphs.

It has been many years since a librarian said to me, "Nancy Drews aren't the kind of books we like to have in the library," and many more years since Carleton Washburne and Mabel Vogel decided to consign series books to a typewritten *Supplement*. But children continue to read series as voraciously today as they did in the days of Optic and Finley. It may be true that, in terms of literary quality, many of these books are merely the stepchildren of real literature. But generations of young readers have relished their comforting mix of security and excitement and have grown into adults whose memories of series bring nothing but satisfaction. As Ilene Cooper wrote in the *New York Times Book Review*, "The attachment many of us have for these books is rather like the way we feel about members of our own families. It would be nice if they were all bright, witty and wise. Instead they tend to repeat themselves, and we always pretty much know what they're going to do next. Still, they're with us, helping us make it through. We make allowances."[96]

NOTES

1. Franklin K. Mathiews, "Blowing Out the Boys' Brains," *The Outlook*, 18 November 1914, 653.

2. Lewis Terman and Margaret Lima, *Children's Reading: A Guide for Parents and Teachers,* 2d ed. (New York: Appleton, 1931): 78.

3. Roxanna Anderson, "A Preliminary Study of the Reading Tastes of High School Pupils," *Pedagogical Seminary* 19 (1912): 444.

4. Edna Yost, "The Fifty Cent Juveniles," *Publishers' Weekly,* 18 June 1932, 2406.

5. Dorothea Lawrance Mann, "What about Books for Girls?" *The Independent,* 13 November 1926, 557.

6. Higginson quoted in Richard Darling, *The Rise of Children's Book Reviewing in America, 1865-1881* (New York: Bowker, 1968), 57.

7. Higginson quoted in *A Descriptiv* [sic] *List of Books for the Young* (Cambridge, MA: W/M Griswold, 1895), 158.

8. Margaret Anderson, "A Child's Garden of Books, Part II," *The Bookman,* December, 1913, 447.

9. Ruth Abbott, "A Suggestive List of Children's Books for Christmas," *Elementary School Journal* 20 (November 1919): 226–33.

10. Grace Isabel Colbron, "Choosing the Children's Library," *The Bookman,* October, 1915, 196.

11. Alice A. Chadwick, "Reading for Children," *The Outlook,* 11 September 1897, 122.

12. Josette Frank, *What Books for Children? Guideposts for Parents,* rev. ed. (New York: Doubleday, 1941), 91 (italics Frank's).

13. Carleton Washburne and Mabel Vogel, *Supplement to the Winnetka Graded Book List* (Winnetka, IL: Winnetka Individual Materials, 1926).

14. Montrose Moses, "The Children's Christmas Book Shelf," *The Independent,* 18 December 1911, 1325.

15. M.B.C. True, "What My Pupils Read," *Education* 14 (October 1893): 99–102.

16. *Catalogue of Books in the Children's Department of the Carnegie Library of Pittsburgh,* 2d ed., 2 vols. (Pittsburgh: Carnegie Library, 1920), n.p.

17. Anne Campbell Rinehart, *What Pittsburgh Junior High Pupils Read* (Pittsburgh: Henry Frick Educational Commission, 1931), 32–33 (italics in original).

18. Lucy M. Kinloch, "The Menace of the Series Book," *Elementary English Review* 12 (January 1935): 9.

19. R. Anderson, 444.

20. Frank, 90.

21. Terman and Lima, 85.

22. "Fit For Boys," *The Nation,* 9 January 1921, 75.

23. Graham Taylor, "The Civic Value of Library Work with Children," in Alice Hazeltine, ed. *Library Work with Children* (New York: Wilson, 1917): 129.

24. Eliot quoted in Clara B. Mason, "Some Library Experiments in Nebraska," *Journal of Addresses and Proceedings of the National Education Association* (1903), 966.

25. Talcott Parsons, "Professions," in *International Encyclopedia of the Social Sciences,* vol. 12. ed. David Sills (New York: Macmillan/Free Press, 1968), 545.

26. Parsons, 536–37.

27. As described in Robert Dingwall, introduction to *The Sociology of the Professions: Lawyers, Doctors, and Others,* eds. Robert Dingwall and Philip Lewis (New York: St. Martin, 1982), 4.

28. Dingwall, 4.

29. Some sociologists refer to such occupations as nursing, elementary-school teaching, social work, and librarianship as "semi-professions." As Richard Simpson and

Ida Harper Simpson explain in "Women and Bureaucracy in the Semi-Professions," (in *The Semi-Professions and Their Organization,* ed. Amitai Etzioni [New York: Free Press, 1969], 196–265), semi-professionals "lack autonomy . . . they are more account-able for their performance" than are the most prestigious professionals. When one exam-ines the social impact of the semi-professions, however, it is clear that these groups es-tablish cultural authority in the same manner as the more prestigious professions.

30. Louis R. Wilson, "Historical Development of Education for Librarianship in the United States," in *Reader in American Library History,* ed. Michael Harris (Washington, DC: NCR Microcard, 1971), 186.

31. John D. Pulliam, *History of Education in America,* 4th ed. (Columbus, OH: Merrill, 1987), 85, 111, 113.

32. Caroline M. Hewins, "How Library Work with Children Has Grown in Hartford and Connecticut," in Alice Hazeltine, ed. *Library Work with Children* (New York: Wil-son, 1917): 48.

33. The column was reprinted as "New Writers for Girls," *The Literary Digest,* 31 January 1914, 205–6.

34. Frances Jenkins Olcott, *The Children's Reading* (Boston: Houghton Mifflin, 1912), 170.

35. Mary E.S. Root, "Not To Be Circulated." *Wilson Bulletin* 3 (January 1929): 446.

36. "Children's Reading," *The Independent,* 11 November 1922, 276.

37. Mark I. West, "Not To Be Circulated: The Response of Children's Librarians to Dime Novels and Series Books," *Children's Literature Association Quarterly* 10 (Fall 1985): 139.

38. M. Anderson, 315.

39. Herbert, quoted in "New Writers," 206.

40. Montrose Moses, "Books for Young People," *The Independent,* 12 December 1912, 1360.

41. "Children's Reading," 276.

42. Colbron, 196.

43. "Children's Reading," 276.

44. Ernest F. Ayres, "Not To Be Circulated?" *Wilson Bulletin* 3 (March 1929): 528.

45. Richard Ohmann, "The Shaping of a Canon: U.S. Fiction 1960–1975," *Critical Inquiry* 10 (September 1983): 200.

46. Ibid., 580.

47. Ibid., 584.

48. Burton Bledstein, *The Culture of Professionalism: The Middle Class and the Development of Higher Education in America* (New York: Norton, 1976), 90.

49. "The Winnetka Graded Book List," *Peabody Journal of Education* 3 (January 1926): 236.

50. Elizabeth White, "Recent Experimentation in Children's Reading," *Elementary English Review* 3 (September 1926): 233.

51. Arthur Melville Jordan, *Children's Interests in Reading* (Chapel Hill: Univer-sity of North Carolina Press, 1921, 1926).

52. Willis Lemon Uhl, *Scientific Determination of the Content of the Elementary School Course in Reading,* University of Wisconsin Studies in the Social Sciences and History, no. 4 (Madison, 1921).

53. Danylu Belser, "The Reading Interests of Boys: A Committee Report," *Elementary English Review* 3 (1926): 296.

54. Jordan, 1.

55. Carleton Washburne and Mabel Vogel, *The Winnetka Graded Book List* (Chicago: American Library Association, 1926): 11.

56. Ibid., 6.

57. Ibid., 51.

58. Ibid., 42.

59. Ibid., 43.

60. Deidre Johnson, "*The Winnetka Graded Book List* and Its *Supplement*," *Dime Novel Roundup* 50 (June 1981): 62.

61. Washburne and Vogel, *The Winnetka Graded Book List*, 43.

62. Arthur Bostwick, "Again, the Winnetka List," letter to the editor, *Libraries* 31 (May 1926): 221.

63. E.G.H., Review of *The Winnetka Graded Book List*. *Library Association Record* 4 (December 1926): 243.

64. S[terling] A[ndrus] Leonard, "The Winnetka Reading List," *Elementary English Review* 3 (1926): 122.

65. Francis J. Macelwane, Review of *The Winnetka Graded Book List*. *Catholic Educational Review* 24 (1926): 314.

66. G[uy] T. Buswell, "Two New Book Lists for Children's Reading," *Elementary School Journal* 26 (1925-26): 551.

67. White, 233.

68. Frank Shuttleworth, *A Critical Study of Two Lists of Best Books for Children*, Genetic Psychology Monographs, vol. 9, no. 4 (Worcester, MA: Clark University, 1932).

69. A Group of Librarians, "The Winnetka Graded Book List." *Elementary English Review* 3 (1926): 235.

70. Ibid., 236.

71. Carleton Washburne and Mabel Vogel, "A Reply to the Critics of the *Winnetka Graded Book List*," *Elementary English Review* 4 (1927): 8.

72. Ibid., 27.

73. Bertha Hatch and Annie Spencer Cutter, "Notes on the Winnetka Supplement," *Elementary English Review* 4 (1927): 53.

74. "An Open Forum on the Winnetka List," *Elementary English Review* 4 (1927): 12.

75. "Why Study the Winnetka Supplement?" editorial, *Elementary English Review* 4 (1927): 55.

76. Peter Soderbergh, "The Stratemeyer Strain: Educators and the Juvenile Series Book, 1900–1973," *Journal of Popular Culture* 7 (Spring 1974): 867.

77. "Supporting Evidence," editorial, *Elementary English Review* 4 (1927): 29.

78. Carleton Washburne and Mary S. Wilkinson, *The Right Book for the Right Child: A Graded Buying List of Children's Books*, 2d ed. (New York: John Day, 1942), xii.

79. Edward Stratemeyer, accounts ledger, Stratemeyer Syndicate Records, New York Public Library, Manuscripts and Archives Collection.

80. George Dunlap, *The Fleeting Years: A Memoir* (New York: privately printed, 1937), 193.

81. Kay Vandergrift, "Female Advocacy and Harmonious Voices: A History of Public Library Services and Publishing for Children in the United States," *Library Trends* 44 (Spring 1996): 701.

82. Olcott, 184.

83. Terman and Lima, 77.

84. Yost, 2405.

85. Montrose Moses, "Books for Young People," 1360.

86. Ohmann, 209.

87. Ibid.

88. Yost, 2407.

89. Olcott, 178.

90. Rinehart, 47.

91. Jordan, 15.

92. Bostwick, 222.

93. Terman and Lima, xii.

94. Ibid.

95. "Why Study the Winnetka Supplement?"

96. Ilene Cooper, "Sweet Are the Uses of Predictability," *New York Times Book Review*, 18 November 1992, 52.

Chapter 12

Romance in the Stacks; or, Popular Romance Fiction Imperiled

Alison M. Scott

"Do you know, you haven't told me your name."
"Bonnie." She blushed. "Bonnie Bell—sounds like a romance writer."
"Is that what you write?"
"No. Gosh, I'd die of embarrassment."
 —Characters in the mystery novel *Mudlark* by Sheila Simonson,
 both of whom are writers of genre fiction.[1]

"Plagiarism? How can you tell when all this stuff sounds the same anyway?"
 —*Newsweek*, from a story describing plagiarism accusations
 leveled against the best-selling romance writer, Janet Dailey.[2]

No matter what critical perspective we embrace, popular romance lies at the
bottom of our hierarchy of taste.
 —Beth Rapp Young, "Accidental Authors, Random Readers,
 and the Art of Popular Romance"[3]

As scholars, historians of the book are constantly engaged, one way or another,
in the search for resources with which to work, seeking the material—print,
manuscript, artifact—that might provide the information from which we can
generate new insights into the past and present and synthesize new knowledge of
the ways that the written word engages the human spirit, mind, and heart.[4] Those
of us who are also librarians have another role in this scholarly endeavor: we
have the responsibility of ensuring that the resources for this scholarly inquiry
are acquired and made accessible, so that those who seek can find. And in this,
librarians have a central, though little recognized, position in the formulation,
development, and execution of research. Percy Bysshe Shelley pointed out in
1821 in *The Defense of Poetry* that "poets are the unacknowledged legislators of
the world." So, too, are librarians the unacknowledged legislators of scholarship.

This is to say that much of the research into the history of the book is driven by, directed toward, or drawn by resources that are available for use in libraries, archives, and other institutional research collections. It is librarians, one way or another, who decide what will be preserved and at hand for use in those research collections, and they are no less influenced by attitudes about cultural value than other members of society.

As an academic librarian and the director of a research collection, it is my belief that what librarians preserve, scholars will use, as long as those materials remain accessible. The libraries of the world are filled with treasures that have been and will remain part of the vital resources of scholarship and that will continue to offer new occasions for analysis and synthesis for years to come.

The obverse is also true. What of the materials that librarians did not collect, and what of the collections that got away—the manuscripts that were pulped, the books that were dispersed in secondhand shops, the objects that went to the garbage dump? We know little or nothing of them because they failed to become part of the available repertoire of accessible, permanent, institutionalized research collections. We can neither learn from these lost resources nor integrate what they could have told us into our understanding of culture. We can only be certain that decisions concerning the inclusion or exclusion of items from research collections will influence the direction that scholarship will take, even as those decisions are themselves influenced by social, cultural, and institutional attitudes toward cultural material.

Such is the case with the romance novel, a valuable, endangered species of research material, and a class of book that constitutes a major portion of the contemporary bibliographic marketplace in North America. Romance novels are those paperback volumes defined by the Romance Writers of America as "[c]ontemporary or historical romance novels numbered and sold as part of a regular package, usually issued monthly. Loveswepts, Harlequins and Silhouettes are examples. These books are also known as category [or series] romances."[5] They are commonly known in the United Kingdom as the Mills & Boon novel and in North America, they "are often (and erroneously) lumped together under the generic term 'harlequin.'"[6] Series romance novels are almost universally scorned by the academic, literary, bibliographic, and library establishments, as well as by broad segments of the general public, and they have been almost universally scorned by academic and research libraries for reasons that have little to do with their potential to reward serious inquiry.

To understand better the scorn for romances, it is important to examine the genesis and formulaic nature of the genre. The origins of the romance novel may be found in the eighteenth century, for "[t]he roots of gothic and romantic fiction for women go back to the beginning of the novel itself as a literary form. . . . The tensions of women's romances, the way the fictional world operates, were very much a part of *Pamela* and its host of imitations."[7] By the twentieth century, the romance novel had taken on specific generic attributes and become a formulaic story of a woman's successful search for happiness, through the resolution of conflicts with a socially and emotionally desirable man. As one study of the romance explains, "A [modern] romance novel is defined as a book whose primary focus is a romantic relationship between a man and woman that ends happily. The happy ending is one of the primary requirements of a romance, and it's one of the reasons *Bridges of Madison County* is not a romance novel but is instead simply fiction."[8] This "happy ending" is typically made manifest by marriage or its promise, a settled, monogamous, socially recognized union between heterosexual protagonists.[9]

So formulaic is the genre that authors who wish to publish their novels in any of the series issued by major publishers such as Harlequin must follow series guidelines that designate elements of plot, characterization, and setting. Some series guidelines provide very general instructions: "Silhouette Romance requires talented authors to portray modern relationships in the context of romantic love. Although hero and heroine don't actually make love until married, sexual tension is a vitally important element."[10] Other guidelines are quite specific: "We are looking for historical and contemporary romances set in Ireland. No magical or fantasy elements. The romance should take precedence over political and religious turmoil, not vice versa."[11] Series romances may therefore be more identifiable by intentionally formulated house styles of plot, setting, and characterization than by their individuality as original works of fiction.

To speak more bibliographically, the paperback novels that embody these generic traits appeared in England after World War II, issued in numbered series by the London-based firm of Mills & Boon. The successful formula arrived in Canada and the United States in the 1950s, when the Toronto-based publishing house Harlequin Enterprises began reprinting Mills & Boon titles. Harlequin quickly began publishing original stories but retained the practice of issuing volumes in numbered series (as had been the practice of major American paperback houses, such as Avon, Dell, and Pocket Books, since the 1930s). Harlequin eventually added the month and year of publication to the cover of their books, along with the series number.[12] This practice gives retailers the capability of ready maintenance of current stock and offers scholars the opportunity for specific historical contextualization.

Series romances are issued in a set number each month and are marketed less frequently in traditional bibliographic outlets—bookstores and newsstands—than through the mail by subscription and in other retail outlets frequented by women, such as department, grocery, and drug stores. Publishers of series romances also place advertisements in their own books, in women's magazines, and, increasingly, on cable television. Harlequin, the publisher that pioneered these techniques, was so successful in its efforts to market series romances that numerous rivals have entered the field over the last four decades. Harlequin has itself expanded its own series offerings, ranging from devotional romances featuring deeply religious Christian heroines to explicit tales of sexual romance and intrigue, providing a remarkable example of product diversification and marketing innovation. Harlequin and its competitors, including Silhouette, Zebra, Heartsong, and Fawcett, are the publishers of brand-name fiction, and the general category of romance novels includes dozens, if not hundreds, of volumes published each month: romance novels comprise nearly 50 percent of the mass-market paperbacks sold annually in the United States.[13] Series romance novels represent, therefore, a valuable asset for their publishers and a remarkable break-through in the rationalization of the production and distribution of books, an area of performance that has historically represented the greatest challenge to the publishing and bookselling industries.

Series romance novels are also the most scorned genre of popular fiction. As critic Kay Mussell observes, "Two centuries ago, critics and moralists argued against the proliferation of novels and lending libraries because novels were sus-pected of corrupting the morals of innocent young girls who were presumed to make up the bulk of the audience. Today, romances are shunned as trivial and attacked as unrealistic and subversive. Disdaining to read them, critics and re-viewers have instead been satisfied to relegate them to the garbage heap of fic-tion—along with that other unfavored literary genre, pornography—in a gesture of contempt that denies the validity of both the books and their readers."[14] These novels are typically regarded by all except their readers with undisguised deri-sion and disdain and are dismissed as the worst sort of escapist trash. Series romances may be, and have been, readily characterized as formulaic narratives of wish fulfillment and their readers viewed as passive consumers of the worst that popular culture can create for a mass audience.[15]

We must acknowledge what is known to any reader of genre fiction: many individual volumes within a genre, as formulaic fiction, have clear aesthetic de-ficiencies that may justify exclusion from academic consideration within the con-text of canonical valuation and the practice of literary criticism. And, as mass media critic Ien Ang has noted, much feminist scholarship, with its critical atten-tion to the ways that the romance formula reiterates and reinforces existing hier-archies of power and desire, has helped contribute to a generally negative and dismissive view of romances held by literary, feminist, and other academic crit-ics.[16] However, unlike other areas of popular fiction, such as mystery, science fiction, and adventure, the entire genre of romance is typically understood by reference to its worst examples or what are thought to be its worst attributes. As one reader remarked, "Romance is a form of literature beloved by readers and loathed by literary critics. This didn't used to bother me; I just accepted the given that all romance fiction was hackwork. . . . No decent critic would every say, 'All literary fiction is good,' or 'All stories about war are bad,' and yet the bias against romance was almost universal. Yes, a lot of the writing in romance fiction is abysmal, but so is a lot of the writing in mystery, SF, and literary fic-tion, and only the romance gets condemned as an entire genre."[17]

Pejorative views of series romance fiction are not limited to the literary es-tablishment or the academy: they penetrate popular culture, as well. The best-selling fantasy and science fiction novelist Marion Zimmer Bradley writes that "I am often asked why I personally think romances, even when combined with a few fantasy elements, are a bad thing which no self-respecting woman should read. I feel strongly that romances, even the ones which make six figure incomes for their very well-meaning and hard-working authors, perpetrate the most harm-

ful of old stereotypes; the one which encourages women to think their primary—maybe their only value—is the finding of the right man; that all their
troubles will be ended upon the procurement of love and marriage. . . . I, who am
the kind of omnivorous reader who reads the back of toothpaste cartons, can't
stomach the average romance. They are more thoroughly tied to formula than the
worst hack fiction in the outfield."[18] Bradley goes on to argue that the bad influence of romance novels is so profound and pernicious that women, raised on "a
steady diet of this kind of reading" and incapable of distinguishing between
harmful fantasy and true reality, are unfit for the workplace, unfit for mother-
hood, and unfit for genuine love.[19] In short, the modern romance novel, a mere-
tricious and debased literary form, creates helpless, though willing, victims.

Contempt for romance novels is often extended to romance readers, who
routinely endure what the romance novelist Susan Elizabeth Phillips describes as
"leisure harassment."[20] Jayne Ann Krentz, another romance author, elaborates:

Few people realize how much courage it takes for a woman to open a romance novel on
an airplane. She knows what everyone around her will think about both her and her
choice of reading material. When it comes to romance novels, society has always felt free
to sit in judgment not only on the literature but on the reader herself.

The verdict is always the same. Society does not approve of the reading of romance
novels. It labels the books as trash and the readers as unintelligent, uneducated, unsophisticated, or neurotic.[21]

The low status of romance novels may be attributed to their aesthetic and
political deficiencies, yet the extremely low level of regard, even in the marketplace where money usually brings some respect, suggests that something else is
at work. The scorn that romances garner relates substantively to the fact that
romances are women's reading. An article in *Romance Writers' Report* asks,
"[W]hy isn't romance thought of more highly? Why doesn't it command more
respect even though it makes up half the paperback market and a sizable share of
the hardback market? Even though the latest statistics say that romance generates
over a billion dollars a year?" The article then asserts, "Romance isn't valued
because it examines, and elucidates a woman's view of the world and her place
in it. . . . These are the experiences and issues that have not been legitimized by
the legion of scholar/critics who determine what has value and what does not in
our culture."[22] Or as Jennie Crusie notes, "Sociologists have long recognized a
phenomenon called 'feminization,' which means that anything that becomes associated solely with women falls in general esteem."[23] Romance novels are objects designed for women's self-indulgence, for moments when their readers,
typically beyond their twenties, married, with children, in the working and middle classes, do something for themselves.[24]

Owing to their lack of prestige and concomitant lack of respect, romance
novels are granted little place in institutions intended to preserve respected parts
of our cultural heritage. The Tulsa Public Library, for instance, appeals to the
library's mission as cultural guardian to justify their decision to move away from
extensive investment in genre fiction: "We believe that the library should serve a

higher purpose than merely satisfying our patrons' immediate cravings. . . . We concluded that in pursuing the popular, we were losing sight of our mission."[25] The library's efforts, not surprisingly, have a disproportionate effect upon romance readers: the authors note, without regret, that "we have probably disenfranchised some readers of romances, who grumble that we don't have enough for them to read."[26] No other category of popular fiction is singled out for exclusion, and the librarians feel no need to justify their deliberate alienation of a significant part of the reading public from the aims of a public library.

Public libraries that have bowed to the demands of their readers for series romances have, in most cases, failed to catalog them, circulating these items as "one Harlequin" or "one Silhouette" rather than as specific bibliographic entities, such as *Marriage by Mistake* by Mollie Molay (Harlequin, 1996) or *The Groom, I Presume?* by Annette Broadrick (Silhouette Desire, 1996). Further, public libraries that do carry series romances do so for current consumption, on the apparent theory that one romance novel will serve to meet romance readers' desires as well as another. No public library, to my knowledge, has made efforts to form permanent collections of series romances or to replace a worn-out or lost copy of a series romance with another copy of the same text. This is, in any case, difficult to accomplish because of the short time during which series novels remain available from publishers and distributors, and it is now nearly impossible to acquire early series romances for inclusion in library collections.[27]

Despite the growing prominence of popular culture studies in American universities, academic and research libraries have, with a very few exceptions, also failed to incorporate romance novels into their research collections, even as other popular genres with equally formulaic reputations (though with more prestige), such as mysteries and science fiction, have been integrated into research collections and have generated an extensive and active body of research.

One of the few exceptions to the rule of the exclusion of popular culture materials from academic research libraries is the Popular Culture Library of Bowling Green State University, which was founded in 1969 to support curricular work and research in popular culture. In the last thirty years, the Popular Culture Library has made every effort to incorporate series romance novels into its collections, just as other research libraries have acquired fifteenth-century printed books, medieval manuscripts, modern first editions, and other research materials of permanent and traditional research value.

As of May 15, 1998, the Popular Culture Library held 10,154 cataloged series romance novels. Of these, 334 were published before 1970, during the "cradle period" of the series romance, by Bantam, Dell, Harlequin, Paperback Library, New American Library, Lancer, Prestige, Avalon, and Valentine. These books were at the time of their publication among the earliest examples of the production and distribution of brand-name, mass-market fiction for women, and they are now the most difficult to find, both in libraries and in the secondhand-book market.[28]

Of these 334 series romance novels, 30.84 percent—103 titles—are unique to the Popular Culture Library, as demonstrated by holdings statements in the bibliographic database, WorldCat: no other libraries report owning them.[29] In another eighty-one cases, the Popular Culture Library is the only *research* library that holds these books; they are also owned by some public library collections (but only in fourteen instances do more than five public libraries own any of these eighty-one titles). Thus, more than half of these early series romances—55 percent—are a permanent part of only one research library.[30]

Of the same group of pre-1970 series romances, 78 are owned only by the Popular Culture Library and one other research library.[31] In another fifty-seven cases, two research libraries report holdings, as do from one to five or more public libraries. (In only seven instances do more than five public libraries hold any of these fifty-seven titles.)

Thus, of these 334 early romances, 319, or 95.5 percent, are part of the permanent collections of only one or two research libraries; in only two instances are any pre-1970 series romance titles held by more than five research libraries. The full results of this holdings survey, shown below in Table 1, reveal a remarkable pattern of absences.

Table 1
Series Romances, Published before 1970[32]

N = 334	PCL Only	+1 Other Research Library	+2 Other Research Libraries	+3 Other Research Libraries	+4 Other Research Libraries	+5 or More Other Research Libraries
PCL Only	103	78	1	1	0	0
+1 Public Libraries	23	25	2	3	0	1
+2 Public Libraries	17	13	1	0	1	0
+3 Public Libraries	17	10	2	1	0	0
+4 Public Libraries	10	2	1	1	0	0
+5 or More Public Libraries	14	7	0	0	0	0

By way of contrast, consider the case of the paperback science fiction books published by the New York publisher Ace Books. The firm was founded in 1952 and is best known to book collectors for its practice of issuing two short novels as a single volume, bound *dos-à-dos*. Ace specialized in publishing cheap science fiction, Westerns, and other popular adventure stories, frequently reprinting material originally published in pulp magazines twenty and thirty years earlier. The company is a contemporary of Harlequin Enterprises, and their books appeared in the North American market at about the same time.[33] Since science fiction, a mainstay of Ace's list, has sometimes been dismissed as an escapist and formula-driven genre, read primarily by adolescent and adult males, we might, therefore, expect that science fiction, particularly of the kind published by Ace, would have comparatively little presence in research libraries and other leading repositories of respected, respectable, cultural material. The expectation is, however, not the reality. The Popular Culture Library holds 236 Ace science fiction titles published before 1970. Of those, the Popular Culture Library is the sole reported owner of record of only thirteen books (6.35 percent), whereas 88.98 percent—210 books—are held by four or more research libraries; in many cases, individual volumes are held by more than ten research libraries throughout North America. Science fiction, in the form of cheap paperback reprints, seems to have been thoroughly institutionalized in traditional research libraries.

However, as science fiction has been the chosen recreational reading of many thoughtful and well-regarded individuals, it could be argued that the cheap science fiction published by Ace has been institutionalized by association with more serious literature utilizing the conventions of science fiction.[34] A colleague who spoke with me about this project as a work-in-progress suggested that a survey of a class of books that he believed would be equally as scorned by research libraries might make a more suitable comparison to romance novels. On this recommendation, I surveyed volumes held by the Popular Culture Library from a radically different generic tradition, books that represent stereotypically male reading interests in violence, intrigue, and sex, the long-lived "Nick Carter/Killmaster" stories. Written under the house name of "Nick Carter," these eponymous novels are formulaic spy thrillers (issued in a numbered series), featuring abundant mayhem and death, sexual adventure, and a hero who retains, despite his numerous encounters with designing (and dangerous) women, his bachelor status. Nick Carter is the adult, twentieth-century reincarnation of the nineteenth-century dime novel hero, Nick Carter, Detective, and the logical extension of the Stratemeyer Syndicate's and others'efforts to systematize the production of fiction.[35] The series, though no longer in print, was quite popular in its time, despite the fact that, as literature, the randomly chosen Killmaster novel is no better, and often much worse, than the randomly chosen romance novel.

A survey of reported library holdings carried out in May 1998 yielded the following results, which are strikingly similar to the results of the survey of science fiction holdings. Two of the seventy-three Nick Carter novels, 2.73 percent, are held only by the Popular Culture Library; twenty-nine, or 36.98 percent, are held by four or more research libraries (including the Popular Culture Library). The full results are summarized in Table 2.

There are, of course, major differences between series romances and the Nick Carter novels, even beyond the extensive differences between genres. Romances published in a single series are written by many different authors while the Killmaster adventures are all ostensibly written by the same author. Killmaster books feature the single recurring hero, Nick Carter, while romance novels must feature different main characters, for if an essential attribute of the conclusion of a romance story is a happy marriage, heroines will not and cannot have repeated romantic adventures. Both these circumstances may inspire more particularized reader loyalty toward Nick Carter. Additionally, the Killmaster series books were published more recently than the romance novels discussed above, and, as a result, have probably suffered less attrition through loss and physical deterioration than the older romances have. And finally, markedly fewer Killmaster books have been published than series romance novels, making the collection and retention of these volumes a much less daunting prospect than the systematic acquisition of series romances. These significant differences may help explain the presence of Nick Carter novels in public libraries; they do not explain why Nick Carter has so much more presence in research libraries than romance novels. For this we must again return to the idea of scorned literature: even the most formulaic Nick Carter novel has a higher place on the cultural hierarchy than series romance fiction and is, therefore, incorporated into the working collections of repositories of cultural value with greater frequency.

Table 2
Nick Carter/Killmaster[36]

$N = 73$	PCL Only	+1 Other Research Library	+2 Other Research Libraries	+3 Other Research Libraries	+4 Other Research Libraries	+5 or More Research Libraries
PCL Only	2	7	2	3	1	1
+1 Public Library	1	7	6	4	1	5
+2 Public Libraries	1	2	3	1	4	2
+3 Public Libraries	1	3	3	0	1	1
+4 Public Libraries	2	2	0	2	0	0
+5 or More Public Libraries	2	2	0	1	0	0

What is the result of research libraries' acceptance of the commonplaces of cultural hierarchy? Copies of the rarest of rare books are often easier to find for research purposes than the most popular of series romance novels. As a rare book librarian by training, I am not ordinarily alarmed by rarity. I am, however, alarmed at the apparent rarity of series romance novels, which were and are so widely popular and available, and so widely read, and which are so poorly represented in the research libraries of North America. We are seeing an extension of what Joanna Russ described in *How to Suppress Women's Writing*, because libraries are implicated in, and supporters of, cultural hierarchies of value and prestige. To the degree that series romance fiction, as women's reading and as popular reading, is excluded from research collections, the inevitable result will be the difficulty, if not impossibility, of research into the full measure of the bibliographic culture of the late twentieth century. We do not now know what the study of the series romance novel will yield to serious investigation, because the work has not yet been done, and the possibilities for fruitful research have been obscured by the scorn accorded the romance in libraries and in the academy. Nevertheless, the series romance novel's position in the intersection between literary creativity, the economics of publication and distribution, and readers' desires for fictive experience make these volumes a valuable resource for explorations into the history of authorship, publishing, and reading.

The multitudinous challenges facing future historians and critics as they attempt to understand the culture of late-twentieth-century North America will be increased unless scholars and librarians recognize the value of preserving the full range of contemporary publications, including the much maligned, much ridiculed, much scorned, series romance novel.

NOTES

1. Sheila Simonson, *Mudlark* (New York: Worldwide, 1995), 10. *Mudlark* was originally published by St. Martin's Press in 1993; Worldwide, which issued the paperback reprint, is an imprint of Harlequin Enterprises.

2. Marc Peyser and Yahlin Chang, "The Queen of Hearts Gives Up Her Throne: Purloined Purple Prose May Sink Janet Dailey," *Newsweek*, August 11, 1997, 74.

3. Beth Rapp Young, "Accidental Authors, Random Readers, and the Art of Popular Romance," *Where's Love Gone?: Transformations in the Romance Genre*, special issue of *Para-Doxa* 3: 1–2 (1997): 30.

4. This paper was delivered, in different forms, at the Popular Culture Association annual conference in March 1997 (held in San Antonio, TX) and at the Society for the History of Authorship, Reading, and Publishing in July 1997 (held in Cambridge, England). My thanks to those whose comments on these presentations and on drafts of this paper materially improved the construction and content of this essay.

5. Romance Writers of America, "What Is a Romance Novel?" 1997, <http://www.rwanational.com/inforom.htm>.

6. Cathie Linz, Ann Bouricius, and Carole Byrnes, "Exploring the World of Romance Novels," *Public Libraries*, May/June 1995, 149. Even Janice Radway adopts this inaccurate, though understandable, usage: see, for example, *Reading the Romance: Women, Patriarchy, and Popular Literature* (Chapel Hill: University of North Carolina Press, 1984), 4–5.

7. Kay Mussell, *Women's Gothic and Romantic Fiction: A Reference Guide* (Westport, CT: Greenwood Press, 1981), 3.

8. Linz, Bouricius, and Byrnes, "Exploring the World of Romance Novels," 144.

9. Until the 1970s, the heroine was a single woman, without prior history of serious romantic involvement with a man; in the later 1970s, widowed or divorced women make their entrance as the heroines of romance; in the late 1980s and the 1990s, single mothers (occasionally pregnant with another man's child at the beginning of the story) begin to appear.

10. *Silhouette Tip Sheet Guidelines* (New York: Silhouette Books, 1995), quoted in Anita Michel, "Re-reading the (Series) Romance: Toward a Typology of Recent Series Romance Novels," master's thesis, Bowling Green State University, 1997, 39–40.

11. "Market Update," *Romance Writers' Report* 18: 6 (June 1998): 46.

12. For a history of Harlequin, see Margaret Ann Jensen, *Love's Sweet Return: The Harlequin Story* (Bowling Green, OH: Bowling Green State University Popular Press, 1984); for an extended discussion of romance publishing history in general, see Chapter

One, "The Institutional Matrix: Publishing Romance Fiction," in Radway, *Reading the Romance*, 19–45.

13. Linz, Bouricius, and Byrnes, "Exploring the World of Romance Novels," 144.

14. Kay Mussell, *Fantasy and Reconciliation: Contemporary Formulas of Women's Romance Fiction* (Westport, CT: Greenwood Press, 1984), 16.

15. For a summary list of the common slurs leveled against romance novels, see Jennie Crusie, "Defeating the Critics: What We Can Do about the Anti-romance Bias," *Romance Writers' Report* (June 1998): 38–39, 44.

16. Ien Ang, *Watching Dallas: Soap Opera and the Melodramatic Imagination* (London: Routledge, 1985), 118–119.

17. Jennie Crusie, "Defeating the Critics," 38.

18. Marion Zimmer Bradley, introduction to *Sword and Sorceress VI: An Anthology of Heroic Fantasy* (New York: DAW Books, 1990), 7–8.

19. Marion Zimmer Bradley, introduction, *Sword and Sorceress VI*, 9.

20. Susan Elizabeth Phillips, private communication with author, June 21, 1997.

21. Jayne Ann Krentz, introduction *to Dangerous Men and Adventurous Women: Romance Writers on the Appeal of the Romance* (Philadelphia: University of Pennsylvania Press, 1992), 1. A cottage industry of paperback-sized opaque book covers advertised as "protective" has emerged in the United States, allowing readers to disguise, as well as protect, their reading material. These book covers may be purchased in most retail book stores, and through many mail-order catalogs, as well as other retail outlets where series romances are available.

22. Sharon Stone, "Blame It on Homer (or, Go to Your Room)," *Romance Writers' Report* 16: 8 (June 1998): 45.

23. Crusie, "Defeating the Critics," 38.

24. "Harlequin readers are overwhelmingly women of whom 49 percent work at least part-time. They range in age from 24 to 49, have average family incomes of $15,000–20,000 and have high school diplomas but haven't completed college." Fred Kerner, Vice-President for Publishing, Harlequin Enterprises, quoted in Radway, *Reading the Romance*, 55.

25. Nancy Pearl and Craig Buthod, "Upgrading the 'McLibrary,'" 117 *Library Journal* (October 15, 1992): 37.

26. Pearl and Buthod, "Upgrading the 'McLibrary,'" 39.

27. Ingram, a major book wholesaler with a national customer base, keeps series romance novels in stock for no more than six months. See Linz, Bouricius, and Byrnes, "Exploring the World of Romance Novels," 144.

28. These 334 volumes represent an unknown, but probably relatively small, fraction of those titles published in romance series before 1970. The bibliography of series romance is not well developed and series romance novels have not made their way into rare-book collecting, a field well known for the development of extensive bibliographical apparatus. One of the commonly available price guides for a popular audience entirely excludes Harlequins from its lists (John Warren, *The Official Price Guide: Paperbacks* [New York: House of Collectibles, 1991]), and "the *first* and *only*" guide for collectors of romance books, *Collecting Romance Novels* by Dawn Reno and Jacque Tiegs (Brooklyn, NY: Alliance Publishing, 1995; back cover blurb, emphasis in the original) devotes less than twenty-five pages (of 118) to lists of romance novels, and does so alphabetically by author's name; this volume also concentrates on "books written from the 1970s to the present" (vii), rendering it useless for investigations into the earlier history of the modern romance novel.

29. WorldCat reports holdings for libraries in North America, the United Kingdom, Australia, New Zealand, as well as a few institutions in other Pacific Rim nations and Europe.

30. For the purposes of this discussion, libraries' status as "public" or "research" collections were inferred from the WorldCat holdings identification codes. School, military, prison, state, and community college libraries were counted as public libraries, and my working assumption is that these libraries are acquiring and cataloging materials primarily for current consumption; four-year college, university, national, and special libraries were counted as research libraries, and my assumption is that materials added to these libraries will, by and large, be permanent additions to collections intended to support scholarship. This working assumption will, of course, be incorrect in some cases; however, as I am primarily concerned with the absence of series romances from research libraries, a university library's decision to catalog "disposable books," for instance, a circulating collection of paperback books for recreational reading, does not materially affect the argument.

31. In most cases, the other research institution is the Michigan State University Library, in East Lansing, another library that has devoted serious and long-term efforts to the collection and study of popular culture materials; the National Library of Canada also reports holdings of a few of these volumes.

32. The survey of reported holdings in WorldCat of pre-1970 series romances held by the Popular Culture Library, Bowling Green State University, Bowling Green, Ohio, was performed May 15–28, 1998.

33. For brief but informative histories of Ace Books, see Thomas L. Bonn, *Under-Cover: An Illustrated History of American Mass Market Paperbacks* (New York: Penguin Books, 1982), 74–75 and Piet Schreuders, *Paperbacks, U.S.A.: A Graphic History, 1939–1959* (San Diego, CA: Blue Dolphin Enterprises, 1981), 100–1.

34. See Michael L. Lewis, "From Science to Science Fiction: Leo Szilard and Fictional Persuasion," in *The Writing on the Cloud: American Culture Confronts the Atomic Bomb*, ed. Alison M. Scott and Christopher D. Geist (Lanham, MD: University Press of America, 1997), 95–105, for a discussion of one important instance of the use of science fiction for highly serious purposes.

35. The titles in this series held by the Popular Culture Library were published by Award (1964–1976) and Charter (1982–1986).

36. The survey of reported WorldCat holdings of Nick Carter/Killmaster was performed May 15–31, 1998.

Selected Bibliography

Adams, Charles Frances, Jr. "Fiction in Public Libraries and Educational Catalogues." *Library Journal* 4 (September-October 1879): 331–38.

Adorno, Theodor, and Max Horkheimer. "The Culture Industry: Enlightenment as Mass Deception." *The Cultural Studies Reader*, ed. Simon During, 29–43. New York: Routledge, 1993.

Allmendinger, Blake. *Ten Most Wanted: The New Western Literature*. New York: Routledge, 1998.

American Boys' Series Books 1900 to 1980. Tampa: University of South Florida Library Associates, 1987.

Anderson, Margaret C. "A Child's Garden of Books." Parts I and II. *The Bookman* 38 (November 1913): 315–22; (December 1913): 437–47.

Atkinson, William P. "Address," *Library Journal* 4 (September-October 1879): 359–62.

Avery, Gillian. *Behold the Child: American Children and Their Books 1621–1922*. London: The Bodley Head, 1994.

Ayres, Ernest F. "Not to Be Circulated?" *Wilson Bulletin* 3 (March 1929): 528–29.

Benton, Mike. *The Comic Book in America: An Illustrated History*. Dallas, TX: Taylor Publishing Co., 1988.

———. *Superhero Comics of the Golden Age: An Illustrated History*. Dallas, TX: Taylor Publishing Co., 1992.

Billman, Carol. *The Secret of the Stratemeyer Syndicate: Nancy Drew, the Hardy Boys, and the Million Dollar Fiction Factory*. New York: Unger, 1986.

Bishop, W[illiam] H[enry]. "Story-Paper Literature." *Atlantic Monthly*, September 1879, 383–93.

Bledstein, Burton. *The Culture of Professionalism: The Middle Class and the Development of Higher Education in America*. New York: Norton, 1976.

Bold, Christine. *Selling the Wild West: Popular Western Fiction, 1860–1960*. Bloomington: Indiana University Press, 1987.

Bonn, Thomas. *Heavy Traffic and High Culture: New American Library as Literary Gatekeeper in the Paperback Revolution*. New York: New American Library, 1980.

Brett, W.H. "Books for Youth." *Library Journal* 10 (June 1885): 127–28.

Brown, Bill, ed. *Reading the West: An Anthology of Dime Westerns*. Boston: Bedford Books, 1997.

Brown, Janet Elder. "The Saga of Elsie Dinsmore." *University of Buffalo Studies* 17 (1945): 75–131.

Buswell, G[uy]. T. "Two New Book Lists for Children's Reading." *Elementary School Journal* 26 (1925–1926): 548–51.

"The Cheap Libraries." *Publishers' Weekly* 12 (1877): 396–97.

Cixous, Hélène. "The Laugh of the Medusa." *Signs: Journal of Women in Culture and Society* 1, no. 4 (1976): 875–93.

Collins, Max Allan and James Traylor, *One Lonely Knight: Mickey Spillane's Mike Hammer*. Bowling Green, OH: The Popular Press, 1984.

"Communications in Favor of Excluding Libraries from Second-Class Mail Privileges." *Publishers' Weekly* 65 (1904): 1255–56.

Comparato, Frank E. *Books for the Millions*. Harrisburg, PA: The Stackpole Company, 1971.

Comstock, Anthony. *Traps for the Young*. 1883. Reprint, with an Editor's Introduction by Robert Bremner, Cambridge, MA: Harvard University Press, Belknap Press, 1967.

Cowley, Malcolm. *The Literary Situation*. New York: Viking, 1954.

Crist, Judith. "Horror in the Nursery." *Collier's*, 29 March 1948, 22–23.

Darling, Richard L. *The Rise of Children's Book Reviewing in America, 1865–1881*. New York: R.R. Bowker Company, 1968.

Denning, Michael. *Mechanic Accents: Dime Novels and Working-Class Culture in America*. New York: Verso, 1987.

Dingwall, Robert, and Philip Lewis, eds. *The Sociology of the Professions: Lawyers, Doctors, and Others*, 1–8. New York: St. Martin, 1982.

Dizer, John T. *Tom Swift and Company*. Jefferson, NC: McFarland, 1982.

Doll, Carol. "The Children of Sophie May." In: *Research about Nineteenth-Century Children and Books*, edited by Selma K. Richardson, 97–116. Monograph—University of Illinois Graduate School of Library Science, no. 17. Urbana-Champaign: University of Illinois, 1980.

Douglas, Ann. "Soft-Porn Culture." *New Republic* (30 August 1980): 25–29.

E.G.H. Review of *The Winnetka Graded Book List*. *Library Association Record* 4 (December 1926): 242–43.

Fiedler, Leslie. *Love and Death in the American Novel*. 1966; New York: Anchor, 1992.

Foley, Barbara. *Radical Representations: Politics and Form in U.S. Proletarian Fiction, 1929–1941*. Durham: Duke University Press, 1993.

"For It Was Indeed He." *Fortune* 9 (April 1934), 86–89, 193–94, 204–10.

Foucault, Michel. *The History of Sexuality. Volume I: An Introduction*, translated by Robert Hurley. New York: Vintage Books, 1990.

Frank, Josette. *What Books for Children? Guideposts for Parents*. Rev. ed. New York: Doubleday, 1941.

Gabilliet, Jean-Paul. "Cultural and Mythical Aspects of a Superhero: The Silver Surfer 1968–70." *Journal of Popular Culture* 28:2 (Fall 1994), 203–13.

Gaines, Ernest J. "Viewpoint: Closed Circuit Children's Books." *Library Journal* 95 (April 1970): 1455.

Garber, Marjorie. *Vested Interests: Cross-Dressing and Cultural Anxiety*. 1992; New York: Routledge, 1997.

Girls' Series Books 1841–1991. Minneapolis: Children's Literature Research Collections, University of Minnesota Libraries, 1992.

Goodstone, Tony, ed. *The Pulps: Fifty Years of American Pop Culture*. New York: Chelsea House, 1970.

Goulart, Ron. *Cheap Thrills: An Informal History of Pulp Magazines*. New Rochelle, NY: Arlington House, 1972.

———. *Dime Detectives*. New York: Mysterious, 1988.

———. *Over 50 Years of American Comic Books*. Lincolnwood, IL: Publications International, 1991.

———. "Wartime," *The Funnies: 100 Years of American Comic Strips*, 143–66. Holbrook, MA: Adams Publishing, 1995.

Greenberg, Clement. "Avant-Garde and Kitsch." In: *Mass Culture: The Popular Arts in America*, edited by Bernard Rosenberg and David Manning White, 98–110. New York: The Free Press, 1957.

Group of Librarians. "The Winnetka Graded Book List." *Elementary English Review* 3 (1926): 235–38.

Gruber, Frank. *The Pulp Jungle*. Los Angeles: Sherbourne, 1967.

Hagler, Philip E., and Desmond Taylor. *The Novels of World War I: An Annotated Bibliography*, 313–449. New York: Garland Press, 1981.

Hall, David D. "Readers and Reading in America: Historical and Critical Perspectives." *Proceedings of the American Antiquarian Society* 103 (1993): 337–57.

Harper, J. Henry. *The House of Harper: A Century of Publishing in Franklin Square*. New York and London: Harper & Brothers, 1912.

Harris, Art. "Mickey Spillane, Still Hammering," *Washington Post*, 24 October 1984, sec. D: 1, 9.

Haviland, Virginia. "The Travelogue Storybook of the Nineteenth Century." In: *The Hewins Lectures 1947–1962*, edited by Siri Andrews, 25–63. Boston: The Horn Book, 1963. Originally published as *The Travelogue Storybook of the Nineteenth Century*. Boston: The Horn Book, 1950.

Hazeltine, Alice, ed. *Library Work with Children*. New York: Wilson, 1917.

Hersey, Harold. *Pulpwood Editor: The Fabulous World of Thriller Magazines Revealed by a Veteran Editor and Publisher*. New York: Stokes, 1937.

Hewins, C[aroline] M. *Books for the Young: A Guide for Parents and Children*. New York: F. Leypoldt, 1882.

Higginson, T[homas] W[entworth]. "Address," *Library Journal* 4 (September-October 1879): 357–59.

[Higginson, Thomas Wentworth.] "Children's Books of the Year," *North American Review* 102 (January 1866): 236–49.

Holsinger, M. Paul. "Thirty-Nine Cent Americanism: The Fighters for Freedom Series." *Newsboy: The Official Publication of The Horatio Alger Society* 30 (1992): 16–23.

———. *The Ways of War: The Era of World War II in Children's and Young Adult Fiction*. Metuchen, NJ: The Scarecrow Press, 1995.

———. "World War Combat in American Juvenile and Paperback Series Books." In: *Pioneers, Passionate Ladies and Private Eyes: Dime Novels, Series Books and Paperbacks*, edited by Larry E. Sullivan and Lydia Cushman Schurman, 147–62. New York: Haworth Press, 1997.

Holt, Henry. Letter to the Editor. "On the Decline of the Book-Buying Habit." *Publishers' Weekly* 32 (1887): 18–19.

"International Copyright. The Copyright Controversy." *Publishers' Weekly* 22 (1882): 866–69.

Jagusch, Sybille, ed. *Stepping Away from Tradition: Children's Books of the 1920s and 1930s*. Washington, DC: Library of Congress, 1988.

Jensen, Margaret Ann. *Love's $weet Return: The Harlequin Story*. Bowling Green, OH: Bowling Green State University Popular Press, 1984.

Johannsen, Albert. *The House of Beadle and Adams and Its Dime and Nickel Novels: The Story of a Vanished Literature*. Vols. 1–2. Norman: University of Oklahoma Press, 1950.

Johnson, Deidre. *Edward Stratemeyer and the Stratemeyer Syndicate*. New York: Twayne Publishers, 1993.

———. "Nancy Drew—A Modern Elsie Dinsmore?" *The Lion and the Unicorn* 18 (June 1994): 13–24.

Johnston, Richard. "Death's Fair-Haired Boy," *Life* 32 (23 June 1952): 79–80, 82, 85–86, 89–90, 92, 95.

Jones, Daryl. *The Dime Novel Western*. Bowling Green, OH: The Popular Press, 1978.

Jones, Dolores Blythe, comp. *An "Oliver Optic" Checklist:· An Annotated Catalog-Index to the Series, Nonseries Stories, and Magazine Publications of William Taylor Adams*. Westport, CT: Greenwood Press, 1985.

Jordan, Alice M. *From Rollo to Tom Sawyer and Other Papers*. Boston: The Horn Book, 1948.

Jordan, Arthur Melville. *Children's Interests in Reading*. Rev. ed. Chapel Hill: University of North Carolina Press, 1926.

Kaestle, Carl F., Helen Damon-Moore, Lawrence C. Stedman, Katherine Tinsley, and William Vance Trollinger, Jr. *Literacy in the Unites States: Readers and Reading since 1880*. New Haven: Yale University Press, 1991.

Karetzky, Stephen. *Reading Research and Librarianship: A History and Analysis*. Westport, CT: Greenwood Press, 1982.

Kilgour, Raymond L. *Lee and Shepard: Publishers for the People*. N.p.: The Shoe String Press, 1965.

Kinloch, Lucy M. "The Menace of the Series Book." *Elementary English Review* 12 (January 1935): 9–11.

Krentz, Jayne Ann, ed. *Dangerous Men and Adventurous Women: Romance Writers on the Appeal of the Romance*. Philadelphia: University of Pennsylvania Press, 1992; New York: HarperPaperbacks, 1996.

LaFarge, Christopher. "Mickey Spillane and His Bloody Hammer." In: *Mass Culture: The Popular Arts in America*, edited by Bernard Rosenberg and David Manning White. Glencoe, IL: Free Press, 1957.

Legman, Gershon. *Love and Death: A Study in Censorship*. New York: Breaking Point, 1949.

Leonard, S[terling] A[ndrus]. "The Winnetka Reading List." *Elementary English Review* 3 (1926): 122–25.

Lupoff, Dick. "The Propwash Patrol." In: *The Comic Book Book*, edited by Don Thompson and Dick Lupoff, 62–86. New Rochelle, NY: Arlington House, 1973.

———. "The Propwash Patrol Flies Again." In: *The Comic Book Book*, edited by Don Thompson and Dick Lupoff, 174–204. New Rochelle, NY: Arlington House, 1973.

Lupoff, Dick, and Don Thompson, eds. *All in Color for a Dime*. New Rochelle, NY: Arlington House, 1970.

Macelwane, Francis J. Review of *The Winnetka Graded Book List*. *Catholic Educational Review* 24 (1926): 313–14.

Mackey, Margaret. "Filling the Gaps: The *Baby-Sitters Club*, the Series Book, and the Learning Reader." *Language Arts* 67 (September 1990): 484–89.

Mathiews, Franklin K. "Blowing Out the Boys' Brains." *The Outlook* 108 (18 November 1914): 652–54.

Mattson, E. Christian, and Thomas B. Davis. *A Collector's Guide to Hardcover Boys' Series Books, or Tracing the Trail of Harry Hudson*. Newark, DE: Mad Dog Books, 1997.

McCann, Sean. *Gumshoe America: Hard-Boiled Crime Fiction and the Rise and Fall of New Deal Liberalism*. Durham, NC: Duke University Press, 2000.

Mitchell, Lillian Herron. "Not To Be Circulated." *Wilson Bulletin* 3 (April 1929): 580, 584.

Mott, Frank Luther. *Golden Multitudes: The Story of Best Sellers in the United States*. New York: Macmillan, 1947.

Mussell, Kay. *Fantasy and Reconciliation: Contemporary Formulas of Women's Romance Fiction*. Westport, CT: Greenwood Press, 1984.

———. *Women's Gothic and Romantic Fiction: A Reference Guide*. Westport, CT: Greenwood Press, 1981.

Noel, Mary. *Villains Galore: The Heyday of the Popular Story Weekly*. New York: Macmillan, 1954.

North, Sterling. "A National Disgrace." Reprinted in *Childhood Education* 17 (October 1940): 56.

Nyberg, Amy Kiste. *Seal of Approval: The History of the Comics Code*. Jackson: University of Mississippi Press, 1998.

O'Brien, Geoffrey. *Hardboiled America: Lurid Paperbacks and the Masters of Noir*. Expanded ed. New York: Da Capo Press, 1997.

Ohmann, Richard. "The Shaping of a Canon: U.S. Fiction 1960–1975." *Critical Inquiry* 10 (September 1983): 199–223.

Olcott, Frances Jenkins. *The Children's Reading*. Boston: Houghton Mifflin, 1912.

"An Open Forum on the Winnetka List." *Elementary English Review* 4 (1927): 10–12.

"Our Comic Culture." *Educational Forum* 6 (November 1941): 84.

Palumbo, Donald. "Adam Warlock: Marvel Comics' Cosmic Christ Figure." *Extrapolation* 24:1 (Spring 1983): 33–46.

———. "Comics as Literature: Plot Structure, Foreshadowing, and Irony in the Marvel Comics' *Avengers* 'Cosmic Epic.'" *Extrapolation* 22:4 (Winter 1981): 309–24.

———. "The Marvel Comics Group's Spider-Man Is an Existentialist Super-Hero; or, 'Life Has No Meaning without My Latest Marvels!'" *Journal of Popular Culture* 17:2 (Fall 1983): 67–82.

———. "Metafiction in the Comics: *The Sensational She-Hulk*." *Journal of the Fantastic in the Arts* 8:3 (December 1997): 310–30.

———. "The Pattern of Allusions in Marvel Comics." *Proteus: A Journal of Ideas* 6:1 (Spring 1989): 61–64.

Parry, Sally E. "'You Are Needed, Desperately Needed': Cherry Ames in World War II," 129–44. In: *Nancy Drew and Company: Culture, Gender, and Girls' Series*, edited by Sherrie A. Inness. Bowling Green, OH: Bowling Green State University Popular Press, 1997.

Parsons, Talcott. "Professions." In: *International Encyclopedia of the Social Sciences*, vol. 12, edited by David Sills, 536–47. New York: Macmillan/Free Press, 1968.

Piersel, W.G. "A Graded Book List for Elementary-School and Junior High School Reading." *The School Review* 34 (October 1926): 630–31.

"The Postal Bill as Passed." *Publishers' Weekly* 15 (1879): 280–83.

Prager, Arthur. *Rascals at Large, or The Clue in the Old Nostalgia*. Garden City, NY: Doubleday & Co., 1971.

Radway, Janice A. *Reading the Romance: Women, Patriarchy, and Popular Literature.* 2d ed. 1984; reprint, with a new introduction, Chapel Hill: University of North Carolina Press, 1991.

Rinehart, Anne Campbell. *What Pittsburgh Junior High Pupils Read.* Pittsburgh: Henry Frick Educational Commission, 1931.

Root, Mary E.S. "Not To Be Circulated." *Wilson Bulletin* 3 (January 1929): 446.

Rosenberg, Bernard. "Mass Culture in America." In: *Mass Culture: The Popular Arts in America,* edited by Bernard Rosenberg and David Manning White, 3–12. New York: The Free Press, 1957.

Ross, Catherine Sheldrick. "'If They Read Nancy Drew, So What?': Series Book Readers Talk Back," *Library & Information Science Research* 17 (Spring 1995): 201–36.

Sabin, Roger. *Adult Comics: An Introduction.* London: Routledge, 1993.

Sanders, Minerva A. "Report on Reading for the Young." Fabyan House Conference Proceedings. *Library Journal* 15 (1890): 58–64.

Schurman, Lydia Cushman. "The Librarian of Congress Argues against Cheap Novels Getting Low Postal Rates." In: *Pioneers, Passionate Ladies, and Private Eyes: Dime Novels, Series Books, and Paperbacks,* edited by Larry E. Sullivan and Lydia Cushman Schurman, 59–71. New York and London: The Haworth Press, 1997.

———. "Those Famous American Periodicals—The Bible, the *Odyssey* and *Paradise Lost*—or, the Great Second-Class Mail Swindle." *Publishing History* 40 (1996): 33–52.

Server, Lee. *Danger Is My Business: An Illustrated History of the Fabulous Pulp Magazines.* San Francisco: Chronicle, 1993.

Shove, Raymond Howard. *Cheap Book Production in the United States, 1870 to 1891.* Urbana: University of Illinois Library, 1937.

Silver, Rollo G. "Rollo on Rollo." *The Colophon.* New graphic series. No. 2 (1939): n.p.

Simpson, Richard L., and Ida Harper Simpson. "Women and Bureaucracy in the Semi-Professions." In: *The Semi-Professions and Their Organization,* edited by Amitai Etzioni, 196–265. New York: The Free Press, 1969.

Smith, Erin A. *Hard-Boiled: Working-Class Readers and Pulp Magazines.* Philadelphia: Temple University Press, 2000.

Smith, Henry Nash. *Virgin Land: The American West as Symbol and Myth.* New York: Vintage Books, 1950.

Society of Phantom Friends. *The Girls' Series Book Companion 1994.* N.p., 1994.

Southern, Terry. "An Investigation of the Mid-Century Literary Phenomenon in Which Mr. Spillane, a Popular Novelist of the Day, Chooses to Assay the Role of His Hero, Mike Hammer, in a Motion Picture Interpretation of a Book, Thereby Inciting Curious Speculation." *Esquire* 60 (July 1963): 74–76, 112.

Stern, Madeleine. *Imprints on History: Book Publishers and American Frontiers.* Bloomington: Indiana University Press, 1956.

———, ed. *Publishers for Mass Entertainment in Nineteenth Century America.* Boston: G.K. Hall & Co., 1980.

Stimpson, Catharine R. "Reading for Love: Canons, Paracanons, and Whistling Jo March." *New Literary History* 21 (1990): 957–76.

Tebbel, John. *Between Covers: The Rise and Transformation of Book Publishing in America.* New York: Oxford University Press, 1987.

———. "Specialized Publishing." Part IV in *The Expansion of an Industry, 1815–1919,* vol. 2 of *A History of Book Publishing in the United States,* 481–607. New York: R.R. Bowker Co., 1972–81.

Tebbel, John, and Mary Ellen Zuckerman. *The Magazine in America, 1741–1990.* New York: Oxford University Press, 1991.

Terman, Lewis, and Margaret Lima. *Children's Reading: A Guide for Parents and Teachers.* 2d ed. New York: Appleton, 1931.

Thompson, Don. "OK, Axis, Here We Come!" In: *All in Color for a Dime,* edited by Dick Lupoff and Don Thompson, 121–43. New York: Ace Books, 1970.

Thurston, Carol. *The Romance Revolution: Erotic Novels for Women and the Quest for a New Sexual Identity.* Urbana: University of Illinois Press, 1987.

Tompkins, Jane. *West of Everything: The Inner Life of Westerns.* New York: Oxford University Press, 1992.

"Troubles of Literary Pirates." *Publishers' Weekly* 30 (1886): 555–56.

U.S. Senate Subcommittee to Investigate Juvenile Delinquency, Juvenile Delinquency (Comic Books), Hearings, April 21, 22 and June 4, 1954.

U.S. Senate, Comic Books and Juvenile Delinquency. Interim report of the Committee on the Judiciary, Subcommittee of Juvenile Delinquency, 84th Cong., 1st sess., 1955.

Vandergrift, Kay. "Female Advocacy and Harmonious Voices: A History of Public Library Services and Publishing for Children in the United States." *Library Trends* 44 (Spring 1996): 683–718.

Wagner, Geoffrey. "Popular Iconography in the U.S.A." *Parade of Pleasure.* New York: Library Publishers, 1955.

Washburne, Carleton, and Mabel Vogel. "A Reply to the Critics of the Winnetka Graded Book List." *Elementary English Review* 4 (1927): 6–9, 27.

———. *Supplement to the Winnetka Graded Book List.* Winnetka, IL: Winnetka Individual Materials, 1926.

———. *Winnetka Graded Book List.* Chicago: American Library Association, 1926. Reprinted as *What Children Like to Read: Winnetka Graded Book List.* New York: Rand McNally, 1928.

Wertham, Fredric. "The Comics—Very Funny." *Saturday Review of Literature,* 29 May 1948, 6–7.

———. *Seduction of the Innocent.* New York: Holt, Rinehart & Winston, 1954. Rpt. Port Washington, NY: Kennikat Press, 1972.

———. "What Parents Don't Know about Comics." *Ladies' Home Journal,* November 1953, 50–53.

West, Mark I. *Children, Culture and Controversy.* Hamden, CT: Archon Book/Shoe String Press, 1988.

Where's Love Gone?: Transformations in the Romance Genre. Special issue of *Para-Doxa: Studies in World Literary Genres,* 3: 1–2 (1997).

"Why Study the Winnetka Supplement?" Editorial. *Elementary English Review* 4 (1927): 55.

Wilson, Louis R. "Historical Development of Education for Librarianship in the United States." *Reader in American Library History,* edited by Michael Harris, 186–194. Washington, DC: NCR Microcard, 1971.

"The Winnetka Graded Book List." *Peabody Journal of Education* 3 (January 1926): 236–37.

Witek, Joseph. *Comic Books as History: The Narrative Art of Jack Jackson, Art Spiegelman, and Harvey Pekar.* Studies in Popular Culture. Jackson: University Press of Mississippi, 1989.

Wylie, Philip. "The Crime of Mickey Spillane." *Good Housekeeping* 140 (February 1955): 54–55, 207–9.

Index

Series titles and characters are indexed under first name (e.g., Nancy Drew, not Drew, Nancy)

About the Editors and Contributors

LYDIA CUSHMAN SCHURMAN is a Professor Emerita of Northern Virginia Community College. She coedited *Pioneers, Passionate Ladies, and Private Eyes* with Larry E. Sullivan and has published many articles on nineteenth-century popular fiction in *Primary Sources and Original Works, Dime Novel Round-Up,* and *Publishing History.* She presents papers at SHARP and at PCA, where she established both the Dime Novel and Reading and Popular Literature Areas.

DEIDRE JOHNSON is an Associate Professor in the English Department at West Chester University, where she teaches graduate and undergraduate courses in children's literature. She is the author of *Stratemeyer Pseudonyms and Series Books* and *Edward Stratemeyer and the Stratemeyer Syndicate* and has published numerous articles on juvenile series. She is also the associate editor of *Dime Novel Round-Up.*

JESSE BERRETT is completing a study of consumer culture and masculinity in postwar America for the University of California Press. His writings on literature and culture have appeared in, among other publications, *American Quarterly, Journal of the History of Sexuality, Journal of Social History, The Nation, Publishers' Weekly, The Village Voice, SPIN,* and *Salon.*

KATHLEEN CHAMBERLAIN is an Associate Professor of English and Associate Dean of Academic Affairs at Emory & Henry College in Virginia. She has published articles on series books in *The Lion and the Unicorn, The Children's Literature Association Quarterly, Nancy Drew and Company: Gender, Culture, and Girls' Series* (ed. Sherrie Inness), and the forthcoming *Defining Print Culture for Youth* (ed. Anne Lundin).

JANET DEAN is Assistant Professor of English at Bryant College. She taught previously at the University of South Dakota. Her essay on the marriage trope in James Fenimore Cooper's *The Pioneers* appears in *Arizona Quarterly*. She is currently completing a book on gender and the frontier in the nineteenth-century American imagination.

SARAH S.G. FRANTZ, a transplanted South African, is a graduate student at the University of Michigan, Ann Arbor, specializing in the eighteenth-century novel. She is currently working on her doctoral dissertation, on masculine emotional accessibility and confessional scenes in Romantic-era literature, with an additional interest in the conservative ideology and aesthetic of the most popular novels of the late eighteenth and early nineteenth centuries.

M. PAUL HOLSINGER is Professor of History at Illinois State University. Along with dozens of conference presentations dealing with various aspects of the popular culture of World War II, especially those designed for youth, he has written or edited such works as *Visions of War: World War II in Popular Literature and Culture* (1992); *The Ways of War: The Era of World War II in Children's and Young Adult Fiction* (1995); and *War and American Popular Culture: A Historical Encyclopedia* (Greenwood, 1999).

AMY KISTE NYBERG is an Associate Professor of communication at Seton Hall University, where she teaches media studies. *Seal of Approval: The History of the Comics Code*, her study of the history of comic-book censorship, was published in 1998. She won the 1996 M. Thomas Inge Award for Comics Scholarship for a paper on comic books and fan culture presented at the Popular Culture Association.

DONALD PALUMBO is Professor of English at East Carolina University, Film Area Chair for the Popular Culture Association, and series advisor to Greenwood Press' "Contributions to the Study of Science Fiction and Fantasy" series. He has published sixty articles and three collections of essays on science fiction and fantasy literature and film, American comic art, and existential literature and philosophy.

ALISON M. SCOTT became the Charles Warren Bibliographer for American History at Harvard University in 2000, after professional positions in Illinois, New York, Massachusetts, and Ohio. Her publications include *The Writing on the Cloud: American Culture Confronts the Atomic Bomb*, coedited with Christopher D. Geist (1997), "They Came from the Newsstand: Pulp Magazines and Vintage Paperbacks in the Popular Culture Library," *Primary Sources and Original Works* (1996), and book reviews for professional and scholarly journals.

ERIN A. SMITH is Assistant Professor of American Studies, Literature, and Gender Studies at the University of Texas at Dallas. She is the author of *Hard-Boiled: Working-Class Readers and Pulp Magazines* (2000) and has also published numerous articles on American popular literature, Canadian and American women writers, detective fiction, and pulp magazines.

MADELEINE B. STERN, a former Guggenheim Fellow, is an independent scholar, author, coauthor, editor or coeditor of nearly forty books, and a partner in the New York rare book firm of Leona Rostenberg and Madeleine Stern. Her works include *Imprints on History: Book Publishers and American Frontiers*, numerous other books about books, and biographies: *The Life of Margaret Fuller, Louisa May Alcott*, and *Purple Passage: The Life of Mrs. Frank Leslie*. After Rostenberg's discovery of Louisa May Alcott's pseudonym, Stern traced the Alcott thrillers and edited numerous collections of them. Her coauthored works with Leona Rostenberg include *Old Books, Rare Friends, Books Have Their Fates*, and *Bookends: Two Women, One Enduring Friendship*.

DAWN FISK THOMSEN specializes in nineteenth-century American popular culture and examined the origins of detective fiction in her Ph.D. dissertation. After an early career in secondary education and twenty years in nonprofit management, she is currently President of DFT & Associates, Inc., a management consulting firm for nonprofit organizations.